AND THEN THE PHONE RANG...

THE LIFE ADVENTURES OF DR. RON HILLER

by
Ronald E. Hiller

FriesenPress

One Printers Way
Altona, MB R0G 0B0
Canada

www.friesenpress.com

Copyright © 2022 by Ronald E. Hiller
First Edition — 2022

All rights reserved.

No part of this publication may be reproduced in any form, or by any means, electronic or mechanical, including photocopying, recording, or any information browsing, storage, or retrieval system, without permission in writing from FriesenPress.

ISBN
978-1-03-913183-5 (Hardcover)
978-1-03-913182-8 (Paperback)
978-1-03-913184-2 (eBook)

1. Biography & Autobiography, Personal Memoirs

Distributed to the trade by The Ingram Book Company

CONTENTS

PREFACE v
CHAPTER 1: The Early Years 1
CHAPTER 2: Spiritual Awakening 15
CHAPTER 3: Student Life – Finding a Wife 23
CHAPTER 4: Launching Out 41
CHAPTER 5: Getting Settled 47
CHAPTER 6: The Phone Rang! 57
CHAPTER 7: What a Trip! 67
CHAPTER 8: Arrival at Warwar 77
CHAPTER 9: Mambilla – Our Mission Field 93
CHAPTER 10: The Church in Mambilla 111
CHAPTER 11: Life and Times at Warwar - The First Four Months 123
CHAPTER 12: Back to Work 137
CHAPTER 13: Mbingo Cameroon 157
CHAPTER 14: Furlough 197
CHAPTER 15: Back to Warwar 209
CHAPTER 16: Canada – Our Home Again 243
CHAPTER 17: Family Practice in Burnaby 253
CHAPTER 18: The Family 263
CHAPTER 19: The Phone Rings Again 297
CHAPTER 20: God's Help Every Step of the Way 317
CHAPTER 21: Retirement is Not Resting 353
CHAPTER 22: Trips and Travels 365
CHAPTER 23: Retired, but Not Resting 411

PREFACE

An autobiography is the telling of the story of one's life experiences. My story has been profoundly shaped by God. As a teenager I was challenged by Romans 12:1-2. This passage told me to offer my body - my ordinary everyday life to God. I committed myself to Him, and this led to a life that I could never have imagined. I experienced, at pivotal moments, God's good and pleasing will directing me. My story is a testimony to God's mercy and grace. I was not always obedient and had times of doubt when things became difficult, but God mercifully forgave me and by His grace, restored me. He never left me alone, even when I felt very alone. God has truly blessed me with a most wonderful godly wife in Marion, four great and uniquely special children, three fantastic in-law children, and seven precious grandchildren.

This autobiography is written to provide a legacy and heritage for my children, grandchildren, and generations following. It has been my prayer for years that all of them put their trust in Jesus as Saviour and Lord. May they be encouraged in their walk of faith. The following scripture passages accurately express my purpose for writing my life story.

> *This will be written for the generation to come, that a people yet to be created may praise the Lord.* Psalm 102:18

> *I have no greater joy than to hear that my children walk in truth.* 3 John 4

I also hope that anyone else who may read my story will be encouraged to offer their ordinary everyday selves to God and so experience His good, pleasing, and perfect will too.

PREFACE

While we were in Nigeria and Cameroon, Marion and I wrote regular letters to our mothers which they kept in ring binders in chronological order. I also wrote a daily diary when we returned to Nigeria in 2005-06. This material was most helpful in writing my story many years later. I could only use a small fraction of the material in order to keep the story flowing. Parts of the story contain some detailed medical and surgical descriptions that would interest readers that have medical and nursing backgrounds.

I want to express my deepest thanks to the following people:

- Dezene and Joyel Huber, and Lori Hiller, my daughters and son-in-law, who edited my story, formatted it, and arranged for the publishing of it into book form.

- Paul Hiller, my son, who helped me solve technical issues with my computer.

- Dr. Harry Senges, a life-long friend, who sent much needed surgical supplies to me in Nigeria.

- Dr. Kurt Gottschling, a fellow family doctor, who welcomed me into his group of family doctors in Burnaby and sent medical equipment to me in Nigeria.

- Drs. Robertson, Gottschling, Wagar, Silverthorne, and Jones who graciously made room for me to rejoin their group medical practice on my return from Africa.

- Dr. Egon Nikolai, a dentist, who gave me basic dental instruments and a short tutorial in extraction of teeth.

- The many people who prayed and supported us while we were in Africa and sent kilo parcels containing food items unavailable to us.

- Grandpa and Grandma Asselstine who consented to my marriage to their daughter Marion. They gave their blessing to our venture to Africa and prayed for us.

- Oma Hiller, my mom, who released us and blessed us in our desire to follow God's call to the North American Baptist medical mission work in Nigeria and Cameroon. She was recently widowed at the time, but was willing to give up her son and daughter-in-law and their two babies, allowing them to go to some unknown, remote corner of Nigeria.

- Marion, my wife, and the love of my life! Without her support and leadership in many ways my life story would not have happened the way it did. She spent countless hours editing drafts of this book, making corrections, giving advice, and encouragement.

CHAPTER 1

The Early Years

My father was born in Drzewociny - Pabjanice near Lodz in Poland on October 12, 1904 as the eldest son of Gustav and Alvine Hiller. His family were German farmers in the area. His grandfather, Johann, and his father, Gustav, were Baptist lay preachers as well as farmers. As a youth he had to sleep under the hay in the barn to protect the animals from thieves and to hide himself from soldiers who were looking to conscript boys for the armies (German, Russian, and Polish) during World War 1. Being the eldest son, he had to work on the farm. Consequently, he had only three winters of schooling. In 1930, at age 26, he and brothers Herbert and Bruno, and sister Hannah immigrated to Canada, arriving at the famous Pier 21 in Halifax. They made their way to Olds, Alberta, to live with an uncle and work on his farm. They learned English – both good and bad words – from their cousins. Dad eventually made his way to Vancouver to work at gardening and even worked a short time in a mine in Anyox, north of Prince Rupert.

For two summers he climbed on top of railcars along with many other men to travel to Alberta to work on the farms and, when harvest was done, he bought a ticket to ride back home to Vancouver. On one trip, riding the rails, the train stopped in Kelowna. Dad along with 300 other "rail riders" got off the train and lit a small fire to get warm and to heat some food. An RCMP officer came and tried to drive them away by pointing a gun at the men. The men slowly bent down and each one picked up a rock and told the officer – if you shoot, you might get several of us, but you will be dead

THE EARLY YEARS

too. The officer wisely put away his gun and pleaded with the men to be peaceful –which they were to begin with. It was very cold riding on top of the rail cars, and the smoke was choking as the train went through tunnels.

These were unemployed hungry men in the depths of the Great Depression, and dad was one of them. He met my mother at a wedding in Kelowna and stayed there to help with harvesting fruit in the many orchards. They fell in love and, with both unemployed and nothing better to do, they got married on November 9, 1935. The next spring dad and mom moved to Vancouver where dad joined his brother Bruno in a gardening business. Dad was a man who knew what hard physical work was all about. He was a devout Christian and deeply involved in church work and fellowship. He served as head usher for decades at Bethany Baptist Church and enjoyed singing baritone in the locally renowned Bethany Male Choir.

My mother was born in Lauter, Germany in Saxony on June 20, 1913 to Otto and Tabea Paschold as their second-oldest daughter. The family of seven children initially lived near Schneeberg. They then moved to Lager Lechfeld in Bavaria where my grandfather, Otto, owned a small clothing factory. Grandfather Otto was pressed into the German army in World War 1. In the mid-wartime (1916) mom's older brother, Paul, died at age eight of complications of a ruptured appendix. After the war, during the Weimar Republic, inflation was rampant with rapidly rising prices. Otto had to put daily income into a wheelbarrow and stop at the bakery for bread on the way home because each subsequent day bread prices would rise again. He had to sell sewing machines and lay off workers in order to make ends meet. Finally, the family decided to immigrate to Canada to seek better opportunities. One souvenir they brought to Canada was a one billion-mark bill which was worthless.

Mom was a 12-year-old girl when the family landed in Quebec City. Her younger brother John, age four, suffered a fractured leg in a fall on the ship, so he and grandmother had to stay in a Quebec hospital until the leg had healed. There was a fear that amputation might be required, and in that case, the family would have to return to Germany. During John's month in hospital, Otto and the remaining five children moved on to a farm near Yorkton, Saskatchewan. Otto went to work, 15-year-old Mary looked after the children and mom, now 13, went to work as a housemaid for a local pastor and his wife.

The family then moved to Nokomis, Saskatchewan for two years and then to a milder climate in Kelowna. Mom and her family were charter members of the newly founded Grace Baptist church. Mom was the organist and had an apple box as a seat. The organ was a pump organ, and by the end of the church services the nails of the apple box got loose due to her vigorous peddling efforts and needed to be re-nailed. Mom did manage to get to grade ten in school and wanted to graduate and become a teacher, but times were tough and the poor economy forced her to leave school and go to work in a bakery. Meanwhile, the Paschold family moved to a farm on bench land in Mission, near Kelowna, overlooking Okanagan Lake. Mom wrote a detailed biography with pictures included, so I will not elaborate further.

I made my entry into this world in the early morning of July 6, 1941. The world was in the middle of the chaos of World War II. My birth brought a bit more chaos for my parents as I had a cleft lip and cleft palate deformity. This deformity required numerous operations to close up. Most of the specialists were in the armed forces to deal with war casualties. A general practitioner tried his best to close up the openings. When I was about five-years old a final attempt was made at surgery followed by radiation to the lower face to try to reduce formation of scar tissue. There was no concept at the time of the dangers of radiation. My poor mother was berated for my crying that tore open my repairs. How can one stop a newborn baby from crying? The end result left me with a permanent hole in the hard palate – connecting to my nose. So my start in life was difficult, especially for my poor parents.

WHEN I WAS BORN WE lived in a tiny house on St. Catherines Street, near 47th Avenue, on the south side of Vancouver. This home was just one block away from the church I grew up in – Bethany Baptist Church. Two years later we moved to 410 East 49th Avenue in a small two–bedroom house with a full basement. I remember dad carrying in sacks of coal and piles of firewood into the basement to burn in the furnace. Every morning he went down to the furnace to get a fire going again to heat the house. The

THE EARLY YEARS

basement also contained many jars of preserved fruits and jams and two large stone crocks of homemade sauerkraut. Mom also had an icebox in the basement to keep food cool. An iceman would come down the back alley regularly to deliver a large block of ice for the box. My cousins and I would get ice chips off the ice truck to suck on. We had a great yard with a large vegetable garden, several fruit trees, and beautiful flowers. Our peach tree was very productive – one year it produced 1000 peaches and then died the next year. I soon learned to plant seeds, weed, and water the garden. Later I learned the fine art of mowing and trimming lawns. Uncle Bruno and Aunt Agnes lived next door and so I as an only child had four cousins to play with – Rolfe, Larry, Ingrid, and Bill.

South Vancouver was known as little Germany due to mass immigration from Germany after World War II. A number of German speaking churches were started among the Catholics, Lutherans, Mennonites, and Baptists. Bethany Baptist was exclusively German speaking in the early years – dad and mom were charter members. During, and just after, the war, Bethany was falsely accused of being a Nazi cell by the local newspaper. People threw rocks, broke windows, broke in, and trashed furnishings and the kitchen. The trustees finally had to install wooden shutters to protect the windows, only opening them for services. We had a ministry to the starving people of post-war Germany in sending care packages of tea, coffee, sugar, and other non-perishables to relief agencies. Mom and Aunt Agnes packed parcels and sewed cloth covers and my cousins and I loaded them on our wagons and hauled them up the hill to the post office on Fraser Street. Our church was truly a family – a tight knit fellowship of faith. I grew up going to Sunday school and church and prayer meetings. Bethany Baptist Church was the center of our German speaking community life. All of us lived close enough to walk to church in rain or sunshine. We were elated when Dairy Queen decided to open an ice cream store at Fraser and 47th Street, which was on our route to church. As we were quite poor, dad and mom could not afford a car until about 1956 when we finally got a Volkswagen bug with the small back window.

September 1947 was when I started to go to school. I spoke only German for my first five years, so for a year mom taught me English in preparation for school. My two older cousins, Rolfe and Larry, walked with me to Sir

AND THEN THE PHONE RANG...

Sanford Fleming School on 49th Avenue and Knight Road, just over a mile away. I did not have a clue as to what was going on. At recess I walked home alone thinking school was over. Mom had to drag me back to finish the whole school day. I did not know my alphabet and was mystified when all the other children opened their books and phonetically read the ABC's. I don't know how I was passed into grade two. In grade two I had a little midget lady named Miss Sutherland as my teacher. I could understand what she was trying to do with us and began a rapid catch-up.

We had some serious issues in the early school years due to being of German heritage. It was just after the end of World War II and there was a great deal of hatred for anything to do with Germany. The name Hiller was very easily turned into "Hitler." Rolfe, Larry and I plus a few other German Canadian kids had to beat up a few of the bullies before we had peace. Having a bit of a feisty nature was helpful. We refused to be anybody's doormat! I did, however, feel very inferior because of the tone of voice I had due to the incomplete repair of my cleft lip and palate. I developed a severe stutter, especially for words starting with g, d, c, and t.

I was taken to a speech therapist and this only made it worse. I also had to have a lot of orthodontic work to bring the right upper teeth forward from their markedly recessed position. Then a tooth grew out of my hard palate and had to be removed. It felt like my brains were being pulled out through my mouth. Then I developed two formed teeth in my right maxillary sinus that required major oral surgery and a series of cautery treatments to close an oro-antral fistula. Needless to say this was an unhappy time with so much fuss and pain with my mouth. No wonder I had a sense of inferiority and developed a stutter.

In time, events occurred that helped me get over these problems. I started to excel in school work and rose to the top in the class. I enjoyed playing soccer and winning some games for our school. I became a schoolboy patrolman. That position required us to control the traffic intersection of 49th Avenue and Knight Road. We wore a uniform belt and hat and carried stop signs to stop cars and school kids. I became a vice captain and gave orders to patrol boys in my unit. I had many good friends at school and in church. We spent many long hours at Sunset Park playing baseball

THE EARLY YEARS

and touch (or flag) football in the summers. Mom got a bit upset at my coming home at dark for supper.

At church we had to attend Saturday morning German classes taught by our Pastor Gerhard Gebauer. We were very upset to have to spend all Saturday morning memorizing German hymns instead of playing sports. We were smart enough to know that our indoctrination in German was an attempt to perpetuate the language and culture in our church and families. We had the seeds of rebellion growing within us! Our church leaders finally realized that if Bethany did not allow English to be used by the youth, Bethany would ultimately lose the youth to English speaking churches or even lose them entirely to church and faith. During the later elementary school years I earned a bit of money picking blueberries in the summer. I walked to Fraser Street and Marine Drive where a farmer met the pickers and took us in the back of a pick-up truck to the berry farms. We were paid five cents per basket we picked. We were dismayed when he only paid part of the agreed fee!

Trips to Kelowna were always a highlight. I was the first grandchild of the Paschold clan so I was spoiled rotten by grandparents, aunties and uncles. Grandfather gave me a special treasure – a U.S 1900 silver dollar. Uncle John taught me how to shoot gophers with a .22 rifle. He was a World War II veteran Canadian soldier serving in the reconnaissance and intelligence corps, and that really impressed me. Mom was horrified to discover what we were doing, especially when I told her we had to stomp on the gophers if they didn't die immediately. We justified ourselves by pointing out that gopher hills in the alfalfa fields damaged the teeth in the hay mower.

Uncle Bob let me steer the family car while sitting on his knee – but he did have his thumb on the wheel! Aunts Lena and Anne taught me clay molding and got me to help bake cookies. Grandmother made great meals and let me have all the dessert I wanted. Luckie, the family dog, played fetch with me as I threw pine cones for hours. I was very sad when my grandparents died. They made me feel valued and loved.

I did have some mischievous moments as I grew up. One Saturday mom made lunch and ate hers early and left on an errand. She left a note for me regarding lunch and told me to wash the dishes. In righteous indignation

I wrote a reply, "I will wash my dishes, you wash yours." That was a huge, huge mistake. You can guess who had to wash all the dishes for all the meals for the entire next week?

On another occasion I was playing in the snow at lunchtime at school. The vice principal came out and gathered all the kids around to admonish them for being too rough with snowball fights. Some children were being hurt by snowballs with rocks in them. I was on the periphery of the crowd of kids behind the teacher and had a snowball in my hand. I realized by the speech being made that I had to get rid of this snowball. So I just lobbed it up in the air and, to my horror, the snowball made a perfect looping arc in the air and landed smack on the back of the teacher's neck. He turned around to see where this came from and so did all the kids – they were all looking at me, so I turned around too and looked behind me - and saw no one. Somehow I escaped punishment for lack of sufficient evidence.

Cousin Larry was two years older than me and often my partner in mischief. One day we decided to try parachute jumping. So equipped with our mothers' umbrellas, we climbed onto the roof of Larry's garage and jumped. Fortunately we landed in the compost box full of rotting grass clippings and vegetable peels. Our mothers were not very impressed at our stupidity, the broken umbrellas, and the stench on our clothes and skin.

We also experimented with smoking but had no money to buy cigarettes. Being resourceful, we picked a bunch of dried brown and yellow leaves from the peas in the garden. A hammer from dad's tool box was used to pound the leaves into the proper consistency and newspaper was cut into proper size to make our own "roll your own" cigarettes. The smoke was horrible and once again we faced our mothers' interrogation and dire punishment. The worst prank Larry and I did was to embed nails into the hot soft asphalt of 49th Avenue on a hot summer day. The nails were carefully angled so that cars coming down the hill would pick up the nails and penetrate the tire and inner tube, resulting in flat tires. Care was taken to hide under the fuschia bushes in the front yard to watch the action to see how quickly drivers could change tires. Our mothers never did find out, but we did feel some guilt because in Sunday school we learned that God sees all we do and He hears all we say.

THE EARLY YEARS

We did have some good moments. We invented a game called "peggie" that we played in the back alley using sticks and tin cans. What we invented was really very similar to cricket – tin cans for wickets and sticks for bats.

Junior high school started in grade seven at John Oliver High School. Our grade seven home room was the woodwork shop where we had to sit on top of workbenches. The home room teacher was a short-tempered man who yelled a lot. On one occasion of anger, he threw a wood chisel at a student. The chisel stuck into the wall narrowly missing the student!

Every hour we had to move to a different classroom for the next subject. At times we had to run across busy Fraser Street for the next class. In grades seven and eight we were segregated into boys-only and girls-only classes. At this time we had a personal development class where a teacher with a great sense of humor tried to teach us about the differences between boys and girls and about the "birds and the bees."

In senior high school we were again in co-ed classes with the brightest kids in division one. I did manage to be in division one throughout grades nine through twelve. I became the president of the Flicker Club that provided movies during lunch hour one day a week. I loved this job as I got to miss an entire afternoon once a week in order to return the film reel to the school board offices by bus.

I also enjoyed playing the position of wide side break on the school rugby team. The role of the break position was to break loose from the rugby scrum and tackle any opposition player who got the ball. A great way to release pent up aggression! We managed to win the British Columbia High School Championship by using some unorthodox but legal American football tactics to confound our opponents. I also very much enjoyed the Inter-School Christian Fellowship (ISCF), which was a club for Christian students to meet for social events, discussions, and listening to guest speakers. By grade eleven I became the president of ISCF at John Oliver.

Singing in the school choir was fun. Teo Repel, our teacher, was excellent. In grade twelve we performed the musical "South Pacific." The boys' favorite song was "There Is Nothing Like A Dame".

Summer times were spent working with my dad and Uncle Bruno at their gardening business. This continued every summer from ages 14 to 22. I took one week of holiday and one week to attend summer camp at

Green Bay Bible Camp in Westbank, near Kelowna. I did most of the lawn mowing and clipping work at palatial homes in Shaughnessy and British Properties in the west end of Vancouver. Cousin Larry and I would have to climb tall trees and prune branches with a hand saw under the direction of Uncle Bruno below.

In addition to gardening, in town, we worked six days a week, 12 to 14 hours a day, at a hunting lodge at Widgeon Creek, which converges with the Pitt River. We slept in the lodge for a week at a time. We logged, built fences, cut firewood, and even climbed naked into a septic tank to clean it. That was a disgusting job! Afterward we were thoroughly hosed off by a fellow worker.

One time we had a pile of logs in a trench that needed to be burned. In order to "do it properly" we inserted old tires between the logs and doused the whole works with gasoline. Larry then threw a flaming stick onto the pile. There was a huge explosion. At the time I was nailing shingles on a shed roof and was slammed flat on my face on the roof. Larry went flying through the air like the dashing young man on the flying trapeze. He suffered singed eyebrows and a few bruises. Miraculously he was not hurt more. Sometimes we had to learn lessons the hard way.

I did learn to drive a jeep and a Bombardier at age 14 at this lodge. Working outside all summer without a hat or shirt resulted in deep tans that we hoped would impress the girls! We were glad to have mom there as a cook for the gang.

Grade twelve was an important year as we had to write provincial exams in order to graduate. The results of these exams also determined if we would qualify for university and whether or not we would get a bursary that would pay one-third of the university tuition fees. So I applied myself to studying and I received good enough exam results to open the door for admission to the University of British Columbia and a bursary. I then faced a difficult decision. Was I to go on to university or should I join my dad and Uncle Bruno in the gardening business? I had worked during the summer with them since age 14 and seemed to do well. In time I would possibly take over the business.

My dad sensed my struggle and gave me encouragement to go to university. He said that he did not have enough money to help pay for

THE EARLY YEARS

school fees and books, but as long as I attended university I could "put my feet under his table". In other words, he would help me with free room and board.

High School graduation was a bit difficult for me as we were to bring a girl to the graduation banquet. At this time of my life I just worshipped girls from afar. I asked at least five girls to accompany me and all turned me down. My old feelings of inferiority arose again and I told my friend Harry that I was not going to attend the graduation. Harry got really mad and chewed out the girls! I finally did manage to find a different girl to go with me, but I felt quite sad. These are only a few of the events of my early years, but we must move on.

MATERNAL GRANDFATHER OTTO PASCHOLD

AND THEN THE PHONE RANG...

MATERNAL GRANDMOTHER TABEA PASCHOLD, ME, AND DOG "LUCKY"

EDMUND (DAD) AND RUTH (MOM) WEDDING PICTURE

THE EARLY YEARS

LITTLE RONNIE HEADING OFF TO CHECK OUT THE WORLD

RON TAKING CALLS IN HIS BACKYARD OFFICE

AND THEN THE PHONE RANG...

DAD AND MOM WITH THEIR ELEMENTARY SCHOOL BOY

HILLER AND SIEWERT COUSINS – RON IN BACK ROW EXTREME RIGHT

THE EARLY YEARS

JOHN OLIVER HIGH SCHOOL CHAMPIONSHIP RUGBY TEAM. RON KNEELING ON EXTREME RIGHT

CHAPTER 2

Spiritual Awakening

Great is the LORD! He is most worthy of praise!
No one can measure his greatness.

Let each generation tell its children of your mighty acts;
Let them proclaim your power.

Psalm 145:3-4

As a child I did not realize the heritage of faith I was born into. Too often we are oblivious of the steadfast faith in God of our fathers and mothers – much to our detriment. There are many lessons to be learned from them that we could apply to our spiritual pilgrimage. Their stories can serve to encourage and inspire us to follow Jesus with all of our heart, mind, and strength. This heritage of faith was present in both my dad's and my mom's families.

My dad's father, Gustav Hiller, was a German farmer living in Poland, a predominantly Catholic country. He was a Baptist lay preacher at a preaching station in Drzewociny, a small farming village near Pabjanice and Lodz. The mother church was in Mierzunzka. Gustav and his wife, Alwina, endured the ravages of World War II living under German occupation. Near the end of the war, when the German armies retreated, roving bands of Polish communists searched out German people remaining in Poland. Many Germans fled westward, but Gustav and Alwina, for unknown reasons, did not.

SPIRITUAL AWAKENING

After finding a dead Russian soldier on the farm, a group of Russian soldiers came and beat up Gustav and shot him in the presence of Alwina and their youngest son Willi. With the help of a neighbour woman, Alwina buried Gustav. This was difficult as it was winter time and the ground was frozen solid. The farm was seized by a Polish family who forced Alwina to serve them as a housemaid and a cook. She and Willi were soon put into separate internment camps. Willi, who had Down's Syndrome, died in his camp of presumed starvation. Alwina saw Willi only once and managed to slip him some bread through the fence separating them.

Alwina somehow escaped and after some hair-raising experiences, made her way to West Germany and was reunited with her son Arthur. She then immigrated to Vancouver, Canada, to be with her children – Mildred, my dad, Herbert, Hannah, and Bruno. My Uncle Herbert was fortunate to get an education in Poland, Canada, and the USA. He graduated from Rochester Baptist Seminary and served as Pastor in North American Baptist churches in the USA and Canada for 50 years. He taught at the NAB Seminary in Sioux Falls South Dakota, and at the Christian Training Institute – now Taylor Seminary – in Edmonton, Alberta. My dad was not educated, but had a strong faith and served for years as a member of the male choir and as head usher at Bethany Baptist Church. I think his middle name must have been "faithful". All the church kids loved him, perhaps because he always had some candy in his pocket to help settle down fussy little ones.

My mom's grandfather, Robert Sieber, was the owner of a garden nursery business in Schneeberg in Saxony, Germany. A picture of the pagoda, their home, and the business center, is among our family photos taken by my mom's brother Bob. Opa Sieber was a pious man - the first, and for a time, the only Baptist in the area. He witnessed wherever he went and on Sundays preached the gospel in nearby villages. This earned him the nickname "Der Heilige Sieber" (The Holy Sieber). Mom's aunt Ella married a Rev. Louis Putensen, a Baptist pastor in the same region.

Mom's uncle Johannes Sieber and his wife Dora were pioneer missionaries in a remote area of the North West Province of Cameroon. They initially went to "Kameroun" prior to World War I. During WW I they were interned in Spain and returned to Germany after the war. After WW I

Cameroon was taken out of Germany's control and became a colony under British and French mandates. In 1928 the German Baptist Missionary Society sent Adolph Orthner, Uncle Johannes, and Aunt Dora to British Cameroon to pioneer mission work in the grasslands. They started mission work in the hot, snake-infested lowlands of the Mbaw plain at Mbirkpa.

Here they started a church and a school and trekked to many other villages to preach the gospel and start churches. Aunt Dora was a nurse and treated many sick people with her limited medical supplies. After an epidemic that caused many deaths, the Siebers moved to the healthier climate of Ndu at 7000 feet elevation. The present Cameroon Baptist Convention Seminary is located at the site of the Sieber home in Ndu. Adolph, Johannes, and Dora extended their evangelism and church planting to Mbem, Belo, Mfumte, Ngom, and Binka to name only a few places.

Cameroonian evangelists such as Robert Jam, Joseph Mamadu, and Robert Nteff were the first to preach the gospel in the grasslands and their ministry opened the door for the first western missionaries. World War II made a huge impact on German missionary work in Cameroon. The British interned all German missionaries forcing them to report to the government in Bamenda. The Siebers made the long 150 km trek from Ndu to Bamenda on horseback and walking when the trails were too slippery for horses. This was during the heavy rains of July 1940. Johannes became ill with chest pain, cough, dizziness, and weakness. Shortly after arrival he died in the arms of his beloved Dora. Aunt Dora buried him outside the government headquarters on a hill in Bamenda. A short time later she was taken overland to Lagos Nigeria and onto a ship with hundreds of other prisoners bound for an internment camp in Kingston, Jamaica. She lived behind barbed wire in hot humid and crowded conditions for five-and-a-half years before being released and transferred home to Germany. During her internment she suffered illness and loneliness and even survived a hurricane that killed 44 people. The Sieber's experiences were recorded in Aunt Dora's diaries and letters, which have been translated into English.

When I worked in Cameroon, I went up the Government Hill and found the gravesite of Uncle Johannes Sieber in the expatriate cemetery. I also was privileged to meet Robert Jam, the pioneer Cameroonian evangelist, and to later attend his funeral. His son Samuel Jam, a good friend of mine, had tape recorded his father's last words of praise to God and a call to his people to follow Jesus. This taped message was played at the graveside. The people were most astonished to hear the voice of a dead man speaking from his grave.

Mom's parents were devout Baptists and were charter members of Grace Baptist Church in Kelowna. My mom was deeply involved in ministry at Bethany Baptist Church teaching girl's Sunday school, organizing the Women's Missionary Fellowship, singing in the mixed choir, and doing lots of kitchen work. I remember her sewing baby clothes on her Singer treadle sewing machine. The products of that endeavor were sent in White Cross shipments to Cameroon.

As I grew older, I became aware of these family heroes of the faith, and their stories made a deep impression on me. At about five years of age I had my tonsils and adenoids removed at Mount St. Joseph's hospital – a Catholic hospital run by Nuns. The day after surgery as I sat on my bed in a large children's ward, a Nun came into the room. All the children ran to her to hold her hand or touch her dress, but I sat firmly rooted on my bed with a fierce look on my face. The Nun immediately noticed this and came to my bed and asked how I was doing. I replied in the most forceful way to be heard by all, "I'm a Baptist!" I am sure there was great mirth in the staff coffee room when the tale of the little Baptist boy was told to the rest of the Nuns.

However, it was my mom who taught me many bible stories by reading Egermeier's Bible Story Book to me. Regular Sunday school attendance, time spent in corporate worship with our church family, and listening to many sermons expanded my understanding of God and His role in the lives of everyday faithful Christians. Children sat through entire Sunday services with their parents, I believe to their great benefit and to the benefit of the adults around them.

Bethany also often held weeklong deeper life services in the evenings. I remember listening to Rev. Herman Palfenier, who was billeted in our home several years in a row. He was a very big man with a huge bulbous nose and a great sense of humor. He would tell jokes at our supper table and laugh uproariously. My dad would join in laughing until tears rolled down his cheeks. Rev. Palfenier was a very engaging speaker and I loved to listen to his preaching. In 1948 Rev. Kujath from Kelowna was the speaker at the week of deeper life meetings. He was so short that he had to stand on a box to be seen behind the pulpit. He was a very powerful preacher and he clearly explained the way of salvation through repentance and faith in Christ who died on a cruel cross, bearing the penalty for our sins. He issued an altar call, inviting those who want to come to Jesus to come forward and pray in the choir room. I felt very convicted and wanted to go forward, but being only seven-years old I asked my dad for permission. Also, part of me wanted to see what was happening in the choir room. My dad asked the advice of two deacons – Albert Hass and Carl Pudlas. Both men encouraged me to go forward, saying, "Do not keep children away from Jesus." I knelt down in the choir room and prayed for forgiveness of my sins and I asked Jesus to come and live in my heart. This was one of the rare occasions when I saw my dad cry. I felt a joy in my heart and on the way home I danced and whooped all the way to Fraser Street.

The following year I was being prepared for baptism. Part of the process was to be interviewed by two deacons and then later to stand in front of the entire church to answer questions. I recall being asked what I would do if someone offered me a cigarette to smoke. Albert Hass, the moderator, intervened and admonished people for asking stupid questions of a young boy. I guess I satisfied everyone with the clarity of my testimony and was approved for baptism. On Easter Sunday, April 17, 1949 I was baptized by Rev. John Schweitzer at the ripe old age of almost eight. I remained deeply involved in church life – attending services and Sunday School. As I got older, I participated in the male choir as a second tenor. All the boys eagerly awaited their fifteenth birthday when they were permitted to try out for that choir. The youth group provided fellowship and was popular, especially because we were allowed to speak English. Attending Green Bay Bible Camp was also a favorite summer time event with great food, fun in the sun, and swimming in Lake Okanagan.

At age 14 I was challenged by the missionary speaker at the camp to seek to do God's will. My good friend, Harry Senges, and I sat under a tree by the water's edge and wondered what God's will for us really was. We decided that the Bible must have the answer, so I did something that I do not recommend. It could be very dangerous! I closed my eyes and opened

SPIRITUAL AWAKENING

my bible and put my finger on the page. On opening my eyes, I saw that my finger was on Romans 12:1-2. I read these verses:

I beseech you therefore, brethren, by the mercies of God, that you present your bodies a living sacrifice, holy, acceptable to God, which is your reasonable service. And do not be conformed to this world, but be transformed by the renewing of your mind, that you may prove what is that good and acceptable and perfect will of God.

This passage told me what God's will was. I was to present myself, my body, my heart, and my mind to God; and to be transformed by the Holy Spirit. Under that tree I prayed to God and committed myself to Him – stating that I would go wherever He wants me to go, and do whatever He would want me to do. In retrospect, this was a divine appointment with God.

After camp that year I went home – back to high school, sports, summer gardening work, and involvement in youth activities. Life became full of time-consuming activity and gradually the promise I made to God at camp faded into distant memory.

JOHANNES (MY GREAT-UNCLE) AND DORA SIEBER, PIONEER MISSIONARIES TO CAMEROON

AND THEN THE PHONE RANG...

GRAVESTONE IN BAMENDA, CAMEROON

HARRY SENGES AND RON AGE (14) AT GREEN BAY BIBLE CAMP

CHAPTER 3

Student Life – Finding a Wife

I had to make a big decision at the time of high school graduation in 1959. Should I go on to university or should I join my dad and Uncle Bruno in the gardening and landscaping business. Doing the latter would have meant instant income and the prospect of eventually taking over the business. I had ideas already of how I would modernize and mechanize the work, such as buying a Bobcat to lift rocks for retaining walls instead of busting a gut lifting and rolling them by hand and with iron crowbars. But I already had enough negative experiences with blistered hands, running into fresh dog poop with a power lawn mower, cleaning septic tanks, and sore muscles to make me reconsider that option. My marks in the grade 12 provincial exams were good enough that I was able to gain entry into the University of British Columbia with a bursary that paid one-third of the school fees. My dad, being poor, stated that he did not have enough money to help with fees, but I had free room and board. So I made the decision to enter first year Arts & Science at U.B.C. in September of 1959. In preparation I bought a desk with an arborite top and the wood stained to look like mahogany. My friends, Egon Nikolai and Wally Eggert built a number of these to make money for their schooling.

Several friends from Bethany Baptist were also attending UBC and living at home, but none of us owned a car to get there. We could not afford to live on campus. Harry Senges, Udo Herke, Walt Heine, Wilf Loch, and I managed to take turns borrowing our respective family cars for a week at a time to form a carpool. Len Strelau joined the car pool in 1960. We had some uproarious times with jokes and banter. One time we were laughing so hard at a joke that the driver at the time, Udo Herke, forgot to straighten out his car after a curve in the road and ran right into the ditch. We all got out and hitchhiked the rest of the way to UBC, leaving Udo behind to figure out what to do next with his family's big Buick in the ditch. One dark and foggy night during my week to drive we had great difficulty seeing the road because of the dense fog on Marine Drive. It was so bad that I made the guys take turns to sit on the front fender to see the white center line and point which way to steer. We just crawled along taking forever to get home. All the fender sitters were nearly in hypothermia.

Classes at UBC were very different from high school. No professor got to know the students as the classes were very large. There was no spoon feeding by the profs. Before we knew it midterm exams were upon us. The English 100 professor failed at least 1/3 of the class, probably to shock us all into taking studies seriously. I was not sure what academic path to follow, so I took a range of studies that included prerequisite courses for a wide number of future options. These courses included English, Math, Physics, Zoology, and German. I found Math the most difficult and spent more time studying it than all the other courses combined. Our math class was held in an old army hut that leaked when it rained, so we had to find dry seats to sit in. I chose German because most areas of study required at least one year of a foreign language. German was easy. I didn't study more than five minutes all year for the exams. I just wrote things in German the way my mom would say it. I got 90% in that course. Mom wondered what had happened to the other 10%, and was a bit miffed when I told her that it was her fault! In subsequent years I added courses in chemistry (inorganic & organic), psychology, philosophy, biophysics, and more zoology.

During my undergraduate years I experienced the first real challenges to my Christian faith. The first challenge was from an outspoken atheist physics professor who seemed to go out of his way to demean Christianity during his lectures. He even entered into a debate with a Christian professor in a campus event. In zoology I encountered the theory of evolution which was presented in an unbalanced manner, as though evolution was not debatable. Then in the philosophy course we spent the first half of the year on arguments for the existence of God. The second half of the year disproving the existence of God. Of course, this professor had us all in a tizzy, as he had spent years studying this stuff and we ignorant students were quite naïve at the process of logical argument and apologetics. I came to appreciate the foundations of faith built into me by my parents and by my church. This biblical foundation and the Holy Spirit within me helped me to stay true to my faith in God. There was also a strong supportive Christian fellowship in the Inter-Varsity Christian Fellowship. A lot of Christian students studied between classes in the Ridington Room of the library where we occupied several tables. For a break we would go for a coffee at the Campus Cupboard Cafe behind the library, or we would go for a walk to the cliff overlooking the entrance to Burrard Inlet. On our walks we discovered abandoned bunkers and gun emplacements used in World War II to defend against possible Japanese attack.

Another big decision loomed in front of me regarding the future direction of study and ultimate career path to follow. I was torn between becoming a pastor or a medical doctor. I wrestled with this for a while and finally decided on becoming a doctor. After weighing all the pros and cons the final deciding factor was my impaired speech. Due to my cleft palate being incompletely closed, I realized that my voice had a nasal tone that would likely reduce my acceptance as a preacher by churches. Little did I know that I would spend much time teaching adult Sunday school classes, preaching in Africa, and speaking in churches in North America while on deputation. It is probably a good thing that I didn't know too much about the future. I had to learn to trust in God one step at a time. With the decision made to apply for medical school, I joined the pre-med club at UBC and chose appropriate courses required as prerequisites for medical school. The pre-med club often showed films during lunch time that featured medical issues. On one occasion I invited some of my car pool buddies to watch a film of the birth of triplets by Caesarian section. It was a very bloody scene and my buddies left, one by one - feeling nauseated, while I sat there eating my tomato sandwiches and enjoying the film.

Summers were spent working with my dad and Uncle Bruno in order to earn money for school fees and books. I did manage to get good enough marks in my courses to continue receiving bursaries to pay one-third of the school fees. Fortunately, I earned enough to continue going to

STUDENT LIFE – FINDING A WIFE

university. It was great to get into good physical shape and develop a deep tan working outdoors.

A very significant event occurred on August 19, 1961. I met Marion! My cousin Walter Sturhahn from Bethany got married that day to Genny Okrainetz from Alta Vista Baptist Church. I first saw this gorgeous 17-year-old girl, Marion Asselstine, at the wedding ceremony and I was captivated by her beauty. I wondered if I would be lucky enough to meet her and talk to her. The reception was held in the large backyard of the Sturhahn farm on Boundary Road. The tables were set under the fruit trees on which lanterns were hung. This was a very romantic setting. The youth from Bethany and Alta Visa served food and coffee to the seated guests. At the end of the meal we were instructed to clear the tables with the guys holding trays and the gals loading dishes on them. I managed to catch Marion's eye and raised my tray as a signal for her to join me in the clearing task. She came to help me and I thought I had just entered heaven! We took the loaded tray to the basement of the house to the dish washers. I managed to corner Marion in the basement and offered her a ride home after the wedding. She hesitated and stated that she could walk, but I protested that it was not good for a girl to walk home in the dark. She finally agreed to a ride home. However, I now realized that there was a logistical problem. I had an obligation to drive four cousins to their home near Cambie street in Vancouver, the opposite direction of Marion's nearby home in Burnaby. And I was driving a little Volkswagen Beetle! Undaunted, I seized the moment and crammed the four cousins into the back seat, ignoring their protests of not enough room, and put Marion in the front seat beside me. I drove the cousins home as quickly as I could, and then slowly meandered the way back to Burnaby via the long and scenic route. This gave me the opportunity to get to know Marion a bit more. I gathered enough courage to ask her out on a date for the following weekend. She agreed to go with me on not just one date, but three nights in a row- to a youth party, an afternoon and evening at the Pacific National Exhibition, and a Sunday evening church service. Thereafter, we dated most weekends except for about four to six weeks when Marion decided to break-up. The break up nearly broke up my heart as I was falling head over heels in love with her. We soon resumed dating again and the feelings of a growing love were mutual.

My parents had a very positive reaction to Marion. On the night of the wedding I got home a bit late, and told mom and dad that I had met a really nice girl. On meeting Marion, they approved of her. Dad initially felt it was too bad that she could not speak German, but after getting to know her, he was almost as smitten with her as I was! Mom and dad came to love her as a daughter.

It was interesting to meet Marion's family and have the spotlight of inspection shine on me. Marion's older siblings were Art, Shirley, Jack, Jocelyn; the younger ones were Leonard and Dennis. Later Sandy joined the clan as a foster brother. Aunt Pearl, a crusty old spinster, also lived in the Asselstine home for long periods of time. Art and his wife, Gwen, had three children. Shirley and her husband, Don, adopted two children. Jack and his wife, Marlene, had six children. Thus as an only child, I was a bit overwhelmed by such a large family. Aunt Pearl was a bit of a hypochondriac and, after finding out that I was planning to be a doctor, she thought I might be all right for Marion. Len and Dennis initiated me by putting my Volkswagen beetle on blocks when I wasn't looking.

Marion's parents were warm, hospitable folks and put me at ease quickly. Dad Asselstine (William Arthur) was a fifth-generation Canadian of Dutch ancestry, traced back to the United Empire Loyalists who came to Canada from the U.S.A. at the time of the American Revolution. The family tree was traced further back to Holland to the time of William of Orange. The Van Ysselsteyns apparently moved to England with William of Orange when he became King of England. There is some even more distant historical evidence that King Clovis, circa 500 AD, granted land to a Veltin Van Ysselsteyn, who built a castle on a rock island (Insel-Stein) in the Ijssel River. The town of Ysselsteyn was built and still stands today. Dad Asselstine was born in 1892 in Sharbot Lake, Ontario, to Sperry and Letoria (nee Wagar) Asselstine. In 1911 the family moved to a farm six miles south of Fleming, Saskatchewan. He married Kate (nee Elmore) in 1924, and they had three children, Arthur, Shirley, and Jack. Kate died of postpartum sepsis after the birth of Jack. A few years later, in 1937, dad Asselstine married Ruth Mildred (nee Elmore), the first cousin of Kate. The Elmore clan had immigrated to Canada from England in the early 1800's and ultimately settled in the Fleming and Moosomin farming area

STUDENT LIFE – FINDING A WIFE

of Saskatchewan. Mom Asselstine (Ruth) graduated from nursing school in Owen Sound, Ontario in 1922. She recalled that, as a student nurse, one of her duties was to pull hairs out of the horse tails when delivery carts came to the hospital. These hairs were used for operating room sutures!

Dad and mom Asselstine moved to Pierson, Manitoba where dad ran a barber shop and an attached pool hall. In the early 1940's they moved to Vancouver where Jocelyn, Marion, Leonard, and Dennis were born. Dad initially worked in the shipyards building ships for use in World War II. After the war he worked for the British Columbia Electric Company as janitor and maintenance man. In 1953 the family moved to Portland Street in south Burnaby. They began to attend the Alta Vista Baptist Church where dad was baptized. He was proud to be a member of the Loyal Orange Lodge, and had no use for Catholics. Mom and dad Asselstine developed a valuable and difficult ministry of taking handicapped children into their home as foster children. Over the years they fostered many such children. One of them, Sandy Spicer, was born with spina bifida and urological complications. He became a permanent foster child and a member of the family.

I continued to get good enough marks at university to earn an annual bursary for one-third of the school fees. During my third year of Arts & Science I took a long shot and applied for admission to the UBC School of Medicine. This was a long shot because almost all applicants had an undergraduate degree, and some a masters or even a doctorate degree. To make things more interesting, there were over 600 applicants for 60 positions in the first year class. With nothing to lose, I applied in the spring of 1962. In the summer I got a nice letter informing me that I was not accepted but was put on an alternate list for consideration if any successful applicants chose a different medical school. I was emotionally prepared to return to UBC for the fourth year to get a Bachelor of Arts & Science degree. In late August, about one week before classes started, I got a second letter that congratulated me on my acceptance into medical school. After informing my happy parents, I phoned Marion at her home and told her I was coming to see her right now – something important happened. I raced up her front stairs shouting "I'm in, I'm in – yahoo!" There were hugs and kisses and great jubilation. Looking back, one could see that God had brought me through a door that seemed impossible to open. He had a plan for me and was making it happen.

My first year in medical school was a real challenge. The transition from high school to university paled in comparison to the huge transition from university to medical school. We had eight hours of lectures and labs every weekday, and four hours on Saturday. The rest of the waking hours were devoted to study and quick meals. First-year subjects included Anatomy, Histology, Radiology, Biochemistry, and Physiology. The first anatomy lab was a very tense time. We were ushered into the dissection lab in teams of four to a table. The cadavers were covered with metal hoods that looked like coffins. With great ceremony we opened up the hoods and had our first look at a room full of dead bodies. The smell of formaldehyde preservative was overpowering. Some students looked quite pale and were near fainting or vomiting. We then began the initial dissection, with bare and trembling hands, making the first incisions. It was difficult to eat lunch afterwards, as the smell of formaldehyde on my hands did not wash off easily. The pace was intense and relentless. We could not allow getting behind in studies because catching up would be extremely difficult. Final exams were very stressful because the pass rate was 75%. If we failed a final exam (mark less than 75%) in any one subject we would have to drop out of medical school. There was no opportunity to repeat the 1st year. Many students suffered anxiety symptoms, loss of sleep, headaches, and abdominal cramps etc. I recall studying late one night and falling asleep well after midnight. Mom noticed my light still on in my basement bedroom. She found me lying on my back fast asleep still clutching a textbook. She had difficulty prying my fingers open and, as I awoke, I panicked, crying out, "I'm going to fail!" Well, I didn't fail and was surprised to rank twenty-third in our class of 60.

In February of 1963 Marion entered the School of Nursing at the Vancouver General Hospital and had to live in the nurse's residence. She sure looked cute in her student nurse's uniform! Her program was a combination of lectures, labs, and practical bedside nursing in the hospital. Early in her first year she was given the task of cleaning and washing a very dirty elderly man. The dirt was so thick and adherent that she had to pick some of it off with her fingernails. She did a great job, but unfortunately

STUDENT LIFE – FINDING A WIFE

the man died the next day. I wondered if his death was due to exposure from lack of insulating dirt!

Life in the residence was quite confining. Students had a curfew of 10 PM. They were granted a 12 PM curfew once a month, and were strictly monitored by "the dragons" who were matrons of the residence. The entrance was called the fishbowl because the matrons had a big window through which they could see everything that went on in the entrance. Boys were allowed only on the first floor to visit the gals in little alcoves with doors that could not be closed! One time Marion and I were at a wedding reception and to our horror we noticed that it was 9:55 PM. We ran to the car, sped down Cambie Street, and dashed through a red light on the way to the nurse's residence. A policeman stopped us and I rolled down my window and said, "Meet you at the nurse's residence." I sped off, with the police car flashing its lights, in hot pursuit. I stopped at the nurse's residence with the police car, still flashing its lights, right behind us. The student nurses leaned out of their windows and cheered Marion on as she made a mad dash for the fishbowl. I told the policeman that I was sorry but Marion had a 10 o'clock curfew. The kind policeman said, "Yeah I know all about it, I married one of those students a few years ago." He had three issues with me speeding, the red light, and failure to stop when apprehended. He took pity on my situation but said that he had to do something, so he gave me a ticket for only one of my misdeeds, the least offensive one of going through a red light. That was the only time I ever thanked a policeman for a ticket. No doubt the cheering student nurses looking on were a special help.

Our dates were quite limited. Sunday night after church and following youth meetings, we would often go to a basement café in the Biltmore Hotel for coffee and orange chiffon pie. Harry Senges was dating Heather Dewar, also from Alta Vista, and they often joined us at the Biltmore. On Saturdays Marion would come to my house for supper with my parents and then she would study in the living room and I went downstairs to study. Then we enjoyed the ride to take Marion back to the residence and, of course, a quick kiss in the fishbowl.

Second year of medical school seemed less stressful, or perhaps I had learned better coping skills. We were introduced to pathology, pharmacology, epidemiology, the history of medicine, bacteriology/parasitology and early clinical skills. Our bacteriology professor was a very intense, prim, and proper man who managed to convulse the class into gales of laughter with his very serious statement, "The whole world is covered in a thin layer of faeces." He was merely trying to impress us with the prevalence of microorganisms. I enjoyed this year more and ranked thirteenth out of 60 by the end.

After six months of probation in nursing school Marion received a cap in a special ceremony. A year later she got a wide bib and white stockings as symbols of advancing levels of nursing proficiency. Early in her training she had to learn how to give an injection. Somehow she managed to put the needle through her own finger on the way into the patient's rear end. Marion just carried on and pushed the plunger of the syringe to get the medicine into the patient before getting the needle out of the patient and her own finger. Fortunately HIV infections were not around at that time. Her first day as a scrub nurse in the operating room was made quite stressful by a surgeon who looked at her and said, "If you don't do this right the patient might die." That was not a great way to instill confidence in a young student! In the final year Marion got a black stripe on her white cap and was put in charge of nursing care for an entire hospital ward.

Marion and I had discussed the concept of marriage by this time and even casually looked at rings. I frantically saved up enough money to buy a ring in December of 1963. On Christmas Eve I told my mom and dad to take their time coming home from the church service. "Visit with some friends for a while," I said. So Marion and I were home alone beside the Christmas tree when I proposed marriage and showed her the ring. I figured she would say yes, but I was still very nervous about it all. She did say yes, and just about then my parents walked in. That sure was a great Christmas! We knew this was going to be a long engagement as Marion was not allowed to marry until the final six months of her nursing school time. Also we were both poor as church mice and could not afford to live on our own.

Third- and fourth-year medical school was much more clinical in nature and our lectures were now at Vancouver General Hospital. We were divided into clinical groups of five or six for hands-on bedside

STUDENT LIFE – FINDING A WIFE

teaching. I had purchased my first car, a used grey Volkswagen Beetle, so that I could travel to clinics held in several different hospitals. We learned clinical examination and differential diagnosis. Rotations were made through Internal Medicine, Surgery, Obstetrics, Gynecology, Pediatrics, Psychiatry and many sub-specialties. This was the pattern for both third and fourth year.

I really enjoyed the more practical aspects of medicine and ended up ranking ninth in my third-year and third at the end of my fourth-year. In the summers after my second and third years I worked at research for Dr. Phil Ashmore, a paediatric cardiac surgeon. Together with Walt Paton, a classmate, we investigated why children frequently developed respiratory distress following cardiac surgery where a heart-lung bypass pump was used. We anesthetized dogs and put them on a heart-lung bypass pump with an oxygenator. They too developed respiratory distress. Treatment with hyperbaric oxygen was investigated. We studied the lungs microscopically and measured surfactant action and lung elasticity. We discovered that the oxygenator, where oxygen was wafted over blood films on rotating teflon discs, caused platelets to clump and plug up lung capillaries. This plugging of lung capillaries reduced lung elasticity and surfactant levels resulting in respiratory distress. We published a scientific paper (under Dr. Ashmore's name) and wrote a graduation thesis on our original research. UBC was only one of two medical schools in North America that required a thesis for graduation. The practical result of this research was the discontinuation of Teflon disc oxygenators and the introduction of membrane oxygenators for use in paediatric cardiac surgery. Much happier babies post op!

Marion and I planned our wedding for June 4 1966, one day after my graduation ceremony. Marion had graduated with a Registered Nursing degree in February and had started working at the G.F. Strong Rehabilitation Hospital. It was good for her to earn a bit of money before getting married. I made a list of wedding expenses (flowers, money for pastor, organist, honeymoon etc.) and was 50 cents short. I jokingly told my mom that I would have to cancel the wedding. She replied, "No way, I will give you the 50 cents, you just better marry that girl." Either she wanted me out of the house, or she liked Marion very much!

AND THEN THE PHONE RANG...

The Medical School graduation was a formal afternoon affair as we filed forward to receive our diplomas and a tap on the shoulder as we knelt before the Chancellor of UBC. I ranked third in the class and was honored with medals of top merit in orthopedics and in obstetrics and gynecology. My dad was so proud that he was in tears to see his son be recognized as a doctor. That evening Marion and I, plus our parents, celebrated by dining out at the fancy Bayshore Inn. We had all the wedding rehearsals and details of planning done ahead of time so we could just relax and enjoy.

The day of the wedding finally came. The cars were decorated, hair fixed, dresses on, flowers in hand, and the entourage to church commenced. En-route it was realized that Marion's mom was missing. Somehow, in all the excitement, everyone left and forgot the mother of the bride. She ended up sitting at home waiting in the hope that she would get a ride to church, which did finally happen. Pictures were taken in advance so that guests could leave the ceremony in the sanctuary and go immediately to the reception in the church basement. It was a great time of celebration that included some of our nursing and med school friends. Harry Senges was my best man, just as I was his best man when he married Heather the year before. Three of my cousins, the Badke boys, had learned to play trumpets and they had planned to play "Rescue the Perishing" at the reception. A mortified Auntie Anne, their mom, changed the number at the last minute. A ladies trio did manage to sing "It's not an easy road that we travel together." Very nice lyrics but a bit funny to sing at a wedding. A male quartet sang a humorous song that they composed called, "Ron and Marion are marryin' tonight." The ladies of Bethany Baptist put together a great meal for us. A happy time was had by all.

After saying farewell to guests and family, we escaped from would-be high-jinks by having Harry stand in the middle of the road as we left so that no one could chase us – a nasty custom of the time. I had also checked in at the Sheraton Villa on the morning of the wedding and stashed our suitcases in the room to avoid possible mischief.

Our honeymoon was spent travelling to Jasper where we stayed at the Jasper Park Lodge in a beautiful setting by a lake and river. We had a little one room cabin in the forest, a short walking distance from the lodge. Breakfast by room service was entertaining as the waiter pedalled a bike

STUDENT LIFE – FINDING A WIFE

to the cabin with a huge tray, loaded with food and coffee, perched on his shoulder. He made an elegant appearance as he artfully swooped off his bike and served breakfast on the little patio table. We could only afford to stay three days, so we managed to go for walks, go on a horseback trip, and paddle a boat in the lake. We were delighted to just relax and realize that student days were over and that we had found each other. Now we could look forward to what would come next.

RON AND MARION'S FIRST DATE – ON GROUSE MOUNTAIN CHAIRLIFT

AND THEN THE PHONE RANG...

WHAT BEAUTY! NO WONDER I WAS SMITTEN

MARION STARTS NURSING SCHOOL AT VANCOUVER GENERAL HOSPITAL

STUDENT LIFE – FINDING A WIFE

MY MEDICAL SCHOOL STUDIES – INSPIRED BY PICTURE OF MARION

ENGAGEMENT – CHRISTMAS 1963

AND THEN THE PHONE RANG...

MY FIRST CAR — "HERBIE"

MARION'S GRADUATION AS REGISTERED NURSE — FEBRUARY 1966

STUDENT LIFE – FINDING A WIFE

RECEIVING MY M.D. DEGREE - UNIVERSITY OF BRITISH COLUMBIA, JUNE 3, 1966

PROUD PARENTS AND FIANCÉE INSPECTING MY DIPLOMA

AND THEN THE PHONE RANG...

CELEBRATING MY GRADUATION THE DAY BEFORE OUR WEDDING

OUR SUPPORTIVE PARENTS ON OUR WEDDING DAY.
LEFT, EDMUND & RUTH HILLER AND RIGHT, RUTH & ARTHUR ASSELSTINE

STUDENT LIFE – FINDING A WIFE

WEDDING PARTY – LEFT TO RIGHT, WILF LOCH, HERB STURHAHN, HARRY SENGES, MARILYN HUMPHRIES, SHARON LOCH, AND MURIEL EDGE. NORMIE & NOLA ASSELSTINE

DR. AND MRS. HILLER – CUTTING THE WEDDING CAKE ON A VERY HAPPY DAY!

CHAPTER 4

Launching Out

What came next was the harsh reality of awakening to an alarm clock and heading off to work. The glorious celebrations of a graduation, the wedding, and the relaxed honeymoon were over and now we had to settle into the daily routines of life. I had arranged to do a year of medical internship in Victoria at the Royal Jubilee Hospital after a prior exploratory trip to Victoria with several classmates. Marion and I packed our few belongings and moved into a third-floor apartment on Fort Street just two blocks from the hospital. The only furniture we had was a mattress on the bedroom floor and an old wooden table with four chairs donated by my parents. We had a roll-away cot that we covered with a wedding-gift blanket and called our living room sofa. Two other married interns and their wives also rented apartments on the same floor.

We went shopping for essentials like a broom and mop, soaps, toiletries, and food staples. The total bill came to $75 which was a huge amount. We had 10 cents left to last us until the first pay cheque. I had to lie down on the sofa to recover from the shock!

Monday morning came in a hurry and it was off to work for both of us. Marion worked as a registered nurse on a surgical floor and got into the flow of work rapidly. She had some bizarre experiences with patients who went into post-operative deliriums. One patient was found stark naked pushing his hospital bed down the hall. Another patient was heard singing loudly to himself, and on checking was found in bed with his intravenous undone and the fluid pouring down on his head. He was simply enjoying a shower! It seems that most of the strange behaviours were by patients of an eccentric prima donna vascular surgeon who had everyone afraid of his temper tantrums. He was known to throw surgical instruments across the operating room when annoyed by some trivial matter. I recall assisting this surgeon on an aorto-femoral bypass operation. He made a huge incision down the entire abdomen and into the groin, stared at the wound, and then walked out of the operating room stating that he did not feel like doing this case today. The family doctor and I were left behind to close this huge incision. The poor patient woke up later thinking the operation was done, only to find out that he had to go through all this again the next day!

As interns we rotated through various departments of surgery, internal medicine, pediatrics, obstetrics, emergency, psychiatry etc. I was unfortunate to be assigned to the emergency department as my first rotation. I was a bit overwhelmed as I walked down the hall towards a nursing station dressed as an intern in my white uniform. Suddenly all the nurses stood up as I approached. I turned around to see who the important person behind me might be, only to find no one behind me at all.

Within an hour of my first day in the emergency room an ambulance crew brought in an elderly woman with chest pain. She promptly went into cardiac arrest as I approached her bed. With the help of a veteran nurse, Miss Harbottle, I got her onto the floor and started chest compressions and ventilations. The alarm went off and soon there were a number of doctors and nurses around to help. A senior cardiologist calmly strolled up and looked at the ECG and stated, "She is dead, stop the resuscitation." Everybody left and here I was, just me, Miss Harbottle, the dead woman on the floor, and a weeping family outside the room. I was advised by another nurse to go and speak to the family. I was bewildered, and could not remember any medical school lecture on what to do with a grieving family, so I tried my best to console them and mumbled something about calling a funeral home.

As I was in the midst of this, another nurse summoned me back to the emergency room where a man lay unconscious presumably from an overdose of drugs. As I approached his bed he stopped breathing and turned blue. I got a bag and mask and ventilated him until he was pink and then intubated him, which was easy after intubating dogs with huge tongues for two summers in the research lab. Fortunately, there was a Bird respirator handy so I connected it to the patient's tube and used the same settings of rate and pressure that we used on dogs. The patient was then moved to the intensive care unit and I became an instant hero in the eyes of the emergency room staff. I did wonder what it was about my approach to patients' beds that made them stop breathing or their heart to stop pumping.

My first day of initiation was not over. Another unconscious man was wheeled in. He was a diabetic and had a very low blood sugar level. While the nurses tried to start an I.V. drip, I found some glucagon, injected it and woke the man up in a big hurry. No need to panic about finding a vein as he could now drink some sweet orange juice. The rest of that first shift was much easier with routine lacerations, infections, and sore tummies. I went home that evening and collapsed on our sofa and announced that I was not going back to the emergency room tomorrow! Marion revived my spirits with a great supper and encouraged me with, "It can't get any worse than today."

We enjoyed our little apartment and gradually added to our furniture by shopping in antique stores and estate sales. As Victoria was known to be a place for the newly wed and the nearly dead, there was a brisk business in selling used furniture from estate sales. We found an old black and white T.V. with rabbit ear antennae for $25. The T.V. plus an old china cabinet made our empty living room look much better. Dad and mom Hiller came for a visit and Marion prepared a great dinner and set the table using the crystal glasses that we got as a wedding gift. Things got a bit tense when the glasses were filled with tomato juice and my dad accidentally knocked his over getting the juice all over the table cloth. He was most embarrassed. The roast was very red and tough, so we joked about having to tie it to the table leg so it would not run away. After that things settled down to a most enjoyable evening.

On another occasion, Wilf and Sharon Loch came for a visit. They had chaperoned us during our courtship days and Sharon was one of our bridesmaids. Somehow Marion managed to burn the toast in a pop-up toaster that didn't pop up, and the apartment filled with smoke. Wilf, being asthmatic soon developed a severe attack of wheezing. So I took him outside for fresh air while Marion and Sharon opened windows and frantically flapped towels to drive the smoke out. Everything settled down and a good time was had by all. One day I came home from the hospital to find all three intern's wives in the hallway trying to get smoke out of their apartments. It was funny to realize that three interns were coming home to burnt offerings for supper on the same day.

Finding a church to attend was a priority for us, so we visited several Baptist churches. One Sunday we went to Central Baptist Church in downtown Victoria. A greeter at the door pointed to a room that had an adult Sunday school class. We nervously entered and found our seats. Within a minute we felt the people behind us tapping our shoulders. Their names were Ben and Joy Warkentin, a couple a bit older than us. They greeted us warmly and invited us to have coffee and dessert at their home that evening, together with several other folks from their church. The morning church service was engaging, and once Pastor Holmes was part way through a terrific message, Marion and I exchanged looks of approval. We had found a great church to be a part of – friendly people and great biblical preaching. The evening with Ben and Joy was enjoyable and Joy's dessert was fantastic. We had many more times of fellowship with them during our year in Victoria and they became life-long friends. Together with Ben and Joy plus some other friends we formed a hootenanny fellowship where we met for singing, accompanied by Ben's guitar. Of course delicious snacks were served.

The year in Victoria passed quickly. I learned a lot from the many excellent doctors on staff. I managed to deliver 22 babies on my own and enjoyed assisting at surgery. There was one memorable case of a patient with mitral valve stenosis. I assisted the surgeon who made a purse-string suture in the right atrium and then inserted his finger into a stab wound he made through the atrial wall. I held the purse-string suture tight around the surgeon's finger as he broke up the stenotic valve by blunt dissection. Talk about brave pioneer surgery, done before echocardiograms and angiography were available! Another interesting case was that of two Christian Scientist ladies who were hit by a car after church – just a few blocks away from the hospital. They were most upset when I informed them that their X-rays showed fractures and that we had called an orthopedic surgeon to see them in consultation. The poor women were in a real crisis of their faith, as they believed in mind over matter.

I was able to visit the offices of several excellent family doctors who allowed me to take histories and to examine their patients. I developed a real respect for these doctors' skill in diagnosis and practical management of a wide range of health issues. I enjoyed obstetrics and surgery, but did not want to specialize in these areas and thus exclude all the other interesting aspects of medicine. So gradually a decision was made to become a general practitioner, now known as a family doctor. This allowed me to be involved in a wide range of medical care. Being a family doctor meant full-service care of patients from cradle to grave. This involved obstetrics; care of babies and adults; office work; admitting patients to hospital and caring for them there; making house calls, visiting patients in nursing homes, doing minor surgery, and assisting surgeons in major operations. Near the end of the internship year I met with Dr. Kurt Gottschling, a family doctor in Burnaby and a member of Ebenezer Baptist Church in Vancouver. Somehow he heard about me and the possibility of my wanting to get into a family practice. We had a long talk and I subsequently met Kurt's partner, Dr. Alex Robertson. After some discussion, I accepted their invitation to join them in family practice in Burnaby. I would be on salary for three years, starting at $800/month, increasing by $100/month each year. After three years I could become an equal associate if mutually agreeable.

We enjoyed many aspects of life in Victoria. There was the charm of all the old big mansions, the Legislature buildings, Beacon Hill Park, the Empress Hotel, the antique stores, tea shops, and the wax museum. The Empress hotel was famous for the fancy high tea served in the lobby. This tea was much too expensive for us. We found a cafe in the basement that served the same fare offered in the lobby at less than half the price. So, we went downstairs for low tea complete with crumpets, clotted cream, and jelly. We made sure to have our fingers crooked in the appropriate fashion.

We valued the many new friendships we made in Victoria, but we did feel somewhat isolated on an island. To travel anywhere else, we would have to drive to Swartz Bay and wait for a ferry and then sail one-and-a-half hours to the mainland. So with mixed feelings we bade farewell to friends after a delightful year and moved on to the next phase of our lives.

LAUNCHING OUT

OUR FIRST APARTMENT IN VICTORIA WHERE I WAS AN INTERN

FELLOW INTERNS AT THE ROYAL JUBILEE HOSPITAL, VICTORIA BC

CHAPTER 5

Getting Settled

Now that my internship was over, I was able to practice medicine independently. No more classes, no more doctors checking out my work as an intern. I was now totally responsible for my clinical decisions and that was an awesome feeling – a curious mixture of pride and fear. The old dictum of do no harm often came to mind. I joined Drs. Alex Robertson and Kurt Gottschling in family practice at the Old Orchard shopping center in Burnaby after my application to join the medical staff at Burnaby Hospital was accepted. This allowed me to have admitting privileges, deliver babies, and perform minor surgery. The office was quite small so the three of us shared five examining rooms in which to see patients, along with a small cloak room.

Marion and I found a two-bedroom apartment to rent on MacKay Street in Burnaby. Our apartment building was next door to an apartment where Herb and Del Sturhahn lived. We now had a bit more furniture that we had gradually acquired at estate sales in Victoria. We appreciated being close again to family and to long-time friends at Bethany Baptist Church. In retrospect it was good to have lived away from family and old friends for a year. It allowed us to develop our identity as a couple, working out all the issues of living together, and setting our own priorities. This helped us form the foundation for a good married life together.

The first day in the office was very slow as only about two or three patients had been booked for me to see. Dr. Gottschling suggested that I make a house call on a lady patient for him, as he was quite busy. The

GETTING SETTLED

patient to be seen had a long history of migraine headaches, so he suggested that I take injectable Demerol and Gravol along in case she was too nauseated to take oral medication. Off I went with a map in one hand and black bag in the other to Dieppe Street in East Vancouver. I knocked on the door and rang the bell but no one answered. The door was unlocked so I entered a dark house with all the blinds closed. The lady was in her bedroom sitting on the edge of the bed and vomiting into a bucket. With some difficulty I got a history from her and, having plenty of time, I did a very thorough examination with emphasis on her neurological status. There was one sign that indicated we were dealing with more than a severe migraine - I noticed a slight difference in pupil size. Examination of her retinae was difficult because she could not remain still for very long. I suspected an intracranial pressure increase, possibly a hemorrhagic event. She needed immediate hospitalization, but I had never admitted anyone to hospital before and did not even know the phone number. I found a phone book and, after convincing the admitting department that I was a real doctor with privileges, I managed to get her admitted. While waiting for the ambulance to come for her I called a Vancouver neurologist, Dr. D. Jones, whom I recalled from my student days at Vancouver General Hospital. After hearing my story, he most graciously offered to come all the way out to Burnaby Hospital to see the patient. Dr. Jones saw her and immediately transferred her to Vancouver General Hospital to be seen by a neurosurgeon. That evening she had brain surgery to put a clip on a bleeding blood vessel in her brain. She had a condition known as a ruptured Berry aneurysm. That evening I sat at home wondering, why do I have such calamities every time I have a first day. I would have been much happier making a house call on a child with an ear infection or a case of chickenpox, instead of this life-and-death stuff.

My family practice grew quite rapidly and I soon became fully booked with appointments. I enjoyed the breadth of work that included office practice, hospital work, delivering babies, minor surgery, house calls, and nursing home visits. Marion and I soon felt a desire to own a house of our own and began to look for one. We found a tiny two-bedroom bungalow on 19th Avenue in East Vancouver, just two blocks from Boundary Road, for sale at $13,500. There was a $5000 government grant available for new doctors to settle into a home and practice, so that became the down payment. Now we were proud owners of a tiny house with a small grape vine covered arbour in the backyard. We enjoyed entertaining our parents and friends with what we referred to as a dinner under the vines. In a short time we realized that this house was a bit old and in need of quite a bit of repair. We started to look around again and found a newly built two-level house on a large lot on Portland Street on the south slope of Burnaby. The builder agreed to take our little bungalow as down payment for the new house which was valued at $38,500. He planned to demolish the bungalow and build a new house to sell. So after a year-and-a-half of practice we had saved up enough money to buy the new house with the help of a mortgage. We enjoyed a beautiful view of the Fraser River flatlands and the Olympic Mountains in the distance.

Another acquisition was the purchase of a brand new, canary yellow Chevy Malibu 327 horsepower, four-door sedan. We bought it at a North Vancouver dealership after very intense bargaining that saw me walking off the car lot three times. The salesman was in hot pursuit each time and finally a reasonable deal was struck. That Malibu was a great car with power to spare. One time I drove up the steep hill on the Hope–Princeton highway at 90 miles-per-hour with the gas pedal not yet fully pressed to the floor. I assured Marion that this was just a one-time test. We also bought dad Asselstine's Ford Valiant as a second car. Marion's dad had cataracts removed before the days of implantable lenses, so he wore very heavy, thick glasses. One day he drove to our house and attempted to park in the carport, but with his impaired vision, he did not see the distance to the back wall very well and hit it with a big bang. Fortunately, I had a big sledgehammer and was able to bash the wall studs back onto the foundation plate to prevent the wall from sagging down. This event seemed to signal the end of his driving career and we offered to buy the car from him.

We were delighted to have our Victoria friends, Ben and Joy Warkentin, and their two sons, Glenn and Grant, move to Burnaby just two blocks away from our new home. Ben got a job teaching high school industrial arts, and Joy was hired as receptionist in our medical office. We had great times going for pizza, sharing desserts, and playing Rook. We also got together frequently for a hootenanny time with Ben and Joy, Wilf and Sharon Loch,

GETTING SETTLED

Herb and Del Sturhahn, and Bob and Nancy Hepting. These evenings consisted of good food, lots of laughter and a lot of singing. Ben played guitar, Herb plucked a mandolin, and I strummed a ukulele. This was so much fun that we met monthly, rotating around our different homes.

In 1968, we discovered that Marion was pregnant and we let our parents know right away. My mom danced around the living room in a fit of exuberance that was a sight to behold! My dad had already quit working due to congestive heart failure. He had rheumatic fever as a boy and almost died then. He even recalled hearing his parents discussing his funeral. Now there were times when I raced to my parents' home at night to inject a diuretic to reverse a bout of pulmonary edema, having got there before his family doctor arrived. It was very sad to see his tears as he looked out his kitchen window watching the work gang loading up the tools for the day's work, mourning his inability to join them anymore. But his face really lit up when he saw Marion in her pregnant state.

The monthly income from family practice seemed so generous to Marion that she decided to enroll as a student at the Northwest Baptist Bible School and Seminary in 1967. Marion had dreamed of being a missionary as a young girl, so going to bible school was a natural thing to do. She wrote her final term paper while in the early stages of labour. Thus her hospital nursing career came to an end.

Bruce was born on March 16, 1969 at Grace Hospital. It was customary at the time for prospective fathers to be excluded from labour and delivery, so I sat in a dingy waiting area, nervously reading long out-dated magazines, along with other fathers-to-be. Finally, I got to see Bruce all wrapped up and in the arms of Dr. Dan Froese. Bruce looked a bit egg-headed as he required forceps assistance to be delivered. We were proud and nervous parents as we brought our bundle of joy home five days later. We made a lot of rookie parent mistakes. All four grandparents came to visit and I tried to ensure that everyone had equal time with Bruce, so I gave everyone ten-minutes holding time!

In September of 1969 we flew to Palm Springs for a short vacation. We were there about a week when mom phoned to tell us that dad had a heart attack and was in hospital. Apparently he had two cardiac arrests in the emergency department, was resuscitated twice and was admitted to the cardiac care ward. We rushed home and went straight to his bedside from the airport in order to see him and talk with him. Later that night he suffered a massive stroke that left him in a coma. We were fortunate to have gotten home in time to see him before this catastrophe. It was painful to see him in such a condition. He remained comatose for over a week when he had another cardiac arrest. We had to quickly decide to not try resuscitation again. The funeral was a large one as dad was loved and respected by many people. He was a role model, exhibiting character traits of honesty, gentleness, and faithfulness to God, family, and church. He was buried in the Ocean View Cemetery in Burnaby, next to the grave of his mother. His death left mom a widow at age 56. She worked hard to support herself as she continued her job at the Oakridge Woodwards in the specialty foods section.

We carried on with the various issues of life. Church work was important to us. Marion was involved in women's ministries; as a Sunday School teacher; with hospitality and kitchen duties; and was a camp nurse in the Pioneer Girls Club. I served on the church board, sang in choir, taught Sunday school, and helped with Boys' Brigade.

Medical practice got to be very busy as our all-Christian group of doctors attracted a lot of Christian patients. The phone seemed to never stop ringing when I was on-call. One very sad case occurred when a young mother brought her toddler boy in because she felt he seemed a bit lethargic. When I entered the examination room the child was standing, holding on to a chair. He was about 14 – 16 months old and had an obviously protuberant abdomen. I laid him on the exam table and felt a large hard irregularly shaped mass in his upper abdomen. This was obviously an ominous tumor that the mother had not noticed. I gently put the mom's hand on the child's tummy to have her feel this, and then I tried to explain to her the seriousness of the situation. She stoically tried to restrain tears but couldn't. I cried with her. An immediate referral was made to the Oncology Department of Children's Hospital. Sadly the little boy died a few months later. However, the mom became pregnant and I had the joy of delivering her new baby, and placing it into her arms.

There was plenty of humor in the office as well, which helped to break up the tense emotional times. A man with a hernia came to see me one

GETTING SETTLED

day. When Joy called the man's name to come to the examination room, he quickly jumped to his feet and his pants promptly fell down to his ankles. He shuffled rapidly down the hall trying to pull up his pants at the same time. Joy got all red in the face trying to restrain herself from laughing. A couple of teenaged girls in the waiting room giggled and tried to hide their faces behind magazines. The whole office found this incident uproarious. The poor man was just trying to be ready for examination and had undone his belt and zipper but forgot to hang on to his pants when getting up.

WE ENJOYED THE FELLOWSHIP OF friends and even managed a trip to Hawaii with Ben and Joy Warkentin. By this time Marion was about four or five months pregnant with Lori. We stayed for a wonderful week at the Napili Shores on Maui.

We were really getting settled into the routines of adult married life with a nice house, two cars, a busy medical practice, great friends, active church involvement, a son, and another baby on the way. We felt that we had arrived into a lifestyle that could go on for a very long time.

Suddenly our comfortable existence was shattered when, one morning at about 4:30, the phone rang.

OUR NEW HOUSE ON PORTLAND ST., BURNABY BC

AND THEN THE PHONE RANG...

MARION GETTING GARDENING ADVICE FROM MY DAD

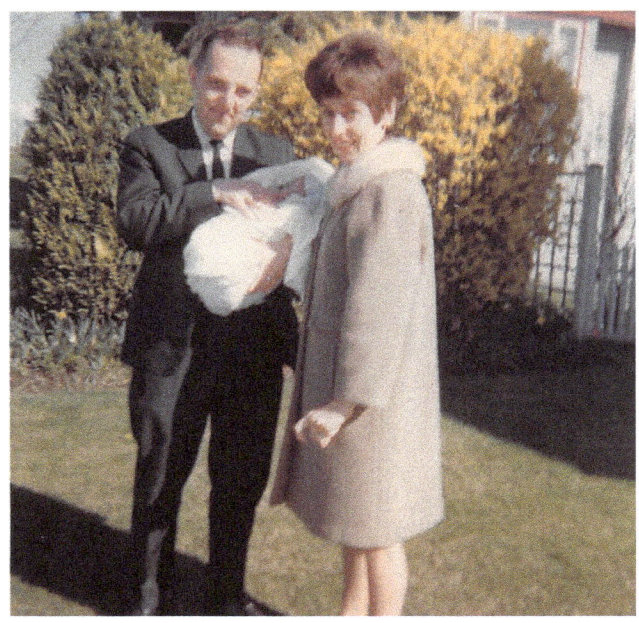

OUR FIRSTBORN SON, BRUCE, ARRIVED ON MARCH 16, 1969

GETTING SETTLED

BRUCE CHECKING OUR FIRSTBORN DAUGHTER, LORI WHO ARRIVED JULY 25, 1970

HOOTENANNY GANG — SHARON LOCH WITH BEN WARKENTIN, ME, BOB HEPTING AND HERB STURHAHN

AND THEN THE PHONE RANG...

HOOTENANNY GANG HERB STURHAHN, MARION, DEL STURHAHN, JOY WARKENTIN, NANCY HEPTING & WILF LOCH

CHAPTER 6

The Phone Rang!

There is nothing unusual about a phone ringing in the house of a busy family doctor doing obstetrics on-call, even at night. But there was something different about *this* phone ringing at five o'clock in the morning. I answered with the expected sleepy hello, trying not to wake up too much, but just enough to deal with the issue at hand. I heard a deep firm voice say, "This is Dr. Schilke here, I would like to know if you would be ready to go to Africa."

Dr. Richard Schilke was the General Secretary of the North American Baptist Missionary Society and was well known for getting straight to the point. He was in his Forest Park, Illinois office at 7 AM Central Time, and not concerned about little things like time zones. I was now wide awake, wondering about what was going on. Dr. Schilke went on to explain that three missionary doctors were coming home in the next two years, one to retire and the other two going on furlough. Somehow, via his vast network, he learned that I was a Christian doctor and a member of a North American Baptist church. His plan was for me to be posted to Warwar Hospital on the Mambilla Plateau in Nigeria to replace Dr. Willy Gutowski (going on furlough), and then transfer to one of the hospitals in Cameroon. By this time I was sitting on the edge of my bed trying to figure out if this was real or just a very vivid dream. I responded, asking for some time to think about this request.

Needless to say, I was in a state of shock. I told Marion about the phone call and she seemed quite delighted at the prospect of missionary work. As

THE PHONE RANG!

a young girl she had decided that she would be a missionary – in response to her mom's question, "What do you want to do with your life?" She had thoughts of going to India where her church denomination had missionary activity. Later, in our courtship years, we had discussed the possibility of mission work as a married couple. But as for me, the years of school, internship, and getting settled in medical practice absorbed all my energy. The idea of missionary work was essentially forgotten. Now the issue of missionary service was front-and-center again – do we or don't we go? Marion was ready to start packing our bags, but I was not.

I had to struggle with the concept of actually being a missionary. In my mind missionaries were spiritual giants, a special breed, role models of commitment and service, and at a level of piety that the rest of us ordinary people could never attain. I knew that I was not like that. I was just an ordinary guy trying to serve God. I did not fully realize how God uses the ordinary and the humble of this earth to achieve His purposes, and that the great things accomplished in God's kingdom are done by the power of the Holy Spirit and not by human wisdom. When Jesus ascended to heaven, He entrusted the proclamation of the gospel to fishermen, a tax collector, a former zealot, and several other very ordinary guys. The book of "The Acts of the Apostles" has been renamed by some as the book of "The Acts of The Holy Spirit." At this point in my life I did not fully comprehend what God can do when one is available to Him. Jesus demonstrated God's power in feeding 5000 men after only two fish and five loaves of bread were made available. It is all too easy to read that account in the gospels and gloss over the personal application.

I also felt fearful of going to Africa with a family. Marion was now pregnant with our second child. I would be exposing them to an unknown lifestyle and the risks of tropical diseases. I felt a fear of the unknown. I also felt poorly equipped theologically to go where I might be called on to preach or teach. My medical training and experience to this point had not prepared me to be the only doctor in a hospital where I would have to do surgery and anesthesia on my own. Finally, I had to consider leaving my recently widowed mother to fend for herself. I, her only child, would not only leave, but also take her grandchildren away for four years at a time.

The struggle of indecision lasted about two weeks. I was unable to get refreshing sleep and paced the hallway for hours at night. I tried to bargain with God by witnessing to patients wherever possible. More people heard the four spiritual laws in those two weeks than in all the prior years of medical practice as I tried to show God that He really needed me here in Burnaby. As I prayed about this issue, God reminded me of the process by which He had prepared me. I came to a saving faith in Him as a child, I was raised in a Christian home and belonged to a mission minded church. I then recalled attending Green Bay Bible Camp at age 14. Now my trip through memory lane became sharply focused. Missionary speakers at camp had challenged me to seek God's will for my life, and I recalled my finding Romans 12:1-2 to contain the answer:

> *I beseech you therefore, brethren, by the mercies of God, that you present your bodies a living sacrifice, holy, acceptable to God, which is your reasonable service. And do not be conformed to this world, but be transformed by the renewing of your mind, that you may prove what is that good and acceptable and perfect will of God.*

My response had been to give my body, my life, to God to use for whatever purpose He would choose. Now, many years later, I felt that He was calling me to this task He chose for me in Africa. I finally swept away all the excuses, recommitted myself to Him, and said yes, I will go to Africa. An immediate peace flooded my soul. I could now see how God had led and prepared me for this. He led me to university, protected me in tests of faith by academia, opened the door to medical school, and gave me the gift of a wonderful godly wife who had a love for people of other cultures.

After a discussion with my ever-ready Marion, I called Dr. Schilke and informed him of our decision to go to Africa on one condition. Realizing the need for further surgical training, I asked for time to do one year of surgical training. Dr. Schilke readily agreed to that request. That night I slept like a baby. During my time of sleepless struggle Marion was able to sleep soundly and did not know about my pacing the floor. We both feel God gave her sound sleep so as to prevent her from influencing my decision. This decision to answer God's call had to be the result of God working in my heart, no one else.

THE PHONE RANG!

I informed my partners, Drs. Robertson and Gottschling, of my decision to go to Africa as a medical missionary. They were sorry to see me leave, but were very supportive and understanding. I was able to arrange for a one-year surgical residency at the Vancouver General Hospital from July 1970 to June 1971. The director of the surgical residency program was Dr. R. E. Robins, a devout Christian and member of Granville Chapel, a Brethren church. I obtained a surgical residency position at a time when there was a long list of applicants for the standard four-year program. A one-year position was most unusual. Our house on Portland Street sold within one week of listing it for sale, and we moved in with my mom on 49th Street in Vancouver. She moved into the basement suite and we occupied the main floor. I also tearfully said good-bye to my canary-yellow Chevy Malibu and sold it to our friend Wilf Loch, who promised to take good care of it. Through all these many changes we could see the hand of God expediting every step of the way.

July 1st arrived and I was now a surgical resident at Vancouver General Hospital on East 8. The year was divided into six months of general surgery, two months of urology, two months of orthopedics, one month of anesthesia, and one month of obstetrics and gynecology. I started with a six-month rotation in general surgery. The workload was very strenuous. We started every day at 6 AM with making rounds on about 40 patients and then assisting at surgery from 8 AM to mid-late afternoon. Then we had to admit new patients by doing complete histories and examinations and writing orders. We could not go off duty until all new patients were admitted.

As a first-year resident, I also had to arrange the surgical slate for the following day and call the patients to come in. Preference for operating times was given to Dr. A.D. MacKenzie, the head of the Department of Surgery and next to Dr. R.E. Robins, the head of the Residency program. It was a bit awkward having to deal with complaints from surgeons who were lower down on the pecking order and wanted more operating time. What made the work most difficult was being on call every second night. That meant staying at the hospital overnight to deal with post-operative complications of patients and to see every patient who came into the emergency department and needed a surgical consultation. We were called by the emergency physicians to see these patients, assess, admit, prepare them for surgery, notify the staff surgeon on call that night, and assist at the surgery. The majority of the emergency consultations were for acute painful abdominal conditions. We rarely got more than a couple hours of sleep. The next morning, we were up doing rounds at 6 AM and starting the day's surgery at 8 AM. I don't know how I ever got through such a difficult schedule.

The surgeons were excellent teachers. Dr. MacKenzie was a world-renowned expert on thyroid conditions and did a lot of very difficult surgical cases referred to him by other surgeons – even from those out of town. He demanded excellence. When assisting him, he would ask many questions about patients he had on the ward, and if I knew the results of the most recent tests done and the patient's condition, he would gradually turn over more and more of the operating procedure to me and he would become the assistant, which was great. As Chief of Surgery he also demanded punctuality. The patient had to be anesthetized, prepped, draped, and ready for surgery by 8 AM. The dictum was the knife hits the skin at eight! One time a surgeon made a big abdominal incision precisely at 8 AM. The patient sat bolt upright and screamed. The patient was wrestled back down and received a very rapid induction of anesthesia. The embarrassed surgeon forgot to check with the anesthetist if it was okay to start. Hopefully the poor patient did not remember any of this!

Dr. Robins and Dr. Hildebrand were Christians and knew about my being on a one-year crash course to prepare for medical missions. Dr. Hildebrand had been a missionary doctor in the Congo and had to leave suddenly during the Simba rebellion. He understood very well what I was going to experience in Africa. They often had me be the surgeon and they assisted me, carefully teaching and talking me through the operation. I did have very steady hands and a gentle touch with tissues. It became apparent that I had an aptitude for surgery, and this became known to all the staff surgeons on East 8. As a result, I got to do a lot of surgery, ultimately at a level of a second- or even third-year resident level. One time, Dr. Hildebrand had scheduled a vagotomy-pyloroplasty on a patient with chronic peptic ulcers to start at 8 AM. Dr. Hildebrand was not feeling well and wanted a short nap. He instructed me to start the operation with an intern to assist me. He indicated that he would join us in a few minutes. I

THE PHONE RANG!

proceeded to prep and drape the patient and began to open the abdomen. I looked over my shoulder but did not see Dr. Hildebrand. So, I proceeded to "kocherize the duodenum" (mobilize the duodenum from its attachments). Another shoulder check revealed no Dr. Hildebrand. So, I kept on going with stay sutures and opened the stomach, cutting through the pylorus into the duodenum. Still no Dr. Hildebrand in sight. On we went, to close the stomach and duodenum transversely so as to enlarge the pyloric passage from stomach to duodenum. I was just putting in the last sutures when Dr. Hildebrand appeared and looked over the drapes and said, "Nice work boys." He then scrubbed in and checked our work, found it satisfactory, and then finished the procedure by doing the vagotomy (cutting the vagus nerves going to the stomach). I then closed the abdomen, wrote the post-operative orders and dictated the operative report.

Once a month grand rounds were scheduled for all the surgeons and residents to attend. Interesting cases were presented by the senior resident which the surgeons, radiologists, and pathologists then discussed. Monthly complication rounds were also held in which all the surgical complications were reviewed and discussed. One older surgeon was very knowledgeable in these rounds as he was quite a rough surgeon and had a lot of complications. I once assisted him in the drainage of a large subphrenic abscess (under the left diaphragm). We had just opened the patient when the surgeon became pale and sweaty. The anesthetist quickly called a second anesthetist to stand by the operating room door in case the surgeon collapsed. The surgeon finally sat down and was persuaded to leave. Suddenly I was the surgeon with an intern to help me. The idea was for me to pack the wound and wait till another surgeon could be found to come in and take over. As it was nighttime, there was no other surgeon handy in the building. So I proceeded with blunt dissection and quite easily found and opened a huge abscess. We suctioned out the pus, irrigated the area with saline, instilled some saline with the antibiotic tetracycline added, inserted big drains and closed the abdomen with retention sutures. The anesthetist seemed quite pleased with the proceedings and was glad to wake the patient up. I learned a lot from the rounds and even had the opportunity to put it into practice. One aphorism I learned here and applied many times later was where there is pus, there must be steel. In other words, if there is an abscess anywhere, a steel knife is needed to drain it. Antibiotics alone are almost useless.

During the six months of general surgery I got to do countless hernias – preferably by the modified McVey method, about thirty cholecystectomies, several common duct explorations, thyroidectomies, partial gastrectomies, pyloroplasties, colon resections, mastectomies, and some skin grafts. Dr. Robins did a lot of head and neck surgery and I got to help him with excisions of parotid gland tumors. This was very meticulous as the facial nerve had to be identified and the tumor mass dissected carefully away from the nerve. Nerve damage would result in facial muscle paralysis and sagging of one side of the face. These operations took up to five hours to complete.

On July 25, 1970 Marion went into labour. I had come home at about 8 PM after 36 hours of exhausting work. I inhaled some supper, fell into bed and drifted into a deep sleep. I was unaware that Marion was up for hours with labour pains. This was two weeks before her due date and things were not ready in the house. So, Marion busily prepared the cradle, packed a bag and then tried to wake me up. It took a while to rouse me enough for me to understand the situation. I told her to call the doctor. She tried but the contractions were so hard that she could not see the numbers on the dial phone. Now I really woke up and we sped off to Vancouver General Hospital, leaving Oma in charge of Bruce. Marion was immediately examined and whisked off to the delivery room. There an intern delivered our little girl – Lorena Ruth. The obstetrical residents were busy doing a Caesarean section and were not available. This all happened so quickly (5-10 minutes), that I was still standing in the hall holding Marion's suitcase when Lori's arrival was announced. When we took Lori home, two-year-old Bruce came near for a quick look, poked her with his finger, and promptly went off to play with his truck.

The year went by quickly. The rotations through urology and orthopedics were very helpful in gaining experience in handling fractures, amputations and urological problems. The time spent in anesthesia was invaluable as there would be no anesthetist in Warwar. I learned how to administer a good spinal anesthetic and about the basic principles of general anesthesia. The month in obstetrics and gynecology was done at Grace Hospital, a Salvation Army hospital for women. The main procedures I learned there

THE PHONE RANG!

were lower segment caesarean sections, total hysterectomies, salpingo-oophorectomies and repair of anterior and posterior vaginal prolapses. Dr. W. Thomas taught me by allowing me to be the surgeon and him assisting me. I recall one very difficult hysterectomy on a patient with a very large uterus and a narrow pelvis. The procedure required repeated clamping and cutting down both sides of the uterus, deep into the narrowing pelvis. Dr. Thomas was sweating profusely as he assisted, but he never took over when things were difficult, letting me experience what a tough case is all about. We were successful and I think he was more relieved than I was.

The time had come to get ready for travel to Nigeria. Dr. Schilke was a master administrator, getting flights, bus and hotel vouchers, visas, registration with the medical council of Nigeria, and arranging the shipment of our cargo. Marion did the bulk of our shopping for clothes and shoes. We got a lot of help from Kiddies Kobblers in deciding what shoes to get for two children for the next four years. We ended up with two pairs of shoes per year for Bruce and Lori in gradually increasing sizes. We got five 45-gallon steel drums with lids and gaskets to pack for shipment to New Orleans and on to Douala, Cameroon. Shipments to Lagos, Nigeria were very expensive and risky. In Cameroon we had personnel nearby to get our drums through customs and then truck them to Bamenda and ultimately to Warwar in Nigeria. I was fortunate to get some excellent medical and surgical textbooks, including Maurice King's classic "Medical Care in Developing Countries". The surgeons at Vancouver General Hospital gave me a silver dermatome – a special knife for taking skin grafts from donor sites. The cutting blade was a stainless-steel razor blade, which allowed removal of a piece of skin almost two inches wide. I also got a gift of money from the women's missionary fellowship of Bethany church that was used to buy a gold handled needle driver, Metzenbaum dissecting scissors, and a variety of surgical clamps. These were packed in my carry-on bag – something I wouldn't dream of doing today.

Dr. Schilke arranged for our financial support and assigned us to a number of supporting churches. We visited the Vancouver area churches just prior to departure to inform them of our mission and for them to get to know us and pray for us. Finally the time came for us to leave for yet another difficult first-time experience.

AND THEN THE PHONE RANG...

PICTURE OF "NEW MISSIONARIES" GOING TO NIGERIA & CAMEROON

SHIPPING OUR CARGO IN STEEL DRUMS TO CAMEROON

THE PHONE RANG!

OUR LAST SUNDAY BEFORE GOING TO NIGERIA

CHAPTER 7

What a Trip!

It was August 24, 1971 – a day of mixed emotions. There was the excitement of going on a venture into the unknown, wondering how we will manage. But there were also the teary good-byes with friends and family who gathered to send us off at the Vancouver airport. Four years seemed like a long time to be away, especially from Marion's elderly parents and my recently widowed mom. We boarded an early-morning flight to Toronto. We were very tired due to all the last minute packing details and good-byes. I had not slept much for two nights as the mounting tension kept my brain on high alert. So we were very emotionally spent by the time we settled into the plane. Marion huddled down with Lori and pulled her baby blanket over both their heads and had a good cry. That released a lot of tension, making her feel much better. Bruce was delighted with being on an airplane, and especially interested in pushing the flush button in the washroom and seeing the noisy swirl of blue water in the toilet. He dragged me down the aisle every half hour for this purpose. I thought if this keeps up he should be completely toilet trained before we see Africa. It was good to travel with children as they provided diversion from thinking too much about the teary farewells. The cabin crew was fantastic, serving up a beautiful breakfast and helping us on and off the plane with all our carry-on bags and diaper bags.

We had three hours of layover time in Toronto before our flight to Rome. We retrieved our bags from the carousel, and when checking them onto the Rome flight, the Canadian Pacific Airline ticket agent demanded

WHAT A TRIP!

payment for extra baggage. We were not aware of such charges and did not have enough money. We were informed that this flight was an international flight and the rules were different from domestic flights. Being novice travelers, we did not know this. I argued that CP Air put us on the flight to Toronto realizing that we were en-route to Nigeria and did not inform us of extra charges. How could they seemingly change the rules on us part way through our trip? Finally the agent consulted with a manager and they allowed us to check our bags without paying an extra fee. We found a family room where we tried to get Lori to nap. Marion suddenly discovered that her dress was coming apart at the seams. She was wearing a new polyester dress (a novelty at the time), but realized that the threads were not polyester. The stretching of the material popped the threads. So I scoured the airport looking for a sewing repair kit. Imagine the scene of Marion sitting in her slip and sewing up her dress by hand, and me trying to amuse the kids and keep strangers out of the room. She got done just in time for us to board the plane.

The plane landed at the Fiumicino airport near Rome in the late afternoon. Rome was hot and humid and I was soon soaked with sweat. I carried passports, tickets, a camera, and three bags. Marion carried Lori, a cuddle seat, and a bag. Bruce carried his little Hawaiian Airline bag full of his favorite cars. The flight to Kano, Nigeria did not leave until 3 AM. In view of this 16 hour lay-over, Dr. Schilke had arranged for a room at the Anglo-American hotel in Rome and travel vouchers for bus transfer to the hotel. However, the bus company at the airport had a wildcat strike going on, so we got CP Air to give us a different voucher for another bus company. Unfortunately this bus just dropped us off at the central bus terminal in Rome.

There we were, with bags and kids at sundown with no idea where the hotel was. We hailed a taxi and made sure the driver knew where the hotel was. On the way I whispered to Marion, "We have no lira (Italian money), so when we get to the hotel, we need to get the kids and our baggage out of the taxi and into the hotel before I deal with paying the driver." We did exactly that after taking what seemed to be the scenic route. The taxi driver was irate when I presented him with Canadian dollars to pay for the fare. I knew the exchange rate and actually gave him about double the fare. The hotel desk clerk was fluent in English and helped me appease the driver with the extra money. The clerk also helped arrange for a sympathetic taxi driver to take us back to the airport later that night.

It was now suppertime, so we walked to a local restaurant that was more like a cafeteria. The food was very greasy and unappetizing, but when you are tired and hungry you can eat anything. It only took three hours for diarrhea to start. Back at the hotel we noticed that Lori was developing quite a high fever that caused another concern.

We got back to the airport without a hitch, but boarding the plane was another matter. It was parked at least 150 yards away from the terminal. So, at 3 AM we trudged out to the plane, Marion carried one-year old Lori, my hands were full with carry-on and diaper bags, so 2½-year old Bruce had to walk, hanging on to the diaper bag. We got to the top of the stairs when Bruce balked at stepping over a gap between the stair landing and the plane – like a cow at a cow gate. The stewardess just stood there and watched until a well-dressed big Nigerian lady behind us berated her with a loud commanding voice, "For goodness sake, help the poor child on board!" We finally got seated and noticed that Lori was not just very hot, but she was also starting to exhibit some twitching in her face. We feared that she might develop febrile convulsions. We asked the stewardess for some water and were told to wait till they had served drinks to everyone. It took over an hour to get a bit of water to help her swallow an aspirin needed to help cool her down. By this time Marion was in tears and we were both exhausted. It took a while to settle down.

Sleep was not possible for me so I just stared out the window into the black of the night. At about 5 AM I noticed points of fire on the ground. It took a minute or two to realize that we had crossed the Mediterranean Sea and were now over the dark continent of Africa. The fires were probably burn-off flares from oil refineries. I felt a mixed sense of excitement and fear. Finally we were nearing our destination. It was morning when we landed at Kano airport in northern Nigeria. Stepping out of the plane was like stepping into an oven due to the high temperature and humidity. The passenger in front of us pulled out his camera and took pictures as he descended the stairs. Soldiers carrying assault rifles met him at the bottom of the stairs and hustled him away to be interrogated. I quickly learned that officials in Nigeria were very sensitive about security, as the Biafran civil war had ended just a short time prior to our arrival.

It took a long time to get through immigration as everyone crowded forward. There was no lining up. At the customs area we had to put all our bags in front of an official who interrogated us. "Who are you? Why are you here? Where are you going?" And on and on the questions went. Behind him stood a big man in a fancy uniform who carried a swagger stick and supervised the proceedings. They wondered if we had money to be exchanged into Nigerian currency. I hesitated, as I felt like this was becoming a shake down. They wanted me to open our bags, and pointed to the diaper bag for starters. I was carrying feverish and crabby Lori at the time, and I gave her thigh a little pinch. Lori came to the rescue in great style by letting out a tremendous wail. That noisy bawling seemed to really disturb the customs officials and they just waved us on through. They were either soft-hearted family men or they simply did not want to put up with the noise.

There was another five-hour delay for our final flight to Jos, where Harold and Marg Lang were to meet us. Apparently there had been a plane crash in which an important army official was killed. The airline gave us a complimentary hotel room and breakfast. This time our bus voucher worked and we were taken to a hotel near the airport. As we travelled in the bus I noticed a distinct pleasant odor that I had never sensed before. It was earthy and different, perhaps due to different vegetation, open-air markets with produce, meats, and palm oil. There were many people walking along the road, some with donkeys loaded high and wide with cargo. Women were dressed in colorful cloth wrappings – some with babies tied to their backs and some carrying baskets balanced on their heads. An agent from the Nigerian Airline travelled with us to help us get to the hotel. I think he revealed the real reason for helping us when he repeatedly asked us to exchange our money. I was reluctant to do this because we had to declare all of the currency we had with us at the airport. I carried emergency money in various denominations such as British pounds, German marks, and American dollars. Apparently these amounts are closely checked on departure from Nigeria. The hotel was nice and clean. They served us a tasty breakfast on a shaded patio restaurant. We enjoyed a bath and lay down on the bed in our air-conditioned room, but were afraid to sleep in case we missed our flight to Jos.

We got back to the Kano airport and found a pushing, noisy crowd at the check-in booth. There seemed to be a problem with where the plane was going – maybe to Kaduna, or Zaria, or Jos. This was most disconcerting. We finally joined in the unaccustomed pushing and made our way onto a plane in the hope that it was actually going to Jos. The plane was an old DC-3 propeller driven aircraft with a narrow, sloping aisle. We climbed upwards to our seats at the front of the cabin and found ourselves looking at the baggage compartment, separated from the passengers by a big net. We were given only two seats and had to hold our children on our laps. Marion's seat back was broken and was left in a reclining position. As the old DC 3 taxied and powered down the runway, the baggage shifted towards us and everything in the plane rattled like it was about to fall apart. I figured that if God had really called us to Nigeria, He would see to it that we would get there in one piece. Fortunately the distance from Kano to Jos was only about 300 miles, so it was a mercifully short flight. Harold and Marg Lang were at the bottom of the stairs of the plane to welcome us. We had no idea what they looked like, but their white skin suggested their identity. They hugged us and we immediately felt we had known them for years. What a sense of relief.

The Langs showed us Woyke House Hostel where they served as house parents for 16 missionary children from Nigeria and Cameroon who were attending Hillcrest School in Jos. We had lunch and supper there and met the 16 children. The Langs then took us to the Sudan Interior Mission's guesthouse where we were to stay while in Jos. The guesthouse was run by a retired SIM missionary lady and her Nigerian husband. We were given a nice cool two-room unit on the ground floor. That night we slept like babies. We had not slept for two nights prior to leaving Vancouver and then travelled without sleep for over 32 hours. The multitude of tensions on our trip all conspired to make us completely and utterly exhausted. The next morning Lori's fever was gone but she was covered in a faint rash, which I diagnosed as roseola. The food in the guesthouse dining room was fantastic. A couple nights of good sleep, afternoon siestas, and great food revived us.

WHAT A TRIP!

Marg Lang took us shopping in Jos. The Kingsway store one block away even had small shopping carts and a great variety of food, much of it imported from England. Marg helped us pick out Laughing Cow cheese, canned foods, sugar, flour, rice, jams, peanut butter, TreeTop orange juice concentrate in glass bottles, and tinned spam. She also helped us buy dishes, cooking utensils, linens, and a Singer treadle sewing machine from retiring SIM missionaries. The market was very interesting and contained little booths loaded with produce, cloth, tools, soda drinks, and local arts and crafts. We heard a lot of, "Come here and buy this – very cheap, very cheap." Our budgeted $1000 disappeared in a hurry. SIM had a Bible bookstore behind the guesthouse called Challenge Books, which was a great resource for churches and missionaries. We discovered that Jos was a favored place for the administrative headquarters of many mission agencies as the climate was temperate at five thousand feet elevation in the center of Nigeria. The airport and Hillcrest school were also great assets.

After five days of rest and shopping in Jos we were ready to travel to Warwar, a very remote village on the Mambilla Plateau where our hospital was located. Plan A was to fly in a Christian Reformed Church Mission Cessna from Jos to Serti and then drive four hours in a Land Rover to Gembu, the main town in Mambilla. Unfortunately the CRC missionaries had booked all their planes for their annual conference, so Plan B was to drive all the way from Jos to Mambilla. Dr. Willi Gutowski drove a canvas-backed Landrover from Warwar to pick us up. He brought along Barb Kieper, a nurse-midwife, who was returning to Warwar after a furlough. We somehow managed to pack all our travel bags and purchases (including a six month supply of toilet paper), plus Barb's cargo into the vehicle and set off on a journey of about 650 miles. Barb was the driver. Marion sat in the middle seat with Lori on her lap, and I sat by the window with Bruce on my lap. Willi sat in the back of the canvas-back with one leg draped out over the tailgate and the other in our laundry tub. We were packed in like sardines in a tin! We were barely out of Jos when Barb informed us that there were no gas stations or bathrooms to use. The rule for pit stops was to find tall grass or bushes, stop the vehicle and men went to one side of the road and women to the other side. Thus toilet paper was an essential item.

We also carried several five-gallon jerry cans full of petrol, jugs of drinking water, and food for lunch.

The first leg of the trip was on a paved road through Bauchi and Gombe. At Gombe we detoured northeast to Mubi where Barb had to officially sign in to Nigeria because she was an American. The paved road contained many potholes as the contractor building the road had laid only a thin layer of pavement to make more profit. Heavy trucks soon broke up that pavement. We spent the night in a guesthouse in Biu (near Mubi), and then came back to Gombe and resumed our trip to the Mambilla plateau. We crossed the Benue River at Numan on a small barge that was propelled by a small outboard motor. There was a long line of cars, Land Rovers, and trucks waiting to cross the river. On the other side the roads were red dirt and full of potholes and washboard. Barb was quite skilled at dodging a lot of holes going at considerable speed. So we had to hang on tight. Every bridge had a sign "danger – weak bridge." Not one bridge had intact railings due to numerous accidents such as trucks tipping over.

It was the height of the rainy season and the roads were wet, but we were fortunate in that there were no monsoon-like rains during our trip. The second night we slept at Serti, where the Christian Reformed Church mission had a maternity center and mission station. The station also had an airstrip that was used by the CRC Cessna and Navaho planes. Marg Koiman, the station midwife, was very friendly and hospitable and gave us a nice supper and had beds ready for all of us. Serti was at a low elevation - hot, sticky, and full of snakes. We had to keep our eyes open for them and avoid walking at night without a flashlight. We were tired after two 14-hour days on the road cramped up in the Land Rover with children on our laps.

The next morning we set off for Mambilla. After driving twenty-five miles we reached an escarpment. The road here was a series of steep switchbacks nine miles long that ascended to the 6000-foot elevation of the Mambilla plateau. The air was much cooler and very tolerable at this height. The road however was much worse. The rains had transformed the red dirt road into muddy quagmires in places where culverts were not cleaned out. Trucks had also carved deep ruts in the road, so at times we drove beside the road in deep grass to get around the bad places.

WHAT A TRIP!

Progress was much slower, but very interesting. The plateau had rolling hills covered in green, high grass with interspersed groves of eucalyptus trees. There were large herds of cattle owned by Fulani herdsmen. The cows were very large and had a big hump on their back and long curved horns. The villages we passed through had houses made of sun-dried mud blocks and roofs of either thatched grass or corrugated zinc, a sign of wealth. There were market stalls in the center of the village lining the road. They contained produce, cloth, sugar cubes, tins of sardines, sandals, and tools. We stopped briefly in Nguroje to pick up Ruthie Juvoh, a teenaged worker at the Warwar hospital who was returning from a short leave. We finally got to Gembu, the main town and administrative center of the Mambilla Plateau. Ken and June Goodman greeted us. They were veteran missionaries with many years of service in Cameroon and Nigeria. Ken was the Field Secretary (Director) of the Mambilla Baptist Mission (MBM), and June was the Field Treasurer. They lived in a metal Quonset-type house at the edge of the government hospital in Gembu.

After lunch with Goodman's we drove down a steep and very rough hill to the edge of the Donga River. Barb drove the Land Rover from there onto a small raft slightly longer than the vehicle. The Land Rover had to be driven through deeply rutted and slippery mud onto planks to get up from the mud and onto the raft. The raft was then pushed across the river by six men using bamboo poles, pushing up stream in slow flowing water and then frantically pushing through the fast central current that sent the raft downstream. The hope was that the raft would end up at the right place on the other side, where the same planks were used to drive off. We passengers got into dugout wooden canoes, which were pushed across the river in the same manner as the raft. Our feet were in muddy water and as we crouched down and held on to the edge of the canoe our fingers were in the river. Having got safely across, we then drove up the steepest, roughest switchback road I have ever seen. The only way to get up was to put the Land Rover into first gear and low range. The road then leveled off for several slow rough miles. Parts of the road were dotted with manure patties deposited by cows, known as the Mambilla paving crew. The road then descended into the valley of the Warwar River and Warwar village itself. This too was steep and very slippery when wet. It was like driving on ice, and there was no edge to the road. We drove through the center of the village and crossed over a small creek and climbed up to the Warwar mission station. We had finally arrived. Praise God we made it. What a trip!

CROSSING THE DONGA RIVER TO GET TO WARWAR

DEEP MUDDY RUTS ON BOTH SIDES OF THE DONGA RIVER

CHAPTER 8

Arrival at Warwar

Minnie Kuhn, a Canadian missionary nurse-midwife working in Warwar, was standing at the top of the road to the doctor's house to greet us as we drove up. She faked a frown and hollered, "What took you so long?" She then broke into a broad smile and gave us a most hearty welcome. She was relieved to see us all arrive because she was left in charge of the hospital with no doctor present. She had admitted an expatriate man, on contract to the government's Ministry of Forests, who had suffered a non-surgical leg injury and was sick with pneumonia. Minnie immediately got Willi to see the patient while she supervised her cook who was getting supper ready for the weary, hungry travelers. Meanwhile we unpacked the Land Rover and inspected the house that was to be our home.

The house was built by pioneer missionaries using sun-dried mud blocks which were later faced with stone and cement mortar. The roof was corrugated zinc and the floor was stone. An open style kitchen faced onto the dining area. The dining area was adjacent to a large living room with a stone fireplace and furnished with a three-seat sofa, two armchairs, and a small pump organ. The master bedroom contained a queen bed and a small armoire. This bedroom served as a hallway to a smaller children's bedroom containing a crib and a bunk bed. There was a bathroom with a full tub, sink, and toilet. A screened, covered porch off the dining room allowed for cross-ventilation. The porch looked out to a terraced garden and beautiful bougainvillea bushes and poinsettia trees that were over ten feet tall. We would not lack for fruit, as the house was surrounded by

ARRIVAL AT WARWAR

papaya, mango, guava, avocado, lime, and orange trees as well as banana trees and coffee bushes. There was a smaller, three-room building containing a kitchen with a wood burning stove, a store room, and a tool room for the station labourers. Minnie and Barb shared a smaller two-bedroom house of similar construction. The two guest houses were along the driveway and nestled under a circle of palm trees bearing palm-oil nuts. The houses were round mud huts with thatched grass roofs. The walls were plastered and painted and the floor was cement. Two smaller grass-roofed huts served as bathroom and a kitchen. A small garage was used to store drums of petrol (gasoline), kerosene, and diesel. The living conditions were rustic and simple, but we soon felt very comfortable.

Minnie provided a great supper for us. Over coffee we chatted and shared a bit about our histories. Minnie grew up in a large family on a farm near Rabbit Hill, Alberta. She was a very well-trained nurse with considerable administrative ability. She had served as the night supervisor of nursing at the Royal Alexandra Hospital in Edmonton. Prior to coming to Cameroon as a missionary nurse, she went to the School of Frontier Nursing and Midwifery for additional training in midwifery. She now had 19 years of experience as a nurse-midwife in Cameroon and Nigeria.

BARB KIEPER WAS ALSO A farm girl from Fessenden, North Dakota. She not only learned to drive tractors, trucks, and combines, but also knew how to do mechanical repairs. Like Minnie, she was a nurse, and had attended the midwifery school in Hyden, Kentucky. Barb worked for a number of years as the only nurse-midwife at the Mbem mission station just across the border in Cameroon. On a number of occasions she drove a Land Rover over treacherous roads on rainy nights to transfer patients with complications to Banso Baptist Hospital for emergency surgery. Hearing their stories at supper revealed to me that Minnie and Barb had a wealth of experience from which I could learn. They both exhibited a love for the people they came to serve, and had a desire to see them come to faith in Jesus and to join His church.

A rapid orientation began the next day with Dr. Willi Gutowski who was leaving in less than a week for furlough. His wife Anita and three daughters Sandy, Melody, and Lisa had already left for home. Willi graduated from medical school at the University of Manitoba in Winnipeg about the same time I graduated. He and Anita had worked for four years in Warwar, Willi being the first permanent resident doctor. Prior to this, Dr. Jerry Fluth had visited briefly to assess the need for a hospital with a doctor. As Willi and I made rounds, I began to realize how primitive the facilities were compared to hospitals at home. The buildings were sited on sloping land and thus arranged in terraces. On the upper level was the nicest building, the maternity block, built with cement blocks and roofed with corrugated zinc. This building contained labour and delivery rooms, a postpartum ward, and an operating room at the far end. Behind the maternity was a shower stall and a deep pit latrine with a cement slab floor containing the appropriate holes. The front of the building had a wide covered cement verandah with wooden benches for patients to sit and visit.

The delivery tables were crude wooden tables with vinyl covered pads. The operating room had an old operating table that could be tilted by a hand crank. The lighting was provided by two sheets of corrugated plastic semi-transparent sheets that served as a sky-light for day time surgery. The light was augmented by louvered glass windows that allowed for cross-ventilation as well. Screens kept most of the flying vermin out. A small building adjacent to the operating room contained a small three-quarter-horsepower Brig-Stratton generator with a gas motor. This was used at nighttime for emergency surgery to power two four-foot neon lights that were mounted on a wooden frame that could be lowered down over the patient. Beside the generator house was a concave, cement slab that served as the hospital laundry. Soiled, used sheets were dumped on the slab, water and soap added, then two women would stomp all this with their bare feet. After this agitation the laundry was rinsed, wrung out and hung up to dry in the laundry shed – an open-air affair with posts, weld mesh for walls, and a zinc roof.

Having toured the nice part of the hospital, we moved on to the wards. On the top level were two cement block buildings with zinc roofs and cement floors. They contained four beds each with a divider forming two bed sections. The beds were Vono beds that consisted of metal frames with metal springs and a thin mattress. These two buildings were used for post-operative patients who were carried there from the operating room

ARRIVAL AT WARWAR

on a canvas stretcher by two teenage youths. The upper level also had two round mud huts with dirt floors and a thatched grass roof. These each had four beds that were wood slats on a wooden frame supported by legs that raised the bed to two feet off the floor. The patients would place their grass mats on the bed while their caregivers and relatives slept on the dirt floor under the bed! Beside the center post of the hut were three large stones and a cooking pot on which the caregivers could prepare food. The doorway was so low that we had to bend way down to get in. There was a small twelve-by-twelve window with a wood shutter that admitted a bit of light. It was difficult to see the patients on cloudy, rainy days, especially when the hut was full of smoke from the cooking fire. We learned to make people smile and their white teeth, now visible, helped us locate them. To hang an intravenous drip, we tied the I.V. bag to one of the eucalyptus rafters. Under these circumstances we treated patients with pneumonia, meningitis, malaria, amoebic dysentery, tetanus, and other serious maladies.

The lower level of the hospital grounds had a long rectangular mud block building that was plastered and painted. The floor was cement and the roof was zinc. Three large rooms were wards for men, women, and children. There were Vono beds but no linens. At one end there was a dispensary where medicines were kept and where outpatients received injections. A smaller room served as a consultation area that was equipped with a small wooden table, an examining table, and three chairs for a patient, an interpreter, and a consultant. Behind this building was a long rectangular shed, open on one side. This was the waiting room for patients. There were several pit latrines as well as huts in which caregivers cooked food. It was interesting to see how people segregated themselves by tribal groups in their occupation of the cooking areas. At a lower level were four round mud huts similar to the ones on the upper level. These huts with four beds in each were used as the isolation ward for patients with highly contagious conditions such as tuberculosis, measles, and fulminant diarrheas.

While Willi and I made rounds on the in-patients, Minnie Kuhn accompanied us and made notes on the patient's chart from our clinical observations and the verbal orders for treatments to be done. These charts were then given to the hospital staff to institute the treatments ordered. One staff person carried a pan of water, soap and a hand towel for us to wash hands between patients. While rounds were going on, Barb was in the dispensary to organize the 100 to 200 outpatients. Some of them had orders for a series of daily injections such as penicillin for their pneumonias. These patients were not quite sick enough to be admitted, and as we had a limited number of beds, they went to sleep in Warwar village and came every day for treatment. Other people who came for initial consultation were organized into three groups. Sick children were seen first, then the women, and finally the men. When in-patient rounds were done, and a quick coffee break taken, we went to see the out-patients. This took until mid-afternoon to complete. Finally, we went back to the house for a late lunch. By this time I was well into a case of culture shock! How will I ever manage in these conditions? This feeling was exactly what I had experienced on my first day as an intern in Victoria and on my first day of family practice in Burnaby. It was *déjà vu* all over again!

I was amazed at the staff. They were all teenagers who had completed grade seven. Minnie had gathered applicants for hospital workers and gave them a written exam to test their English comprehension and general knowledge. A short list was made and these people were interviewed and the most suitable applicants were hired. In this process the applicants had to present a letter of commendation from their church pastor as well. The successful applicants were then taught basic hygiene, nursing care procedures, some anatomy, pharmacology, and pathology. The girls were taught how to care for pregnant women and to do uncomplicated deliveries. The boys were taught how to assist at surgery and to do simple lab work such as hemoglobins and recognition of parasites on stool samples. They were housed in separate male and female dormitories near the maternity. Shortly after our arrival there was another intake of workers and Marion was given the role of nurse educator, teaching them the above subjects. Barb and I were called in as guest lecturers to augment the classes. In order to survive such a huge daily patient load we realized that we had to teach, teach, and teach some more. Only then could we increasingly delegate responsibility to a more competent trained staff. There was one fully trained indigenous midwife, Esther Lackson. She had gone to the midwifery school at Mkar Christian Hospital on a scholarship. She was

ARRIVAL AT WARWAR

a very capable and dependable person who was given a supervisory role over the rest of the staff, especially in the maternity.

Headman Joseph supervised the rest of the staff. They were adults who worked as laundry women, carpenters, night watchmen, general laborers, and even a horse boy and mail carrier. Joseph was an older, grey haired man, who was a respected elder in the Warwar Baptist Church. He was among the first four Christians to be baptized in Mambilla. He was like a kindly father to all the staff and very much respected. He would arrive at the hospital at 6 AM and pound a wake-up drum just outside our house. He gave out tools and assigned work to the labourers such as cutting the grass, digging pit latrines, clearing culverts, repairing the road, and doing general clean-up. Philip Munyah and Stephen Lamba were carpenters capable of building doors, window frames, rafters, and furniture, using only hand tools. They also did repairs, simple plumbing, and did maintenance and running of the station generator. Their workshop was an open-air affair of two workbenches with vises, under four posts and a zinc roof.

The two main tribes on the Mambilla Plateau were the Fulani and the Mambilla. The Fulanis were basically herdsmen and travelled around to graze their cattle. Some of them had settled down on permanent compounds. They were tall and slender with light brown skin and fine features. The women were very beautiful with tribal markings, dangling jewelry and colorful flowing robes. The Fulani people were Muslim and many observed the five daily times of prayer. A lot of them were so-called folk Muslims, who did not really understand the tenets of Islam. They were a dominant people group who ruled over the Mambillas for many years. The Mambilla people were farmers whose main crop of maize was carefully stored for an entire year to feed the family. The women tended the maize and the men raised cash crops such as coffee and bananas. The money was used to buy clothes, pay school fees, toiletries and other necessities. The Mambillas were of darker pigmentation and heavy set. The Christians of the plateau were mainly from the Mambilla tribe. Many Mambillas were pagan or animists who had a well-developed worldview that included a dimension of powerful spirits. When illness occurred, they would consult with the witch doctor or medicine man to determine the cause of the illness, and then proper atonement had to be made. The Fulani and Mambilla co-existed, but at times animosity would flare up into violence, especially when a Fulani herder allowed his cows to get into a Mambilla's corn field, destroying that family's food source for the coming year. Smaller tribal groups such as Yambas and Nsunglis also lived in Mambilla. They were part of much larger tribes in Cameroon. A plebiscite in 1961 created a new artificial border along the Donga River when North Cameroon voted to become part of the newly independent state of Nigeria. The people in South Cameroon voted to stay as part of Cameroon. This new border ran through traditional tribal lands dividing people of the same tribe into Cameroonians and Nigerians. There were also a few traders, teachers, and government officials from tribes such as Takum, Ibo, and Hausa that sporadically migrated to Mambilla.

Marion had been busy occupying the house. The house had been unoccupied by humans for over a week and the premises were now usurped by many different little creatures such as cockroaches, spiders, ants, flies, and even termites that left traces of dirt on the cracked cement of the living room floor. Marion declared war, and by the time I got back to the house it was obvious that Marion had the upper hand in the battle that raged on for several more days. She was ably assisted by James, our cook, who came to work for us from the Gutowskis. He was a big, amiable, gentleman with a real love for children. Bruce and Lori got special treats from his kitchen. James had a great sense of humor, a big grin, and an infectious laugh. He was convulsed in laughter when Marion once asked him to chop wood. His response was, "I no fit chop dat wood ma, ee no go fine fo mouth." In Pidgin English the word chop means to eat (chop with your teeth). Marion meant for him to cut firewood for the stove, not eat the wood! James would spend the day cleaning, cooking on the wood stove, and heating water for doing dishes and laundry. After supper he put a large washtub on the stove to heat water for our baths. We used one pail of hot water for the children, one pail for Marion, and I got whatever was left over. Our water came from a spring in the hill above the hospital. The water was stored in a cement and stone cistern from where it was piped to the hospital and the houses. We had a Katadyn filter on our kitchen tap to screen out the dirt. This water was then boiled, stored in empty bottles in the kerosene refrigerator, and used for drinking. We had shipped a washing machine powered by a

ARRIVAL AT WARWAR

small gasoline engine, but this, along with five steel drums of cargo, did not arrive for six months. So doing laundry was a real hard chore when all we had was an old fashioned washboard!

On the evening of our second day at Warwar, Willi knocked on our door and proceeded with further orientation. He said, "Come out here, I want to show you something." He showed us a large hairy, black tarantula sitting on fire wood just outside our kitchen door. Now it was Marion's turn to go into acute culture shock. She did not like spiders, and a tarantula was just too much. The glamour of being a missionary rapidly dissipated as she stared at this creature. After toying with the tarantula, Willi crunched it under his foot and, much to Marion's dismay, informed us that the mission station was located on a tarantula hill. Marion had a real fear of these big, hairy-legged spiders, but was afraid to pray and ask God to remove this fear. She figured He would cause her to see many more of them in order for her to get accustomed to them. It took three months of being afraid, especially at twilight time, before she finally claimed 2 Timothy 1:7, "*For God has not given us a spirit of fear, but of power and of love and of a sound mind.*" She prayed, "Okay Lord, however You want to do it, I ask You to take the fear away." The Lord gradually removed the fear and she even became a bit sympathetic of the plight of the poor tarantulas as I crushed them for daring to enter the house.

As mentioned, the orientation to medical mission work at Warwar with Willi was short. One day was spent doing hospital rounds, one day doing some last-minute plumbing, and one day going to Mayo Daga for a clinic. Weekly Friday clinics were held in distant villages when roads were passable. The Land Rover was loaded with boxes of medicines and hospital staff. Then off we went for a four-hour trip on rough dirt roads after crossing the Donga River. There were several hundred people waiting for us. The local church pastor gave a short evangelistic message and a prayer that God would use our medicines to heal the sick people. One of the hospital staff then presented a health talk stressing proper hand cleaning before food handling, covering pots of food to keep flies away, and the use of latrines. The image of flies having little brown feet that carried fecal matter to food was particularly vivid. Children were vaccinated against measles, diphtheria, whooping cough, and tetanus. Pregnant women were checked for anemia and hypertension and were given antimalarial medicine and iron pills. Sick people were seen by Willi, children first, then women, and finally men. Prescriptions were written on scraps of paper and on Christmas cards sent from North American Baptist Conference churches. Hospital staff dispensed prescribed medicines and gave dosing instructions. The local church people prepared a meal for the clinic workers consisting of Fufu (corn meal cooked with water and shaped into loaves), soup (a stew with pieces of meat and leafy greens cooked in palm oil), and a cola type of drink. This food was completely foreign to me and I was a bit reluctant to eat this, using fingers only, after handling sick people all day. But I ate anyway and began to enjoy it. The diarrhea on the following day was not too severe! Minnie taught us the missionary version of the song, "Where He leads me I will follow, what He feeds me I will swallow." On Saturday Willi did last minute packing and bade farewell to friends and staff.

At daybreak Sunday we were woken by a loud pounding noise just outside our house. Women were pounding corn (maize) into flour using a mortar and pestle. They were preparing a welcome meal for us. We first walked down the hill and across a small valley and up through Warwar market to the Warwar Baptist church. On our way we saw many huts made of sun-dried mud blocks and roofed with either zinc or thatched grass. Around these compounds were farms growing mainly corn, carefully tended by the women. The small market contained open shops selling rice, sugar cubes, salt, tinned sardines, Bic pens, note books, palm oil, and produce. Some shops carried mainly cloth and sandals. One shop was owned by a Moslem man who sold candy and medicines. He was nick-named Maalam Bon-Bon because of his candies. In his shop he even gave injections of vitamins and various antibiotics with little evidence of sterile precautions. His shop was Warwar's version of an unregulated drop-in clinic. As he was a Moslem maalam, he visited Moslem patients at the hospital.

The church was a few steps beyond the market. It was a round mud building with plastered walls, a grass thatched roof, a dirt floor, and four arched doorways. At one end was a raised section of the floor that served as a platform where the pastor and elders sat behind a small wooden pulpit. The congregants sat on curved rows of mud blocks, capped with

ARRIVAL AT WARWAR

cement, each row slightly higher going from front to back. Women and children sat on the left and the men and boys on the right. The singing was exuberant, often in a chant, led by a worship singer who would sing a phrase which the congregation repeated in response. The singing was accompanied by musicians rhythmically beating various sized drums, blowing cow horns, shaking noisy gourds, and clanging sticks on pieces of metal. Everyone participated by clapping their hands to the lively beat. No one falls asleep here! Announcements and a welcome to strangers were made by Headman Joseph. Two choirs sang several songs in English and in vernacular, either Mambilla or Fulfulde. The offering time was done to even more lively music and singing as people danced down the aisles to bring offerings of money, corn, fruits, and live chickens to the front of the church. This process could take 15 to 30 minutes. The non-monetary offerings were either sold by auction or given to the poor. When all were settled back in their seats, the pastor would preach a lengthy sermon. The delivery was loud and very forceful. The pastor would preach in pidgin English and an interpreter would repeat each line in Fulfulde and at times a second interpreter spoke in Mambilla. The services would typically last at least two hours. In this service we were officially recognized and welcomed and called to the platform to say a few words of greeting. Everyone wanted to see the new doctor's family and hear them speak. All were especially attracted to little Bruce and Lori. Sunday school preceded the service with an hour of lessons held in the open air with attendees sitting on narrow wooden poles propped on mud blocks. My rear end was glad when this was over and I could sit on a flat cement bench in church.

After church we went home and shortly after we heard drumming and singing as the church people came up to our house carrying welcome gifts of flowers, branches, baskets of corn, eggs, peanuts, and even live chickens. On arrival they began to dance to the beat of drums, cow horns, and shakers. After a couple of hours of this dancing, Willi and I joined in for a few minutes, much to their amusement. They made welcome speeches and presented their gifts to us. A cow had been slaughtered and Fufu prepared. The pastors and elders joined the missionaries and us to eat inside the house while the rest of the people ate outside. Non-Christian villagers, ambulatory hospital patients, caregivers, and even some Fulanis gathered around to join the celebration. Drumming and dancing continued until twilight. We felt very grateful and humbled by such a rousing welcome. Not only had we arrived at Warwar, we had now been welcomed and commissioned by the people.

WARWAR VILLAGE VIEW FROM ACROSS THE WARWAR RIVER, HOSPITAL BUILDINGS ON UPPER RIGHT

MINNIE KUHN (L) AND BARB KIEPER (R) GREET US AT WARWAR

ARRIVAL AT WARWAR

MOMS WITH BABIES AWAIT IMMUNIZATIONS AT THE MATERNITY WARD

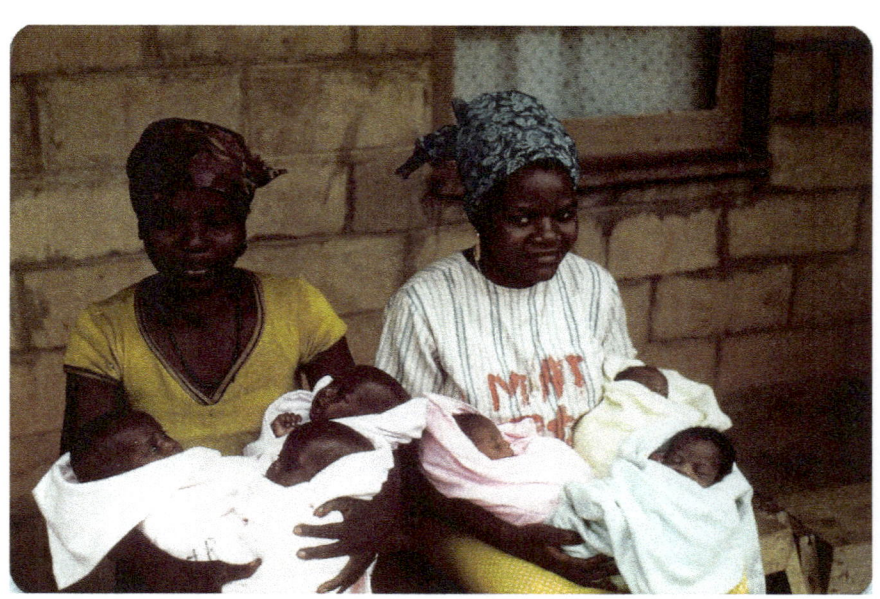

TWO SETS OF NEWBORN TRIPLETS

AND THEN THE PHONE RANG...

MAKING ROUNDS IN A 4-BED HOSPITAL "WARD" — A MUD HUT!

TEEN-AGE WARWAR HOSPITAL STAFF WITH CHAPLAIN (WEARING A HAT)

ARRIVAL AT WARWAR

MIDWIVES L-R ESTHER CHUFOR, SABINA MAMLA & ESTHER LACKSON

"HEADMAN" JOSEPH GINDAL BEATING THE 6 AM WAKE-UP DRUM

AND THEN THE PHONE RANG...

WARWAR VILLAGERS WELCOMING US IN FRONT OF OUR HOUSE

WELCOME GIFTS INCLUDED LIVE CHICKENS AND LIVELY DANCING

CHAPTER 9

Mambilla – Our Mission Field

Monday morning had come, and Dr. Willi Gutowski was on his way home. It was overwhelming to suddenly be left in charge. The first night after Willi left, we had to do an emergency C-section on a lady in distress with prolonged labour that was not progressing. This was my initiation to the operating room. A staff member swept the dirt out of the operating room and wet mopped the floor. With coaching from Barb, I got the three-quarter horsepower generator started so that we could have some light. I then, with shaky hands, got a spinal anesthetic into the patient and tilted the head of the table back. After scrubbing up and getting gowned and gloved, Barb handed me a piece of stained cloth the size of a large napkin. I looked at this, wondering what it was, when Minnie loudly mentioned, "I don't think the new doctor likes our drapes." So, that was a drape! I placed it on the patient along with others in preparation for surgery. I was quite nervous as there was no anesthetist to monitor the patient, or an experienced obstetrician on the other side of the table to assist me. I soon discovered the talents and experience of Minnie and Barb. We prayed for God to guide us and for a safe delivery of a healthy baby. The surgery went well. I got some more teasing when Barb announced that we would not be doing much more surgery in the future as, "The new doctor is using up most of our suture material tonight." She noticed my two-hand method of tying square knots to secure bleeders and stitches. When using that method, one throws away six or eight inches of suture material after every tie, which is what we did back home. So, I quickly switched to instrument ties. We finally finished, and mother, baby and me were doing fine – except that I was the only one sweating!

Within the next week I did several C-sections (one for a ruptured uterus), hernia repairs, an eye enucleation, tubal ligations, and a laparotomy. The hospital was full to overflowing with sick patients. The highest inpatient count had been around 40 or 42 patients, and now we had 47 or 48. All the floor space was used, so we seriously contemplated cutting some high grass to make lean-to shelters for the overflow. Besides seeing all the inpatients, we had around 300 to 400 outpatients daily. Some came for a series of antibiotic injections and others, newly arrived, came for consultation. It was still the rainy season and thus we saw a lot of people with malaria, pneumonia, tuberculosis, and dysentery.

There was a small cluster of round mud huts with grass roofs just above the maternity building. Pregnant women would come during the final month of pregnancy and stay in a hut, together with their care-giver, until labour started. They would then come to the maternity for an enema and a bath and admission to the labour and delivery room. There was an average of three or four deliveries a day, which is around 1000 – 1300 deliveries a year. Minnie and Barb encouraged pregnant women to come to Warwar prior to delivery so that other medical issues could be dealt with. The inducement to do that was a free layette for the newborn that included a receiving blanket and baby clothes, generously supplied in White Cross shipments by the women of our churches in North America.

Soon after our arrival in Warwar both Bruce and Lori got sick with fever and colds lasting about a week. They were given treatment for malaria despite being on malaria prophylaxis. They were just starting to improve when Marion started spotting blood. She spent three days on bed rest, but by September 15, 1971 she developed uterine contractions and heavier bleeding. That night she delivered a stillborn boy at about 22- weeks of gestation. He had been dead for a short while and had a large meningomyelocele in his neck area. Minnie and Barb were very attentive as I dealt with this by the light of a flashlight. We named him Michael. Minnie took care of his burial. We were not grief stricken as we realized that the deformity would have been lethal regardless of when he was born. Marion subsequently developed a fever and a chest cold that required treatment with antibiotics, antimalarials, and further rest.

Marion finally improved and we thought we were done with illness. Not so! Now it was Bruce's turn to get sick. He developed a fever, cough, wheeze, and hoarseness. He had the same symptoms a few months before in Canada and was admitted to hospital with acute laryngotracheobronchitis, and was treated with antibiotics, steam, and oxygen. A pediatrician and an ear, nose, and throat specialist sat up with him all night in the emergency department, debating as to whether or not to do a tracheotomy (which ultimately was not required). Now he was doing the same thing all over again, but there was no pediatrician or ENT specialist here in the bush, and no steamer or oxygen available. We rigged up a kerosene heater on which to boil a kettle of water and fashioned a tinfoil tube to vent steam to his crib that we covered with a sheet. There was no equipment available to do an emergency tracheotomy. Minnie and I found a foley catheter and cut it to size, and put it in a sterile surgical pack with scissors, forceps, and a scalpel. We hid this pack in the house so as not to alarm Marion. I then went outside the house and wept, and cried out, "God, what have I done to my family in bringing them to this remote bush?" God heard my cry of anguish by reminding me of Matthew 28:19-20:

> *Go therefore and make disciples of all nations, baptizing them in the name of the Father and of the Son and of the Holy Spirit, teaching them to observe all things that I have commanded you; and lo, I AM WITH YOU ALWAYS, even to the end of the age.*

Jesus spoke with all authority in heaven and earth, and this promise gave peace to my troubled soul. I interpreted the promise of Jesus being with me always as His presence being with me ALL THE TIME, and in ALL CIRCUMSTANCES. I could then humbly pray and ask God for His strength to help me through the difficulties we were experiencing. This message was so clear that it seemed like I actually heard it with my ears!! We were happy to see Bruce gradually improve and fully recover.

The medical work was carried out in a routine pattern, interrupted by various emergencies. Each day we were awakened at 6 AM by Joseph

Headman's drumming outside our bedroom. Devotions with the staff were held at 6:30. Breakfast was at 7 AM and ward rounds started at 7:30. At 6 PM every day we had what we called the night show, where the staff brought very sick children to our kitchen door to be seen and admitted. These were children who had been carried in by parents, arriving long after the outpatient clinic was over. The very sick kids often had malaria and severe anemia with hemoglobin levels less than 4 grams (normal is 11 to 14 grams). They were gasping for oxygen and needed immediate blood transfusions. Others had pneumonia, tuberculosis, dehydration from diarrhea, or meningitis. None of them could wait until morning for treatment. It made me wonder how many little kids died *en route* to the hospital and were never seen by us.

The typical week went as follows:

MONDAY – detailed ward rounds were done with either Minnie or Barb writing clinical notes and orders on charts which I dictated while examining the patients. During rounds, the staff organized the outpatients and gave the daily series of injections on ambulatory patients. The majority of these were being treated for pneumonias, tuberculosis, and skin infections. Some of them came for dressing changes. The average number of these walking wounded was 100 – 150 each day. The hospital chaplain, a local pastor, followed us on rounds and spoke with the patients and caregivers, comforting them, and praying with them. He also gave a short devotional talk and a prayer at the outpatient shed prior to the start of treatments. After ward rounds, we usually made a dash to the house for a quick coffee break and strategy time with Minnie and Barb to deal with the issues of the day. I then went to the consulting room and, with Joseph Headman interpreting, I saw about 150 new patients and others who had completed their course of treatment. Following these consultations, we had a gynecology clinic where more privacy was arranged for pelvic exams. Most of these patients presented with infertility issues. Others had genital infections, pelvic pain, and lower abdominal masses due to ovarian or uterine tumors. Every Monday about 30 to 35 women attended this clinic. Lunch time was variable, and only after all patients had been seen. Lunch was followed by a short rest and then station work was done. I would go around with Joseph to inspect the general condition of the hospital grounds and give instructions for digging pit latrines, garbage pits, ditches for water drainage, and doing repairs of leaky roofs. This was also time for supervising the carpenters and masons as we were building a small laboratory using sun-dried clay blocks.

TUESDAY - ward rounds were a bit less detailed because this was surgery day. The cases for surgery were electively booked, many on new patients seen the day before. The most common operation was repair of hernias, both inguinal and femoral. Other common cases were hysterectomies and or oophorectomies for tumors of the uterus and ovaries. We also did skin grafting for burns, debridement of dirty wounds, drainage of osteomyelitis, circumcisions, tubal ligations, repair of cleft lips, and bowel resections for volvulus with gangrene of bowel. I will comment later on some unusual cases that required emergency surgery. It was interesting to note that circumcisions were in high demand and routinely requested shortly after birth. However, since there was no surgery available for many years, we seemed to be doing catch-up circumcisions on boys in their early teens. One time a village elder brought about eight teenage boys from his village for circumcisions. He had them all lined up on the outpatient veranda. I foolishly pulled out my Swiss Army knife, opened the blade and asked, "Who will be first?" That was a mistake. The boys scattered and ran like frightened rabbits. It took the elder half a day to round them all up again, reassuring them that I was just teasing. I vowed to never do that again!

As mentioned before, the operating room floor had to be cleaned of mud and mopped. Our instruments had to be washed carefully after each case, dried, wrapped in cloth packs, and sterilized in a pressure cooker! Fortunately, we had some sterilizer tape that would indicate sterility by change in color. We had enough instruments to do several cases which allowed time for the first sets to be re-sterilized for use again. There were two sets of instruments kept in reserve for emergency C-sections.

Anesthesia was mainly by spinal injection. A few cases requiring general anesthesia were done with use of open-drop ether which was poured onto four-ply gauze stretched over a wire mask. To shorten the ten-minute wrestling match caused by ether induction disorientation, we initially used a mixture of ether and chloroform for no longer than one minute, as chloroform can be lethal if given much longer. Some cases could be done using local anesthetics for nerve blocks. I was quite amazed at the low rate of post-operative wound infections in clean cases, considering our really primitive conditions. The infections we did have seemed to respond to simple antibiotics such as penicillin, ampicillin, chloramphenicol, tetracycline, and sulphonamides. I do believe that God was intervening to bring about healing. We prayed with all the patients prior to surgery and a good number of them came to faith in Jesus.

After surgery was done, I went to the out-patients area to see the most seriously ill patients that had been triaged by our staff. Esther Lackson, our Nigerian midwife, and two older boys, Zebulon Wanmi and Paul Chufor, were capable of consulting, diagnosing and treating simple cases of pneumonia, intestinal worms, malaria, scabies, and dehydration from gastroenteritis. Lunch was usually late on surgery day. Marion revived us by bringing a Thermos of coffee and cookies or fruit to the operating room for us to enjoy between cases.

WEDNESDAY – The schedule for Wednesday was the same as Monday. Wednesday was also the antenatal day. At least 150 women came for their routine pregnancy check-up that included blood pressure measurement, hemoglobin, abdominal palpation and measurement of uterine growth, listening to the baby's heart rate, and treatment of any concurrent medical problems. The women were given iron and vitamin supplements to last for a month. This clinic was run by Minnie, Barb and Esther. What a noisy place with 150 women all talking at once! Many mothers also brought young children along for immunizations. Infant and maternal health and preventive measures such as immunization and education were a high priority. It was estimated that only 50% of babies born lived to reach age five. So prevention and early intervention was critical. Our caseload was about 900 deliveries in 1971, rising to 1500 in 1978. After all inpatients and outpatients were seen I had lunch and proceeded with station work.

THURSDAY – The routine was the same as Tuesday, when elective surgeries were done. Newborn circumcisions were done in assembly line fashion, with our female staff holding a row of babies. Foreskins retracted, clamps applied, snip-snip down the line, and then cautery and release of the clamps. For cautery we used a kerosene stove to heat the heads of nails held in forceps. The red-hot nail heads were then applied to the cut edge of foreskin to provide hemostasis. We could do 10 circumcisions in about 15 -20 minutes.

FRIDAY – This was clinic day. There were many villages in Mambilla that were situated far away from Warwar, and it was difficult for the people there to access health care. As already mentioned, public health and infant-maternal well-being were high priorities in Mambilla. Every Friday we would travel to a distant village, and people in the surrounding villages and farms would gather for the clinic. Five such villages were regular clinic sites. Thus, we could see pregnant women every five weeks and also establish a regular immunization schedule for the children. Measles was a real threat in Mambilla as about 50% of infected children died if untreated. The mortality rate for kids with measles treated in hospital was still high at 10%. The measles strain prevalent must have been particularly virulent. Also, most children had a load of intestinal worms, anemia from malaria, and malnutrition which greatly compromised their ability to fight off measles. Invariably these measles-infected kids would get respiratory symptoms and pneumonia. So earlier in the week Marion would pack several boxes of medicines and early Friday morning I would load the Land Rover with staff, medicine boxes, and a freezer box with vaccines and drive for three or four hours to the clinic site.

We set up inside the local church. The local pastor would present a devotional of an evangelistic nature and pray for the sick. One of our staff would give a health talk using large cards with pictures. Presentations included use of latrines, hand-washing for food handlers, keeping flies with brown boots off the food, rehydration for gastroenteritis patients, and the need for immunizations. The midwife (Esther, Minnie, or Barb) then immunized children – usually 100 to 200 of them, and then examined the pregnant women, giving iron and vitamins. Women at 36-weeks of gestation were referred to the pregnancy village at Warwar hospital. I, with the help of interpretation by the local pastor, saw the sick people. The children were seen first, then women, and finally men. The sickest people were put in the Land Rover and brought to the hospital that evening. There was not always room in the Land Rover for everyone who required hospital admission. Those folks were given initial treatment at the clinic and the family would then arrange for carriers to carry the patient on a homemade stretcher many miles to the hospital. Not all would survive the trip, especially those with advanced meningitis, cerebral malarias, or pneumonias. Some of the adults I saw seemed to be a bit hypochondriacal and presented with a vast array of impressive symptoms. They would describe, in Pidgin English, abdominal pains with such phrases as, "A worm dey fo belly where e da holla so tey, and e don bite me belly an run fo e house, I wants medicine were e go chuckara (destroy) de house so de worm he go die." In proper English, "There is a worm in my abdomen that makes a lot of noise and causes pain. The worm then runs to his house (protected area). I want medicine to destroy this house and kill the worm."

Some men complained of impotence, having very unrealistic expectations of performance. They were very happy to receive an injection of vitamin B which was an impressive dark red color. In their estimation the more painful the shot, the more powerful the medicine! The next best medicine was a liquid, and so liquid worm medicine was appreciated. Mere pills were not as highly regarded.

It was really sad to see how many people suffered with various illnesses, often in end-stage pathology, rarely seen in North America. It was particularly heartbreaking to see children in congestive cardiac failure with a loud heart murmur who were going to die a horrible death. They could have had life-saving surgery if they had been born in Europe or North America. Malnourished children with Kwashiorkor presented with swollen legs, hugely distended abdomens and thin red-grey hair. They simply needed protein in their diets. We tried to help the malnutrition issues by bringing seedlings of mango and guava trees to be planted in the church compounds for everyone to use. Inclusion of groundnuts (peanuts), avocados, sardines (available in many bush markets), and milk into diets was encouraged. We ended the clinic by doing dental extractions of rotten teeth, using a set of forceps and elevators donated by my dentist friend Dr. Egon Nikolai, who gave me a 20 minute crash course in proper extraction technique. With only one set of forceps and no portable sterilizer available, we reused the instruments after cleaning with them alcohol soaked white cross bandages. We were tired and hungry after seeing as many as 400 or 500 people. The women of the local church supplied us with food – Fufu and njamajama (leafy greens) in palm oil with chunks of beef or chicken, all washed down with soda pop. The trip back to the hospital was often in the dark, which made crossing the Donga River even more of an adventure.

SATURDAY – Being away all Friday made it necessary to do very detailed rounds of inpatients, especially the newly admitted ones. The daily routine was similar to that of Monday.

SUNDAY – Rounds were done more quickly, concentrating mainly on the sickest patients. We then trooped our way across the valley to the Warwar church for Sunday School and a church service lasting three hours. Afterwards we were ready for lunch and then maybe a little nap. After the night show and supper, we had a fellowship time in our living room with the hospital staff. Devotionals and bible studies were held and the staff learned to use the four spiritual laws, Campus Crusade material, in witnessing to patients and families. They enjoyed singing, especially when I was able to play the song on the pump organ. On some Sundays we visited various churches by Land Rover in order to get to know the people and pastors and to bring words of encouragement to the congregations. It was still the rainy season in early September when I loaded up the canvas-back Land Rover with hospital staff who were going to sing at the church in Mbamga. To get there we had to drive across a little creek. During the church service there was a big rainstorm that did not concern me, as the rain stopped by the time the service was over and we had eaten lunch with the pastor. On the way home we saw that the little creek we had crossed earlier in the day had become a swollen torrent of water. In total ignorance I proceeded to drive across and was almost swept downstream as the water came up over the hood, causing the engine to sputter. Fortunately, the creek was not very wide and I had enough momentum to get to the other side, with the vehicle starting to point downstream. I thought to myself – that sure was a stupid rookie missionary mistake!

TO RUN A MEDICAL WORK in a remote place like Mambilla took a lot of creative administration not taught in nursing or medical schools. We needed a regular supply of medicines that was affordable and unadulterated. Medicines could be bought in many village markets, but the labels did not necessarily indicate what was in the bottle. We were aware that many medicines in labeled bottles were, in fact, just compressed corn starch. The mission agencies in Nigeria involved in medical work co-operated in setting up the Central Pharmacy in Jos. A pharmacist was hired to compound the medicines and make up liquid batches of worm medicine, cough meds, and topical creams. A business manager organized purchase and importation of medicines from pharmaceutical companies in Western Europe and North America at reduced prices or even as donations. At Warwar we had a drug storage room with cards for every medicine dispensed and how much remained. We did an annual inventory to determine how much of each kind of medicine was used in a year. We then placed an annual order for the drugs based on the amount used in the past year plus 10% for anticipated increased requirements. Central Pharmacy packed our order in steel drums and sent a shipment quarterly on a small truck that could get as far as Gembu. We then made a number of trips, crossing the Donga River each time, to get the drugs from Gembu to Warwar.

At times we had to make a special order when supplies got too low. To pay for all these medicines, and to pay staff salaries, buy fuel for vehicles and the hospital generator, and supplies of soap etc., we had to charge patients for drugs and for surgery. In order to balance the budget of the entire medical work we charged the patients three times the cost of the medicines they received. The missionaries' salaries were not included in the hospital budget. In some cases of hardship, we reduced the fees for very poor people and for patients that required a lot of medicine and surgery. In order to preserve the dignity of a poor family, we would give a healthy male caregiver, often the husband, some work such as cutting grass with a machete or digging, which would pay the debt. There were a few rich men who came to the hospital driving their own vehicles. These men were charged at least ten times the cost of the drugs, and they felt proud when we told them that the extra charges were to help their poor country folk. Minnie also arranged staff work rotations and handled discipline issues that would crop up with the young staff that we had. Both Minnie and Barb were determined to maintain the best possible standard of care and behaviour, so as to be a testimony to the entire community. On one occasion several of the girls were summoned to Minnie's house to deal with yet another misdemeanor. The girls pleaded, "Please Ma, forgive and forget."

Minnie replied, "I forgive you, but you keep doing the same things, over and over, so you don't let me forget!"

A SHORT TIME AFTER OUR arrival we went to greet the Chief of Mambilla in Gembu. There were lesser chiefs in each village, called Kashalas, who were subservient to the paramount chief of Mambilla. He had a palace in Gembu surrounded by high mud walls and guarded by servants. We were ushered into a large room where he sat on a throne perched on a low platform. He wore long flowing blue robes and had an ornate turban. We discovered that he was recently elevated to the position of Lamido by the Sultan of Sokoto, which was a high rank in the Moslem aristocracy, just below an Emir. We greeted him, brought him some appropriate gifts, and introduced ourselves and our purpose to help his people. He responded with warm greetings and gave me a plastic replica of St. Peter's Basilica in Rome, complete with a picture of the Pope looking out one of the windows. I wondered where he would have gotten this trinket, perhaps from a Catholic missionary? Our dialogue was facilitated by an interpreter. The chief dismissed us after a few minutes and thanked us for coming to help his people who were suffering. We respectfully backed out of the room and left. We did not see the rest of his palace where he housed his many wives, concubines, and children. It was of strategic importance to visit the chief, pay our respects, and explain our work to him. In return, he would serve as our protector.

Marion and I realized that medical work was just a part of our responsibility. Marion had a heavy load of work trying to run a household without the modern conveniences to which we were accustomed. She had to learn how to operate, clean and refuel a kerosene refrigerator. Drinking water was prepared by using a Katadyn filter on the kitchen tap to remove sediment from the water, which was then boiled for sterility. If she wanted butter, she had to make some. The Monday laundry day started with heating water on a wood stove. Our wash machine was *en route* somewhere in a freighter on the Atlantic Ocean, so Marion had to do diapers and sheets on an old-fashioned washboard. Clothes were wrung out by hand and hung as early in the day as possible in the rainy season. The rains were daily, usually starting in the early afternoon, so, at the first sight of a rain drop a mad scramble began in order to get all the clothes off the line. Ironing was done using a heavy iron that was heated on the wood stove. James, our cook, was very helpful in this chore. Thursday was spent teaching our staff and packing the medicine boxes for clinics. Marion was also station hostess and kept the two grass-roofed rest houses free of black widow spiders and spotless for visitors. She and James did a lot of baking and prepared for the midmorning coffee breaks. We hired a part time garden boy, Stephen, who would, under Marion's supervision, till soil, weed the vegetable garden, and water the plants and flowers. Every ten days was market day when mobile traders would present their goods for sale in the Warwar village market place. A cow was butchered in plain view from our house. James would run down and buy fresh meat, including liver, before flies climbed all over it. On several occasions I went down to inspect the meat and once had them bury the cow due to obvious bovine tuberculosis. That was expensive for the cow owner. There were no banks available for most people, so cows became essentially a walking bank account. The sale of a cow was like a cash withdrawal from the bank account. Marion also prepared food for the biweekly missionary fellowship times for all the missionaries- Ken and June Goodman, Minnie, Barb and us. The maternity walls were looking shabby, so Marion started painting them and continued on to do the in-patient wards as well. Every day the staff would bring money collected from patients to her to be counted, put in the safe, and the amount entered in a ledger. Marion also learned how to run a hand cranked mimeograph machine to make copies of a typed stencil. She produced materials for the Mambilla Baptist Convention and our chaplain, as well as the hospital. This was not easy, as the equipment was old and warped and often printed unevenly. At times she even resorted to using a spirit duplicator.

I had the dubious joy of doing payroll every month for the medical staff, laborers, laundry women, night watchmen, carpenters, masons, mail-runner, horse-boy, etc. – a total of over 40 employees. The currency was Nigerian pounds, shillings, and pence. It was a bit of a trick to figure out what to pay a laborer who worked 21-and-a-half days a month at four shillings and six pence a day. Joseph headman kept a tally of work days for the laborers and tradesmen. The British, who ran Nigeria as a protectorate, developed a daily ready reckoner book to help figure out salaries. This was a great help. When Nigeria switched from the British monetary system to Nigerian Naira and Kobos, a special government team came to our hospital to exchange currencies for people. There was considerable mistrust and hesitancy among the people to part with the pounds, shillings, and pence to which they were accustomed. The older mommies stood at the periphery of the exchange proceedings and watched, nervously clutching their old money tied in a corner knot of their *lappa*, a cloth wrap-around skirt. Finally, they screwed up enough courage to part with their hard-earned money for the shiny new stuff.

Barb taught me how to do a lube job and oil change on the Land Rover. I ended up having to replace broken rear axles, which could be a challenge if the broken bit stayed inside the shaft. I then had to take the good axle out and use a narrow rod inserted in the good side, pass it through the rear differential and tap the broken piece out the other side. Replacing a broken leaf in a rear leaf spring was even more difficult as several jacks were employed to bend the repaired spring far enough to reattach it again. Plumbing was not too difficult as we had a pipe threader and pipe cutter. Willi left a supply of oakum, so with the oakum and some paint, I could make water-tight joints. Philip, the carpenter and handyman, was anxious to help and soon I could leave projects for him to do on his own.

THE WATER SUPPLY FOR THE entire mission station and hospital was inadequate during the dry season. Philip and I climbed up the hill above the hospital and found a spring that had a good flow rate, even in the dry season. We did not know how to tap a spring, so we did the next best thing by building a small dam to collect the water in the creek bed. We inserted a pipe in the dam and covered the opening with mesh to keep leaves out. A fence was erected around our catchment site to keep the cows and people out. A one-inch metal pipe line was assembled and buried underground to transport the water about one kilometer down a 400-foot drop in elevation to a cement-lined stone cistern. The oakum and paint were all used up on this project! In order to break up the water pressure, we placed a steel drum, with a float valve attached, in the pipeline half way down the hill. The water in the cistern was then distributed to the hospital and various houses. To heat water for the laundry women, we placed a steel drum on its side on top of cement blocks and piped water to it with a control tap at the drum site. Beneath the drum was room to build a fire using eucalyptus wood. A vent pipe was inserted in the drum to prevent rupture when the water got hot.

Firewood was always in demand for the laundry, our fireplaces, and for patients to cook food. The Mambilla plateau was essentially a grassland savannah with a limited number of trees. Years of cutting down eucalyptus trees had deforested most of the land. The State government established a forestry department to deal with this problem. I struck a deal with the expatriate head of the forestry department. If he would supply us with seedlings, we would plant them on the hill above the hospital. He agreed to help and supplied us with 5000 seedlings. I got Joseph to get all the workers busy planting trees. In three to four years we could begin to harvest wood. New shoots sprang out of the stumps and we pruned off the small shoots, saving only one or two to regrow. Thus, we produced a sustainable supply of firewood.

October 4, 1971 was a very sad day as we watched Minnie Kuhn leave Warwar to go home for deputation. She was like a den mother to our family during all of our illnesses and difficult orientation. I realized how much I had depended on her wisdom and encouragement. Her absence was another reminder to depend totally on God, who does not go on furlough, but stays with us "even to the end of the age," or in a more literal translation "the whole of every day."

AND THEN THE PHONE RANG...

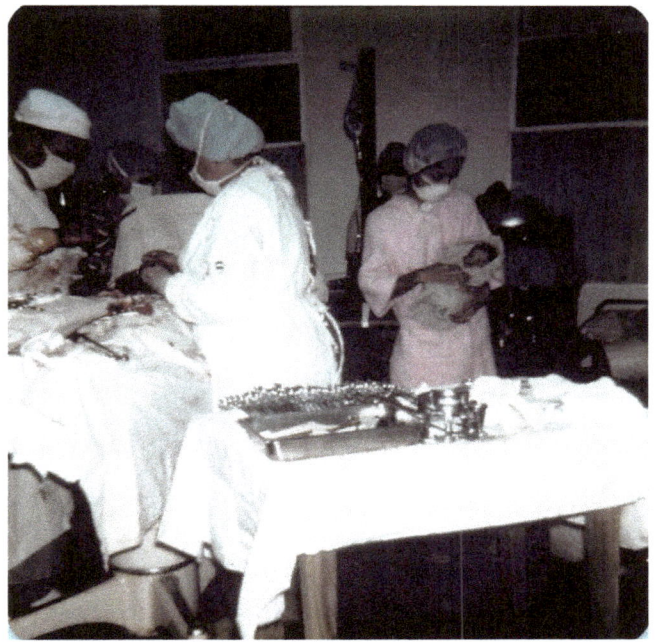

NIGHTTIME C-SECTION. MARION IN A KIMONO CARES FOR BABY

MAMBILLA "AMBULANCE" CARRYING SICK PERSON TO HOSPITAL

MAMBILLA – OUR MISSION FIELD

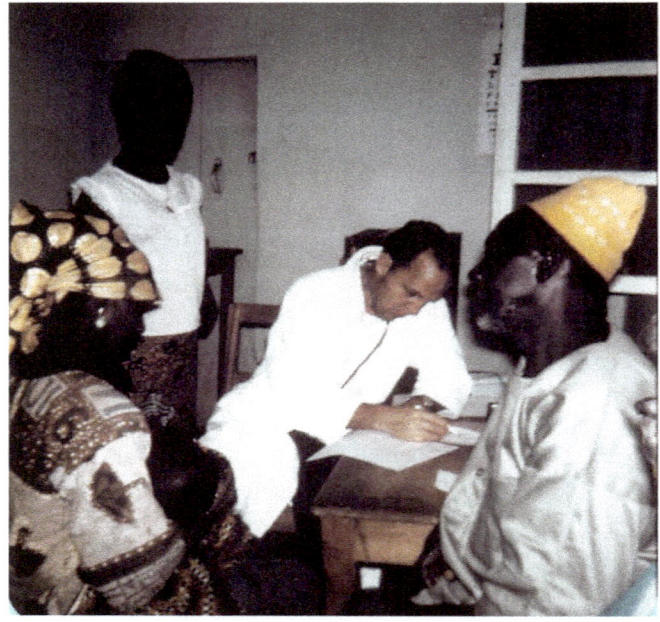

OUTPATIENT CONSULTATION, JOSEPH "HEADMAN" INTERPRETING

CHAPLAIN SPEAKING TO WAITING PATIENTS AT A CLINIC

AND THEN THE PHONE RANG...

BRUCE SUPERVISING VEHICLE REPAIRS

CHAPTER 10
The Church in Mambilla

The gospel of Jesus Christ was introduced in Mambilla by Joseph Mamadu around 1929. He was a pioneer Cameroonian evangelist who came to faith and was mentored by the German-American missionary Carl Bender and Cameroonian pastor Joseph Ebakise Burmley. In 1922 Mamadu was sent north to his home village where he established the first grassland Baptist church. After evangelizing and planting churches in the Mbem area of Cameroon, he crossed the Donga River to enter Mambilla (then still part of Cameroon) to preach the gospel. The first resident American missionaries in Mambilla were Dr. and Mrs. George Dunger who, in 1938, opened a mission station at Warwar. Missionary work was limited by a clause in the residence permit that restricted evangelizing to the confines of the mission station and to non-Muslims. That restriction resulted in a strategy of bringing people to the mission station where local people came to faith and were immediately trained to go to villages as lay evangelists.

One of the consequences of World War II was the internment of all the German missionaries in Cameroon, including my great uncle Johannes and aunt Dora Sieber. Only three American missionaries were left, the Dungers and Laura Reddig. The Dungers left Warwar and settled in Ndu, Cameroon in order to administer the grassland mission work at a more central location. They turned over the mission work in Mambilla to Rev. Robert Jam. He was a Bikom Cameroonian who was trained by coastal missionaries and pastors while he worked in the coastal plantations. Robert Jam established the first

THE CHURCH IN MAMBILLA

church in the Belo area at Wombong in 1931. A year later he transferred to Ndu where he received further mentoring and training from Johannes Sieber. Robert Jam then worked as an evangelist for three years in Mbem and seven years in Mfumte where he planted 11 churches. He moved to Warwar in 1942 and stayed in the Warwar area for five years. During this time he founded and dedicated ten new churches. God richly blessed this wonderful Cameroonian evangelist. I had the honor of meeting him in his final years of life while we worked at Mbingo. His son, Samuel Jam, was a nurse and then chaplain at Mbingo Baptist Hospital and became a good friend of our family. I attended Robert's funeral in 1974 at his home village of Mughef near Belo, Cameroon. His son, Samuel, had taped Robert's final words of encouragement to his beloved Bikom people. As the relatives and friends sat around the casket, they were astonished to hear Robert's voice speaking to them. It was a powerful moment of testimony to the glory of God!

In 1947 North American Baptist missionaries Rev. and Mrs. Gilbert Schneider were posted to Mambilla and settled in Warwar. They built the mission house at Warwar that we eventually occupied. At this time, they found about 183 Christians in six churches. In addition to evangelization, the Schneiders were involved in agricultural development. One of their projects was the raising of a herd of cattle that was later driven to the New Hope Settlement for leprosy patients at Mbingo, Cameroon. Other missionaries came to Warwar for short periods of time after the Schneiders left. There was a period of three years when no missionaries lived in Mambilla. During the later half of the 1950's Rev. Ken and June Goodman taught short-term Bible courses to Christians in Mbem and Mambilla. These were later called leadership training courses. In 1961 the Goodmans were permanently posted to Mambilla and ultimately settled in the small town of Gembu, the administrative center of the Mambilla Plateau. By this time there were 35 churches and between 2200 and 3000 members.

There was a desperate need for medical care in Mambilla. Joseph (Headman) Gindal had some training in simple medical treatment from missionaries at Warwar, so he carried out rudimentary health care. A delegation from Warwar/Mambilla came to an Annual Missionary Conference in Bamenda, Cameroon to demand that a missionary doctor, missionary nurse, and missionary evangelist be posted to their area. No such personnel were available, but Minnie Kuhn heard this plea and volunteered to be posted to Warwar. Minnie arrived in Warwar in 1964 where she worked with Joseph, using two 4 bed wards for sick patients and the delivery of babies. It was obvious that a small hospital with a doctor was needed. Barb Kieper joined Minnie in the late 1960's, and in 1967 Dr. Willi Gutowski and wife Anita came to Warwar as the first resident doctor. A maternity, in-patient ward, and outpatient facility were built. The Warwar dispensary and maternity became the Warwar Hospital.

The number of churches in Mambilla gradually grew, but there was a serious lack of trained pastors. Some Mambilla men were able to get Bible school or seminary training at Ndu, Cameroon after attending the Goodman's preparatory short term Bible school classes. These men, Timothy Yula, Moses Ishi, Abraham Jiminda, Peter Tomnyi, Phillip Sol, Daniel Njilmer, Moses Kwolde, Isaiah Kah, Paul Abah, Moses Juvoh, James Buvoah, Peter Jumvuh, Stephen Ndibil, and Alexander Jandong became the leaders of the Mambilla churches. They were known for their passion, energy, initiative, and powerful preaching. After Mambilla became part of Nigeria in 1961, it became increasingly difficult for young men in Mambilla to travel to and afford the training at Ndu. Visas and legal papers became very difficult to obtain. When Timothy Yula graduated from the six-year theological course at Ndu, the leadership of the Mambilla churches decided they needed their own Bible school in Mambilla. Our NAB Missions did not have the funds or personnel to establish such a school. So, the enterprising Mambillas started their own Bible School in a three-room mud block building on the site of the church in Mbamga. Abraham Jiminda served as the first principal. He was a deeply devout man who knew the scriptures well and could deliver excellent messages. I was ministered to by his preaching and his humble walk with God. The following is a quote from a letter I wrote to my mother, dated April 4, 1972 :

> *The Bible school here was started by several African pastors on a "shoe-string." Mambilla boys can't afford to go to Ndu in Cameroon. They started in Sept, 1971 with 10 men in a prep class (mainly to learn English), and 10 men in 1st year Bible school. Two African teachers are running this – no missionary is available to help teach. The boys are almost starving for lack*

> of food, and they almost had to close down a couple of times. Next year the two teachers will not be able to handle prep class plus 1st and 2nd year Bible school. This is our most urgent need as over ½ of our churches have no pastor. Some churches have "church teachers" with only grade 7 education plus a few Bible courses. In a field of 90 plus churches we have only 7 ordained pastors – one is away for further training, two are field pastors, and one is principal of the Bible school. That leaves three ordained pastors in Gembu, Warwar, and Furumi.

The budget for the Bible school came from donations from the Mambilla churches. Many churches also donated food that we collected on our medical clinic days and brought to the school with the hospital vehicle. It was amazing to see the determination of the Mambilla Christians to get a Bible school. They realized that training of pastors was essential for the future growth of the church.

In 1970, just prior to our arrival in Mambilla, pastor Isaiah Kah together with Minnie Kuhn and the Goodmans organized the Mambilla Baptist Convention as a separate entity from the Cameroon Baptist Convention. Having legal status allowed the Mambilla Baptist Convention (MBC) to acquire land for a permanent Bible school at Mbu, near Gembu. This led to the development of the Mambilla Baptist Theological Seminary (MBTS), and ultimately obtaining accreditation. It took some time before an official Certificate of Occupancy was obtained. That then allowed the building of the MBTS buildings, funded by our mission. In 1972, when Minnie Kuhn returned from her furlough, we got involved with teaching Theological Education by Extension (TEE) courses. These courses allowed church teachers/pastors to get further training while still serving their churches. Workbooks were given to the students, and every two weeks the students would come to a central location for review of the material, question and answer time, and discussion. This was a huge encouragement to the pastors. Many of them used the lessons learned for their Sunday sermons. I enjoyed teaching my class at Mbamga. We met in the church for our sessions. Chickens roamed in and out of the room, and we just ignored them. However, every time I went to this class I would get chiggers in my toes, despite wearing closed shoes. It seemed that as time went on, the chiggers (parasitic mites) became more painful as they burrowed into the skin of my toes. It was also a painful procedure to dig out the egg sacs without breaking the sac (which would spread chigger eggs all over the toes). We blamed the chickens! The TEE courses became a part of the curriculum of the MBTS.

The churches had to deal with a number of problems. One was the culture of polygamy that was widespread in West Africa. Women did most of the farming and to have more than one wife farming was seen as an advantage. There was also a prestige factor, as a man with several wives indicated that he was wealthy and able to pay the necessary dowry for each wife. The Muslim men were allowed to have four wives and, in the case of chiefs, any number of concubines. Another possible reason for polygamy was the taboo against women getting pregnant while nursing a baby, usually up to two or even three years of age. In the absence of effective birth control, the only certain way to prevent pregnancy was to avoid marital intercourse. The result was that men would seek to get another wife. Having many wives would ensure having a large family that in later years could care for the elderly. The large number of children born would also help to offset the devastation of the high infant mortality rate. The taboo against pregnancy while nursing probably saved the lives of some infants who would be at risk of malnutrition and gastroenteritis if weaned too early. The problem of polygamy was difficult for the churches to resolve. The early missionaries taught that the husband had to keep the first wife and reject all the others before he could be baptized and join the church. This resulted in abandoned women and children. The rejected wife could not return to her parents and most often ended up in a life of either adultery or prostitution. By the time we arrived on the scene, the churches had adopted a more compassionate policy of allowing the husband and all the wives to stay together, be baptized, and join the church. However the man was not allowed to teach or hold a position of leadership. He was also prohibited from acquiring more wives and had to promise to marry off his children monogamously. This affirmed the Biblical teaching of monogamous marriage and at the same time expressed grace to those in a polygamous relationship prior to coming to faith. However, the problem of avoidance of marital intercourse for a nursing mother remained. We tried to introduce birth control methods with some difficulty. Teaching the rhythm method was virtually impossible due to communication barriers and its lack of reliability. Birth control pills were tried and the more educated women were able to use this method. We heard stories that some women took the whole month's supply at once or put them under the mattress. We even learned that some gave the pills to their children! Condoms were not available and most men would rebel at using them anyway.

There were other strains on Christian marriages. The dowry system involved the payment of a bride price by the prospective husband to the bride's family. Most marriages were arranged by the parents of the couple. In a sense, the husband bought his wife and thus she could be considered his property. The Biblical marriage is one of partnership and mutual submission and a sacrificial love of a man for his wife – not an owner of a wife. If the wife gained further education, her family of origin could demand increased dowry payment. If she proved to be very fertile and bore many children, she became even more valuable. A wife being an equal partner instead of a commodity was a difficult concept in such a culture. A further strain on some marriages was prolonged separation when the husband travels away for further education or for employment. Leaving the wife alone at home to tend the farm and the children could easily lead to various temptations of infidelity.

Traditional religious beliefs were very strong. They included belief in the power of multiple gods and spirits of the ancestors over fertility, crops, weather, illness, and forecasting the future. A common feature of animistic religious practice was the offer of sacrifices to the spirits of the ancestors, because if offended, the ancestral spirits could cause sickness and many types of trouble. In Mambilla there was a practice of divination where a medicine man would seek the cause of illness or misfortune by examining the movements of the ngambe spider, a tarantula, inside a clay pot. Our mission station at Warwar was full of these tarantulas! Other practices included examination of scattered bones and the sacrifice of animals where blood was shed. Witchcraft was also widely practiced. Various rituals, such as wearing, or hanging fetishes and charms in huts or farms were done to ward off the evil machinations of the witches. This whole subject of traditional religious beliefs and practices is vast and complicated, and varied in different tribes and regions. A full description would take several books written by anthropologists. The effect of these traditional beliefs was felt by the churches. New believers in Jesus Christ had to renounce the former belief systems. For many this was difficult to do, and some Christians lapsed into syncretism because of fear of offending the ancestors and gods.

In a local church a highly respected elder had a son who got involved in a sexual relationship with another man's wife. The elder gave his errant son some chickens to bring to the angry husband in order to make atonement. The leadership of the church recognized that sacrificing chickens and using their blood in a ritual of atonement was not the Biblical way of dealing with sin. Only the shed blood of Jesus Christ was sufficient to remove our sin. The respected elder was confronted – a very difficult thing to do in a society that venerates the elderly. The elder confessed his wrongdoing and submitted to discipline that required him to step down from leadership for six months. This disciplinary action was a powerful lesson for the members of that church.

THERE WAS A WIDESPREAD TRADITIONAL belief that illnesses had supernatural origins. The concept of a spirit world interacting with and influencing the physical realm was much more accepted and developed in African society than in the Western world. The precise source of a person's sickness could be due to angry gods, offended ancestral spirits, witches' curses, etc. People came to our hospital for diagnosis and treatment of their illness. Joseph Headman would point out to me at times that the patient I just saw was the local traditional healer, witch doctor, or ju-ju man coming for a cure. Our medical treatment was not necessarily the end of the matter, as many cured patients would then consult the traditional healer to determine the root cause of the illness. Appropriate sacrifices would then be prescribed to appease the angry god, offended ancestor, or malevolent witch. We took great pains to pray before every operation and every clinic that God, who is more powerful than any other spirit or god, would give wisdom to the medical staff. We also prayed that God would use the medicines we had to help people get well. Our chaplain would also preach to waiting patients and counsel individuals regarding their need for spiritual healing and the removal of the curse of sin that comes through faith in Jesus Christ. The pastors of our churches did a great deal of teaching to help Christians conquer deep fears of the spirit world, often citing 1 John

4:4, *"Little children, you are from God and have overcome them, for He who is in you is greater than he who is in the world."*

Bribery and corruption were endemic in Nigeria and Cameroon. Bribes were routinely paid to police and judges to bend the justice system in one's favor. Government officials readily accepted, and in fact required, kickbacks in order to process documents. Bribes were required by school principals so children could gain entrance into secondary school. We were aware of instances where the bribe consisted of girls having to sleep with the principal. Contractors would pay government officials in order to obtain contracts to build roads or buildings. At times the work was never done and the money somehow vanished into thin air between officials and contractors. It was difficult for Christians to live out the Biblical principles of honesty and integrity in such an environment. The church responded with strong teaching against corruption. But still the question remains, what do parents do to get a bright child into advanced education? How does the Mambilla Baptist Convention obtain a Certificate of Occupancy for the Bible School property? These people learned to pray very earnestly! The position of the mission was to never pay even a tiny bribe because no bribe ever remains tiny and no issue is important enough to compromise one's testimony. We spent many an hour on the hot dusty roadside at a border crossing to Cameroon, waiting for the border guard to give up the idea of getting a bribe. In time it became well known that missionaries will not pay bribes and will do without the service requested. So the expectations for bribes and the concomitant hassles diminished. Because of the endemic corruption with money, there was some lack of trust, even in the churches in terms of offering money to fund the MBC ministries. The lack of training of MBC leaders in accounting practices contributed to this lack of trust. June Goodman was particularly adept at bookkeeping and managed the MBC accounts and also taught leaders about proper accounting and reporting. Rev. Daniel Njilmer, pastor at Warwar, was one of the leaders who earned a high level of trust with his solid integrity in handling money.

Tribalism was and continues to be an issue with which the churches have to deal. In Mambilla the gospel of freedom from the curse of sin and death found in Christ was embraced with enthusiasm by a tribe that had suffered under the domination of the Fulani and Hausa Muslims. They now felt a sense of freedom from oppression of sin, a sense of freedom similar to freedom from the oppression of a domineering tribe. There was also a recent history of conflict with other tribes over property issues and dominance. Slave trading was still a part of the memory and oral history of the elders. It was difficult in some areas for the Mambilla people to accept people from the Yamba or Ensungli tribes as equal members in the local church. There was very little enthusiasm to preach the gospel to the Muslim Fulani or Hausa, who were seen as oppressive enemies. Even the name, Mambilla Baptist Convention, could imply that the convention of Baptists is for Mambilla people and not for all the peoples of the Mambilla Plateau. As a result, there were churches of the MBC that were predominantly composed of Yamba people yet Yambas and Ensunglis would not expect to be elected into convention level leadership positions. A notable exception was Rev. Abraham Jiminda whose gifts of teaching and preaching were exceptional.

These problems faced by the church in Mambilla are somewhat unique to West African culture. Other problems such as alcoholism, materialism, immorality, and superficial Christianity are found worldwide. Despite the problems, the church in Mambilla grew from 35 churches and 3000 members in 1961, to 117 churches and 8554 members in 1979. There were many devout Christians who took their faith seriously and were active in proclaiming the gospel to their neighbours in both words and good deeds. Our staff and chaplain at Warwar hospital were very active in their witness. The MBC partially funded an evangelist to work in the area down off the plateau to an unreached people group near Baissa. The MBC also funded the operating costs of their Bible School (MBTS) and paid the salary of our hospital chaplain. We did have some interesting conversations with the MBC leadership who complained that the NAB Board of Missions loved Cameroon more than Nigeria because they greatly subsidized the Ndu Seminary's operating budget, but not MBTS. They had some difficulty accepting our answer that the MBTS was in better shape financially in the long run because it was already self-sufficient. We asked them a somewhat hypothetical question, "If all missionaries had to leave Cameroon and Nigeria suddenly, which school would be able to continue?" The immediate problems of the school made long-term thinking difficult. More details of the growth and development of the church in Mambilla will emerge as my story continues.

THE CHURCH IN MAMBILLA

ORIGINAL WARWAR BAPTIST CHURCH

OUTDOOR SUNDAY SCHOOL CLASS AT WARWAR

AND THEN THE PHONE RANG...

BAPTISM IN A LOCAL STREAM

WOMEN PREPARING FUFU FOR SEVERAL HUNDRED PEOPLE AT A FIELD BIBLE CONFERENCE

THE CHURCH IN MAMBILLA

REV. PETER SCHROEDER TEACHING AT MAMBILLA BAPTIST SEMINARY

CHAPTER 11

Life and Times at Warwar - The First Four Months

We were definitely rookie missionaries exposed to a long series of adventures from living in such a remote area. The first four months were overwhelming due to the culture shock and the sheer volume of work done at a fast pace.

DOMESTIC ISSUES

MARION DECIDED TO BECOME A farmer besides all her other duties. She planted a huge garden with 60 tomato plants, corn, watermelons, green peppers, asparagus, rhubarb etc. There was a constant war with birds and grasshoppers who really loved this buffet of veggies. Our North American corn did not grow beyond forming tassels and we learned that sweet corn needs more than 12 hours of sunlight. The African maize did well. We had an abundance of fruits such as mangos, pineapples, guavas, avocados, bush cherries, *paw-paws* (papayas), bananas, and even coffee bushes. She discovered that the papaya trees are either male or female and the female trees needed at least one male tree in the group in order to produce fruit the size of small watermelons! She hired a part-time laborer to do the weeding and watering. Amazingly some seeds sprouted out of the ground within a week of planting.

LIFE AND TIMES AT WARWAR - THE FIRST FOUR MONTHS

Marion's level of animal husbandry was very basic. She got a bunch of young chickens, put them in the hen house and faithfully watered and fed them. After a while she became frustrated because there were no eggs being produced. She consulted with Joseph, the station headman about the lack of eggs. Joseph could hardly contain his laughter when he informed Marion the chickens were all *man-pekin*, Pidgin English for males! She finally got some females and with feeding them milk and ground up cow horns she finally got her coveted daily eggs. She even treated the chickens' head lice by covering their heads with palm oil. Marion also discovered first-hand the animosity present between the Fulani herdsmen and the Mambilla farmers when a Fulani cowboy carelessly let his cows get into Marion's garden. With the help of the garden boy, she managed to catch one of the cows and tied it up. The cowboy, after being properly scolded, was forced to pay Nigerian pounds to get the cow back.

We had a refrigerator in the kitchen for storage of food items and vaccines. It did not occur to us to notice what powered the fridge until one day it began to smoke from a vent at the top. Minnie Kuhn pointed out that the tray under the fridge had no more kerosene and the wick was charred and burned causing the smoke. So, every week I was down on my belly to pull out the tray, fill up the kerosene, trim and re-light the wick, and line up the tray with the vent so as to get a proper blue flame.

There was no wash machine to do the laundry, but Marion found a washboard and did the laundry by scrubbing it on the washboard in a tub of water and soap. She ended up with quite a severe strain of her neck and possibly some cervical disc protrusion that almost incapacitated her. She had such severe neck pain riding in the Land Rover on bumpy roads that we had to stop for her to vomit beside the vehicle. We were very relieved when at Christmas time, four months later, our petrol-powered washing machine arrived at Banso Hospital in Cameroon. There was great rejoicing when it arrived at Warwar and we got it to work.

AND THEN THE PHONE RANG...

BRUCE AND LORI

BRUCE AND LORI ADJUSTED QUITE rapidly to life at Warwar. They learned Pidgin English from the many Nigerian children living on the hospital compound – children of our staff and labourers. Their closest friends were Victo, Guye, Spirie, and Evelyne. They had a few toys that we packed in our suitcases, but in three months most of Bruce's matchbox cars were missing.

Bruce and Lori had their share of adjustment to the various pathogens and bugs of Africa. Within several weeks of arrival at Warwar, Bruce developed a severe case of laryngotracheobronchitis to the point of respiratory distress (see chapter 9).

Bruce did recover but later had a session with Dengue fever. Lori also had bouts with both pneumonia and dysentery. Lori once came into the kitchen crying "a butterfly bit me," when in actual fact she got into some army ants that really know how to bite! Both Bruce and Lori had to take the bitter chloroquine pills for malaria prophylaxis and regular worm medicine to get rid of *Ascaris* round worms. They were also introduced to chiggers that burrow into the outer layer of skin of feet and lay a sac full of eggs. These sacs of eggs had to be carefully removed with a pin or needle without breaking the sac. This was an unpleasant experience but co-operation was easily obtained by bribery with a piece of chocolate.

Bruce and Lori enjoyed running around outside with their African friends. One time they came to the house covered in red mud to call us out to see the mud house they built, complete with sticks and grass for a roof. They enjoyed our two pets, a cat named Sinbad and a puppy named Cinnamon. Cinnamon got sick and died so a proper funeral and burial had to be observed. They observed a lot of things that North American kids never see, such as the birth of a baby or witnessing the African die cry when a patient died. They would watch the grave being dug and the body lowered into it and covered with dirt which was compacted by men stomping the dirt with their feet. Seeing the birth of a baby sure started discussion about the birds and the bees at an early age!

LIFE AND TIMES AT WARWAR - THE FIRST FOUR MONTHS

INTERESTING EVENTS

MINNIE KUHN LEFT FOR HER furlough in October and we felt more isolated and alone even though Ken and June Goodman were in Gembu and Barb Kieper was with us in Warwar. Our contact with the outside world seemed very remote. We had a shortwave radio and were able to listen to BBC, Voice of America, and ELWA (Monrovia) at times. No mail from home came until the end of October, and to our dismay, the first piece of mail was a letter from Revenue Canada! I still don't know how they knew where we were. A surprise letter came from Mrs. Waltereit, the pastor's wife at our home church, Bethany. She must have written and mailed the letter before we left home for Nigeria, as mail from home took at least 4 – 6 weeks to reach us. We felt a bit better once letters arrived regularly from our mothers and friends. We really appreciated getting kilo parcels which were two-liter milk cartons that weighed about one kilogram when fully packed. They were filled with spices, sewing notions, small toys, and, best of all, tins of bacon. The bacon had to be carefully doled out in equal portions and served only when there were no other guests at the table! Harry Senges came to our rescue by sending stethoscopes and blood pressure cuffs to replace the few worn out ones we had.

Within a month our hospital generator stopped working. Fortunately, we had our kerosene fridge to store vaccines. In the evenings we depended on kerosene lamps for light. There was a ¾ horsepower gas generator on hand to supply light for emergency surgery at night. There were two four-foot neon tubes suspended from the ceiling of the operating room. A pulley system allowed us to lower the light down over the operating table. Unfortunately, flying insects were attracted to the light and at times got zapped by the hot neon tubes and fell into the patient's wound! Not being a mechanic, I did not know how to fix the generator. Ken Goodman was handy with mechanical things and, once the necessary parts arrived, he came over to complete a ring job and restore the compression of the generator.

We had four building projects going on: a dorm for male staff, an extension on the female staff dorm, a guesthouse kitchen, and a laboratory building. I found some clean yellow clay and got laborers to dig it up and make sun dried building blocks using a wooden form. Those were very hard blocks – almost as hard as cement. My role was to draw up plans, engage laborers, arrange for wood for door and window frames, rafters and purlins. I also had to arrange for corrugated zinc roofing sheets and nails with rubber plugs. In the late afternoon, after the hospital work was completed, I would inspect the work progress and give instructions for the next day. Getting wood was arduous. Trees were felled, cleaned, and dragged to a slit trench where they were sawn into usable lumber. One sawyer stood on top of the log, the other sawyer was in the trench under the log to saw lengths of wood. A third man sat on the cut end of the log to hammer a wedge into the cut in order to keep the saw from jamming. The wood was then hand-planed smooth and shaped into 2-by-6 and 1-by-12-inch usable wood. I relied on Philip Munyah and Stephen Lamba to supervise the laborers and do the carpentry.

In November the rains stopped and dry season was upon us. The skies were clear, the weather was sunny and hot, and soon the grassy hills turned yellow and brown as the grass dried out. It was not long before the hills were blackened by grass fires that, in most cases, were purposely lit with the idea that, when the rains returned, the new grass would be lush and green. The fires were also started for hunting. Fires were lit at the bottom of the hills and the updraft of air would carry the fire rapidly up to the top. Hunters with spears and homemade guns would wait over the crest of the hill to kill animals fleeing the fire. The missionary homes and hospital buildings were at the top of a hill and thus were vulnerable to fire damage. Joseph headman supervised the burning of firebreaks all around the compound in the cool of the evening when there was no wind. It was a spectacular sight.

A number of visitors came to Warwar and Marion, as station hostess, made sure that meals and beds were ready. She was grateful to have a cook help with cooking and laundry. It was exciting to meet famous missionaries from Cameroon like Tina Schmidt, Trudy Schatz, Myrna Goodman, and Fred & Dot Holzimmer. The guest rooms were two round mud block huts with plastered and painted walls, cement floors, grass roofs, and ceiling board. They were quaint and comfortable once we made sure there were no snakes, tarantulas, or black widow spiders inside!

LIFE AND TIMES AT WARWAR - THE FIRST FOUR MONTHS

MEDICAL WORK

WE WERE EXTREMELY BUSY AND the sheer volume of the patient load often left us exhausted. The following quotes come from letters written to my mother.

> Nov. 1/71 "The medical work is busy as ever. We have a measles epidemic now that kills kids like flies. We are cramming 10 patients plus family into mud huts designed to hold 3. They sleep 2 to 3 on a single bed and the rest sleep on the dirt floor under the bed".
>
> Nov. 8/71 "We did a Caesarean section 4 days ago in which Marion had to help as scrub nurse. This was the first time she saw me operate. We are training her to help in surgery in case Barb is away on leave or at a clinic and we have emergency surgery to do. We didn't fight about anything – for once I was absolute boss and master! - until I got bawled out for getting blood on the floor!! We are now averaging 50 – 56 patients in a hospital that has a bed capacity of 40. Our big ward had 8 beds in it until we had to squeeze 14 beds into it. There is no room to walk in there – you have to literally climb over beds and get patients to come to the foot of the bed to be examined. I am throwing people out left and right but still have to admit one to two new ones the same day. We have babies with meningitis sleeping on cement and dirt floors. I was feeling tired and finally smartened up. I now insist on lying down for a ½ hour in the mid-afternoon and woe betide anybody that bothers me then."

There was an interesting case of a woman presenting with a large four-pound lipoma, a tumor of fat, on the right side of her neck and back. It was the size of a football and made her look like a 2-headed woman from behind. She was very self-conscious and covered her head and the tumor with a large shawl to partially hide the mass. Barb Kieper saw her in the outpatient's area and booked her for surgery the next day. I was shocked to see this case and wondered how I was going to remove this. Open drop ether anesthesia was impossible because she had to lie on her side for me to access this mass. So, I injected a large amount of local anesthesia and managed to remove this lipoma with some difficulty. The woman was so relieved and happy that she accepted Jesus as her Saviour. Now she had two burdens removed – the burden of the tumor and the burden of her sin! This all ended well, but I made a new law of the Medes and Persians, as written about in the book of Daniel, that I would be the only one to book surgeries from now on.

There was great excitement one night at about 11 PM. We heard several Land Rovers roaring up the hill beside our house with great honking of horns as they sped to the hospital. There had been a serious accident when a drunk driver hit a cow and rolled the vehicle. There were six injured people. The worst injury was to the Wakili, second only to the powerful chief of Mambilla, whose word was law in all of the Mambilla plateau. The Wakili was semi-conscious with his face chewed up with multiple lacerations. The worst wound was on his left upper eyelid which was split open vertically. He was confused and belligerent when handled, so we sedated him with largactil and paraldehyde. The next several hours were spent in sewing him up. It was tricky to get the tarsal plate of his upper eyelid perfectly approximated. I had no idea how important a man he was in the community until after we were done treating him. The other injured included the Wakili's son, a sergeant in the Gembu police force, a leprosy inspector, and several others. The leprosy inspector had compound, comminuted fractures of the radius and ulna of both forearms. We cleaned his open wounds and set the fractures as best we could without the help of X-rays and loaded him up with antibiotics. Barb and I worked on all these men from 11 PM until 4:30 the next morning. I was too wound up to get much sleep, and a full day of work awaited us at 6:30 AM. The Wakili's son took several days to regain full consciousness and, thankfully, was able to see out of his left eye and open and close his eyelids. A few days later the Chief of Mambilla came to see what had happened. The superintendent of police for the entire province also came to investigate the incident. Also present were various ministers of works, roads, and administration. Our quick treatment of all the injured apparently made a very favourable impression

LIFE AND TIMES AT WARWAR - THE FIRST FOUR MONTHS

on all the dignitaries. Marion quickly prepared cookies, banana muffins, tea, and coffee for all the V.I.P.s. At the time Ken and June Goodman were in the far distant city of Maiduguri, capital of the North East State, on official business for the mission. The Minister of Health there had heard about the accident and our treatment of the injured and asked the Goodmans about our work at Warwar.

Sad things also happened. A woman who was 28-weeks pregnant came to the hospital in labor, and was bleeding heavily. The baby was in an undeliverable transverse position and already dead, as no fetal heartbeat was detectable. The woman was pale and shocked from blood loss, so we transfused several units of blood into her, gave her a spinal anesthetic, and did a destructive delivery of the dead baby, removing it piece by piece. We saved the woman's life but it was very sad to lose the baby. Life is a very precious gift from God.

We had to terminate the services of a Cameroonian midwife who had been sent to Warwar to help with maternity work in the absence of Minnie Kuhn. This midwife was found to be grossly incompetent in that she failed to report fetal distress in a laboring mother that she was monitoring. The baby died unnecessarily when a Caesarean section could have saved its life. The grieving mother had a history of 11 pregnancies and only one live child. The midwife was unrepentant and quite incensed that we would terminate her service at Warwar. I had to spend time fixing the Land Rover so that Barb Kieper could drive this midwife back to Cameroon.

Some very essential supplies began to arrive by mid-November. Harry Senges sent filiforms and followers so that we could dilate urinary strictures caused by gonorrhoea infections. He also sent some #1 and #0 chromic sutures with swedged-on needles that were most helpful in getting control of bleeding when closing a uterus in a Caesarean section. Our mothers sent out numerous kilo parcels with various foods, spices, small clothes, and sewing notions that Marion requested. We were glad to receive our four big suitcases that were air-freighted to Kano and finally delivered to Gembu. We finally got extra pants for Bruce and some shoes for Lori who by this time had to wear cheap flip-flops that we got in the local market.

AND THEN THE PHONE RANG...

WE ATTENDED OUR FIRST ANNUAL field Bible conference for the Warwar field of churches. This was held at the beginning of the dry season every year. I quote from my November 22, 1971 letter, as follows:

> *The meetings were held in the open air under a partial roof made of bamboo sticks arranged in a lattice work and covered with broad leafed grass – very comfortable. The Bible studies were excellent, on the topic of "The Spirit Filled Life". The messages were by Rev. Abraham Jeminda, the Warwar field pastor (equivalent to our regional ministers). He had 3 years of Bible School and 3 years of Seminary at Ndu, Cameroon. He was an excellent speaker and could easily hold his own in North America – a really great guy! I also had to speak and give an annual medical report. The kids liked the open-air atmosphere and witnessed chickens wandering around, a dog fight, and even a galloping riderless horse which added to the African flavor of things. There was a report on the start of the Mambilla Baptist Bible School that year. The initiative and leadership were all done by Mambilla pastors who had seminary training at Ndu, Cameroon. There were 10 students in the prep class to learn English better, and 10 men in the first year Bible school. There were contests for church choirs where they were judged on their uniforms, marching, and singing ability.*

Our chaplain also gave a report on his work at Warwar hospital. He noted that in October alone he recorded 30 conversions to Christ, including four former Muslims from the Fulani tribe. We came home to Warwar for a special church service on Thanksgiving Day. This service included a baptism which made it a very long day. The service started at 9 AM with singing and announcements. Then a procession was formed, led by the pastors and choir with the baptismal candidates behind them. All the rest of the congregation followed the procession through the village market and down to the river for the baptism. The singing and drums attracted many villagers who came to see what was going on. Before the actual baptism, the pastor gave a message. After the baptism we all marched back to church for more singing, a thanksgiving offering where people danced

LIFE AND TIMES AT WARWAR - THE FIRST FOUR MONTHS

to the front of the church to deposit offerings of money, corn, chickens, a very long sermon, and finally the communion. We got out of church at about 3 PM – tired and hungry. The people continued with celebrations and escorted the newly baptized people to their homes. There was a great feast with more singing and dancing until darkness sent people home.

We were delighted at the news that we had received visas for travel to Cameroon. That allowed us to attend the annual Cameroon Missionary Fellowship (CMF) Conference 18 – 22 December 1971 in Bamenda. By this time the Wakili was up and walking around and soon ready for discharge. We arranged for Dr. Gwen Evenhouse, a Sudan United Mission doctor, to oversee the medical work at Warwar in our absence. We got to our neighboring mission station at Mbem, Cameroon and were amazed at the beautiful station, with flowering bushes, painted buildings, and very nice missionary houses. Ruth Rabenhorst ran a dispensary and maternity at Mbem and Rev. Fred and Dot Holzimmer served as Mbem field missionaries. The kids were really impressed when Uncle Fred made ice cream using salt and ice water in a large bucket with the ice cream made in a smaller bucket which was rotated round and round inside the ice-filled larger bucket.

We travelled on to visit Ndu, the site of the Joseph Merrick School for boys and the Cameroon Baptist Theological Seminary. It was a very impressive station with beautiful buildings. It was emotionally moving for me to see the place that was founded by my great uncle Johannes and aunt Dora Sieber who were pioneer missionaries in the area. On our way to Bamenda we visited Banso Baptist Hospital and Mbingo Baptist Hospital. I marvelled at the huge hospitals with well-trained Cameroonian staff and well-built facilities.

As mentioned, the CMF conference was held in Bamenda, the capital city of the Northwest Province of Cameroon and the site of the Cameroon Baptist Mission headquarters. The Cameroon Baptist Convention also had their central offices on the same compound. There were almost enough rest-houses to accommodate all the North American Baptist Conference missionaries in Cameroon and Nigeria. Some of the single missionaries stayed at the government rest-houses on a hill above the mission station. The food was wonderfully prepared by veteran cooks who worked for some of the missionaries in Cameroon. It was great to finally meet all the famous missionaries that we had read about in the Baptist Herald magazine. We really felt accepted as part of a huge family of God. With all of our initial troubles and feeling a bit homesick, I was emotionally vulnerable. When I heard Penny Dubland (nee Jucht) sing, "I'm so glad I belong to the family of God," the dam broke and I dissolved into tears that would not stop. The pent-up tension and pressure of the past four-and-a-half months was finally released. This was a time when the missionaries could relax and be refreshed with good biblical teaching, sharing, sleeping in, eating too much, laughing, and, most importantly, restoring their commitment to obeying God's call.

While in Bamenda we travelled up the hill to the government office buildings. Behind one of the offices was a small expatriate cemetery. The cemetery was overgrown with grass, but we were able to find headstones and wooden markers of missionaries buried there. We found the burial plot of Johannes Sieber that had a small wooden marker with his name still legible on it. We took a picture of it to show our family at home. In later years my cousin, Eric Spletzer, came to Cameroon as a short-term missionary and he brought a more permanent plaque for the grave site.

PART OF THE FUN WAS a Christmas party with singing and hilarious skits. Curt Radke, dressed in a Santa Claus outfit, came roaring into the meeting room on a motorcycle and distributed gifts to the kids. After the conference we spent Christmas at Mbingo with Jerry & Monie Fluth, Geraldine Glassenap, Laura Reddig, Pat Lenz, and George and Carol Black. Lori began to cry on Christmas eve when being put to bed after hanging her stocking on the bedpost. When questioned, she sobbed out, "I don't want Santa Claus coming on my bed with the motorcycle."

All good things must come to an end so we packed up and made our way back to Warwar, stopping at Banso to load up our drums of cargo that had been shipped from Vancouver and had finally arrived.

LIFE AND TIMES AT WARWAR - THE FIRST FOUR MONTHS

BRUCE AND LORI WITH PLAYMATES

BUILDING A HOUSE, STARTING WITH THE ROOF!

AND THEN THE PHONE RANG...

CROSSING THE DONGA RIVER BY DUGOUT CANOE

ANNUAL CAMEROON/NIGERIA MISSIONARY FELLOWSHIP IN BAMENDA.
BRUCE & LORI IN THE FRONT ROW LOOKING BACK

CHAPTER 12

Back to Work

We returned to Warwar refreshed and rested after a wonderful trip to Cameroon. The love and acceptance by our missionaries made us feel more at home with the new family we now had in Africa. Now we could unpack our drums that we brought from Cameroon to Warwar. It was like a huge Christmas gift opening time to get clothes and equipment. A butane-fired water heater was purchased in Cameroon, so now we had hot water any time we wanted it. No more bucket brigade for bath water from the washtub on the cookstove.

The kids provided a lot of humour for us. Lori spluttered and choked a bit on some milk. Bruce immediately shouted out an order for a mix of penicillin/streptomycin to be injected into Lori. Bruce also carefully examined his toy tractor and announced that it was "pregnant and needs surgery." We wondered if he was going to launch a career as a doctor. One day there was a freak rainstorm with bits of hail – very unusual for here. Lori came roaring into the house holding her head and crying "ouch-ouch." She was not impressed at all!

The medical work was as busy as ever. I quote from my letter of January 10, 1972 to my mother:

> *On Saturday I went on a clinic to Kushuku. I crossed the Donga River by canoe with medicine boxes, the chaplain, and three ward helpers on Friday night and slept at Gembu. At 7 AM we drove 45 miles (in two hours) to reach Kushuku. I had "chop" with the pastor, a meal of fufu, palm oil, and chicken.*

BACK TO WORK

I drank my own filtered and boiled water. Then I saw 318 patients in 4 ½ hours and drove back to Gembu for supper with the Goodmans' at 7 PM. By 8 PM I was at the Donga River to cross by canoe again with zinc nails, plumbing supplies, paint, and our medicine boxes. Barb met us at the river with the Land Rover and we got home about 9:30 – an average Saturday clinic day. Up at 6 AM Sunday for hospital rounds. Among the newly admitted patients I discovered several new meningitis cases and one case of tetanus.

In the first six days of January we delivered 31 babies, including one anencephalic baby that died. We also had several children admitted with cancrum oris, which is a horrible infection of the mouth that causes extensive sloughing of necrotic tissue. The poor child is left with a huge hole in the cheek with missing areas of bone and teeth. The mortality rate is 70% to 90% in hospitals where plastic surgery is available. The children are usually quite malnourished and have concomitant infections of intestinal worms and malaria. I also saw several babies with tetanus who were born at home and had cow dung applied to the umbilical cord stump. The babies were so stiff that one could lift them with one hand under the head and one under the heels without the child bending at all. I was now doubly convinced of the need for proper maternity care and for immunizations. It broke my heart to see these kids die a horrible death that was preventable.

Soon after our return to Warwar we realized that we had run out of some essential medicines like tuberculosis drugs, worm medicines, and analgesics. The patient volume had increased far beyond the estimated annual increase. So an emergency 600-mile trip to Jos was required. We used the Goodman's Volkswagen bus as it had a large space for cargo. Marion came along with Bruce and Lori so she could shop for food items. We set off on the long dusty trip with the bus loaded with empty drums in which to pack drugs, and empty butane tanks to refill. James, our cook, pastor Paul Yangchi, and a truck driver also accompanied us. The driver was to rent a truck to carry the medicines purchased in Jos back to Warwar. What a noisy trip! It was deafening to drive on washboard and potholed dirt roads with empty steel drums and tanks banging together in a VW bus with worn out shock absorbers. Then at twenty-five miles from Numan and the

Benue River, the left rear torsion bar broke. We managed to creep slowly to the Sudan United Mission (SUM) compound in Numan where we stayed overnight. The SUM mechanic was unable to fix the torsion bar or shock absorbers, but he advised us to lighten the load and drive very slowly to Jos. Fortunately the road to Jos on the other side of the Benue River was paved and had fewer potholes. So the next morning we put our drums and tanks and three Nigerian passengers on a truck headed for Jos. Our drive to Jos, 280 miles away, took over 10 hours. The VW was repaired and loaded with food, drugs, plumbing supplies and light bulbs. The heavier drums and full butane tanks were put on a truck for our driver to bring home. With banking and insurance business done, we set off for home, 600 miles away. We realized that with our heavy load, the vehicle would not manage to get up the nine-mile steep hill to the Mambilla plateau. We unloaded half the load plus James and Paul at the Christian Reformed Church mission compound in Serti. I drove the half load plus Marion and the kids to the top of the hill where we unloaded everything at the side of the road. Marion and the kids had an extended picnic while I went back down to Serti to get the men and the cargo. When everyone and everything was back in the VW, we made our way to Gembu. The next day we proceeded to the Donga River where all the cargo and people were loaded onto dugout canoes to cross the river where Barb Kieper met us with the Land Rover. What a relief to get back home to Warwar.

About this time Jean Berkin was on her way to Warwar as a six-month short-term missionary. Jean was a laboratory technician who worked for the R.C.M.P forensic lab in Regina. In preparation for her arrival, Marion decided to paint the inside and the outside of the rest house in which Jean would stay. Marion got on a roll and also painted Barb's house and then proceeded to the maternity ward, which looked quite shabby. Barb helped by moving things out of the maternity ward so Marion could get the paint job done quickly. Barb carried a bed outside and then came back in, rolled up a mattress and carried it outside. A newly delivered mother came into the ward and was frantically looking for her baby. Barb muttered "oh-oh" and ran outside, unrolled the mattress, and found the lost baby.

We were glad to have Jean Berkin come and train some of our teenage boys in laboratory work. The lab building was completed, and I found my microscope in one of our drums, so Jean could get to work. The staff learned how to do a simple urinalysis, complete blood counts, and a thick smear to identify malaria. Stool samples were checked for various intestinal parasites. Blood cross-matches were very basic. We could do ABO typing but no Rh typing. For blood transfusions we took a drop of blood from the donor and mixed it on a slide with a drop of the patient's blood. If there was no agglutination (clumping of red cells) seen by microscopy, we would proceed with the transfusion. The odds were in our favor as only 5% of the population here were Rh negative. Besides doing lab work, Jean got all our White Cross supplies organized in the storage room – a huge job.

The Mambilla Missionary Field Conference made the decision to not build a new hospital at Mbu, but rather expand and improve the Warwar site of the hospital. Mbu later became the site of the Mambilla Baptist Bible School and Seminary. This decision meant that we would build missionary housing, an outpatient building with a medical storeroom, a surgical building with an operating room and wards, and renovate the existing old outpatient building into medical wards. The NAB Missions Board approved this plan and a special project was set up to receive donations. Curt Radke was posted to Warwar, arriving in July 1972, to take charge of the building. Curt was a member of our home church, Bethany Baptist, and was a short-term missionary in Cameroon teaching in the secondary schools. We realized that our water system was inadequate for a larger hospital and that there was insufficient firewood for caregivers to use for cooking meals. We also needed sand for making cement building blocks and timbers for rafters, window frames, and doors. So, prior to Curt's arrival, we started the following hospital building projects:

- Five thousand eucalyptus tree seedlings donated by Mr. Chapman, a British man in charge of the Ministry of Forests, were planted on the hill above the hospital and grew rapidly. They can be cut down every five years and then they grow a new tree from the stump. Thus, we had a renewable source of firewood.

- A spring was located on the hill above the hospital. We did not know how to properly tap a spring, so we made a simple dam and put a pipe in it with a mesh cover to keep grass and leaves from clogging the system. A fence around the site kept the cows and people out. We dug a 3000-foot trench to bury the two-inch pipe. There was a 400-foot drop in height down to our 2500-gallon cistern. To ease the pressure in the pipe, we installed several steel drums in the line with toilet tank float valves to control the flow.

- Men were hired to operate our primitive sawmill as described in the previous chapter.

- It was dry season and the low water level in the Warwar River exposed large sand banks. After the hospital work was done, I drove down to the river with the canvas-back Land Rover and hauled sand to stockpile it for making cement. We also hauled cement from Gembu before heavy rains made the Donga River crossing more difficult.

Marion had her hands full as station hostess. We had to host a meeting of 11 missionary doctors working in the North East state of Nigeria. The meeting was to discuss a uniform approach to the government regarding charging fees to patients. The government hospitals provided free medical care financed by the wealthy oil-rich government of Nigeria. But the people preferred the higher-quality care in the mission hospitals. In order to survive, the mission hospitals had to charge fees. There was some concern that the government would decide to take over the mission hospitals. Marion had trouble trying to find enough beds and cots for all these people plus provide all the meals. We were grateful to have James as our cook. It was good to have some painting done beforehand so the place did not look so drab and shabby. The conference went well and many of the doctors planned to come back for a holiday in the relatively cool air at our 4500-foot elevation. There were numerous visitors from Cameroon from time to time and Marion took good care of them. She became brave enough to smash all the big black widow spiders in the rest houses herself, but insisted that I had to deal with the tarantulas.

We had a big fight in our house one evening. Barb's cook Moses, a Yamba, got one of our Mambilla ward workers pregnant. She was the daughter of a prominent pastor. She came with her parents to our house one evening to give us, and Barb, this unhappy news. Her father was quite agitated and left with a steel rod and a cutlass in his hands to look for

Barb's cook. Our field pastor who was coming to the meeting met the girl's father at the door, disarmed him, and brought him back inside. Barb's cook was summoned, and he appeared quite nonchalant about what he planned to do about this situation. The father and the field pastor got so upset at the cook's attitude that they began to beat him. So, we all dove in and broke up the fight. The poor father was very subdued when the rather large Barb ended up sitting on his head! The cook finally agreed to pay the father the cost of the daughter's education and the loss of future dowry, as she was now, in that culture's opinion, spoiled goods.

A huge surprise greeted us on Easter Sunday morning. All of the ward workers went on strike! So, Barb, Jean, and I made rounds, gave out all the medications, did the injections, and changed the wound dressings. We then saw all the outpatients and ended up missing church. We were not very happy. Apparently, the teenage ward workers ran out of money. They had just received their monthly pay the day before with a ten-shilling increase in salary. They counted their money and realized that they had no money left for food after subtracting the amount they owed to various creditors. Foolishly they had incurred big debts for new clothes and shoes for Easter and now were broke. Joseph Headman was very angry and scolded them for withholding medical care from their own people. Their worries increased when I threatened to terminate them all and close the hospital down until we could hire some mature people as ward workers. They were reminded that if this happened, they had no chance to be recommended for a mission scholarship to midwifery or nursing school. Their parents were likely also to beat them, as was the custom in Africa for such disgraceful behavior. They all saw the light and quickly returned to work the next day. We realized that they were still teenage kids and so we forgave them and helped them with money management by paying them weekly instead of monthly until all their debts were paid. A few weeks later we hosted a week of evening deeper life sessions for our staff in our living room. The guest speaker was Rev. Abraham Jeminda, a gifted and devout man of God.

More bad behavior happened. Bruce and his friends Victor and Sperry were caught stomping on a small chicken wire enclosure where new chickens were kept. The little chicken coop was destroyed. Joseph Headman caught them in the act and got a twig and gave all three of them a good switching on their bums. Further punishment was dispensed. Sperry, the oldest, had to carry several head pan loads of sand from the river. Victor was put on house arrest for several days. Bruce confessed his complicity and had to work punishment by carrying firewood to the kitchen wood box. He then audaciously requested payment for his work. This request was of course denied. He finally realized the enormity of his misdeed and asked if he would go to hell. He was reassured that friends of Jesus don't go to hell, only enemies of Jesus go there. Some very earnest prayers were made, and critical lessons were learned.

Marion was shocked one day when our cook, James, announced that he was leaving our employ, with only one day of notice. He got a job as a cook in the state governor's official residence in Gembu, a job he had applied for a year previously. He packed up his things to go to Maiduguri for special training. Just about this time our washing machine broke down, so Marion had to do laundry by hand using an old-fashioned washboard. Luckily, we found Zaccheus to come and help Marion as a houseboy. In time he also learned some simple cooking skills. If all this wasn't bad enough, the station generator also broke down, reducing us to the use of kerosene lamps at night. Fortunately, the small stand-by generator was still working and available for emergency night-time surgery. It was time for a break! We took a short local leave and travelled to Mbem, Ndu, and Banso for a week. Eleanor Weisenberger, Nursing Matron at Banso Baptist Hospital, served us a special treat of wieners and sauerkraut for supper.

I was grateful again for my friend Harry Senges who sent out some very helpful medical supplies. These included chromic catgut sutures with swedged-on needles for difficult surgeries like caesarean sections and hysterectomies. He also sent some filiforms and followers to help deal with urethral strictures in men. A man came to Warwar with a history of not passing urine for five days. He was in agony. Using the narrow filiforms I found a passage to the bladder through the narrow urethral stricture and then dilated the passage with the followers. It was successful and the patient went home happy. The prevalence of venereal disease was fairly high and would result in urethral strictures and even multiple fistulas with urine draining from several passages (the term watering can scrotum is

BACK TO WORK

mentioned in old urological textbooks). I also saw a very rare posterior triangle hernia protruding from a man's lower back. Once I recognized what this was, it was quite easily fixed. Another one-year-old child presented with a finger that was almost completely cut off. It took some time to get this reattached. Fortunately, there was some blood supply left in one tiny artery. Another one-year-old fell and landed with the front of her neck on a wire fence. Her neck was cut wide open and her trachea was severed. Fortunately, the carotid arteries, jugular veins, and esophagus escaped injury. We had no tracheostomy tubes, so a piece of urinary catheter was inserted to maintain her airway. We later managed to close the wound, but she was at high risk to develop tracheal stenosis later on.

July 1972 marked almost one year from our arrival in Nigeria. The original plan was for us to transfer to one of the hospitals in Cameroon. However, plan A usually doesn't happen, so we soon learned to make plan B or C better plans. Harold and Marg Lang were going home on furlough after serving as house parents at Woyke House, the NAB children's hostel in Jos. Pete and May Schroeder were assigned to replace the Langs, but were unable to get visas for Nigeria because they would take away jobs that Nigerians could do. Plan B was that Dr. Willi and Anita Gutowski, returning from their furlough, would remain in Jos as house parents until Christmas before proceeding on to Warwar. So now we, the Hiller tribe, would stay in Warwar until Christmas before transferring to Cameroon. I flew from Serti to Jos to meet with the Langs and Fred Folkerts, the field secretary of the Cameroon Baptist Mission, to sort out all these details. Curt Radke had also arrived in Jos at that time and we purchased a 1.8 ton flat deck Fiat truck for use in the Warwar building project. The Fiat was loaded with building supplies, medicines, and food – and Curt and I drove back to Warwar. It was great to have Curt, the handyman and builder, on the station. In short order he repaired the station generator, the ailing Land Rover, and our tape recorder. He immediately got the excavation going for the nurse's duplex and showed the laborers how to mix cement to make very strong building blocks. Bruce and Lori loved watching all the action. Lori's vocabulary was expanding rapidly and she was calling Bruce a "ling-a-ling." One day she was mildly ill and in bed for a nap where she was heard singing, "O Jesus is a wock in a wearwy land, a wearwy land."

AND THEN THE PHONE RANG...

Bruce also had a musical repertoire – singing, "praise the Lord for what He's done" and "everybody happy, say amen" while building things with LEGO blocks.

We finally hired an experienced cook named Stephen who came from Cameroon after working for Elmer and Ellen Breitkreuz at Ndu. This was a huge help to Marion, who had developed a very painful neck from doing laundry by hand as mentioned earlier. There was great rejoicing when our gas-powered washing machine finally arrived, as the laundry load had increased with Curt boarding with us. Marion's neck pain was evident one night while we were doing an emergency caesarean section at 3 A.M. Barb was away on clinic, so Marion was assisting as the scrub nurse. It was a difficult procedure on a baby with a face presentation that was stuck in the mother's pelvis. After a struggle we finally got the baby out. As we closed the uterus, Marion almost fainted and had to break scrub and vomit in a bucket. Meanwhile I closed the abdomen without help, having to swat the flying bugs off the drapes. Mom and baby were fine, but not Marion.

News came that my mother, Oma to everyone, was coming with my cousin Carol Spletzer (now Church) for a visit. There was great excitement and a flurry of preparation, which included deworming the kids beforehand so Oma would not be upset. Prior to Oma's visit, Bob and Ruth Rapske from Bethany Baptist, came for a visit. It was a very unique experience for them. Ruth slipped while crouched in the canoe crossing the Donga River. She landed on her backside in the muddy water at the bottom of the canoe and got thoroughly soaked. Bob also got a surprise while taking pictures of a woman delivering a baby (after obtaining the mom's permission). While he was focusing his camera, the mother's membranes suddenly ruptured, and Bob was showered with amniotic fluid. So, both Bob and Ruth were baptized to life in Africa. They were good sports and were able to laugh at their adventures.

Finally, the day came. Oma and Carol flew from Jos to Serti where we picked them up for the drive to Warwar. Minnie Kuhn returned from furlough and Barb's mom also came for a visit. Warwar church put on a great Mambilla welcome for the moms, Carol and Minnie. There were speeches, exuberant singing, dancing, gifts, and feasting. In the middle of all the celebrations we had to attend to the delivery of a set of twins,

BACK TO WORK

plus do an emergency caesarean section. During this time Dr. Helen Marie Schmidt from Cameroon came for a visit together with her parents. All these visitors kept Marion busy. Fortunately, she had the gift of hospitality and somehow managed to find enough beds and food for everyone. We put Oma and Carol to work immediately. Oma spent many hours with the Singer treadle sewing machine making new surgical drapes and mending surgical gowns and instrument wrappers. Carol helped Minnie in cleaning and organizing the medical supplies room that contained all the drugs and White Cross boxes. A complete inventory of our medicine supply was done to enable us to make the annual drug order to the central pharmacy in Jos. I took Carol along to Mayodaga for a clinic. She was astounded at the huge crowd of over 450 patients waiting to be seen.

It was now late-October 1972 and time for a local leave. Pete and May Schroeder, Fred Holzimmer, and Harold Johns (NAB photographer) visited Warwar and we hitched a ride with them to Cameroon for a two-week visit of our mission stations. The stations included Mbem, Ndu (site of the CBC Seminary and Joseph Merrick Boys Secondary School), Banso, Mbingo, Bamenda, Douala, Victoria (now called Limbe – site of the Saker Baptist College, a girl's secondary school), and Buea. It was a bumpy ride down the Sabongari hill into the Mbaw plain in Cameroon with 10 of us crammed into the Land Rover. The Sabongari hill road was a steep, twisting path full of big rocks and gullies from erosion by rain. It was more like a creek bed than a road! The gals reveled in the shopping opportunities in Bamenda and Victoria. Bruce and Lori enjoyed the beach and swimming pool in coastal Victoria. Fred Folkerts, field secretary for the Cameroon Baptist Mission, and I flew from Douala to the capital of Cameroon in Yaounde where we worked on entry and residence permits for our family as well as registration with the Medical Council of Cameroon.

All this was to prepare the way for us to move to Cameroon in 1973 to work at either Banso or Mbingo hospital. Dr. Helen Marie Schmidt and I had to examine missionary Ida Forsch as she was having angina symptoms suggestive of a possible impending heart attack. We arranged for her immediate repatriation to America for further tests and treatment. In 24 hours, she was on a plane going home. After two weeks of leave it was time to return to Warwar. We arranged for a mission vehicle to take us to the border with Nigeria just beyond Mbem. We had to cross the Mbori River, which was waist-deep and impossible to drive through. Curt Radke met us at the river with a Warwar vehicle and we waded across the Mbori, African style, carrying our children on our backs and all the shopping cargo on our heads. We were now back in Nigeria. We had enough time for the kids to have a bit of a swim in the river.

WE GOT HOME TO WARWAR in time to paint the new rest house in preparation for a visit by Dr. Richard Schilke, the General Missions Secretary of NAB. It was confirmed that we would move to Cameroon as soon as we obtained the necessary authority number from the government of Cameroon. We found house parents for the Woyke House in Jos, so the Gutowski family would come to Warwar just before Christmas. We now had to vacate the doctor's house at Warwar and move into the rest houses until we had permission to move to Cameroon. We used one rest house as the family bedroom and the other one for our living and dining room. There were two smaller mud-block and grass-roofed houses that were used as a kitchen and a bathroom complete with a shower. The rainy season had started, and it was quite an ordeal to take the children to the bathroom at night in a rainstorm. We had to get an umbrella, shoes, and a flashlight to make the trip outside to the little house. One night, Marion was shocked when she opened the bedroom door to go outside with Bruce and ran into a horse that had put its head under the grass roof right by the door. The last straw came when she encountered a snake crawling up the side of the bathroom door. From that time on we used a chamber pot in the bedroom at night. We were quite happy to have this thunder-mug, as it was called. I had my own encounter with a snake when I went into the bathroom to have a shower. I was completely undressed when I noticed something move. The *something* was a four-foot-long green snake, possibly a green mamba, between me and the door. I grabbed a towel and flicked it at the snake to get it to hopefully move out the same way it came in. It slithered along and went headfirst into to hole in the cement that was the shower drain. This drain went into a rock soak-away pit covered with dirt. I waited awhile to see if the snake would return. Since it did not show up, I proceeded to shower while very carefully watching the drain hole. I never did see the snake again, so it must have drowned or found some other way out of the rock pit.

Oma, Carol and Jean Berkin returned home at the end of November. We drove them to Serti to catch a flight with the CRC plane to Jos. Curt Radke managed to get a new diesel generator running and hooked it up to the entire hospital and staff and missionary houses. So now we enjoyed electric lights for about three hours every night. The return of Minnie Kuhn plus the arrival of two newly trained Nigerian midwives, Sabina Mamla and Esther Wiribun, greatly eased the workload at the hospital. The midwives and missionary nurses took night call shifts in rotation and I was on call all the time for situations that required a doctor. Our statistics for the year showed almost 1000 babies delivered and about 100,000 people seen as in-patients, out-patients, and mobile clinic patients. The chaplain reported 100 conversions to Christ in two-and-a-half months. The Mambilla Baptist Convention had 90 churches with only 19 trained pastors. The Bible School had 22 students enrolled in the first two years.

In mid-December we all travelled back to Cameroon for the annual Cameroon Missionary Fellowship (CMF). It was a huge entourage with 24 people in four vehicles. All the Mambilla missionaries plus parents and children from Woyke House in Jos travelled together. At CMF I was elected as program chairman and Marion was in charge of the children's program for the following year. We also discovered that we were posted to Mbingo Baptist Hospital once our government authority number arrived.

On return to Warwar, Willi Gutowski and I split up the doctor responsibilities. Having two doctors around was a real treat – we could consult each other on difficult cases. One such case involved Bruce. He did not feel well one day and complained of fever and joint pain all that day. By 1 AM he was delirious, chattering away at high speed, twitching and very hot. He was found to have a very stiff neck and tight hamstring muscles of his legs. This looked like meningitis. I woke up Willi to come and see Bruce. Willi did a lumbar puncture to get spinal fluid for analysis in the morning. We then loaded Bruce up with intramuscular injections – 4 million units of Penicillin G, 1000mg of Sulfadiazine, followed a short time later with another 4 million units of Penicillin and some Phenobarbital. We gave six injections in eight hours to the poor kid. Once everything that could be done was done, I went outside in the dark night and cried my eyes out and prayed with all my heart and soul. By morning Bruce had improved considerably. He was kept on medications and bed rest until his neck and leg stiffness was gone.

The adventurous antics of our children kept us ever watchful. On one occasion the Gutowski and Hiller kids decided to play hospital. Bruce, the doctor, and Sandy, the nurse, treated their (not so patient) patients – Lori, Melody, and Lisa. They found some pills in a box that someone had left unattended and decided to prescribe them for each other. Within a half-hour Lori and Lisa were staggering around like a couple of drunks and soon the rest were also staggering and sleepy. We discovered that the pills were Phenobarbital – a sedative and antiseizure drug. We tried unsuccessfully to make them vomit. They were then given strong coffee and taken on walks until the danger period was over before we let them sleep. To our great relief, they all recovered. We must have caught them before they had taken too many pills.

One day an elderly woman came to the hospital and presented with a huge abdominal tumor. The tumor was so large that she looked like she was 12 months pregnant with triplets! She had previously treated lepromatous leprosy that resulted in severe deformities – missing most of her fingers and toes. We booked surgery and I did the operation with Willi Gutowski assisting and Dr. Jerry Fluth observing, as he was visiting from Cameroon. We discovered the abdominal mass to be a huge ovarian tumor full of fluid. In order to remove this tumor, I had to extend the incision from her sternum to her pubis. Even then we could not adequately mobilize the mass. A trochar was inserted into the mass and we drained out 12 liters of fluid before we could start to mobilize it! The uterus and small bowel were densely adherent to the mass, so we had to carefully dissect it free. We managed to complete the operation in 90 minutes from incision to closing. The patient recovered well without complications. There was some postoperative humor with dressing changes. A newly trained Nigerian midwife had just come on staff and she had put on high and mighty airs, thinking she knew everything. She was told to change the abdominal dressing and then lay a small bag of little stones on top of the dressing, the pretext being that the patient would be able to walk better as she had been accustomed to a large weight in her abdomen prior to surgery. The next day on rounds we discovered the bag of stones on the patient. All of our junior staff and the patient roared with laughter. The new haughty midwife blushed with embarrassment. It was the first time I saw blushing in dark Nigerian skin. Needless to say, she was cured and became a lovely pleasant staff member.

A huge surprise came one day when the Chief of Mambilla arrived as a patient. He had developed a urethral stricture, likely the result of sexually transmitted infection from one or more women in his huge harem. We quickly cleared out a four-bed ward and put a single bed in it for him. A special latrine was dug for his exclusive use. Once again, the filiforms and followers were used with great success and big doses of antibiotics were prescribed. At least ten different Land Rovers filled with government officials and tribal leaders from Gembu arrived to visit the Chief. When he was feeling better, the Chief announced that Federal money had been allocated to pave the roads from Serti to Gembu, build a bridge across the Donga River, and then pave roads to Cameroon and to Warwar as well as roads to Baissa and Mayo Daga. As I write this account 45 years later, there still is no bridge over the Donga River and only the road from Serti to Gembu is paved.

During the time the Chief of Mambilla was a patient, the Chief of Jongoagia arrived at Warwar in the late stages of tetanus and died within 12 hours of admission. He got tetanus from a dirty needle used in a bush injection of an unknown substance. The Chief of Mambilla dispatched the police to arrest the man who gave the injection. We never found out what happened to him. The Chief of Mambilla was finally discharged and very grateful for the treatment he had received. He gave us a full-grown cow and had it butchered for us as an expression of his gratitude for our treatment. What a feast! Our first steaks in Africa! We made a barbeque by cutting an old metal drum in half and putting a piece of weld-mesh on it as a grill. It worked to perfection to give us a wonderful meal of steaks.

AS WE HAD TWO DOCTORS at Warwar, Willi and I decided to make extended treks to visit the outlying churches on the Warwar side of the river. I went first on an 11-day trek by horseback and on foot to visit the churches of the Kara association. Medicines, food, and bedding were packed into four boxes, one for each of our four carriers. Stephen Ndibil,

AND THEN THE PHONE RANG...

Warwar field pastor, and Samuel, a hospital worker came along as well. I rode on Schnitzel, a clumsy brown horse. He was so slow and clumsy that he stumbled over a branch and fell forward onto his nose. I saw this coming and leapfrogged over Schnitzel's head and landed on my hands and knees in front of him. Schnitzel got a real bawling out after I helped him back on his feet. Pastor Stephen rode on Humbug, so named because he had a stubborn streak. Humbug would always attempt to lie down and roll over when crossing a stream or river, thus baptizing the rider. He was a true Baptist horse! A circle tour was planned to visit 13 churches in 11 days. The routine was to trek to a village in the early morning, meet with the church to discuss their progress and problems, see sick people in the afternoon, eat supper, do some informal visiting, and then sleep.

I quote from a letter to Oma dated Feb. 12, 1973:

The tour was in a circle. As each place was 2 – 2 ½ hours by horseback, we usually got up at 6 AM for prayers and breakfast and on the way by 7 AM so as to travel when it was still cool. At this time of year it gets to be very hot from 10 AM to 3 PM. I usually slept in little mud houses and at one place, in Bang, in a house made entirely out of grass. The door was only two feet high, so entry was by crawling on hands and knees. I learned to take a bath with only a head-pan of water by moonlight. This was quite an art and can be cold in the nighttime breeze with cold unheated water from a spring. I took along a low camp cot and a mosquito net. Many places had corn stored in the rafters and rats eating the corn at night kept dropping stuff down. The mosquito net made sleep possible. I also learned to brush my teeth without water – you just keep brushing and spitting till all the toothpaste is gone. Without a filter, boiled water had all sorts of stuff floating in it. It's not too bad if you hide it with coffee and keep your eyes closed when drinking. I will relate only a few of the highlights.

1. BANG – a long dusty hot trek. Arrived Sunday at 10:30 AM in Bang village high on a dry dusty desert-like hill. All the houses were made of grass. Visited the Kashala (local chief)

BACK TO WORK

who was sick and resting in his compound. This man wants a church in his village (for prestige?). He even showed the single Christian in town a plot that could be used for a church. We witnessed to the Kashala and he accepted Christ as his Saviour. Two old men listened to the gospel witness and said that they and their families would come too if a church was built. We then went to the marketplace and sat under a huge tree and soon there were about 25 men gathered to talk to us and to see "the white man." Stephen, the field pastor, got to his feet and gave a salvation message. We then went behind a fence and examined about 130 sick people and gave medicines from our trek box. While we were doing this, all the men remained under the tree and spent over an hour discussing the things they had heard. They wanted to know more about this man called Jesus, having never heard of Him before. This area seemed very receptive to the gospel, so as we travelled on, we challenged other area churches to find, support, and send an evangelist to go to Bang.

2. TITONG – a village with a very sick church with a useless, ineffectual, and uneducated pastor. The deacons were constantly squabbling, and the head deacon was a thief. A church property boundary dispute was settled when I had the chief of the village come and mark off the boundary for all to see. This hopefully settled a four-year long dispute. There was one old man who had become a Christian recently. He had a small carved wooden idol that he wanted to get out of his house, so he gave it to me to take away (this idol ultimately ended up in a garbage can back in Canada). When we left Titong we saw many Juju men all around us in the hills preparing for a Juju celebration. I saw some of them up close – dressed in black stockinet over their heads and feathers and clanging metal ornaments on their arms and legs. They shouted and danced in a frenzy and looked like they were possessed by evil spirits – very frightening. Women were not allowed to see them and would be severely beaten if they did. Children ran home screaming in fright. I really sensed the presence of evil and darkness in that place.

3. DEMBE – Two old Kashalas came to meet us. They were obviously very drunk with mimbo (local corn beer). They thought that I was a god and they knelt down in front of me and tapped their heads on the ground, chanting some type of prayer. Our carriers had quite a time trying to set them straight regarding my real identity! After the usual long day of church visiting, seeing sick people, and supper, we settled in a hut for the night. At about midnight there was a loud banging at the door that woke all of us. After a lot of loud excited talking, we realized that there was a woman in a village about one hour's walk away who was trying to deliver twins. The first baby was delivered but the second one was stuck. So, pastor Stephen and I followed the messengers through the bush for well over an hour by the light of a kerosene bush lamp. The village square was full of anxious people waiting to see what would happen. We were ushered into the mud hut where we saw the pregnant woman lying naked on some banana leaves on the dirt floor. The first baby was lying on a filthy rag with the umbilical cord still attached to the placenta inside the mother. In the center of the hut was a fire and a number of old women sat around looking very worried. All I had with me was a syringe, needles, Penicillin, Ergotamine, two forceps, 4-inch White Cross squares, and some Dettol antiseptic. Before we started anything, I asked Pastor Stephen to pray in the vernacular language so that all present could hear and understand the prayer. We borrowed the husband's hunting knife and put it, with some tough grass, into a tin can of water and set this on the fire to boil so that we could cut and tie the umbilical cords with some semblance of sterility! The first baby's cord was cut and tied, and he was wrapped in a warm cloth. I learned that the local Juju man had tried for 6 hours with incantations and torture to try to get the second baby out. On examination I found the baby's head still high up, so with considerable

pressure on the perineal muscles, I got the woman to push and within a few minutes the second twin was born alive and screaming. The babies and the mother were all given generous doses of Penicillin in view of all the obvious contamination that had occurred. Instruction was given to the villagers that they immediately carry the mom and her twins to Warwar for further treatment. A note was written to Minnie Kuhn as to what happened. The mother came to faith in Jesus while at Warwar.

Willi Gutowski conducted a similar trek through the Warwar association churches. We tallied up our combined statistics and found that we had visited 26 churches and examined and treated over 1000 patients. The visits were a real encouragement to the small rural churches. Marion was the guest speaker at a three-day women's conference in Furumi. She gave Bible lessons to teach about 120 women to come out from among them and be separate. Marion, Bruce, and Lori slept in the church. All of them got chiggers in their feet from the dirt floor where chickens had been running about. One pregnant woman went into labour at the conference but did not deliver the baby until she was taken back to Warwar. Willi and I both got permission from our wives to grow beards. Anita and Marion both realized that men had to grow a beard at least once in their lifetime to prove that they really could do it. I sported a foo-man-chu-type of beard on my chin that I could reverently and thoughtfully stroke as I mused about nothing in particular and looked intelligent all the while. The novelty soon wore off on Marion and I finally was commanded to shave it off.

Our time at Warwar was rapidly coming to a close. We packed all of our cargo onto the Fiat truck so that Curt could drive it to Cameroon. We bade farewell to the many friends among our staff and in the town of Warwar. There were many precious memories of experiences and meals that we shared with them. They had become our close friends. We flew to Jos for a short local leave and attended a five-day workshop conducted by the Lay Institute of Evangelism and met Bill Bright, the founder of Campus Crusade. Fred Folkerts and Dr. Jerry Fluth came to Jos with our Authority Number to enter and work in Cameroon. So, we said good-bye to Mambilla, Nigeria and headed off to Mbingo, Cameroon.

AND THEN THE PHONE RANG...

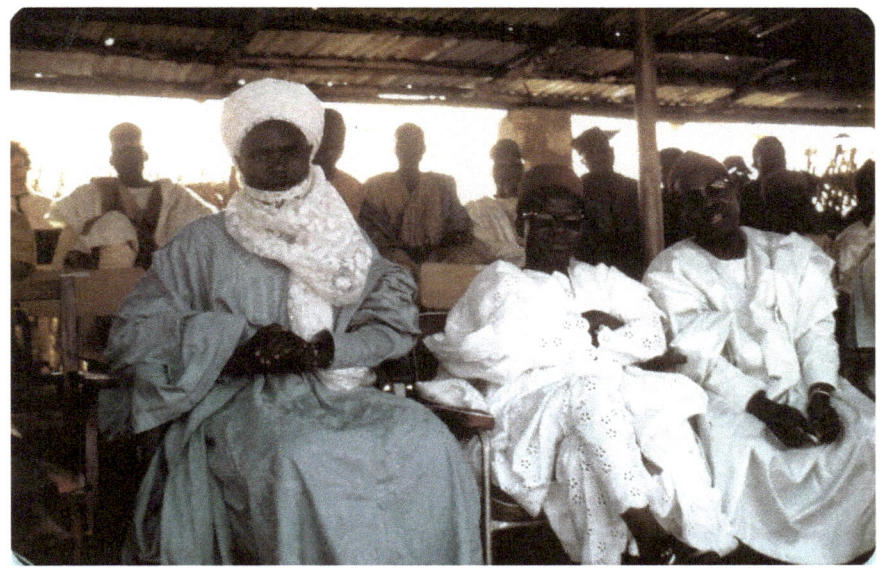

PARAMOUNT CHIEF OF MAMBILLA IN THE BLUE ROBE

GOING ON AN 11-DAY TOUR OF REMOTE VILLAGES

CHAPTER 13

Mbingo Cameroon

GETTING THERE

It was hot, it was humid, sweat rolled down our bodies, and we were miserable. We were travelling from Jos, Nigeria, to Bamenda, Cameroon on our transfer from Nigeria to Cameroon. The Land Rover was loaded with supplies and people – our family plus Fred Folkerts, and Jerry and Monie Fluth who met us in Jos. The trip took us from the cool plateau of Jos down to the low, hot, humid plains, through the towns of Bukuru and Vom, and across the Benue River at Makurdi. We stayed overnight in the Christian Reform Church rest house at Mkar. The temperature was well over 100ºF and the humidity about 90 – 95 % – like a sauna. We drank lots of tepid water and slept fitfully without sheets or mosquito nets. Our alarms went off at 4:30 AM so that we could travel in the relative "cool of the morning." Five hours later, just three miles beyond the village of Obudu, we heard a terrible noise in the Land Rover transmission. Suddenly we had no gears except for fourth gear. We limped our way back to Obudu, drained out the transmission oil, finding very little of it plus some bearing chips.

It was time to improvise. The women, children, and cargo were left at a "rest house" in Obudu. Fred, Jerry, and I made a run for Ogoja, 38 miles away, using only the fourth gear. Maintaining adequate speed in fourth gear was tricky, especially going up hill. Fortunately, there was very little traffic to slow us down. We were relieved to arrive at the Ministry of Works where a young Dutch volunteer mechanic offered to help us. I had just purchased a set of socket wrenches in Jos and we used them to take out the front seats, disconnect the clutch and drive shaft, and remove and dismantle the gearbox. We found a spoiled bearing that caused the main shaft to seize and shear right off. Some spare parts were found in a junkyard and the reassembly began. It seemed like there were 1000 nuts, bolts, and washers! It was so hot that our sweaty shirts could be wrung out, leaving a puddle on the floor. At 5 PM the place closed so the Dutch mechanic put us up on cots at his home. We got supper for 15 shillings at the Government catering rest house in an air-conditioned dining room with three big fans going. It was so cold and windy there that I thought I saw whitecaps in my soup bowl! We had very little money left and Barclay's bank would not cash our cheques until the Dutch mechanic vouched for us. By 4 PM the next day we got the Land Rover reassembled and we returned to Obudu to find our families. Our wives were not enthused about the rest house that had dirty sheets, only one small towel for all of them, and no drinking water. Fortunately they had a hand operated filter pump to get some drinkable water. They survived on beans, mangos, and bananas.

It was after 6 PM by now and the deplorable conditions in Obudu caused us to pack up everything and drive to Ikom near the border with Cameroon. We got to the Government catering rest house five minutes after closing time at 9 PM. As there were no available rooms for us, we went into town and found a "hotel" to stay in. The beds were OK but there was only one bucket of water and one towel for all of us. This was put in the "washroom" that was, in actual fact, a urinal stall. The toilet also had not been flushed for days. Supper consisted of a few leftover beans. Jerry and I found some Coca-Cola in the market, which we drank, and then went to bed dirty and sweaty. It was too hot to sleep until after 3 AM. We were up and travelling by 6 AM and, after a two-hour wait to cross the border on the other side of the Cross River, we got to Mamfe for lunch and to the Cameroon Baptist Convention Compound in Bamenda by 4 PM. We all made a beeline for Edith Schroeder's house for a cold drink with a real ice cube in it, and then straight to our guesthouse for a tub bath.

AND THEN THE PHONE RANG...

SETTLING IN

CURT AND BARB, WITH ALL of our cargo, came from Warwar in the Fiat truck and canvas-back Land Rover. They arrived in Bamenda an hour before we got there. The next day we got a Cameroon driver's license, got our passports stamped, and shopped for food. Then we drove out to Mbingo Baptist Hospital – our home for the next two years. We camped out in the Fluth's spare bedroom for four days while a house on the top of the station hill, called the machine shed, was prepared for us. This house was originally a storage building for equipment and later turned into a school and finally renovated to serve as a missionary home, used primarily by Laura Reddig. All of our cargo was piled into one room and we only unpacked what was necessary for the two months we lived there. The view from the machine shed house on a hill high above the hospital was spectacular. We could see the sloping compound below us and to the side we saw several waterfalls cascading down from a ridge high above the property. When the Fluth family left on furlough we moved back down the hill into the Fluth house. All this moving around was too much for Sinbad, our Siamese cat. He disappeared for a year and then returned for a short time, only to leave again. The Fluths loaned us their cat, PeeWee, who helped get rid of the numerous mice in the machine shed.

Mbingo was a large 2000-acre station with a 50-bed general hospital, a leprosy hospital, and a village settlement for leprosy patients with deformities. A small sloping airstrip, grassland for 500 head of cattle, a coffee plantation, staff housing, a church, small farms, and even a small market place beside the main road made this a very unique mission station. Leprosy patients under active treatment had small houses near the leprosy hospital. A village called New Hope Settlement was situated at the bottom of the long sloping property. This village was inhabited by people who were cured of leprosy and no longer required treatment. They could not return to their homes because the severe deformities caused by leprosy made them outcasts from general society. The men of this village tended the coffee farm and cared for the cattle. This gave them some income as well as milk and meat. The women wove baskets and embroidered tablecloths and handkerchiefs for additional income. Thus these folks had income and fellowship in their own community. A special well was dug for them giving easy access to water. The well area was covered by a gazebo type of roof to create a sheltered center where the community could gather.

MBINGO STAFF

AFTER DR. JERRY FLUTH LEFT on furlough I was appointed as Medical Officer in charge of Mbingo Baptist Hospital, with a main involvement in leprosy work. Dr. Helen-Marie Schmidt, a general surgeon was in charge of the general hospital work. In addition to leprosy work, I also saw general outpatients and did surgery. The operating theater had two operating tables so Helen and I could do two operations at the same time, or assist each other on more complex cases. Helen was a great surgeon and I learned a great deal from her. Geraldine Glassenap, known as "Gigi", was in charge of the nursing and support staff and was an extremely capable administrator. Pat Lenz was an excellent physiotherapist who was very involved with treatment of deformities and rehabilitation for leprosy patients. Nurse Laura Reddig, on furlough when we got to Mbingo, was the veteran missionary who had a heart of compassion for the poor state of leprosy patients and who had started the entire leprosy work at Mbingo. When she returned from furlough we saw how the people loved her as they welcomed her back home. They considered her to be like a mother.

The Cameroonian staff was well trained, dependable, and did excellent work. Moses Tawah was the treasurer and business manager and his wife Rachel worked as a midwife. Samuel Jam was the chaplain and was also a fully trained nurse. He became a special friend with whom I could confide. His wife Theresa was a midwife. David Mfikwe was our leprosy inspector who cared for the needs of our many leprosy patients. Johnson Kananjing was our very capable senior nurse who assisted at surgery and did outpatient consultations. Stephen Gwaksi was our surgical nurse who ran the operating room and assisted at surgery. Elias Toh ran the outpatient department and did the interpreting for us. Pa Shadrach was the station foreman in charge of the laborers and cowboys. He was a very robust and fit man, full of boundless energy, and always present where the action was.

Pa Lenga was the nurse in charge of the leprosy hospital where patients were admitted for special treatment such as complications of leprosy or surgery (amputations, skin grafts, or tendon transfers).

LEPROSY WORK

I SPENT THE FIRST SEVERAL months tagging along with Jerry Fluth to learn about diagnosis and treatment of leprosy. Leprosy is an infectious disease caused by *Mycobacterium leprae* resulting in skin lesions and nerve damage. The severity of symptoms range from mild (tuberculoid) skin lesions only, to severe (lepromatous) skin thickening and anesthetic hands and feet caused by swelling of the myelin sheath around peripheral nerves. This swelling is due to an inflammatory reaction to the leprosy bacilli. The severity of the disease is determined by the extent of natural immunity in the patient. Unaffected people have a strong immune response to the bacteria resulting in resistance to leprosy. The lepromatous patients have little or no immune response and the tuberculoid patients have only a partial immune response. Initiation of treatment with dapsone can cause severe reactions such as painful neuritis and allergic reactions such as erythema nodosum leprosum. Because of numbness in hands and feet, many patients develop wounds due to walking with a stone in a shoe that is not felt or burning their hands while tending a cooking fire. With no pain, these wounds are neglected and become infected. They then require antibiotics, wound debridement, and even skin grafting. Some infections may progress into osteomyelitis (bone infection) that may require amputations. Nerve damage also can result in deformities of hands and feet. Dr. Fluth learned to do some tendon transplants and grafting to improve the function of deformed hands and feet. I worked with the physiotherapy people to make special molded soft Plastazote shoes to custom-fit deformed feet, and make above- and below-knee prosthesis for amputees. The leprosy hospital had a trained leprosy inspector, and a prosthetics technician who was a former leprosy patient. Every day a row of patients would sit on the verandah bench of the leprosy ward with their feet in buckets of water to soak and clean their wounds. Nurses would then redress the wounds using the White Cross bandages sent by the ladies of our NAB churches.

I obtained permission from the Public Health Officer for the Northwest Province to visit all of the government leprosy clinics in order to do a disability survey of all the leprosy patients. Pat Lenz, David Mfikwe (Mbingo leprosy inspector), and I made a number of trips to visit all the clinics of the province. This project took a year to complete and at the end of it I wrote a nine-page typewritten report to the Ministry of Health. We had examined 1725 leprosy patients. There was a 30% incidence of significant deformity of hands, feet, eyes, and face. In these 30% the rate of foot deformity was 94%. Several hundred patients were discharged from treatment as they were either cured or did not have leprosy in the first place. Recommendations were made for earlier referrals to Mbingo to minimize the severity of deformity and the formation of a mobile shoe clinic, funded by the government, to make individually fitted protective shoes for patients in their home villages. Within three weeks of submission of this report I was called to Bamenda to meet with the Chief Provincial Health Officer to discuss the report and its recommendations. Present at the meeting were all the Chiefs of Zone for the various health divisions of the province who were in charge of all the health centers, maternity wards, and clinics. We had a good meeting and I hoped that improved leprosy care in the province would be the result. Part of my leprosy work was teaching two-week courses in leprosy diagnosis and care to students from the Banso Hospital School of Nursing.

MARION WAS VERY BUSY

ON THE DOMESTIC SCENE MARION was happy to receive the services of Laura Reddig's cook, Paul Nkesi, who was available to help us during Laura's furlough. He was a gourmet cook who served up exotic dishes like toasted avocado pear sandwiches or guava pudding etc. Marion visited all of our hospital staff in their homes, which built up very good relationships. She also gathered up all the kids for weekly meetings of the "good news club" for singing and Bible stories. Bruce and Lori had lots of playmates, initially with the Fluth children – Kathy, Karen, Kristie, and Ken; the Lemke children – Milton, Marvin and Marie; and later with the Hoepner children - Kris, Jerry, and Brenda. Marion was put in charge of sewing and embroidery projects for the women leprosy patients. She gave out cloth with designs stamped on them for the women to embroider, which they sold to bring in some income. Marion was also appointed as station hostess to extend hospitality to visitors. This was a big job. At the dedication of a new missionary house Marion served juice, sandwiches, and cookies to 250 people, and two hours later hosted a buffet dinner for 50 missionaries.

At Christmas time all the missionaries from Belo, Mbingo, and Bamenda came for a special dinner at Mbingo. Marion was appointed to cook the turkey. A huge turkey was found and Marion was warned that free-range turkeys have big strong muscles and can be quite tough to eat. This turkey was too big to fit in any pressure cooker in the kitchen. Someone suggested using an old hospital sterilizer. Ed Hoepner, station manager, set it up for Marion on some cement blocks in the yard and lit a roaring fire under it. Marion watched it carefully, waiting for a pfft-pfft sound from the pressure release valve on top. After a while Ed returned to see how things were going. There was no pfft-pfft sound, so Ed and Marion decided to open up the lid to inspect the turkey. They looked in and, much to Marion's horror, they saw the bleached bare turkey bones and all the meat bits floating in the water below. Ed exclaimed, "Looks like he done die, ma." When he saw the look on Marion's face, he beat a rapid retreat and took off in his truck. Once Marion recovered from the initial shock, she managed to make a wonderful casserole with layers of dressing and turkey bits and gravy. Helen Marie found some tins of Pacific oysters in one of her many drums to add to the menu. It took Marion a very long time before she was able to laugh at this experience!

On another occasion we held a dedication service for the opening of a new hospital ward plus a kitchen, laundry, and storage room. Among the dignitaries were the American Ambassador to Cameroon, the District Officer, the Chief Medical Officer of the Northwest Province, the Chief of National Security, and the Fon of Laikom. In total about 1500 people showed up. I chaired the meeting in the Mbingo 1 church. Ed Hoepner handled the ribbon cutting. Helen Schmidt conducted a tour of the facilities, and poor Marion and Marie Hoepner prepared light refreshments for the 1500 people. Marion and Marie then prepared a dinner for 50 dignitaries and missionaries. It was an exhausting day for everyone!

MEDICAL WORK

A ROUTINE DAY AT MBINGO Hospital was as follows :

- 6 :00 AM – wake up
- 6:45 AM – staff devotions
- 7:00 AM – ward rounds on in-patients and then outpatient consultations
- 10:00 AM – coffee in Gigi's office with senior staff
- 10:15 AM – outpatient consultations and surgery
- 12:00 PM – lunch
- 12:30 PM – 6 PM – surgery, repeat in-patient rounds, administration
- Evenings – supper, family time, Bible studies, paper work, emergencies

Surgical emergencies could keep us busy at all hours. The emergencies seemed to come in bunches. One week we had two hysterectomies, one huge ovarian cyst, two hernias (one a child), one cholecystectomy, and five skin grafts (one very extensive), plus several Caesarean sections. One wild night Helen Schmidt called me at 11 PM to help with a patient who was in shock from a gastrointestinal hemorrhage. He was vomiting copious amounts of blood all over the floor and passing bright red blood rectally. He was in total shock with no recordable blood pressure. I managed to start two IVs, get Dextran (plasma expander) and saline into him, and pump out his stomach. I then anesthetized him with chloroform (initially) and then open-drop ether. Helen operated and found a huge duodenal ulcer which she over sewed and then did a vagotomy and pyloroplasty. Remarkably the patient survived!

AND THEN THE PHONE RANG...

Another week we operated on three women with ruptured ectopic pregnancies. Each one had their abdomen full of blood and was going into early shock. We had a unique way of rapid blood transfusion – using a medicine cup, we scooped blood out of the abdomen, poured it through sterile gauze into bottles of ACD anticoagulant, and transfused it back into the patient. There was no need to seek donors and no concern about mismatched blood. That same week another woman with a full-term pregnancy was brought to the hospital with abdominal pain and was in such deep shock that we could not find a pulse or recordable blood pressure. Fortunately, we found two women willing to donate blood. Helen and I got IVs started and started to operate using only local anesthetic. She had a dead baby floating freely in her abdomen. Her uterus had ruptured from top to bottom, right through her cervix, and was inverted inside out (like a sock). We sewed up the torn uterus and then ligated her fallopian tubes to prevent further pregnancies. She had two previous Caesarean sections and was unmarried. She had not wanted another Caesarean section for this pregnancy so she stayed home to deliver this baby. On another weekend Helen and Marion went to a women's leadership conference and Gigi was in Douala, so I was alone when two more patients with ruptured ectopic pregnancies arrived, one of them in shock. To make matters worse, all our trained Cameroonian staff happened to be on leave. So, I had to operate with the help of totally untrained staff.

NON-MEDICAL EVENTS

MAY 20TH IS NATIONAL DAY in Cameroon – the anniversary of Cameroon becoming a United Republic. This being a holiday, a group of missionaries from Mbingo drove to Fundong, the district headquarters, to attend the celebration. We met the District Officer (equivalent to a Governor) and the Fon (paramount chief) of the Bikom tribe. We sat in the V.I.P. section to watch the flag-raising, march past of military and dignitaries, and awarding of medals. Then came traditional dancing, including Juju dancers. The dancers wore a stocking-type covering on their heads and masks covering their faces. Feathers were tied to their heads and arms and noisy rattles to their ankles. The dancers stomped so vigorously that the dust flew and the ground vibrated. All this sound and fury was too much for Bruce and he began to cry. When the ceremonies were done, we had a picnic lunch and then attended a cocktail reception at the District Officer's residence. Fortunately, there was a choice of soft drinks for us Baptist missionaries. This was an important issue as alcoholism is a huge problem in Cameroon, even among Christians. So, we had to be careful not to send a wrong message by drinking alcohol ourselves.

A week later we made a trip to the coast with Oryn Meinerts in order to pick up a new Land Rover for Mbingo Hospital. We stopped at the treasury in Kumba to pick up a cheque for the vehicle and stayed overnight in the Victoria rest house at Saker College. The next day we drove to Douala to do some shopping and to order drugs for the hospital. We had a nice picnic lunch beside the pool at the Seamen's mission and the kids enjoyed a swim in their pool. The new Land Rover was ready for us and we drove it back to Victoria through a monsoon rainstorm. The next morning Oryn and I decided to inspect the vehicle and drove it onto a grease pit. To our surprise we discovered that the whole driveshaft, rear differential, and oil pan was loose and almost falling off! We spent the next hour tightening every bolt that we could find. One of the tires was only half inflated. It was a good thing that we decided to check things out. This averted a disaster on the trip back home.

At times we conducted medical clinics in remote villages. One of these clinics was described in a June 1973 letter to my mother as follows:

> *Last week I took Dr. Barry Simpson, a visiting volunteer dentist from Athens Georgia, on a clinic trip to Fundong on a Thursday and then on Friday – Saturday to Awoh (Fomenji). Rev. Pete Schroeder, field missionary for this area, and his son, Tim, came along. Tim had just finished high school and came to Cameroon for the summer. Awoh is in a very remote area. To get there we had to drive over unbelievable roads that required 1st gear and low range in the Land Rover to get up steep rutted hills. We had to cross six bridges made of sticks that swayed as we drove over. The passengers had to get out and walk over for safety. At the end of the road, we left the*

vehicle and trekked for three miles straight down, carrying boxes of medicine, a portable dental chair, a small generator, and a compressor. At one point the path was only 18 inches wide with a sheer drop of over 1000 feet on either side. Leaning over, one could not see the bottom! It seemed like we drove up the side of a volcano and now were going down into the crater with fog and clouds below us. We crammed about 200 people into a room that evening to show slides and filmstrips onto a sheet hung on the wall. The pictures told animal stories and ended up with a gospel message. The next morning we held clinics, both medical and dental. At noon we packed all our gear and climbed up the steep hill – three miles "straight up to heaven" with not one level spot on the way. It took between one and two hours to get everyone plus equipment to the top. The chief of Awoh met us at the top and showed his gratitude for our visit by presenting us with a snow-white billy goat ram. We managed to tie him up and pack him into the Land Rover along with all our staff and equipment. It was late in the day before we got home after driving down that horrible road.

Dr. Barry Simpson was a very extroverted and excitable man and talked non-stop. As we drove through a small village, a chicken at the side of the road began to run along-side of the vehicle instead of away from us. The chicken was flapping its wings and half flying along making a great deal of noise. He finally hit a small bush and flew up and into the passenger's window, landing right on Barry's lap. I don't know who did the most flapping and clucking – the chicken or Barry! We all had a great laugh after releasing the chicken. The following day we took Barry to Banso where he did two more weeks of dental work. After dropping him off, we went on to Ndu to attend the Bible School graduation ceremony. I took Bruce with me and he was very proud to be the "motor-boy." On the way back home to Mbingo we encountered a very heavy monsoon-like rain. A 200-yard section of the Ndop plain was under 30 inches of fast flowing water. All the taxis were stopped. Our Land Rover had higher clearance so we plowed right through the flood, much to the delight of our "motor-boy."

MBINGO CAMEROON

In the month of July, 1973, the Fluth family went home on furlough (home assignment) and so we moved down from the machine shed house into the "Fluth house." This was much closer to the hospital, which was really appreciated when I was called to the hospital for an emergency on a rainy night. Marion got busy washing walls and sewing curtains for the windows. In addition to our other duties, Marion was put in charge of the women's ministries of Belo Field and I became the Belo Field missionary and advisor to the Belo Field Council of Churches. We both travelled to Belo so Marion could meet and plan the next year's women's work with the Belo women. I met with the executive of the Belo field council of churches and also with the entire council representing 54 churches. I discovered that the Belo people could be quite feisty and lively when debating issues. They almost came to blows over one particular issue. I also attended a three-day pastor's conference where I taught lessons on the necessity of a Holy Spirit filled life as a prerequisite to a fruitful ministry. This was followed by a seven-day tour of some of the association churches with the Cameroonian field pastor. Marion went to a three-day women's leadership training course in Wum, which was a three-hour drive away. She taught lessons on Naomi and Ruth, how to organize and run a church women's ministry, and how to sew pants for little children. Back at Mbingo I taught a class for 18 of our staff on how to be filled with the Holy Spirit. They were then encouraged to go out in pairs as witnessing teams for several weeks at a time with church support.

THE FON OF LAIKOM

HELEN AND THE BELO FIELD pastor joined Marion and me for a visit to the Fon of Laikom. He was the traditional paramount chief of the Bikom tribe that lived in our area of Cameroon. His palace in Laikom was high up on a hill from where one could see 50 miles away in three directions on a clear day. We drove up a mountainous road that only mountain goats and Land Rovers could climb. The reason for our visit was to build good relationships with the Fon. It helps to have the chief's support if problems should ever arise. His compound was huge with many houses for himself, his servants, and his many wives. The compound had a stone wall around it and was quite dirty due to the many sheep wandering around inside. There was a big stone throne in the inner courtyard and the Fon had chairs set up around the throne for us to sit and visit. We presented him with gifts – a bag of cement, a bag of salt, and some sugar. He gave us some Fanta (soda pop) to drink and then gave us some woven bowls, a promise of Bikom robes, and a live-and-kicking sheep. He then showed us his prepared burial site and had two men blow notes on huge elephant tusks. He also showed us his open-air court of law, where all major decisions affecting the tribe were made by the Fon and his elders and advisors. I wondered if he had a premonition of impending death, causing him to show us his burial site. It was good for us to show our respect for the traditional ruler of the Bikom people.

We visited the Fon again several months later as he invited us to a celebration in memory of all the great men of the Bikom tribe who had died long ago. As we arrived, we saw a Juju man dressed with feathers, rattles on his ankles, and stockinette over his head. He was chasing people as he danced around an open field to the beat of many drums. The people had to bow down and kneel in his presence to avoid a beating. To make matters more threatening, he wielded three spears to frighten everyone as he approached them. He saw me coming from our vehicle and danced over to confront me. People all around me on their knees called out "get down, get down." There was no way that I would get down or bow to a Juju who represented evil spirits. What kind of message would be given to the observers if I, as a representative of Jesus Christ, bow down to this man? I was holding on to Bruce and Lori and felt their hand grip get very tight, as they were frightened. The man came very close and I heard him panting behind the stockinette that was over his face. He proceeded to jab my chest with his spears to force me to get down. I had no idea if he was drunk or drugged. Would he really harm me in the compound of the Fon who invited me to come? We had a staring contest for what seemed to be a long time. He finally gave up and danced away as the people on the ground around me murmured expressions of awe and wonder. We proceeded to the Fon's inner sanctum where Ed Hoepner and I presented him with some medicines and two bags of salt. He in turn gave us a dinner of rice and slit open and boiled cow intestines, which were quite salty.

The final time that I saw this Fon was when he summoned me to come and see him because he was ill. I packed a bag of sundry medicines and proceeded to make a "hut call" together with a staff member to interpret. It was late afternoon when we arrived and the palace courtyard was full of curious people wondering what the Fon's problem was. I examined the Fon in his bedroom and discovered that he was in heart failure with swollen ankles and a chest full of rales. I advised him to come with me to Mbingo Hospital where he could get adequate treatment. He declined this offer as the Fon in Bikom culture is god-like and could not be seen publicly as weak. Fons also do not eat in public for the same reason. All that I could offer him was an injection of a diuretic to ease his breathlessness for a while. I informed him that without further treatment he would probably die soon. He agreed to my offer to pray for him, which I did. The prayer included thanks to God for the wonderful plan of salvation for those who trust in Jesus. He thanked me, and told me not to leave yet. He gave instructions to a servant who soon returned with robes. The servant put two aprons on me, one in front and one in back, and then put a full-length robe on as well, with beautiful embroidery around the neck. A Bikom hat completed the outfit. I was then dismissed. As I walked out into the courtyard all the people gasped and got down on their knees. I was bewildered at this. My interpreter then told me that the special embroidery on the robe's neck meant that I had become a "Chia Fon", a member of the Fon's inner circle of advisors. Years later I wore the robe at a mission conference in Kelowna. A Cameroonian pastor, who was a Bikom man, was at the conference. He was amazed to see the robe on me as he recognized the significance of the neck embroidery. He immediately understood when I told him how I obtained the robe.

The Fon died a short time later, so Jerry Fluth, Ed Hoepner, Gigi Glassenap, and I attended the funeral. The palace compound was full of Bikon men all stripped to the waist as is the local custom. Even one of the former Prime Ministers of West Cameroon was there, stripped to the waist, as he was a Bikom man. We presented the new Fon with symbolic gifts of salt (to help feed all the guests) and a blanket (to bury the dead

Fon). We were escorted to the burial hut to see the dead Fon on a cot. Men were digging a grave outside at one corner of the hut. Fons had been buried at the corners for many years. When the gravediggers came upon the bones of a deceased Fon, a shelf was dug to place the bones to the side. Armed soldiers watched the proceedings to ensure that the old, now banned, custom of burying a live child with the Fon did not happen. The child was supposed to look after the needs of the Fon in the afterlife.

TREKS IN REMOTE AREAS

WE MADE A TOUR THROUGH the Wum association to visit churches and conduct medical clinics. The area is quite remote, rural, and undeveloped by Cameroonian standards. Our team consisted of Ed Hoepner (missionary), Moses Chongsi (field pastor), Barnabas Ngong (evangelist), Samuel Jam (nurse and hospital chaplain), and myself. In eight days we visited 14 churches, conducted two baptisms, and held eight medical clinics in which we saw about 850 sick people. The first day we left Mbingo at 5 AM and visited the main church in Wum to conduct a large clinic. We then drove for miles into the bush to the end of the road. There we got seven or eight carriers to tote our boxes of medicines, food, and bedding. As we started the trek a heavy monsoon-like rainstorm descended on us. We walked for several hours through tall, wet elephant grass, up and down hills, and waded through three streams. One of the streams was waist deep with a swift current that nearly swept us down a waterfall. I learned later that it helps to carry something heavy on your head to help stabilize yourself when in swift currents. We finally arrived, very tired and soaking wet. Sitting in wet clothing that evening was unpleasant. Our clothes were still very wet the next morning due to the humidity. Getting dressed was like putting on a wet bathing suit. We saw about 140 sick people after a church service and then trekked back to our vehicle through the three streams again. Ed Hoepner was getting a real initiation in pioneer missionary work. We visited two more churches and drove to Benakuma which was at the end of another road. There we held an open-air evangelistic service in the market and saw another 150 people in the midst of another downpour of rain. Luckily we found a little kiosk with a zinc roof in which to examine patients. We finished seeing the last person at 9 PM using the light of a bush lamp and the headlights of our Land Rover. The next day we trekked 4-5 hours into really dense forest and then thick tangled elephant grass. Our destination was a small church in a very primitive remote place. This was only the second time that the people there saw a white missionary and the first time to see a doctor and western medicine. The women wore only a string around their waists with some grass attached to front and back. It was good to see a number of young energetic Christians. We were able to encourage them in their faith and we also saw many sick people. We could only charge them 5 – 10% of the usual fee for medicine as they were obviously very poor. Some children got free medicines. Ed and I decided to heat up some spaghetti for a change from the local cornmeal fufu. This caused quite a commotion as some people thought that white men eat worms. My electric shaver also created a stir especially among the kids. Not much is private in such a place! The next day another two-and-a-half-hour trek took us to a similar place with a similar agenda. The following day we made a very long return trek to the Land Rover and a drive back to Wum. I discovered the value of raw sugar cane as a thirst quencher and source of energy on a long hot trek. After a good sleep we travelled to Munken, which was also in a remote location. There were only about 20 -30 Christians in a vast area. It was a hilly walk into the village from the end of the road. We held a worship service in the little church and helped with the baptism of four people. A medical clinic was held for the people who saw western medicine for the first time. The area around Munken is large and relatively unevangelized, so we planned to return again later for a whole week with medicines and two-by-two witnessing teams. We drove around the ring road through Ndu where we attended a Sunday church service together with Willi and Marie Mueller. Monday we got home, very tired, but in time to teach a two-week leprosy course to a class of Banso nursing students.

    Marion also did a four-day visit to five churches in the Wum Association to conduct teaching sessions for the women's groups. Two of the churches could only be reached by trekking in the bush. So Marion walked for one hour to one church and over three hours to the other one. She found the three-hour hike through the jungle very interesting but quite tiring. She slept in little mud block huts with grass roofs with very low doorways and no windows. This gave her intense nasal congestion. She also had to wade through rivers that were not too deep as there had been little rain. The women really appreciated the visit and the helpful teaching.

On another occasion I went on a ten-day trek into a very remote area called Mamfe-Overside. Samuel Jam again came along as well as Peter Jam, the Belo Field pastor. We also had eight carriers to tote boxes of medicine, food, and camp cots. Mamfe-Overside was a new region of evangelistic outreach and there were four small churches established. We drove through Wum and Benakuma to the end of the bush road and then trekked for two-and-a-half days to get there. After going through thick elephant grass for many hours we then descended several thousand feet to reach the very hot and humid lowlands. Along the way we boiled water that we got from streams to keep hydrated. Sleeping out in the open was interesting as we were now in an area infested with snakes. The people in this area also never saw a white doctor with medicines before and were again awed that I ate "worms" from a can of spaghetti! It was so hot at night that a sleeping bag was intolerable. I slept with a sheet over my head to try to keep mosquitos away, but despite the sheet and a burning coil of insect repellant, the mosquitos bit me many times right through the sheet. I was a bit fearful of getting malaria. One night the people showed me a place to sleep by a fire pit that had a "gazebo," consisting of four poles and a roof of palm branches. I settled in to sleep only to be awakened by loud grunting noises. Apparently where I put my camp cot was the place where local pigs also used to sleep. So about once every hour that night I had to drive them off with a stick!

I discovered that the people of the area remember the last time they ate a person. The government had sent two agents to the area to take a poll. The people did not trust this as they thought that they would now have to pay huge taxes. So they killed and ate one of the agents and beat the other one and let him go free so that he could tell the government what happened. As a result, they did not see any more government officials in the area. I also discovered an interesting part of their belief system involving illness. They believed that when an important man got ill, he must have done something very bad. In order to atone for the misdeed, they would tie a goat or sheep to a tree with a short rope. The animal would die of starvation due to the short rope that prevented grazing. The animal's death was considered to be the appropriate atonement for the man's transgression. This belief was an excellent opening to present the gospel of Jesus Christ's sacrificial death on the cross to atone for all of our sins. Our team discussed using this redemptive analogy for witnessing in this area.

We visited the four small churches to encourage the people to persevere in their faith and to tell others about Jesus. We saw about 500 sick people, many of whom had malaria and thyroid goiters. I suspected that the soil of the area might be low in iodine content, causing so many goiters.

EVANGELISM

ALL OF OUR EFFORTS INVOLVED working in God's expanding kingdom. The medical work, church visitation, committee meetings, Field Bible Conferences, treks to remote areas, and leprosy clinics were all part of God's kingdom work in Cameroon. At Mbingo Baptist Hospital we had morning devotions and prayer with the staff. The chaplain gave a gospel message to the waiting outpatients and then made hospital rounds to encourage and pray with the in-patients. As we visited churches, we gave words of encouragement to the churches and met with the pastors to give them support; often we preached sermons.

Ed Hoepner and I, two pastors, and two laymen visited Fungom, a remote village, for five days of medical clinics. People from surrounding villages came for medical care. Ed, the two pastors, and two laymen took local Christians in teams of two to visit the surrounding villages to preach and to do personal witnessing. In the five days there we recorded 228 people who prayed to receive Christ as their personal Saviour. This area had only one small church and a few small prayer groups. We hoped that a number of new churches would now be started. From a hilltop one could see for miles across the Katsina Ala River towards the Nigerian border. This was a huge unevangelized area. The two laymen were so excited about potential evangelism that they persuaded the Mbingo church to take on this area as a mission project. We later flew over the area with the Missionary Aviation plane to survey the lay of the land.

On another occasion Ed and I went to the major village of Fundong on a Sunday. I preached a 40-minute sermon on the great commission and taught the four spiritual laws of evangelism. After the message all the people marched to the nearby market place with the choir leading the way with enthusiastic singing. We were joined on the way by a second church. The large market had about 2000 – 3000 people and our procession got everyone's attention. Some men brought a table along for Ed and a pastor to stand on. It was Ed's turn to do some open-air market preaching using a battery powered loudspeaker. About 2000 people heard the message and the choir songs. After the message we retreated to a nearby house where I challenged all the Christians to go back into the market to do follow-up individual witnessing. Ed looked a bit worried when he saw all the people in the market. I encouraged him by remarking, "Don't worry Ed, Billy Graham had to start out with small crowds too!"

One rainy Sunday I visited Mugheff church and had to preach the sermon. I sat on a chair on the raised platform beside the pastor. It was a long wait as a number of choirs had to sing several songs each. The congregation also sang for a long time and then there were prolonged announcements followed by the collection of the offering in which people danced to the front of the church to deposit money, chickens and farm produce. It was almost time for the sermon when I happened to look down at my lap and noticed something white. To my horror I discovered that the bottom end of my white shirt was protruding through the zipper part of my pants. I quickly slid my small bible over to cover the disaster scene. Beads of sweat broke out on my forehead as I frantically tried to devise a plan to recover gracefully and unnoticed, a difficult thing to do while sitting on a raised platform with several hundred eyes looking at me. There was no time left as the pastor had just introduced me and motioned for me to come and preach the message NOW! I broke all records for the ten-yard dash from my chair to the pulpit! I was grateful that the pulpit was a large wooden one that I could hug. In this case the pulpit was not a barrier to communication with the congregation. There was a long silent period in which I struggled to get my brain out of panic mode and to remember the content of my sermon notes. I did manage to preach the message, being very careful to stay behind the pulpit and not begin to walk back and forth. I was a bit distracted by simultaneously planning a dignified graceful exit. It was the custom in that church to walk down the center aisle and greet the people as they exited the door of the church. I got down the aisle with my bible strategically placed. It was pouring rain outside, but I bravely held my folded umbrella in front of me, getting soaking wet as I shook hands. I finally got a private moment to investigate what happened. The zipper handle was pulled all the way up in the proper position, but the zipper had come apart from the bottom up. The whole zipper was, as we say in German, "Kaput!" Needless to say, I never wore those pants again despite Marion's offer to sew in a new zipper.

Besides conducting a Good News Club for children, Marion was also in charge of the Belo Field women's work. This involved writing lessons for women's groups in the field and also teaching in churches. This required some trekking to remote villages such as the Wum association trip already described. We arranged for Paulina, a 14-year-old local girl to help care for our children at busy times. She was a delightful young lady who became like an extended family. Marion had the opportunity to witness to her and to lead her into faith in Jesus. What a joy it was to hear Paulina's testimony and see her get baptized.

While conducting a leprosy tour in Wum, I met Susie, a Swiss girl who ended up in Douala for an impromptu holiday. She went on a Safari through Mamfe-Overside and ended up in Wum. After hearing about our work at Mbingo, she expressed a desire to see the place. So I took her home to Mbingo. Marion spent time with her to show her our hospital and she was keenly interested in all that was going on. What Marion noticed most was that Susie was open to the message of the gospel. It was a privilege for Marion to introduce her to the Lord Jesus. Her heart had been prepared by the Lord. With tears of joy in her eyes she said wonderingly, "Do you suppose I had to come all the way to Africa to find Him?"

AND THEN THE PHONE RANG...

CHURCH WORK

THE CAMEROON BAPTIST CONVENTION OF Churches had churches in the Northwest and Southwest provinces of Cameroon among the English-speaking people. The convention was divided into various Fields that encompassed large regions of major tribes. The Fields were further divided into Associations of churches in smaller local areas. Each Field elected a Field Pastor to be a pastor to the pastors, and to visit and encourage the local churches. Mbingo hospital and compound were part of the Belo field of about 60 churches. Part of our work was to visit and interact with the local churches and to attend the annual Field Bible Conferences held at the beginning of dry season in November. I was assigned to be the Field Missionary which involved attendance at the Belo Field Council of Churches where decisions were made regarding policies, budgeting, church planting, and the election of officers. One difficult issue involved two associations that threatened to withdraw from the field due constitutional disputes. This had to be handled carefully so that reconciliation would happen and that other associations would not also want to withdraw. I discovered that the Belo people were quite feisty and lively in their debates. At another Field Council a few months later there was even more commotion. The field pastor resigned and refused to give reasons for his resignation. Two churches and two pastors were put on discipline for withholding part of the thanksgiving offering. One pastor came down the aisle of the church swinging his fists in anger and I feared that things might get a bit violent. In the end all the issues were somewhat settled.

Our first Belo Field Conference was in Fundong in November 1973. The lady missionaries started meetings on a Thursday with children, youth and women's ministries. Ed Hoepner and I joined the meetings on Friday to Sunday. The theme was, "Looking unto Jesus, the author and finisher of our faith." The sessions were held on an open field under a shelter made of poles holding up a thin cover of grass and palm branches. A total of 3000 people were present out of a total membership of over 7000. It was a big job for the local churches to house and feed all those people. The churches brought their thanksgiving harvest offering to make up the next year's field budget. It was a riotous occasion with dancing, singing, and whooping as the churches in each association danced up to the chairman with their offerings. They really knew how to make a joyful noise unto the Lord! Time was given to presenting reports and for Bible teaching. It was a great time of fellowship.

A year later the Belo Field Conference was held in the remote village of Akeh. Marion described this experience in a letter to her mom in 1974, as follows:

> *We drove part way to the village of Anjin and then had to trek the rest of the way to Akeh. That was quite an adventure! The kids were so excited about finally going on a trek that they could hardly sleep the night before. We had carriers for our cargo (camp cots and bedding) and to carry the kids. It took about 9 hours to get there. We took a gentle pace and had a picnic along the way. We had to climb a long steep hill, which seemed to take forever to get up. Then the path crossed a gradually rising grass covered plateau with beautiful wild flowers. The weather was sunny with a cooling breeze. We went through two forests full of twisted moss covered trees. The bird calls in the forests were something special to hear. We walked and walked until we got to the edge of the plateau and then descended down to Akeh. The descent was very steep, like going down into a canyon. It took us 2 ½ hours to get down. By the time we got to the bottom, our knees were like jelly and our toes got blistered from pressing against the end of our shoes. Bruce and Lori were carried most of the way down the steepest part. As we neared Akeh village Bruce and Lori wanted to walk to see who would get there first. The old "mommies" were amazed to see us walking into the village with two children – Bruce leading the way striding along with a walking stick in his hand. It was a great Bible Conference. The local people housed and fed us well. We had a two-room mud-block house with a new latrine beside it and a nice hedged in spot for bathing. The Hoepners occupied one room and our family was in the other room. We women got initiated to the delights of bathing by moonlight on a big green banana leaf, using a bucket of water*

to throw on ourselves. We stayed from a Wednesday to Sunday and on Monday trekked up the steep hill back to our vehicle. Ron went to Akeh a day earlier and was able to have long conversations with the local pastors.

Somehow I was elected as chairman of the Cameroon Field Committee (CFC) that oversees all of the Cameroon Baptist Mission (CBM) work in Cameroon. This position also made me chairman of the Personnel, Property, and Transport Committee, Scholarship Committee, plus member of the Finance, Medical, Education, and Evangelism Committees. All of these committees reported to the CFC for approval of their recommendations, which were then submitted to the NAB Board of Missions. I was also elected chairman of the Cameroon Missionary Fellowship, which meant that I had to plan the annual missionary retreat held at Christmas time. I was given a pile of 21 thick files to go through in order to do a proper job. We handled a lot of business such as posting and housing of missionaries, assigning mission vehicles, and approving a new constitution for Banso Baptist Hospital.

A major issue to be dealt with was the ongoing relationship between the Cameroon Baptist Mission (CBM) and the Cameroon Baptist Convention (CBC). I had to chair a committee to revise the bylaws of the CMF to deal with the organizational relationship with the CBC. There were intense discussions about turning over all properties and mission work to the CBC, as opposed to continuing to exist as a separate organization in partnership with the CBC. A joint CBC–CBM committee was formed to discuss integration of CBM into the CBC. The meetings were not easy as there were differing ideas and concepts. In order for full integration to work, the missionaries and the NAB Board of Missions would have to trust that the leadership of the CBC had matured to a level of competence to govern the joint work of the national church and the missionaries. After a number of meetings we arrived at a position of total integration of all CBM properties and work under the CBC. One result of these efforts was the inaugural ceremony of establishing the Medical Authority of the Cameroon Baptist Convention. This ceremony was held at Mbingo Baptist Hospital on the final day of the Cameroon Baptist Convention biennial General Session. Oryn Meinerts, the Field Secretary of the CBM read a document of transfer of all hospitals, maternities and dispensaries from our Mission to the CBC. Many dignitaries including the Fon of Babanki and the representative of the Governor of the Northwest Province of Cameroon were present. Marion, with help from others, prepared food for over 100 guests. It was an interesting journey to see how the North American Baptist Mission work in Cameroon was all ultimately put under the full direction and ownership of the Cameroon Baptist Convention.

SAD TIMES

EARLY ON A SUNDAY MORNING in October 1973, Fred Holzimmer came to Mbingo with the news that Dr. Les Chaffee was very ill at Banso Hospital. Dr. Dieter Lemke was treating him for a viral pneumonia that gradually produced a low blood pressure and shock. He was given antibiotics and oxygen. It was felt that he had developed viral myocarditis causing heart failure. He was given digoxin and steroids that got him out of shock but he was still in critical condition. Dr. Lemke requested that I come to Banso to help. I raided our drug supplies for medicines that might be of help and then drove as fast as I could from Mbingo to Banso. Marie Hoepner came along as she had worked for five years as a nurse in an intensive cardiac care unit in the USA. When the oxygen supply became low, Dr. Lemke got more tanks from a welder in Banso town. Dr. Chaffee rallied for a few hours but then went into profound shock with no recordable blood pressure for one-and-a-half hours and then died at 9 PM. We tried everything we could think of to treat him and felt a sense of crushing defeat and failure as we watched him die. His wife Edna kissed him goodbye and thanked God for the life they had together. I really questioned God as to why He allowed this to happen. Didn't God know how much we needed Dr. Chaffee and how much the sick people of Cameroon needed him? Dr. Chaffee was the pioneer missionary doctor for NAB and started Banso Baptist Hospital in 1949. He had returned to the USA and after retirement came back to Banso to help in the medical work. Now he had died with his boots on, serving God. The funeral was held at 2 PM the following day. In the morning Dieter Lemke supervised the carpenters in building a

AND THEN THE PHONE RANG...

casket and digging a grave. Marlis Lemke prepared a floral wreath. I helped by seeing all of the outpatients at the hospital. Messages were sent to the missionaries at the coast and Mbem and all of them arrived at Banso with minutes to spare. Thousands of people attended the funeral. We used a Land Rover as a hearse, which I drove. Dr. Chaffee was very tall so we had to lower the tailgate to get the long casket in. The drive from the church to the gravesite was up hill so we put two men in the Land Rover to hang on to the casket to prevent it from sliding out. Dr. Chaffee was buried at a prominent site right at the entrance to the hospital. It was truly a sad time. But this event gave us occasion to celebrate a life well lived in the service of God and to reflect on how God uses all of us in the advancement of His kingdom.

In late January 1974 Bobe Robert Jam, one of the fathers of the Baptist churches in Cameroon died. He was in his 80s. As a youth he travelled to the coast of Cameroon where he heard the gospel and came to saving faith in Jesus Christ. After some time at the coast, he returned to the grasslands and began to evangelize long before any of our NAB missionaries arrived. He started over 30 churches in Belo, Ndu, Mbem, Banso, and Mambilla fields. He was highly regarded by all as one of the fathers of the Cameroon Baptist Convention. Even on his deathbed he was witnessing and encouraging Christians. His legacy was passed on to the next generation as one son, Elijah, was Field Pastor of the Bamenda Field, another son, Samuel (my good friend), was a nurse and hospital chaplain at Mbingo, and a nephew, Peter, was the Belo Field pastor. Thousands of people attended his funeral, which was a victory celebration of a true saint of God. No sad songs or typical mourning was allowed. George Dunger, who knew Robert Jam since the 1930's spoke at the memorial service. Samuel Jam knew that his father was dying and he arranged to tape Robert Jam's final words of encouragement. As the people stood around the grave site, Samuel suddenly played the tape for all to hear his father seemingly speaking from the grave words of testimony of the goodness of our God. This made a huge impression on all present. It was a sad, but yet wonderfully victorious day.

Several months later Elijah Jam, the Bamenda Field pastor, brought his wife to Mbingo hospital. They had been married for three years in which time she had one stillborn baby and was now in her eighth month of another pregnancy. She developed some complications so this baby also died and a caesarean section was done at the government hospital in Bamenda to remove the dead baby. A series of complications occurred, including hemorrhage, infection, and pneumonia. She was brought to Mbingo where she was treated with blood transfusions, antibiotics and surgical drains for her peritonitis and IV fluid replacement. Despite all our best efforts, she died three days later. We were all in tears as we read a letter from Elijah thanking us for our effort. He wrote about his beloved girl and the closeness they had known while she was alive. There were many other sad occasions, each one reminding us that our God is not just a God to be praised in mountain-top experiences, but He is also our God in the dark valleys. Psalm 23 states, *"Yea, though I walk through the valley of the shadow of death, I will fear no evil: for you are with me; Your rod and Your staff, they comfort me."*

WILD TIMES

MOST DAYS WERE QUITE MANAGEABLE with respect to workload and pressure. However there were some days that were wild and crazy. Our family had attended a new missionary orientation time in Bamenda from a Thursday to Saturday. I gave a talk on missionary health in the tropics. Within 10 minutes of arriving home at Mbingo at noon, the roof metaphorically caved in around my head. I was the only doctor present when a woman with a sick child arrived. The woman was seven-months pregnant. I looked at the floor and saw a growing pool of blood at her feet. We hustled her into the operating room, started IV fluids and prepared her abdomen for possible surgery. I did a pelvic examination and found a placenta previa that was pouring out blood. We gave a spinal anesthetic and got the baby out by caesarean section within two minutes of incision. The woman went into shock with a blood pressure of 60/0. Just at that time a staff worker came into the operating room and stated that a huge truck loaded with 130 boxes of white cross supplies had arrived, and asked, "Would I come immediately to show them where to unload the boxes as the driver was in a hurry to leave?" With utmost restraint I politely suggested that the driver could go jump in the river and I continued on with the surgery. The woman recovered well, but the premature baby weighing only three-and-a-quarter pounds died 12 hours later. We got the white cross boxes unloaded and I went home for a bit of supper. Supper was very quick as I was called back to the hospital to see a man vomiting blood and passing bloody stools. He was also in shock with a blood pressure of 55/0 and a hemoglobin level of only 4 grams (12–14 is normal). What should we do as there was no one around to give him a general anesthetic? We started an IV and got some blood into him which got him out of shock. I anesthetized him with chloroform initially and then open-drop ether. A Cameroonian nurse was given a crash course in anesthesia and I proceeded to operate on the man with only one assistant who was a young man with grade seven education. He was the surgical assistant and scrub nurse all rolled into one. We found a huge bleeding duodenal ulcer with much scarring. I over-sewed the ulcer and did a pyloroplasty. He was too sick to also do a vagotomy. I finally got to bed at 2:30 AM realizing that there was a full day of work ahead. The patient recovered well and went home.

Helen Schmidt and I had a 24 hour tsunami wave of work hit us. We started by making rounds on 75 in-patients and then did a caesarean section for a prolapsed umbilical cord. This was followed by surgery on a patient with a ruptured ectopic pregnancy. We then saw over 180 sick out-patients. At 5:30 in the afternoon a Land Rover came bringing a Fulani woman with a bowel obstruction and in shock. She had a strangulated hernia which we resected and repaired under open-drop ether anesthesia once we got her out of shock. So supper didn't happen till after 8 PM. At midnight Myrna Goodman, our nurse/midwife at Belo drove in with a woman that required a caesarean section. I did not see my bed till the wee hours of the morning. The next day was surgery day where we had eight more major surgeries plus the usual in-patient rounds and seeing out-patients. Our wards were overflowing with patients recovering from surgeries. We were totally exhausted!

Another day a very sick woman arrived at 4 PM. She had a caesarean section done a month previously at a government hospital. She developed a wound infection, so the wound was opened and re-sutured. Her condition deteriorated and her husband put her on a bed in the back of a truck and brought her to Mbingo. She was in terrible shape with pus oozing out of her wound. She tried to drink a bit of milk and within five minutes the milk came pouring out of her abdominal wound. We gave her IV fluids and three units of blood to get her out of shock. At surgery we found the uterus to be gaping open from a classical up-and-down incision. Further examination revealed a six-inch long laceration of the greater curve of the stomach that was also gaping open. It had apparently been sutured with interrupted cotton sutures – which is an absolutely wrong thing to do! Half of this wound had come apart and was draining bile and gastric juices into her abdominal cavity. We could not imagine what kind of butcher had done this surgery and used cotton sutures in a stomach! We closed stomach and uterine wounds and put in a gastrostomy tube to drain the stomach and a jejunostomy feeding tube and several drains to drain the peritoneal cavity. The lady did well for about 16 hours but then developed malaria with a fever of 107–108°F rectally. So now she was back in shock. This was treated with IV Dextran, IV fluids, Nivaquine, antibiotics, and even cortisone, but she was so weak already that she died about 30 hours later. We were incensed at the mistreatment this poor woman suffered in a government hospital. It is no wonder that cases like this cause people to come from far away to mission hospitals. For an encore that night we had to do a bowel resection for a section of perforated small bowel that was gangrenous. Bedtime that day was about 2 AM.

Strange cases kept on arriving. At noon on a surgery day a man brought his wife to Mbingo in a Land Rover. She had suffered a horrible injury to her right leg. On the previous day she was working on her farm when a storm suddenly appeared with heavy rain and very strong winds. As she ran for cover, a tree beside her broke and fell onto her right knee which was raised up in running position. The force of the tree drove her right lower leg deep into the ground. She was pinned down and screamed for help. People came to dig her leg out of the ground and discovered that her entire foot was gone and the flesh of her lower leg was stripped off the bones almost to her knee. It was now getting towards the darkness of evening. Her husband tied a tourniquet around her leg just above the knee to control the bleeding. After some time he found someone with a Land Rover who agreed to take her to the hospital. They managed to drive along a bush road and got to the main road where they ran out of gas. So they spent the night in the Land Rover and finally got some fuel in the morning to enable them to drive to Mbingo. The poor lady was in great pain and in shock from blood loss. IV fluids were started but we needed blood. The only willing donor with the same blood type was the husband. We took about one-and-a-half units out of him and gave him strong coffee and food while his wife received the transfusion. Once she was out of shock, we did a below knee amputation. Not surprisingly the stump became infected a few days later and an above knee amputation was done. Fortunately we were able to make an above knee prosthesis for her so that she could walk again.

The most bizarre case was that of a pregnant woman who was brought to the hospital from the Belo maternity center. She had been in labor for a long time and her cervix was not dilating. The midwife went to the market square to arrange for a vehicle to carry the patient to Mbingo –a distance of five miles. While these arrangements were being made, a maternity worker ran to the market to tell the midwife that the baby's head was visible and about to deliver. The midwife ran back to deliver the baby, but there was terrible damage to the woman's perineum requiring extensive repair. The transport to hospital was very necessary. I examined the woman and could hardly believe what I found. The cervix was still not dilated, and therefore the uterus had ruptured posteriorly and the baby was born through the space between the vagina and the rectum, exploding the perineum. As there was no bleeding of note, I inserted a Penrose drain into the space to drain any potential hematoma and then painstakingly repaired the perineum after loosely closing the recto-vaginal space. I had never heard or seen such a case described in textbooks. I described this case to several obstetricians when we returned to Canada. They also had never seen or heard of such a case.

TRAVELING TIMES

IN JANUARY 1974, AFTER ALMOST a year in Cameroon, we had to return to Nigeria in order to renew our residence permits for Nigeria. Peter and May Schroeder were moving from Bamenda to Jos, Nigeria to serve as house parents at our Woyke House Hostel for missionary children. We decided to travel together in Pete and May's Volkswagen beetle. It was a tight fit for four adults and two children plus baggage. There was only about six inches of clearance under the car. We drove very carefully to avoid getting the car wheels into any ruts that could result in hitting the hump in the road with the underside of the car. We got across the border into Nigeria at Ikom and navigated even more deeply rutted roads and did scrape bottom a few times. While stopping for a coffee break, we noticed a black line in the dirt behind the car. To our horror we discovered that it was oil and saw a growing puddle of it under the car. This was very serious! We quickly jacked up the car and saw oil leaking from a dented cover plate of the oil sump. We removed the plate and tried to catch the draining oil in May's Tupperware container. Here we were in the deep remote bush with the hot sun beating down on us and millions of flies and mosquitoes attacking us. In order to get the bent cover plate straight enough to replace we needed a hammer, which we did not have. As we wondered what to do, we heard a noise in the bush beside us, and lo and behold, a man wearing just a loin-cloth appeared from the bush. In his hand he had a hammer! He was part of a primitive sawmill crew. The hammer was used to help split logs with a wedge while two other men sawed the logs lengthwise. Pete was able to hammer the cover plate flat on a nearby rock. At this time a van came along the road and the driver offered to take May, Marion, and the children to a Catholic convent in Obudu, 19 miles away. That left Pete and me with the disabled car in the hot bush. The gasket for the cover plate was damaged beyond repair so I used a bread knife to fashion a new gasket from a cardboard box. We got the cover plate and gasket bolted in place and poured the oil from the Tupperware back into the car. But there was not enough oil to register on the dipstick. So now what would we do? Then we heard another noise. This noise was made by a small truck approaching. The truck stopped and the driver asked if he could help us. To our amazement he had a big drum of oil as part of his load. We got enough oil to add to our car plus extra oil to carry along in May's Tupperware for possible topping up further down the road. All of these fortunate noises seemed to us to be God answering our prayers for help. God provided a hammer, rescue for our wives and children, and oil just at the right time.

Pete and I got to the convent and found our wives and kids enjoying cold pop and cookies supplied by the nuns. We finally got to Jos the next day, driving even more carefully with the Tupperware full of oil balanced on May's lap

Pete and May settled into Woyke House and got the VW fixed. After getting our residence permits for Nigeria renewed, we flew to Serti on the CRC mission plane and drove up to the Mambilla plateau to Warwar. I replaced Dr. Willi Gutowski who attended a conference in Monrovia, Liberia. Anita Gutowski and the three girls had a local leave in Jos. For ten days we reacquainted ourselves with the medical work at Warwar. It was good to see the growing maturity of the trained staff. Esther Lackson was now the matron (nursing supervisor). Zebulon Wanmi had completed his training, which enabled him to see all the out-patients, treat simple conditions and refer difficult cases to the doctor.

The Fiat truck had been out of commission for three months with a broken rear spring. One afternoon I got the spring off and inserted a new main leaf that we brought from Jos. The next afternoon was spent getting the spring back on. This was difficult as the spring had to be put on under tension. We used several jacks but the Fiat was too light to flatten the spring enough to fit it back on. Finally we got Joseph Headman and several laborers to climb on the back of the truck in order to get the spring fitted properly. The battery was dead so we rolled the truck down the hill to kick-start the motor. We put it in second gear with the clutch pedal down. As we gained speed, I suddenly released the clutch and got the engine started. Running the engine for a while got the battery recharged. It is interesting what a doctor in the bush has to do. Medical school had no courses on this stuff!

Bruce and Lori renewed their friendship with Victor and Guyee in Warwar. One day while hunting for game Guyee managed to kill a dove with a rock. They were impressed with their prowess as mighty hunters. They then proceeded to pluck all the feathers off and roast the bird in an outdoor fire-pit without cleaning out the intestines. Marion became aware of the event when Bruce came into the house to ask for some slices of bread for their meal of roasted fowl. With great ceremony the bird was divided up and placed on banana leaf dishes. Fortunately no one suffered any ill effects. Marion gave them a lesson that killing an animal for food was okay, but killing for the sake of sport was not good.

BACK IN CAMEROON, ANOTHER ENJOYABLE trip was to travel from Mbingo to the Douala airport to meet old time friends Herb and Del Sturhahn. They came to Cameroon in order to visit us and to see the mission work in Cameroon first hand. We spent a week at the coast shopping, swimming, and visiting the missionaries at the Saker College for girls. We then took Herb and Del to Bamenda and Mbingo. Herb accompanied me and several Cameroonian medical staff to the Fungom area for several days of witnessing and medical clinics. Herb was introduced to eating local food and sleeping in a mud house with a grass-thatched roof. He was awakened one night as I chased rats out of the house. Herb and Del were taken to see the Fon of Laikom on a rainy day. Our vehicle could not get up the hill so we trekked up. Poor Del got soaked in the rain and ruined her nice hairdo. We also drove over very rough roads and waded through the Mbori River in order for Herb and Del to see Warwar. On the way back to Mbingo from Warwar we got stuck three times between Mbem and Banso due to heavy rains that caused deep mud holes in the road. We had to shovel mud, carry rocks and sticks, and push to get unstuck. While Del was pulling on a rope, the vehicle suddenly lurched forward and Del landed flat on her back in the mud. I just kept driving using the momentum to get out of the hole. So now Del got covered with a huge spray of mud on her front as I passed by her lying beside the road. Herb broke out in a hearty laugh which he had to suddenly stifle when Del looked at him with a look that all husbands understand. Herb and Del were able to visit most of our mission stations, interact with missionaries, and see the medical work – even witnessing some surgery. They had great experiences that they will never forget.

In January 1975 we had to return to Nigeria to renew our residence permits. There was a refresher course for American nurses overseas to be held in Jos. Ed Hoepner and I loaded our two families and 10 missionary nurses into two Kombi VW vans for the trip. This course enabled the nurses to maintain their professional registration. I was the only one who knew the route so I drove the lead vehicle. Ed and I did childcare for our kids while the nurses were in class. We got our residence permits renewed and also booked our flights home to Canada for the upcoming furlough year. We then spent two weeks working at Warwar hospital while Willi Gutowski and Minnie Kuhn attended important meetings. Marion, Bruce, and Lori flew to Serti in the Christian Reformed Church six-seater Piper Aztec while Barb Kieper and I drove a Land Rover loaded with hospital supplies. I had the interesting experience of delivering a baby in the middle of a clinic in a church in Maisomari. Bruce and Lori also got a refresher course in the birds and the bees as they watched the delivery of a baby at Warwar. We considered this as part of their science lesson! After our time at Warwar we flew back to Jos and then drove one of the Kombi vans back to Bamenda – a long two-day drive.

TIME TO GO HOME

MISSIONARIES SOMETIMES TELL STRANGE, TALL stories. One such story was about how to determine when a missionary was ready to go home on furlough. The story is as follows:

When a fly lands in your soup, a first-year missionary throws out the soup, washes the bowl and gets a refill of soup. A second-year missionary picks the fly out of the soup, throws it away and keeps on eating the soup. A third-year missionary grabs the fly and squeezes it and says, "give me back the soup you stole." A fourth-year missionary just eats the soup, together with the fly and says "that was good protein." This missionary needs to go home on furlough to reacquaint himself with proper table manners.

We didn't eat the flies in our soup, but we were anxious to get home to see family and friends after four years away. In early 1975 we discovered that Marion was pregnant and this was another good reason to go home.

A decision was made by all the missionary doctors in Cameroon and Nigeria that we should be posted to Warwar hospital after our year of furlough. The Gutowski's had indicated that they were resigning from missionary work and hoped we would return to Warwar after our furlough. This decision helped us decide on what to do with our possessions. We packed a big crate and three steel drums with things to ship home. This included some curios – baskets, carvings, paintings and even three ivory tusks. To ship these items home required multiple copies of inventory lists that then had to be approved by four different government agencies in Bamenda. We sold many items to local Cameroonians and the rest we packed for storage and ultimate shipment to Warwar. This kept us very busy as the deadline was March 1, 1975 for the shipment to Canada.

The next few months were filled with extra hospital work as Jerry Fluth cut his hand on a bandsaw. I sewed the wound and then realized that I had to do all his surgical cases for several weeks. Marion had a three-day trek in the Wum Association area where she taught a course to the women of the area. I attended two-and-a-half days of committee meetings of the mission and the CBC and was very glad to hand over all the files to Rev. Ed Michelson. I also managed to fit in a tour of the churches in Esimbi, Fungom, and Mamfe-Overside. The final day of hospital work was May 20, 1975. That gave us a week to visit several mission stations to say farewell and to do our final packing up at Mbingo.

We left Cameroon at the end of May. George Wall, the MAF pilot in Cameroon arranged to fly us from the recently opened Mbingo airstrip to Douala where we signed out of the country. We then flew to Calabar, Nigeria on a route that took us behind the majestic Mount Cameroon. In Calabar we signed in to Nigeria and had to unload all our cargo for inspection. After reloading we flew in a straight line to Serti. This route took us over a part of the Northwest Province of Cameroon. We were able to see Mamfe, Wum, Binka, Oku Mountain, and at a distance Mbingo. From Serti we drove up to the Mambilla plateau with Ken and June Goodman who had just returned from their furlough. We again took over the work at Warwar hospital for two-weeks while the Gutowski's had a local leave. Marion ended up being the chief cook and bottle washer for two weeks as Minnie and Barb had no cooks. So we ate all meals together.

Our faces were finally set for home! We flew from Serti to Jos where Pete and May Schroeder met us. For a final treat before going home, Pete and May took us to the Yankari game reserve for several days. We stayed in a little two-bedroom guest house that had a kitchen. The game reserve was full of baboons, and some tried to get into our house as they smelled food. One did get in and almost stole Pete's dentures! We went swimming in a stream of hot-spring water with a natural pool area. There was even a rope hanging from a tree branch that one could catch and swing out over the pool and drop in. The baboons were watching our every move and we had to be careful not to get too close, or between them and their food. On our drive out of the game reserve we saw a huge elephant standing beside the road near a giant termite hill. Pete stopped the car and decided that he wanted to take a picture. His camera was in the trunk so we all foolishly got out of the car to watch. Pete got his camera out of the trunk. By this time the elephant had turned his back to us. Pete made a loud whistle to get the elephant to turn. He did turn and then suddenly raised his trunk, flared his ears and began to charge towards us giving a loud trumpeting roar. We rushed back into the car, but Pete had trouble getting in because May had slammed the door shut. Luckily the elephant stopped his charge as we drove away in a hurry!

The trip home finally began when Pete and May took us to the airport in Kano for the flight to Amsterdam. In preparation for arrival home we sent a specific request to Oma for a meal of her special chicken noodle soup, farmer sausage, and rye bread. We were weary and excited for the next adventure.

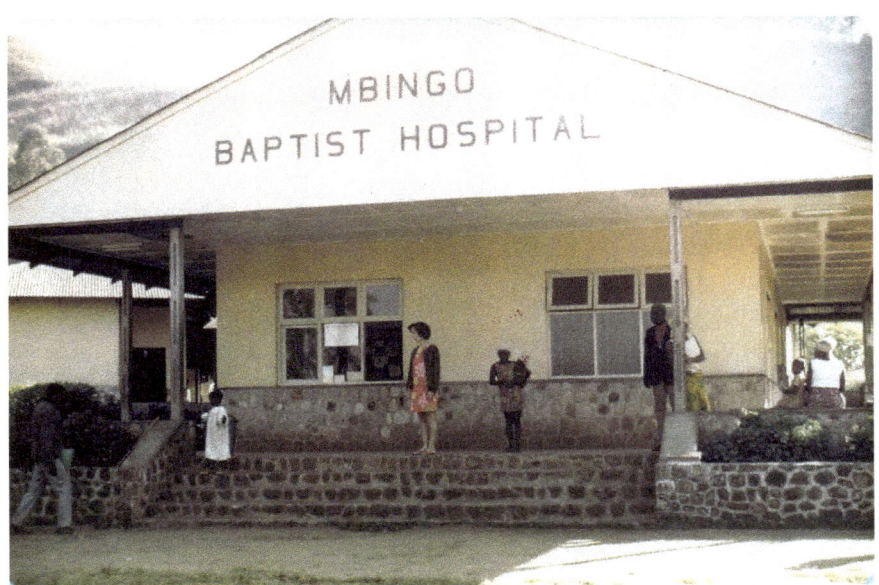

ENTRANCE TO MBINGO BAPTIST HOSPITAL (MBH)

MBINGO CAMEROON

SENIOR HOSPITAL STAFF AT MBH

LEPROMATOUS LEPROSY WITH SEVERE NASAL DEFORMITY

AND THEN THE PHONE RANG...

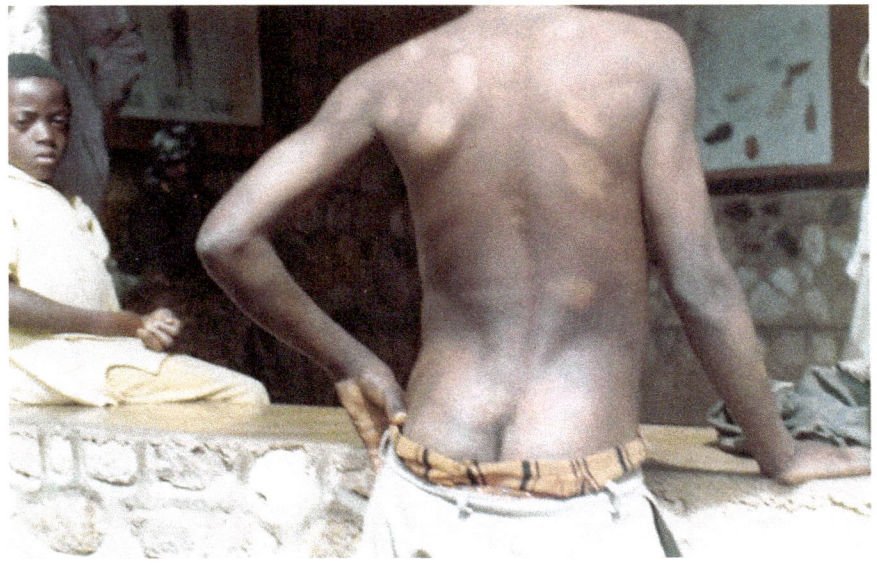

TUBERCULOID LEPROSY

MARION'S GOOD NEWS CLUB FOR CHILDREN

MBINGO CAMEROON

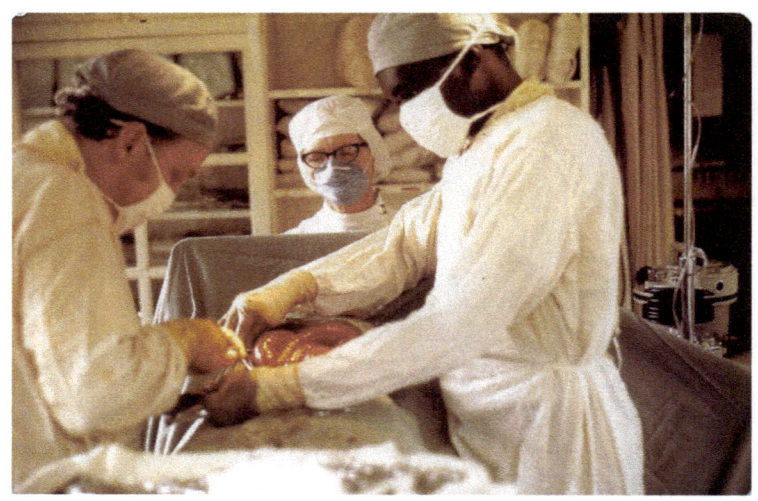

SERIOUS ABDOMINAL SURGERY, LAURA REDDIG
ADMINISTERING OPEN-DROP ETHER ANESTHESIA

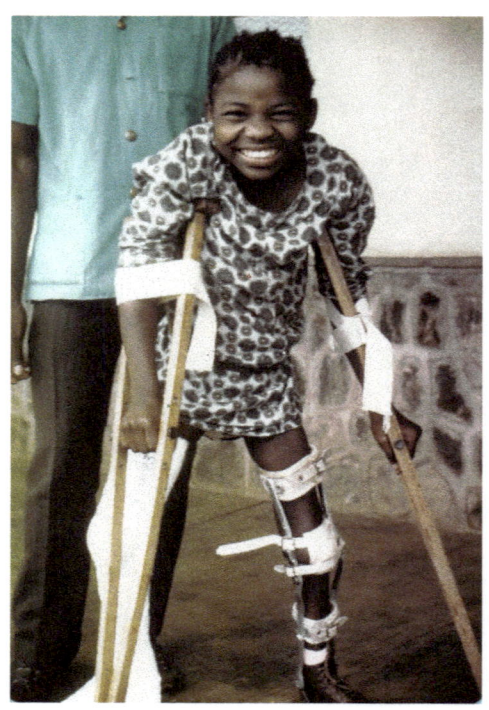

MULTIPLE CONGENITAL LEG DEFORMITIES. HER FIRST TIME EVER ON HER FEET

AND THEN THE PHONE RANG...

THE FON OF LAIKOM

JU-JU MEN ARMED WITH CLUBS

MBINGO CAMEROON

JU-JU MEN WITH MASKS, SPEARS, AND RATTLES

CHAPTER 14

Furlough

It was with mixed feelings that we left Africa to go on furlough. We were excited about seeing family and friends again, but fearful of speaking to large church congregations. Most of all we were very tired. We flew from Kano, Nigeria, to Amsterdam where we stayed overnight. Six-year-old Bruce met an elderly man smoking in the stairwell in our hotel. Bruce went up to him and said, "You shouldn't smoke because the Fon of Liakom smoked and he died." The look on the man's face was priceless! The next day we flew to London where we met my second cousin Peter Herke and his wife. They took us to their home in Maidenhead just west of London. Peter's kids wondered who these important people were as Peter made special efforts to mow and trim the lawns and clean all the flower beds meticulously. Peter grew up in Vancouver and worked in the summertime at gardening just as I had. He had to make sure that things were just right! The Herke's took Marion and the kids on a tour of Windsor castle while I lay on a couch nursing a gigantic migraine headache.

From London we flew to Chicago via Amsterdam and had a debriefing session with Dr. Richard Schilke, the NAB General Missions Secretary. We were encouraged by his wholehearted support. He gave us instructions regarding our deputation assignments which involved visiting and reporting to our supporting churches. This prospect of speaking in front of big groups of people was daunting. What was I supposed to say? Dr. Schilke's advice was just tell the people what you saw God doing in Nigeria and Cameroon.

FURLOUGH

The final appointment in Chicago was a visit to Mt. Sinai hospital to donate stool samples to be examined for parasites. We were given a horrible tasting laxative to drink and then told to sit down and wait for some action. The requirement was to produce three samples of stool – solid, semisolid, and watery. When this was done we were free to leave. We had a flight booked for the afternoon and so we had to produce the three specimens quickly in order to catch the plane. But once our bowels started to move it was difficult to tell them to stop. We made a quick dash to the airport and headed straight to the washroom. Once we were checked-in we made a mad dash to the washrooms by the departure gates. Once on the plane there was another dash to the washroom at the back of the plane.

Our next stop was Minneapolis to see Dr. Peter Fehr for medical exams. We were able to stay with my cousin Larry and wife, Diana and their children Brian and Robin who lived in neighbouring St. Paul. That was a very special treat for us. Finally we got on the last leg of our journey home to Vancouver. As we were landing and the plane's wheels touched the runway we were suddenly jerked back in our seats as the pilot revved the engines and took off again. We circled the airport and then landed safely. Apparently, the pilot noticed a truck on the runway on our first approach and hence the touch-and-go experience.

It was a joyful reunion with Oma, Grandpa and Grandma, and many friends who greeted us. We moved in with Oma. She moved herself downstairs and gave us the main floor with the two bedrooms. She also treated us with chicken noodle soup and farmer sausages – just as we had requested. It was so good to be home again! Our friends' children had grown a lot in four years and some of them were initially hard to recognize.

We arrived in Vancouver at the end of June 1975 and had about six weeks to re-enter the culture at home and get a lot of paperwork done. This time was also spent preparing various presentations to use on church visits. Some presentations were aimed at children and others at adults. Several slide presentations were also compiled for use in evening services and informal meetings. One presentation was called, "My friend Sam" – it focused on the life of Samuel Jam who was a trained pastor and a nurse. This slide presentation showed the work of our mission in Cameroon in theological education, training of nurses, chaplaincy work and medical ministry. Another presentation was called, "Bruce, the missionary kid," with pictures of Bruce showing the work through the eyes of a child. Bruce related what he saw his parents and other missionaries do, and of course, his adventures with his sister, Lori, and various friends. Other presentations were sermons with challenges for people to get involved in God's Kingdom work and calls for financial and prayer support.

Our first assignment was to attend the family camp at Green Bay Bible Camp near Kelowna. This was a very enjoyable, relaxing, and informal time with campers – many of whom we knew as longtime friends.

THE DEPUTATION SCHEDULE WAS AS follows (all dates in 1975):

Aug. 16-19	Family Camp
Sept. 7	Redeemer Baptist Church in Warren Michigan
Sept 13-14	Bethel Community Church in Missoula Montana
Sept. 19	Bethany Baptist Church in Vancouver – Fall Banquet
Sept. 21	Ebenezer Baptist Church in Vancouver
Sept. 28	Rose of Sharon Baptist Church in Richmond
Sept. 29-Oct 4	Missions Conference in Edmonton
Oct. 5	Fort George Baptist Church in Prince George
Nov. 2	Salt Creek Baptist Church in Dallas Oregon
Nov. 6-9	Oregon – Idaho Association meeting in Portland
Nov. 16	Temple Baptist Church in Lodi California
Nov. 19-23	Southern California Missions Conference, including: • Magnolia Baptist Church in Anaheim • Harbor Trinity Baptist Church in Costa Mesa

FURLOUGH

The above list is not complete as I cannot recall many of the other engagements. However there were some interesting experiences on deputation that remain etched in memory. My first major presentation was made at the Redeemer Baptist Church in Warren Michigan. I was really nervous about this. Pastor Adolph Braun gave me a tour of the church on a Saturday. It was huge! The pulpit had a remote control device that raised and lowered the height. There was a phone on the platform by his chair so he could call the ushers for any instructions. His pastor's study had a big bathroom complete with a shower. The more grandiosity I saw the more nervous I became. With the help of the Holy Spirit I managed to speak on Sunday to over 1000 people. Needless to say, I was quite exhausted by the end of the day.

My experience in Missoula was an example of how to over-maximize a missionary's visit to a church. I arrived in Missoula late on a Saturday afternoon and was taken directly from the airport to a combined Men's Banquet and Harvest Missions Festival where I was the featured speaker. The following morning I spoke at the opening session of the Sunday school to a combined group of adults and children. For this event I focused on the kids and told the adults that they could listen in as I told them the story of how Pete Schroeder and I dealt with the oil leak in the VW beetle. I asked the kids if they ever prayed for missionaries and one boy put up his hand – I thanked him for that because we certainly needed God's help to provide a hammer and oil (see chapter 13). I then spoke to the adult Sunday school class and preached in the morning service. After lunch I was taken to my motel room on the highway out of town where I had a short nap. There were no arrangements made for supper, so I walked along the highway to find a restaurant. I was picked up in time to get to church for the evening service where I made a 40-minute slide presentation. Immediately following the service I was asked to speak to a room full of bored looking teenage youth. I was weary and tired and was now expected to inject energy and excitement into this event. This was the most daunting of all the assignments. So there were a total of six presentations made in just 24 hours. I was relieved when this was over.

Marion did not accompany me on out of town deputation assignments, as she was pregnant and expecting to deliver a baby in October. She was busy at home caring for Bruce who was starting grade one and Lori beginning kindergarten. They needed Mom to greet them with a glass of milk and a cookie after school. We were pleased that both kids adapted well to school, although Bruce was accused of carrying a purse because he brought his snack to school in a small Fulani horseman's bag. When asked about the teasing a few days later, he just dismissed the whole thing by saying, "Oh, I just ignored them." Lori was delighted with all the girls her age from the church and neighborhood that came for her birthday party. They also integrated well into the childrens' ministry events at Bethany Baptist Church and started making lifetime friendships with a number of their peers.

On October 16 Marion went into labor. I took her to the Grace Hospital while Oma looked after Bruce and Lori. Marion was doing well in labor but the resident doctor wanted experience in doing a forceps delivery and an anesthetist was called to do an epidural anesthetic. Marion saw the big spinal needle and quickly sized up what was going on. This did not look like a fun time, so she gave a couple of huge pushes to get the baby's head down in a hurry. This made it too late for an epidural and subsequent forceps. Thus, Joyel Marie arrived into the world weighing just under six pounds soaking wet. Because we had lived in Africa for four years, Marion was put into an isolation room so nurses and visitors had to wear masks and gowns to enter. The fear was that Marion might infect someone with some tropical disease like amoebiasis. A very strict head nurse refused to allow me to visit Marion and Joyel after 8 PM.

Marion and Joyel accompanied me on the trip to Southern California to attend a missionary conference there in late November. I spoke at the Magnolia Baptist Church where Dr. Ken Fisher was the lead pastor. There were a number of missionary speakers and the one prior to me was a Russian pastor who spoke of the terrible persecutions going on in Russia. He wished that the churches in North America could experience the same troubles so that they would grow deeper in their love for God. It was difficult to get behind the pulpit and speak following such a dramatic and powerful message. I felt like I was a real anti-climax! It was good to see Rev. Ernie Rogalski, pastor of Harbour Trinity Church in Costa Mesa. He was the pastor who officiated at our wedding while he was pastor at

FURLOUGH

Bethany Baptist. We were very fortunate to be billeted at the home of A.G. and Vickie Sparks and their two girls. There was an immediate rapport and we became lifelong friends. Their girls, Julie and Jill, loved to play and care for baby Joyel, and push her little stroller on social outings.

While at the Oregon–Washington Association meetings I had to speak at a men's breakfast event. The room was full of pastors, area ministers, and prominent lay leaders like Washington State Senator Stan Johnson. I began my talk by saying, "I don't know why I am up here speaking to a room full of theologians and church leaders when I am much better at fixing hernias. Are there any volunteers for this?" The room exploded with laughter and I now had everyone's attention. Actually speaking to various groups and churches became a bit easier as time went on. I discovered a genuine interest among people for the work that God was doing through NAB missions in Nigeria and Cameroon. I found out later that several people answered God's call to them for missionary work following my presentations. That was encouraging to me. God could use me with my poor speech to accomplish His will when I depended on Him to do what seemed impossible.

Christmas time was wonderful. To be at home to enjoy a real Christmas tree, my Mom's great baking, and a turkey dinner with fabulous dressing was a real treat. The Christmas music and choir concert in church stirred up memories and revived my soul. The wonder and mystery of the incarnation of Jesus Christ – the Word became flesh – Immanuel – God with us was the cause for all this celebration.

After Christmas I enrolled in the Northwest Baptist Theological College on Marine Drive in Vancouver. I took several courses taught by Drs. John Pickford, Harold Dressler, Don Hills, Don Carson, and John Richards. I really enjoyed Don Hills' course on Theology because he had a pastoral approach in applying theology to daily life. Don Carson taught the New Testament Survey in a very intensive and stimulating manner. During about the fourth lecture he suddenly stopped teaching half way through the time and said, "Pull out a new page of paper, put your name at the top and numbers 1 to 20 down the left margin." He then proceeded to ask 20 pop quiz questions in rapid fashion. We struggled to answer and people cried out, "Not so fast!" Dr. Carson's reply was, "Either you know the answer or you don't – I expect you to come to class prepared by reading

AND THEN THE PHONE RANG...

ahead." He then collected the papers and announced that the quiz result would be part of our mark for the course. From that time on we came to class prepared!

While on furlough we kept up correspondence with Minnie Kuhn and Dr. Willi Gutowski regarding Mambilla field issues and hospital work. In early April we got the disturbing news that the hospital in Warwar was taken over by the Gongola State Government effective April 1, 1976. It was a real shock to the people of Mambilla who depended on our medical services. The hospital staff were also very worried about their own future. This announcement raised a number of questions such as:

- would the Mambilla Baptist Mission be financially compensated?
- would the present staff be retained or dismissed?
- would fees no longer be charged to patients?
- would expatriate staff be paid by the government?

THE BIG QUESTION FOR US was, would we return to Nigeria and work at Warwar under a government contract and would we still be able to do evangelism? We agonized and prayed about this and finally came to a decision as seen in the following excerpt from a letter written to Dr. Schilke and Rev. Fred Folkerts:

> *The idea of being a civil servant is not pleasant to me. My initial reaction when hearing of the situation in Warwar was to proceed directly to Cameroon on my return to Africa. But after praying about it and talking with Bea Westerman and Dr. Powell, I have decided to go to Warwar and, if necessary, work for the government. Working for the government may do the following:*
>
> - *Keep good relationships intact between our mission and the government – and avoid the adoption of an uncooperative stance by the Mission.*
> - *Keep the Christians of Mambilla satisfied that we are concerned about their welfare.*

FURLOUGH

- *Allow us to explore ways and means of witness and evangelism within new frames of reference.*

If I should work under government contract, I would insist that I be free to do the following:

- *Attend the annual missionary fellowship in Cameroon*
- *Take part in Bible Conferences, committees of the Mambilla Baptist Convention and the Mambilla Baptist Mission Field Committee and in some church visitation and Theological Education by Extension (as time reasonably allows).*

The decision to return to Warwar Hospital was made with some trepidation as I would have to deal with the Government on a number of issues besides the ones listed above. Dr. Schilke also informed me that I was appointed to be the Field Secretary (FS) of the Mambilla Baptist Mission. The Field Secretary's role was to be the official liaison between the NAB Board of Missions and the Mambilla Baptist Convention As such, the individual served as an advisor to the national church and relayed requests and concerns of the National Church back to the NAB Board of Missions. The secular equivalent is an ambassador. The FS was also in charge of the work of the missionaries on the field and was chairman of the Mambilla Baptist Mission, looking after the welfare of the missionaries, and in charge of emergency evacuation plans. I previously thought that running a hospital as the only doctor in charge of a large payroll, ordering supplies, supervising building, seeing all the sick people, visiting outlying clinics, and doing surgery was enough work to keep me busy. Now I was going to learn what busy really looked like!

So we began to shop for clothes and supplies and pack them for shipment to Nigeria via Cameroon. The cargo that we packed and left in Cameroon had been sent on to Warwar in our absence. It was a tearful farewell with our parents as we waited to board our plane. We wondered if that might be the last time we would see Dad and Mom Asselstine again. Dr. Schilke arranged our itinerary with a flight from Vancouver to Calgary, where we had a short airport visit with Harry Hiller, and then on to Chicago for a meeting with Dr. Schilke. We were forced to check

Joyel's stroller into the baggage compartment. As we waited for the stroller to appear on the carousel, sharp-eyed Bruce spotted all of our suitcases rolling down the chute. We thought that they were checked on through to Brussels. We were grateful to Rev. Lyle Wacker who met us and helped us get the bags through customs and checked on the United Airline flight to New York. I had a good meeting with Dr. Schilke who agreed with my planned approach to the Gongola State Government regarding compensation to the mission for the loss of assets at Warwar. He basically gave me a free hand to negotiate with the government on behalf of the NAB.

The Chicago to New York flight was delayed for an hour due to mechanical issues. We were concerned that we might miss our connection with Sabena Air from New York to Brussels. We phoned my cousin, Ruth Pleines, and her husband Richard in New York and asked for their help. I also managed to speak to the pilot who agreed to speed up the flight and he managed to make up some of the lost time. In New York we had 10 minutes to get to the international departure gate. Rich and Ruth drove us there in their car. Rich even managed to get into the baggage section and grab our bags so we could get them to Sabena. Normally such transfer of bags takes 60 to 90 minutes. We got on our flight with no time to spare thanks to Ruth and Richard.

It was a breathless good-bye to North America and on to Nigeria and the many adventures awaiting us there. We were grateful for God's guidance and provision for us as we put our trust in Him.

FURLOUGH

BETHANY LADIES WELCOME US WITH A PANTRY SHOWER

MARION AND MINNIE KUHN — SPEAKERS AT A MISSIONARY CONFERENCE

AND THEN THE PHONE RANG...

ME ON A PANEL AT A MISSIONARY CONFERENCE

BRUCE AND LORI LOVE THEIR NEW SISTER JOYEL — BORN OCT. 16, 1975

FURLOUGH

THE FAMILY PREPARES FOR RETURN TO NIGERIA

CHAPTER 15

Back to Warwar

The children fared well on the flight from New York to Brussels. Joyel slept most of the way in a little bed hung on the wall in front of us. A connecting flight took us from Brussels to Kano, Nigeria, where Pete and May Schroeder met us on their way home from Nigeria. Harold Lang had driven them to Kano in a new Toyota Land Cruiser and then took us back to Jos. Unfortunately, the air freighted school materials for Bruce and Lori did not arrive. After intensive shopping for food and equipment in Jos, Marion and the kids flew to Serti while Willi Gutowski and I loaded the Toyota and drove to Serti via Yola. We joined up in Serti and got to Gembu in time for supper and sleep. The next morning we arrived in Warwar to a joyous greeting from our staff and local Christians.

Within a day of our arrival, Marva Radke went into labour. Barb Kieper and I delivered Aaron Curtis Radke after a difficult labor and a vacuum extraction. Mother and child fared well and even Curt survived the ordeal! There was a great deal of rejoicing.

SETTLING IN

THE GUTOWSKI'S HAD MOVED INTO the rest houses as they were packing up and preparing to return home to Canada permanently. Thus we could occupy the doctor's house on arrival. Marion had to do a lot of cleaning work to get us settled in. The children had a great time playing with the local children and with the three Gutowski girls. Lori made friends with Evelyn Lackson, and Bruce was busy teaching a gang of Warwar boys how to play Canadian football, which ended up being a hybrid of football and soccer. Joyel was feeling quite ignored as everyone was too busy to pay attention to her demands for a lap to sit on.

By mid July we were very alone. The Gutowski family had left for home, Minnie Kuhn was on furlough, Barb Kieper went on a local leave, and the Radkes had moved to Mbu where Curt was supervising the construction of Bible school buildings. We were pleased to see the growth in maturity of our young local staff. Esther Lackson was very efficient and capable as the hospital Matron in charge of all the staff. Zebulon Wanmi and Paul Chufor had received further training and now were able to screen and treat all of the outpatients, referring only the difficult cases to me. They were also able to assist in surgery and do some minor procedures like lumbar punctures, IV cutdowns, and minor suturing. Sabina Mamla and Esther Wiribun had become dependable midwives as well. Without their help I would have been totally swamped.

Marion was very busy settling us into our home without a cook to help. She also looked after many guests that came to our rest houses. She had to launder at least 16 sheets a week in addition to our own. With the help of a young garden boy she planted a large number of vegetables and looked after 15 hens that gave us seven or eight eggs a day.

Within a month Bruce developed a florid case of measles and Lori got tonsillitis. Lori was treated with penicillin but Bruce was banished to his room in isolation and was declared unclean, much to his dismay. Joyel was determined not to be left behind and started crawling all over the house, pulling herself up by a chair and crowing loudly at her great achievement. A local 13-year-old girl, Selina, was employed to wash dishes and do cleaning jobs for Marion. When her work was done she played with the kids. On one occasion Selina was seen washing dishes with a doll tied on her back in proper native fashion. Marion put our station carpenters to work in converting the outdoor kitchen into a school room with a cement floor, ceiling board and desks. Leftover school materials from Sandy Gutowski were used until our air freighted materials arrived.

AND THEN THE PHONE RANG...

The administrative work was huge due to my being the lone doctor of the hospital, Field Secretary of the Mambilla Baptist Mission, and negotiator with the Ministry of Health of Gongola State regarding their takeover of the hospital. In the first six weeks at Warwar I had to attend to the following issues:

- Meet with the Bible school Board of Governors
- File four reports to various Federal Government agencies
- Arrange admission of three girls into midwifery school
- Unpack a huge shipment of drug supplies
- Handle payroll for hospital staff of over 50
- Do a detailed inventory of drugs, equipment, supplies, and buildings in preparation for compensation from the government for their takeover
- Write letters to Fred Folkerts and Dr. Schilke regarding compensation issues
- Teach staff Bible studies
- Teach Theological Education by Extension classes for groups that were normally being taught by the absent Minnie, Barb, and Willi.

All of this work was in addition to being the solo doctor for the hospital full of sick people, seeing outpatients, doing surgery, and going on weekend clinics to outlying villages. I was very grateful for the capable local hospital staff of young people. We slowly learned that when God calls us to do what humanly seems impossible, He makes it possible when we step out in faith and obey the call.

UNSETTLING PROBLEMS

MANY TRIPS WERE MADE TO the Gongola State Ministry of Health offices in Yola, a long day's drive north of Mambilla, in order to settle issues of the

BACK TO WARWAR

Warwar hospital takeover. On one of the early trips in mid August Barb and I had an accident while driving the new Toyota just north of Bali. The dirt road was quite narrow and we had a head-on collision with an army Land Rover that suddenly came around a bend in the road at quite a speed. I got to the edge of the road but we still collided. I could not get off the road, as there was a culvert that would have caused a serious roll over. The steering wheel pinned me against my seat so I had to squeeze my way out. I had some pain in my left abdomen, so I was a bit worried about possible damage to my spleen. Barb remembered that missionary Gary Schroeder died of a ruptured spleen when a cow jumped on his car from a hill beside the road in Cameroon. My passengers were unhurt. An army major in the Land Rover hit the windshield with his head and suffered a laceration above his eye. I put a pressure dressing on it and then a passing vehicle took him to the Jalingo hospital. The police came and examined the scene and made rough drawings for their report. The Toyota was too badly damaged to drive. Fortunately several American engineers passed by and they sent a Land Rover to take us to a police station to make a statement and then took us back to Serti.

I sent a radio message to Curt Radke to come with the Mission Land Rover to take us to Jalingo for a hearing with the District Officer who was administrative governor of the Jalingo district. I knew that I was in trouble because the army has the right of way regardless of the actual circumstances. I had visions of being sent to jail for obstructing the Nigerian army. The jail experience usually involves an initiation of a beating by the guards to show who is boss. The police drawings were totally inaccurate and omitted any mention of the deep culvert I had to avoid. I think that God suddenly gave me a plan of defense. I stated that the whole incident was really an unfortunate accident between two branches of government, medical and military. I informed the District Officer that Warwar hospital was a government hospital. He was skeptical until I showed him my government Authority to Incur Expenditure form showing our hospital budget. I asked him if he had a similar one for his operations. He smiled and nodded and then began to scold the police officers for their shoddy report. I was dismissed and most relieved to be free and able to finish our business in Yola.

AND THEN THE PHONE RANG...

The next big problem came a month later when I woke up at night with severe pain in my right upper abdomen. I noticed that my urine was a very dark brown color and the whites of my eyes were a deep yellow color. I was weak and shaky. I had a fever, chills, and back pain for several days and now it looked like I had hepatitis. But in the dark hours of the night my imagination ran rampant. I began to wonder if I had a common bile duct stone. The possibility of fatal ascending cholangitis began to torture my overactive mind. With the pain I felt, there was no way that I could tolerate a bumpy drive to Serti or to Banso in Cameroon. So my only option was to self diagnose hepatitis and go on five to six weeks of bed rest and hope I was right. I was weak and nauseated and glad to just rest. Marion was a great nurse and brought meals to my bed. It was very boring to just lie there and stare at the ceiling. Over time I saw all kinds of images created by water stains in the ceiling board. It was a moving experience to have three of our laundry women come to the foot of my bed and pray for me in the Mambilla language. June Goodman sent some great bible study tapes by Rev. Pawson, a British pastor. My recovery was slow. Halfway through my bed rest time Marion also got sick with some type of 24-hour bug. So then both of us were in bed. Bruce and Lori took over washing dishes, sweeping up the termites on the floor, feeding Joyel and the chickens, and making coffee breaks.

I praised God for the fact that during the six weeks I was in bed no emergency caesarean sections were required. There was one case of a woman who had been in labor for several days and had an undelivered dead baby. Esther Lackson called and informed me that the baby was in an arm presentation and could not be delivered without some intervention. I managed to walk to the maternity and had to sit and rest a while before proceeding. On examination I noticed that the skin of the baby's arm was peeling off and there was no audible fetal heartbeat. The mother had a fever and to do a caesarean section would be very risky because of probable infection. So I cut the baby's arm off and managed to grab a foot and with some exertion turn the baby into a breech position. I was totally exhausted and sweating, so I sat down and coached Esther through a breech delivery of the dead baby. Antibiotics and IV rehydration was ordered. By now I was too weak to walk home, so Stephen Lamba, our carpenter, took me home by carrying me piggy-back style on his back. The mother recovered quickly and was discharged.

The next problem was a thief in the house. While Marion was teaching school Zaccheus, a former cook, crept into our house and took the office keys from our bedroom closet and raided the office, taking the petty cash plus some Cameroonian francs. Marion noticed the open office door when she came in 15 minutes later and knew immediately that someone had broken in. She recalled seeing Zaccheus near the house that morning so she reported this to Headman Joseph and Stephen Lamba. They, plus another laborer went to the village market and caught Zaccheus with the money. Zaccheus was brought back to the mission compound where he was searched. A crowd of angry people beat him, tied him up, and marched him off to the police in Gembu where he was charged with theft. Bruce and Lori were wide-eyed at all the fuss.

IN MARCH 1977 OUR FAMILY went to the SIM rest house in Miango, near Jos, for a 10-day local leave. We were able to relax, play with the children, read, and enjoy the fine meals prepared for us. A break like this enabled us to recharge our batteries for the challenges ahead. On the way home we flew in the CRC plane from Jos to Serti. The weather was very bad with turbulence that pushed the little plane up and down, back and forth. We gave Joyel some dimenhydrinate so she slept through it all. Lori just shut her eyes, lay back, and toughed it out.

To make matters worse, there was a very thick Harmattan that made it impossible to see landmarks. Harmattan is like a thick dense smog caused by dry season winds kicking up sand and dust from the Sahara desert. After flying for one-and-a-half hours the pilot looked at a map strapped on his leg and at the air speed indicator and said, "We should be over Serti by now, but I can't see anything through all this Harmattan." So he decided to dive down lower to get his bearings. As we dropped in altitude we suddenly saw a mountain right in front of us. We banked quickly to avoid hitting the mountain. As we did this, I spotted a village at the foot of the mountain and reckoned that it might be Mayo Selbe, a village we go through before climbing a steep winding road up to the Mambilla Plateau. The pilot then saw a road which we followed at treetop level going away from the mountain towards what we hoped was Serti 25 miles away. We were all very nauseated as the plane followed a winding road at treetop height. Finally the landing strip at Serti came into view. The pilot had to buzz the landing strip to chase some goats off before actually landing. I was so grateful to survive this scary ordeal that I actually kissed the ground and thanked God for our safe arrival.

DEALING WITH GOVERNMENT

ALL THE MISSION HOSPITALS IN Gongola State, including Warwar, were taken over by the State Ministry of Health. We had agreed to return to work at Warwar hospital and in the process try to provide a transition from the mission to the government. Within days of our arrival in Warwar, a secretary from the Ministry of Health arrived to teach us how to reorganize the hospital to conform to Ministry regulations. This involved budgets, stores records, purchase orders, vouchers, ward inventories, weekly and monthly reports on statistics, reclassification of all staff, and establishing staff salaries. A hospital clerk from Yola was posted to Warwar to do all the clerical work. I soon discovered that he was also a spy, reporting on all of our activities.

I was called to Yola for a meeting with the State Commissioner of Health and the Permanent Secretary along with representatives from mission hospitals in Takum, Mkar, Garkida, and Bambur. We were told that the Government felt an obligation to compensate the voluntary agencies for the takeover of their hospitals. We were then asked to state what we felt was reasonable compensation. Garkida asked only for reimbursement of expendable supplies in their stores. Bambur asked for the same, plus a promise from the government to complete a building project that was under way. I then stated that the Warwar station was started for the purpose of evangelism and that the medical work developed later and as such was a part of our evangelism work. Therefore I asked that the Mission retain the nurse's duplex (built by Curt Radke) for housing of non-medical missionaries. This was rejected because it was required for future hospital staff housing. I conceded their point and then requested sufficient compensation to rebuild mission housing elsewhere. This was accepted as reasonable. Takum representatives demanded full compensation for everything as they felt deprived as a mission from the means of medical evangelism. This line of thought did not go over very well with the Government people at all, who stated that they were just continuing medical care for Nigerians. They claimed that the hospitals were built for the good of the local people, so why should they pay the missions for the buildings. They obviously did not recognize or want to recognize the concept of medical evangelism.

I followed up the discussions with government officials with a letter stating our position on compensation and requested a total of 80,000 Naira ($120,000) as follows:

- 30,000 Naira to replace loss of housing – with details on current cost of cement, zinc sheet roofing, timber, and labour.

- 30,000 Naira to replace the loss of the only resthouse, storage, and maintenance facility that the mission had in Gongola State.

- Reimbursement of the value of the July inventory of drugs in our store which we purchased, and had no way of recovery of the cost without charging patient fees.

- One vehicle to be retained by the mission, the second one given to the hospital.

I concluded this letter stating that the mission considered the hospital buildings, equipment, generator, and one vehicle a gift to Gongola State and to the peoples of Mambilla in order to continue medical care for the local people.

Several months later a group of nine officials from three different government ministries arrived unannounced in order to inspect the hospital facilities, staff housing, and our general operations. One of them was the Permanent Secretary of Health for the state. While I was escorting them around the hospital, Marion and Minnie were frantically putting together a lunch meal that was served in our living room. Care was taken to avoid any pork in the menu as they were all Muslims. On a humorous note – as they were preparing to leave they whispered to one of our staff that they were waiting for Kola nuts from me. Kola nuts were symbolically used in West Africa for special ceremonies and served to honored guests. In this context the request was seen as a request for money from me so that they would make a favorable report. I caught on quickly and called on Joseph Headman who prided himself as keeper of our station Kola nuts. He polished up a small panful of Kola nuts which we presented to the departing officials. They were impressed at our quick thinking in taking their request at face value – they got some Kola nuts, not a bribe! I think they got a bit high as Kola nuts contain a large dose of caffeine, theophylline, theobromine, and nicotine, and were used in the early production of Coca-Cola. Some people get quite addicted to them.

Eighteen months later we finally got a firm promise from the Government officials in Yola that they would compensate the mission for the full amount requested. Up to this time we continued to charge patient fees in order to pay salaries and purchase medicines. This compensation enabled Curt Radke to build missionary housing in Mbamga and at the Bible school at Mbu.

Many more trips were made to the Ministry of Health in Yola in order to sign a Public Service Commission contract for Minnie, Barb, and me. I was given the princely title of Principal Medical Officer in charge of the hospital with an annual salary of $12,415 plus a 20% bonus for working in a remote area. We agreed that the government salaries for the three of us would be put into an Expatriate Fund and that we would continue to receive our regular mission salary. The Expatriate Fund money was then used to build student dorms, classrooms, missionary housing, and a library at the Bible school in Mbu. There was great rejoicing when Johnathan Yep, the executive president of the Mambilla Baptist Convention, finally obtained the Statutory Right of Occupancy for the Bible school at Mbu. The land title and the funds were now available to develop the Bible school fully with the ultimate goal of seminary accreditation. Thus, the Muslim dominated government took away our Mission Hospital and, in turn, funded the Bible school/seminary development!

The many trips to Yola included getting our hospital staff and laborers onto government salaried positions. This was a slow gradual process that brought great relief and joy to our staff. They now had good salaries with pension plans included. Arrangements were also made for drug supplies, new beds, and mattresses. The Ministry of Health also began to build an administration block and staff housing that I had to coordinate.

On one of the visits to the Ministry of Health in Yola I was called aside for a special meeting with both the Commissioner of Health and the Permanent Secretary. They had been informed that we had hired a Christian pastor as a hospital chaplain and were using government funds to do this. I immediately suspected that this information came from the hospital clerk that they sent to Warwar, perhaps as a spy as well as clerk. I launched into a full explanation as follows:

- First, there was a Christian pastor and chaplain who served the spiritual needs of the sick people. He was fully supported financially by the local church. I had earlier insisted that the Warwar church support the chaplain, not the mission or hospital.

- Second, there was a local Muslim leader (Mallam Bon-Bon) who had a shop in the Warwar village market and came to the hospital to visit Muslim patients. We did not interfere with his visitations.

- Third, I reminded them that the constitution of Nigeria allows for religious freedom and that I would ensure that this would be the case at Warwar. At this point they did not want to hear more, but I stated, "I'm not finished yet!"

- Fourth, human wellness involves the spirit and emotion, not just treatment of some physical issues. We are not really well unless we are right with God.

They both nodded their heads and agreed with me and seemed satisfied. I felt that I had to dig in my heels and defend the right of people to hear the truth of the gospel. For me this was a make-it-or-break-it issue as to whether or not I would continue working at Warwar.

The trips to Yola required about 12 to 14 hours of driving on hot dusty rough dirt roads. We carried extra gas in jerry cans and water in metal canisters. In order to keep the water cool, the canisters were covered in canvas and dipped into a stream to make the outside wet. They were then tied to the front bumper of the vehicle. The rush of air evaporated the wet

AND THEN THE PHONE RANG...

canvas that then had a cooling effect on the contents. On one occasion Minnie and I arrived in Yola around suppertime. Our water cans were empty by this time. To our dismay the electrical power to Yola was off as the man in charge of it was out of town. We searched the market for anything drinkable but the shops were all sold out. We tried the government resthouse, asking for water or pop. Minnie, the staunch Baptist missionary, even asked if they had any beer. There was no beer! We finally found a shop that had a large pan full of oranges. We bought them all! The mission resthouse where we were staying had no water except for about one glass full. We had a long discussion as to how to use this. It was decided that we would first brush our teeth using only one sip each and swallow the toothpaste. Next was a small amount to wipe the road dust off our faces. The final little bit of water was used to wash the palms of our hands so we could touch our food. In the middle of the night I woke up and turned on my flashlight to see what time it was. The sudden light resulted in a scratchy sound of several hundred cockroaches scurrying for cover. I made sure to tuck in my mosquito net tightly around my bed for the rest of the night.

On another trip to Yola I drove with Alexander Jandong, a field pastor, who had some official business to do in Yola. As we drove along we came upon a bridge over a small creek. This bridge had no railings – most Nigerian bridges have numerous accidents on them that wreck the railings. As we crossed the bridge we noticed an upside down truck loaded with sacks of grain in the creek below. At the far end of the bridge sat a man swaying back and forth holding his head. Something was wrong, so we stopped. To our horror we saw bodies on both banks of the creek. Some of the people were dead and others were moaning and writhing as they lay dying. Some had heads bashed open exposing brain tissue, some others were disemboweled. There were numerous legs protruding out from under the truck in the shallow creek with the blood from the injured and dead people staining the water. A woman standing by the truck was screaming and pointing at the side of the truck. We heard a child's cry. So we pulled at some of the heavy sacks of grain and managed to extract a live and apparently uninjured little baby and gave it to the mother. We felt utterly helpless at the scene of this disaster. I had no morphine or demerol to ease the pain of the dying. We flagged down a passing vehicle and instructed them to hurry to the Jalingo hospital a few miles back to summon helpers. We drove on to the next village to inform the police and instructed them to get many able-bodied people to help at the scene of the accident. To this day, over four decades later, I can still visualize the terrible scene.

MAMBILLA BAPTIST CONVENTION

THE BIBLE SCHOOL AT MBU developed rapidly after the Statutory Right of Occupancy of the land at Mbu was obtained. Money from the Expatriate Fund allowed the building program to go ahead as mentioned. Small classes were underway already for class two and three. Applications for the new start of class one numbered 24 and included several students from Cameroon. This made a total of 36 students. This was a much needed and critical venture for the future of the Mambilla Baptist Convention. Many churches had young totally untrained pastors who were barely literate. I was involved in some of the teaching of how to prepare a sermon and wrote and taught course material on evangelism. I was very grateful for the semester I had attended at Northwest Baptist Seminary during our recent furlough!

THE THEOLOGICAL EDUCATION BY EXTENSION (TEE) program was developed to help local pastors in their ministry. As mentioned, some were untrained and did not have the necessary funds for Bible school. If they could afford Bible school fees and left home to attend, the local churches would be without a pastor. TEE allowed the pastors to remain home and serve their churches while taking the 10-week courses. The pastors had two weeks to study the course material at home and then go to a central village where one of the missionaries would meet with them to review the course materials and conduct a discussion. The churches benefitted as their pastors used the course subjects for sermon preparation. Local Christian school teachers also began to participate in TEE. Some of the courses were:

- Talking with God - on prayer

- New Testament Survey

- Letters to Seven Churches

- The Shepherd and His Flock

- The General Epistles

We even conducted these courses for 32 of our hospital staff on Sunday evenings. The staff was keenly aware that patients and their families needed to know Jesus and come to faith in Him. They were very helpful to the Chaplain in his rounds and devotional talks.

As Field Secretary I had to meet with the Executive of the Mambilla Baptist Convention and with the General Council annually. My role was to be a listener and to give advice when it was requested. I also transmitted the Convention's requests to the NAB Board of Missions and relayed the NAB response to the Convention. I also had to attend meetings of the Board of Governors of the Bible school. The ultimate goal of the Bible school was to grow and develop into an accredited seminary. The Convention also held an annual General Session where pastors and lay people from all churches attended for days of teaching, celebration, choir contests, and fellowship. The various Fields also held annual Bible conferences in the beginning of the dry season in November. It was interesting to learn that Warwar and Gembu fields recorded a total of 750 baptisms during 1977. I had to do some teaching about the person and work of the Holy Spirit as there seemed to be some confusion and even heresy among some of the churches. One of the issues was the charismatic movement taken to excess. I also taught a four-day Leadership Training Course for 40 pastors on the Gifts of the Holy Spirit using 1 Corinthians 12 – 14.

ANOTHER DUTY OF THE FIELD Secretary was to arrange emergency evacuation plans for all missionaries to get out of Nigeria quickly. The missionaries in Jos who taught at Hillcrest school, the Woyke House hostel houseparents, and the missionary children were 600 miles away from us on the Mambilla Plateau – a two day trip by road. I instructed the Woyke House house-parents to store enough money to pay double the cost of flights for everyone in Jos to fly to safety. The missionaries on the remote Mambilla Plateau were instructed to trek over the border to Cameroon using bush trails to avoid roadblocks. They were to use a trusted local guide and travel at night so as to avoid detection.

MEDICAL WORK

THE HOSPITAL WORK SCHEDULE CONTINUED as before with staff prayer time at 6:30 AM followed by ward rounds, coffee break, and consultation of out-patients until mid-afternoon. A quick lunch preceded administrative chores, supervision of site maintenance, and building projects. On Tuesday we did quick rounds on the most critically ill patients and then did a full slate of elective surgery. Following this we saw patients referred by the out-patient staff as well as new admissions to hospital. Emergency surgery happened anytime when required. On Wednesday the midwives saw antenatal patients – at least 150 to 200 of them – and did well baby checks and immunizations. On Friday and Saturday, we travelled to remote villages for clinics and TEE.

The workload increased year by year. By 1978 we had 75 proper hospital beds plus 25 to 30 beds in mud huts usually at 100% occupancy. On a busy Wednesday in December 1978 after ward rounds, we saw 700 outpatients and 300 women in the antenatal clinic. In the middle of all that we had an emergency caesarean section. The statistics for 1978 were as follows:

- Beds   109
- Hospitalized patients   4973
- Hospital patient days   34541
- New outpatient consultations   30447
- Repeat consultations   72498
- Major surgeries   239
- Minor surgeries   1399
- Babies delivered   1673
- Antenatal attendance   23056
- Caesarean sections   52 (a 3.1% C-section rate!)

AND THEN THE PHONE RANG...

The medical and surgical issues we encountered have already been described, but the following cases were some memorable ones for me.

- Removal of a huge ovarian tumor that was one foot in diameter.

- Saucerization of the entire front of the tibia (lower leg bone) for chronic osteomyelitis. This required removal of the front of the bone and then scraping out all of the marrow tissue.

- Stabilizing a very unstable fracture of both lower bones in the right leg. We had no bone plates and screws, so we did the next best thing. We drilled Steinman pins horizontally through the upper tibia and the calcaneus (heel) and then applied a long leg cast. Curt Radke found a hand drill in the carpenters shop that we sterilized in boiling water. Curt did the drilling while I supervised the proper location. This worked well and Curt was now an amateur orthopedic surgeon.

- Removal of another huge ovarian tumor, the size of a large grapefruit, that was found to be full of hair and fully developed teeth. We showed this only to the operating room staff as the bizarre nature of this would cause a lot of superstitious speculation.

- Amputation of a leg in a three-and-a-half year old little girl. She was bitten by a snake and her parents applied a high tourniquet that cut off blood supply to the leg. When she arrived at the hospital her leg had already turned black and the skin and muscle was sloughing off. What a mess. There was no way to save the leg.

- Repair of cleft lips. The CRC midwife at Serti sent a baby and mother to us thinking that we could easily repair the baby's cleft lip. No, this was not simple. I had never seen a repair done, and we did not have an anesthetist to control the baby's airway. I found a plastic surgery book and spent an evening practicing with paper, cutting out and then approximating the sides of the cleft lip. The next day I took my book to the OR, opened the page, and as I looked at the baby, I was horrified to see that the cleft was on the other side from the picture in the book. So, I had to proceed by flipping the picture to a mirror image in my mind. I had no marking pen so I made little dots of blood with the scalpel tip and quickly cut to join the dots. Copious gauze in the mouth kept the blood away from the throat. Sewing up in layers was quickly done to minimize blood loss. We got the lip nicely lined up. The mother was overwhelmed with joy at the result. Mom and baby went home and soon the word got out that we could repair cleft lips. We ended up seeing a new case every month from all over the plateau. A challenge came when an adult woman came with a shawl over her face covering a huge cleft lip. We managed a good repair. It was worth all my sweat to see her smile when she looked in a mirror for the first time.

- Hernia repairs were done, often several a week. The biggest one was the size of a football. The same day we amputated an arm for cancer. I also repaired a very rare posterior triangle hernia that is described in the fine print of surgery and anatomy books.

- A strange Caesarean section was done one night on the Nigerian wife of the British headmaster of the secondary school in Gembu. We discovered that the baby was in distress during early labour. So we got set up for the caesarean section. I was unable to get a needle in her back for a spinal anesthetic. Again, no anesthetist to do a general anesthetic. The lady was very short – under five feet tall – and had a huge baby. This made it impossible for her to bend forward enough to get a spinal needle in place. If we did nothing we could lose the life of mother and baby. So I called for some local anesthetic which I injected as we cut. Once we got the abdomen open we had to move quickly to get the baby out. At this point we gave the lady some IV medicine to ease the pain. We left the uterus inside the abdomen for sewing up, which is more difficult than lifting the uterus out to do this. The pain of this would have been intolerable. All went well and baby and mother went home after a week. Joyel insisted on helping with the daily baby bath. The happy father gave us three big turkeys as a thank-you gift.

- Caesarean sections were a part of life at Warwar. Our caesarean section rate was very low as the Mambilla women in general seemed

AND THEN THE PHONE RANG...

to have a gynecoid pelvis to allow for natural vaginal deliveries. This must have been a process of natural selection over many generations where women died in childbirth if they had a small pelvis. Our caesarean sections seemed to come in batches – none while I was bedridden for five weeks. Then in a week prior to going to Jos on a trip I had five cases. One very busy day I was confronted with three cases that required immediate surgery. It was a bit of a scrabble as we had only two sets of caesarean section instruments. So we did the most urgent case first, and while doing the second case, the staff boiled the instruments from the first case, wrapped them, and sterilized them in a pressure cooker for use in the third caesarean section. All the mothers and babies did well, but I was wiped out!

- Rabies – one night there was a great noise of fighting animals outside. The next morning a large number of men were running all over the compound to find and kill a rabid dog with their machetes. The rabid dog had attacked many animals in the night, including our dog, Speckie. Speckie had an open wound on his nose and to my horror I saw Marion petting Speckie to console him, using a hand that had a healing cut. To make matters worse, Marion was pregnant with Paul at the time. We paid Philip Munyah, our carpenter and handyman, to take Speckie in the bush and shoot him. I was left with the dilemma of what to do with Marion. Do we give her a series of anti-rabies shots (of dubious quality) or not? If we did, would this affect the pregnancy and little Paul? This was a rare time that I was really angry with Marion because I had to choose a course of action. If only she would have kept her hands off of Speckie! We chose to not immunize and, thank God, Marion and baby were OK.

- Tubal ligations – Many couples were requesting permanent contraception as their families were becoming too large. Birth control pills were not ideal as a constant supply was not always available. Also proper dosing could be unreliable, as some women put them under the mattress as a type of charm. Others took them all at once. So tubal ligations became popular. They were very easy to do postpartum, often with just local anesthetic. One woman who came for a tubal ligation had just delivered her eighteenth baby and had 13 living children!

- Bowel resections – An elderly man presented with a complete bowel obstruction. I opened his abdomen (under spinal anesthesia) and found an obstruction of his small intestine due to a volvulus (twisted loop of bowel). I ended up removing ten feet of black, dead small bowel and doing a primary anastomosis. To my great relief he survived and went home happy. A week later a woman had a similar operation as her bowel was on the point of rupture. Unfortunately she was also very sick with bilateral pneumonia. Despite IV hydration and massive doses of antibiotics, she deteriorated and died two days later.

- We also did amateur dental work to fill the dental caries of Minnie, Bruce, and Lori. I was not too worried about the kids as they were baby teeth.

HOME LIFE

BRUCE RENEWED HIS FRIENDSHIPS AT Warwar quickly and played a lot of soccer using home-made balls of rolled up vines. When the ball disintegrated half-time was declared while a new ball was fashioned. He and his friends built a car out of bits of wood and cardboard and coasted down the hill beside our house. They even figured out a system of brakes. He once watched a caesarean section, held the new baby while I was sewing up, and then wrote an interesting story about the episode. He was very interested in Marion reading, "The Three Musketeers" to him in old English.

Lori was very interested in domestic issues. She learned how to sew an apron, make ice cream, and bake cookies. Selina, our 14-year-old household helper, taught Lori how to pound corn to make the corn flour used to make Fufu. Our pet sheep delivered a little lamb. Lori took over as the mother and named the lamb Frisky. She carried the lamb around like a little baby until it became too heavy to lift.

AND THEN THE PHONE RANG...

Joyel arrived at Warwar as a nine-month-old baby. She was a little social butterfly and happily sat on any available lap to have a chat. By 14 months she was walking and running but had no teeth. Finally she sprouted six baby teeth all at the same time, making her a bit grumpy! As she got bigger she tried to keep up with Bruce and Lori and their friends. A favorite activity was what we called "fighting time tonight" where she and I would get down on the rug and roll around wrestling. She of course had to win. She was very observant as seen by the time she was in the bathtub with her doll. She lifted the doll out of the water and noticed water coming out of the doll's crotch area. Joyel immediately got us to lift her out of the tub so she could seat her doll on the toilet in proper fashion. Marion and I just howled with laughter.

Bruce and Lori were homeschooled by Marion in the mornings. It was very helpful to have Selina watch Joyel for a bit as Joyel wanted to play in the schoolroom and demanded attention. Marion, not being a trained teacher, was a bit concerned that Bruce and Lori would fall behind their peers in Canada. Carla Braun, an NAB short-term missionary teacher at Hillcrest School in Jos, came for a visit to Warwar. She examined the school work the children were doing and assured Marion that Bruce and Lori were actually ahead of their peers who she taught at Hillcrest. By March of 1978 we struggled with the idea of sending Bruce and Lori to Hillcrest School in Jos the following August. Bruce would only be 9 and Lori 8. How would they adapt to being 600 miles away from home and parents for months at a time, living with unknown house parents? Would they somehow feel rejected by us? Would they think that our work was more important to us than they were? Bruce and Lori initially were enthusiastic about the idea, but then reservations set in.

We did manage to take a bit of time off for rest and recuperation. We enjoyed meeting with missionaries from Cameroon at the Mbori river which was approximately at the border with Nigeria. We would swim and wade in the water, eat a picnic lunch, and swap tales. We also managed to go to a SIM rest house and resort in Miango near Jos. This was an all-inclusive place with great meals, restful atmosphere, and even tennis courts and a croquet field. Bruce and Lori even learned to play monopoly there. The total cost for our family for 10 days was only $200 – about 25% of my monthly missionary salary. Marion really enjoyed not having to worry about cooking. A lady did our laundry for us by washing the clothes on a flat rock by a stream, charging us only $1. We managed to go to Miango twice during our three-year tour in Nigeria. The trips to Miango were planned to coincide with necessary business in Jos such as major shopping for food, medicines, and building supplies. Also, vehicle repairs and maintenance could be done at the dealerships headquartered in Jos.

Christmas was a time for celebration. There were church services on Christmas day followed by feasting and dancing late into the night for four days in a row – one day in each of the four quarters of Warwar village. The Ministry of Forestry in Gembu sent a nicely shaped little cypress tree that we set up and decorated in our living room. Bruce and Lori were very busy making a very long paper chain using old Christmas wrapping paper. This was then solemnly draped around the tree. Marion prepared a wonderful feast of roast ducklings with sauerkraut and Weihnachtsstollen, a German Christmas fruitcake. Marion had an old hen sit on a couple of duck eggs to hatch them. The little ducks got big and fat in time for a Christmas Eve dinner. Minnie, Barb, and Reilly and Mildred Neuman (Woyke House house-parents), and their son Sheldon joined us for dinner. After the meal we retired to the living room to open gifts. Before we could start I had to do an emergency caesarean section on a woman who presented with a prolapsed umbilical cord. Minnie was able to hold the baby's head up to prevent compression of the cord which would kill the baby. Reilly and Sheldon helped carry the lady into the operating room with Minnie still holding the baby's head up. They watched the entire caesarean section and were most impressed with all the drama. Both baby and mom were fine in the end. Bruce and Lori were not too impressed with the long wait to open presents!

The day after boxing day we travelled to Bamenda to participate in the annual Cameroon Missionary Fellowship. It was great to visit with all the NAB missionaries in Nigeria and Cameroon. Dr. Richard Schilke (General Missions Secretary of NAB Missions) was our guest speaker. He encouraged us with daily devotional talks. The children really enjoyed their own program that was similar to vacation Bible school. We had to leave a day early as a note from Andreas, our cook, informed us that the Governor of

Gongola State was going to visit Warwar. We hurried home and found that the Governor was visiting Gembu, not Warwar. I managed to get to the meeting that involved all the heads of various government departments. Somehow, I ended up sitting right next to the Governor and had a private talk with him regarding the need for more trained hospital staff and for a bridge over the Donga River.

VISITORS

MARION WAS OUR STATION HOSTESS. This involved maintaining the rest houses, cleaning them and doing the laundry, as well as feeding all the visitors. She entertained SUM and CRC missionaries who came for rest and relaxation time, expatriate travelers, and sick expatriates who were admitted to a rest house as patients. A CRC couple decided to spend their honeymoon at Warwar so Marion prepared their bed with two stuffed monkeys embracing each other on the pillows. Also a number of our NAB missionaries in Cameroon came to Warwar for visits, including parents who were taking their children to Woyke House in Jos.

In December 1977 Dr. and Mrs. Schilke came on an official tour of Nigeria and Cameroon. Dr. Schilke, as mentioned, was the General Secretary of NAB Missions and periodically visited the various mission fields in which NAB was working. I flew to Jos to meet them at the airport to escort them to the various stations in Nigeria. After a visit to Hillcrest School and Woyke House, we flew to Yola to meet with the Gongola State Permanent Secretary of Health and the Commissioner of Health. At this visit they promised Dr. Schilke that the state would pay compensation to the mission for the loss of missionary housing plus all of the other requests that I made for compensation. It was a good face-to-face meeting. We then flew to Serti and drove up to the Mambilla Plateau. The Schilkes were able to participate in a Mambilla Baptist Convention General Council meeting, attend the Bible school Dedication, visit a field Bible conference in MayoDaga, and witness a baptism and Lord's Supper in Warwar. They then proceeded to visit Cameroon and the Cameroon Missionary Fellowship.

BACK TO WARWAR

The Schilkes were very encouraging and supportive of our work. All our missionaries referred to Dr. Schilke as Papa Schilke.

Dr. Ralph and Ardice Powell also visited us at Warwar. Dr. Powell was a professor of theology at Sioux Falls Seminary. He had recently married Ardice who was a former missionary nurse in Cameroon. As they were newly-weds they were very much in love. We observed them walking along holding hands and we had to remind Ardice that such public displays of affection were taboo in West African society. She blushed and immediately remembered. We had a great visit with them and enjoyed some deeper discussions. One time I asked Dr. Powell if I could ask him a question that I always wanted to ask a theologian. The question was, did Adam have a belly button? Dr. Powell started to laugh and suddenly stopped and said, "That is a deep question." In other words, did God create Adam with a belly button or was Adam a name representative of the human race. That led on to a long discussion on creation and evolution and whether the seven-day creation story of Genesis 1 was a literal seven-day creation or not.

Oma came to visit us, arriving in late April 1978. She was able to get a ride from Jos to Warwar with Minnie and Barb who were in Jos for a nurse's refresher course. We had announced Marion's pregnancy to Oma in March, so she came with a bulging suitcase full of baby clothes and maternity items for Marion. Marion's dad sent some seeds along so Marion put our garden helper to work with planting and watering. Oma was able to participate in all the events we were involved in. She even got to go to Yambam, a very pagan village nearby, to whom the Warwar church people witnessed. Joyel bonded with Oma who cared for her while Marion was teaching school to Bruce and Lori. Oma also went to several clinics where she was put to work counting pills which really tired her out after we saw 900 people in two days. In a very brave manner she even managed to smash a tarantula that was trying to get into her bedroom. Minnie Kuhn also put Oma to work sewing operating gowns and repairing hospital linens. Oma also experienced the down-and-dirty life in the bush when we returned home from a welcome party for newly arrived Pete and May Schroeder in Gembu. We left our vehicle on the Warwar side of the Donga River and crossed over in canoes. Curt picked us up on the Gembu side. It was raining heavily that night when we returned home to Warwar. The river canoes had inches of muddy water sloshing in the bottom. The riverbank on the Warwar side was sloppy, wet, muddy, and slippery. The only way up the bank was to crawl on hands and knees which was quite the ordeal for Minnie and Oma.

FAMILY COMINGS AND GOINGS

THE DECISION HAD BEEN MADE to send Bruce and Lori to Hillcrest School in Jos and to live at the Woyke House Hostel. Hillcrest School was run by a board of representatives from a number of mission agencies in Nigeria for the education of missionary children and expatriates. Jos was on a plateau with tolerable weather. It was a large town with modern facilities and a site for a number of mission headquarters. Marion felt somewhat inadequate as a teacher for the higher grades, and worried that the children would not be prepared for integration into the Canadian school system when we returned home. The local schools would not be able to prepare our children properly for their integration into the school systems when we returned to Canada. This was not an easy decision to make as Bruce was 9 years old and Lori had just turned 8. They would be 600 miles away – two fourteen-hour days of driving. Would they be able to cope with the prolonged separation?

On August 7, 1978, Ed Hoepner and I drove to Jos to take Bruce, Lori, and Kristine to Woyke House and Oma to the Jos airport for her trip home to Canada. Marion dissolved in tears as she and Joyel waved good-bye, watching us roll down the hill away from our house. She wanted to come along on the trip but we felt the risk was too high for her state of pregnancy at 32 weeks. Reilly and Mildred welcomed us to Woyke House and showed the kids where their beds were. Poor Bruce got teary eyed after Uncle Reilly reminded all the kids about all the house rules. Bruce was upset because he could not remember all the rules listed. The next morning Lori was covered with mosquito bites as she did not use her mosquito net. Later we found out that Lori developed malaria and needed an injection of anti-malarial medicine. It was discovered that she secretly threw out her prophylactic chloroquine pills because she hated the bitter taste. The injection convinced her that shots were worse than bitter pills. The first day at Hillcrest School went well as both Bruce and Lori immediately found friends. By the end of the first day Bruce learned to ride a two-wheel bike and roamed all over the Woyke House compound.

It broke my heart to say good-bye to Bruce and Lori and leave the Hostel with both of them crying into their cereal bowls. This was the most difficult thing I ever had to do! I was crying too as I drove away. The tears stopped by the time I got to Bauchi 100 miles away. Back home at Warwar I found Joyel a bit out of sorts without her siblings. Marion gave her a kitten to play with which kept her busy for a while. When the mother cat came into the house yowling and looking for her kitten, Joyel grabbed the kitten and told the mother cat, "you go outside, I have this child first!" There was quite an argument between the two of them regarding custody rights. Joyel handled the kitten like a doll and put it to bed and covered it with a lappa, an African cloth wrapper, and even tried to tie it on her back like Nigerian moms do with their babies.

October 1978 finally came and it was time for Marion to deliver her baby. She had several episodes of false labour but on October 14 the real labour started. I put our kitchen table into the bedroom and raised one end with medical books so we had a delivery table. Minnie Kuhn did the delivery while I held Joyel and pushed our cat out of the room with my feet. Paul Ronald weighed in at 7 pounds. We noticed that the umbilical cord had a complete true knot in it. Fortunately the knot was loose. If it had pulled tight during labour I would have been forced to do an emergency C-section. We praised God for the safe delivery. After the delivery Paul, still wrapped up in a towel, was taken outside where many people had gathered. Joseph Headman raised Paul high overhead and shouted out his Mambilla name – Ndalvuri – which means Warwar Boy. Some of our staff and laborers came right into our house singing and dancing up a storm. A chicken was killed and roasted over an open fire and all the people had a bite to eat as Paul was officially adopted as their Mambilla Boy.

It was planned that Dr. Helen Marie Schmidt, from Banso hospital in Cameroon, would come for a visit and be available to help with the delivery. She got a Land Rover ride to Mbem, near the border, and was to proceed to Warwar the next morning only to discover that the Land Rover driver had left early in the morning with a load of peanuts for Banso. Helen did arrive in Warwar four days after Paul was born. We had some early concerns with Paul as he became quite jaundiced. He was put in a basket by the living room window with no clothes on except some gauze to cover his eyes. Rainy season had just started, but there seemed to be enough intermittent sunshine to help deal with the jaundice. Joyel was delighted to have a baby brother but was concerned about his lack of the soft curly black hair that African babies have. She put a head-tie on him to cover up the deficiency.

At the end of October I drove to Jos with Ed and Marie Hoepner to visit our kids. I got a place at Mountain View Hostel where I could sleep with Bruce and Lori on the living room floor as Hoepners used the bedroom. They were excited to hear all about Paul and see some Polaroid pictures. They seemed to have adjusted well to life in Jos. Bruce was riding a bike and had learned to swim. Lori was beginning to relax in the pool as well. She got all As and Bs on her report card and apparently was her teacher's favorite student. Bruce was too busy having fun so his marks were much lower. He was a real aggressive soccer player and ran circles around older boys.

Work at Warwar continued to get busier with hospital issues, clinics, Field Bible Conferences, and TEE classes. On a Wednesday we had 700 patients in the out-patients department, over 300 women in the antenatal clinic, at least 100 in-patients to see, and an emergency C-section in the middle of the morning. We returned to Jos in mid-December to pick up Bruce and Lori for Christmas break. On the day we left Warwar the Chairman and the Secretary of the State Health Services Management Board visited Warwar and wanted me to submit estimates and supervise the construction of a 16-bed maternity extension and a new isolation ward. We got to Jos just in time to see the Christmas program and enjoyed seeing Bruce and Lori perform. Bruce and Lori were overjoyed to see their new little brother, Paul. While in Jos I booked our flights home to Canada with KLM, leaving Nigeria in early June, 1979.

Christmas was a wonderful time of celebration with our entire family. Joyel kept looking out the windows to see if Santa Claus was coming. Bruce and Lori had picked up some smart aleck back talk in Jos that we had to fix with a bit of old-fashioned discipline. Marion cooked a Christmas dinner for 17 people using two scrawny turkeys and it was a big hit. We then travelled to Bamenda for the annual Cameroon Missionary Fellowship where Dr. Ralph

Powell was the speaker. After returning to Warwar, the kids had some time to play with friends, build things with LEGO, and enjoy each other. Lori loved to tie Paul to her back with a lappa just like her African friends did. We had a baby dedication for Paul in the Warwar church together with two of our staff and their new babies. The time came to take Bruce and Lori back to Jos for school. They were not really excited about leaving so we counted out the weeks till we would visit them in March and then again until June when we would be on our way home to Canada. That seemed to help them.

GOING HOME

OUR PLANNED DEPARTURE TIME TO go home on furlough was June 2, 1979. No doctor had been found by the NAB Board of Missions or by the Gongola State Ministry of Health to replace me. We planned for Minnie Kuhn to have full time involvement with teaching at the Bible school and in TEE groups. Pete Schroeder was selected to be the new Field Secretary, so I spent time handing over all the files to him. Barb Kieper, on return from her furlough, would do mobile clinic work and public health on a full time basis. Our trained Nigerian staff, including six midwives, were very capable of dealing with most health issues. We later discovered that the Ministry of Health assigned an ear, nose, and throat specialist to replace me. An occasion arose for an emergency caesarean section. The ENT doctor had never done this operation before, so Zebulon Wanmi and Paul Chufor gave the patient a spinal anesthetic and did a successful caesarean section as the ENT doctor watched. It was really gratifying to realize that during our time at Warwar we had trained teenagers to become midwives and rural health workers capable of doing life saving procedures. Years later one of them became a doctor working in Gembu.

Packing up our household was quite involved as we sorted our possessions into the following categories:

- items to sell, which included all my tools.

- items to give away, this included over 100 books sent to the Bible school.

AND THEN THE PHONE RANG...

- items to ship home, which amounted to four steel drums of cargo.
- items to store in case we returned after furlough time.

Joyel got rather belligerent when all her toys and dolls (except one) were sold or given away.

WE TRIED TO GET THE hospital in good shape before leaving. By tapping into a spring high above the station I worked on installing a new water system with two-inch steel pipe to supply water to the hospital, and nearby neighbors. All the hospital buildings were painted. Seventy-five new beds with mattresses, sheets, and blankets were set up. Also two four-room staff houses were built. A quick trip to Jos was made in March to see Bruce and Lori. While there we celebrated Bruce's tenth birthday and obtained a certificate of Canadian citizenship and a Canadian passport for Paul. We were able to spend three days at Rockhaven, a Sudan United Mission guesthouse that served catered meals. This place was so close to the Jos zoo that we could hear the lions roaring. By this time Lori had learned to swim across the pool and dive like a seal.

Back at Warwar I scrambled around to get some pictures to use for deputation presentations. Marion sent out over 100 letters to family, friends, and supporting churches. We had a flood of visitors at Easter, including Kathy Kroll, Dr. Rod Zimmerman, and Dr. Claudia Rist from Cameroon, plus the Viss family from Serti and the Horsts from Gembu. Cindy Viss and Vickie Horst had recently delivered their babies at Warwar. Marion had to improvise to feed everyone and so sacrificed the last of our turkeys. In the middle of all this company I did three caesarean sections, entertained the guests till 11 PM, then packed until 1 AM for a business trip to Yola – leaving at 4:30 AM. I was really ready for a restful furlough! Kathy Kroll took our four drums of cargo with her to Cameroon for shipment home.

There was a surprise one day when a Land Rover from Gembu drove up to the hospital with the horn blasting. Rev. Johnathan Yep, the Executive secretary of the Mambilla Baptist Convention, was brought to the hospital. He had been pushed through a mud brick wall by a vehicle that backed into him, crushing his pelvis. He had several pelvic fractures but no discernable urological injury. This was perceived as a serious political problem as well because he was the chairman of the G.N.P.P. political party and a candidate in an upcoming election. The Mambilla people were certain that the injury was a deliberate attempt by the opposition party to eliminate him. Consequently several Mambilla people stayed with Johnathan round the clock to protect him. I felt the need for X-rays to determine the extent of injury. So Abel Yiliyu, our trusty driver, took him to Serti for a flight to a hospital in Jos. Johnathan was tied onto three mattresses in the back of the vehicle. A staff member, Alexander Okan, accompanied him on the bumpy ride to give periodic injections of morphine. Never a dull moment!

The final decision was made to return home to Canada and stay there. The factors that we considered were as follows:

- The government take-over of Warwar hospital was complete. We had enabled a relatively smooth transition and all of the trained staff and laborers were on the government payroll and had a pension plan.

- The money from the government compensation for the takeover of Warwar hospital was received and enabled the building of missionary housing.

- The expatriate fund was used to build up the Bible school at Mbu.

- The trained hospital staff was capable of handling most medical issues, and it was hoped that a replacement doctor would be posted to Warwar.

- We felt the need to support our parents. My mom was a retired widow and I was her only child. Marion's mom had recently almost died of a heart attack and later required a pacemaker.

- Lori evidenced some difficulty in adjusting to life in Jos at her young age. She was increasingly insecure about herself and what she could do.

Not one of the above were individually reason enough to stay home in Canada. The combination of all of them helped us make the decision. After much prayer we felt God's guidance in this matter.

AND THEN THE PHONE RANG...

We stayed in Gembu for a week with Pete and May Schroeder to attend the Mambilla Baptist Convention General Conference. We flew to Jos for another week waiting for the Hillcrest school term to end. In preparation for the up-coming flights home Marion taught eight-month-old Paul what the word no meant. This was important for the crowded conditions in planes where food is served on tiny trays. On June 2, 1979 we flew out of Kano to Amsterdam and on to Chicago to meet and debrief with Dr. Schilke. The next flight took us to Minneapolis for medical examinations. Bruce observed that the airlines had special preboarding for handicapped and travelers with children. He piped up with the comment, "Dad, aren't you glad you have so many kids - we get to go on the plane first." While in Minneapolis we visited with Larry and Diana Hiller. Finally we flew home to Vancouver via Seattle, into the waiting arms of family and friends. What a joyous reunion!

CURT RADKE BUILDING AT WARWAR

BACK TO WARWAR

ESTHER (HOSPITAL MATRON AND MIDWIFE) AND STEPHEN LACKSON

ZEBULON WANMI (DISPENSARY ASSISTANT) & WIFE, KATIE

AND THEN THE PHONE RANG...

PAUL CHUFOR (DISPENSARY ASSISTANT) & WIFE ESTHER (MIDWIFE)

SABINA (MIDWIFE) AND GENESIS MAMLA

BACK TO WARWAR

SELINA, OUR HELPER, TEACHING LORI TO POUND CORN FOR FUFU

EXPLORING THE RESTHOUSE AREA

AND THEN THE PHONE RANG...

REV. PETER SCHROEDER WITH SEMINARY STUDENTS AND WIVES

MINNIE KUHN WITH A THEOLOGICAL EDUCATION BY EXTENSION CLASS

BACK TO WARWAR

PROUD SISTERS LOOK AFTER BABY PAUL – BORN OCT. 14, 1978

THE KIDS AT CHRISTMAS IN WARWAR 1978

CHAPTER 16

Canada – Our Home Again

INITIAL IMPRESSIONS

IT WAS A WONDERFUL EXPERIENCE to be greeted by many of our friends and family at the airport. The change in environment really struck us as we drove home. The roads were so clean and had traffic lanes. There was no garbage piled on the sides of the road. The homes were spotlessly clean. The people were so well dressed and lived such an affluent lifestyle compared to African standards. The church buildings were grand and even had padded pews and sound systems. Of course we knew all these things, but the sudden contrast to our Warwar experience still impressed us. Our old friends were much the same but their children had grown and changed so that they were hard to recognize initially.

We moved in with Oma to our family home on 49th Avenue in Vancouver. Oma had moved herself down to the basement suite and insisted that we occupy the main floor. Within a couple of days Marion's dad walked us a few blocks down to Main Street to a furniture store and made us pick a TV set for which he paid. It was his welcome-home gift. The kids were delighted. We soon had to censor some of the violent cartoons and shows that portrayed bad behaviour such as, "Roadrunner" and "Wiley Coyote." It was great for me to see news and sports like football and hockey. Marion enjoyed shopping for clothes and foods that were not available at Warwar.

CANADA – OUR HOME AGAIN

DEPUTATION

WE HAD TO VISIT OUR supporting churches as part of the home assignment as missionaries. Our retirement as missionaries was effective as of the end of 1979, so we began the deputation with a visit to Bismark, North Dakota to attend the NAB Triennial Conference. It was nice to see fellow missionaries who were also on furlough. A missionary orientation and deputation workshop was held at the Bismark Junior College following the Triennial sessions. Before our deputation schedule started in September we attended a family camp at Green Bay Bible Camp with the entire family. The deputation schedule was as follows:

- Sept. 9 – Fort George Baptist Church – Prince George, BC
- Sept. 11 – Bethel Baptist Church – Prince George, BC
- Sept. 12 – College Heights Baptist Church – Prince George, BC
- Sept. 16 – Zion Baptist Church – Terrace, BC
- Sept. 16 – Bethel Baptist Church – Prince Rupert, BC
- Sept. 23 – Rose of Sharon Baptist Church – Richmond, BC
- Sept. 28 – Bethany Baptist Ladies Fall Banquet, Vancouver, BC
- Sept. 30 – Bethany Baptist Church, Vancouver, BC
- Oct. 7 – Salt Creek Church – Dallas, Oregon
- Oct. 11-14 – Pacific Northwest Association – Olympic View Church, Tacoma, Washington State
- Oct. 21-28 – Missionary Conference – Edmonton, Alberta area churches
- Nov. 1-4 – B.C. Missionary Conference – Ebenezer Baptist Church, Vancouver, BC

- Nov. 7-11 – Missionary Conference – Magnolia & Harbour Trinity Churches, Los Angeles, California

- Nov. 14-18 – Missionary Conference – Okanagan Valley (BC side of the border)

- Nov. 24-25 – Lakeshore Baptist Church – St. Catherines, Ontario

- Nov. 25 – Getzville Church – Buffalo, New York

- Nov. 28 – Ridgemont Baptist Church, Detroit, Michigan – I stayed at the home of Uncle Herbert and Aunt Froh Hiller (senior pastor)

- Dec. 2 – Grosse Pointe Baptist Church – Detroit, Michigan

- Dec. 9 – Sunshine Ridge Baptist Church – Surrey, BC

This was a hectic schedule of sermons, reports, slide shows, and meeting people. I did most of the out-of-town visits alone as Marion stayed home to care for our four rascally children. She was able to join me at the Pacific Northwest Association, the Missionary Conference in Los Angeles, and at the Vancouver-area churches. We were able to renew our friendships with the Sparks family in Anaheim and the Rist family in Detroit, as well as have a longer visit with Uncle Herbert and Aunt Froh in Detroit.

The children soon made friends at church and in the neighbourhood. Bruce and Lori were enrolled in John Henderson elementary school just a three-blocks walk from home. They fit in quite well, made friends, and were up to speed in all their subjects. Living with Oma was wonderful for our children as they learned a lot about their heritage and German-Canadian customs.

SADNESS

CHRISTMAS TIME 1979 WAS A very sad time for our family. In mid-December Grandpa Asselstine became quite ill while visiting family in Kelowna. He was hospitalized as he developed a rapidly progressing pneumonia and then kidney failure. He died on December 18. His funeral was held on Christmas Eve at Alta Vista Baptist Church where he was a member. Grandma was feeling quite weak and shaky and was unable to sit in the front of the church, so we sat with her at the back of the church. A few minutes into the service she was on the verge of collapse and we picked her up and carried her home (two blocks away) to rest. Later in the day she rallied a bit so we took her to our place in Vancouver to have a Christmas Eve dinner and have her watch the grandchildren open a couple of gifts. She was unable to eat and collapsed again. She was taken to Burnaby hospital by ambulance and was examined by Dr. Ehsan Qureshi, a very competent internist. She had electro-mechanical dissociation which meant that her heart muscle was not responding to her pacemaker. The prognosis was extremely bleak. The siblings present at the time sadly had to decide not to proceed with heroic interventions that were most unlikely to benefit her. She died within minutes. Our comfort was that she was now with Jesus and with Grandpa and would not have to suffer grief and bereavement anymore. Thus a second funeral happened in the family in the space of one week.

FAMILY PRACTICE

THE DEPUTATION TIME WAS OVER and we were no longer missionaries. It was time to get back to medical work. I had to decide what to do – family practice or finish a surgical residency and become a general surgeon. I had a very tempting offer from Dr. Ted Robins, head of the surgery residency program at Vancouver General Hospital. He extended an offer to rejoin the residency program at the second-year level as he seemed to think I had a natural aptitude for surgery. I was tempted to accept this offer, but when I considered that it would take another three years of residency plus a year of fellowship training and then several years to build up a referral base, I declined the offer. It would have meant some years of near absence from my family to achieve this. This would not be fair to Marion and especially to the children who needed the presence of a father in their lives.

After Christmas I did a two-week *locum tenens* to care for the practice of a doctor in Burnaby who was going on a holiday. This doctor happened to be part of a group of Christian doctors doing family practice medicine together. The originals in the group were Dr. Alec Robertson and Dr. Kurt Gottschling, my former associates. During my time in Africa Drs. Don Wagar, David Jones, and Cliff Silverthorne were added to the group. At the end of my *locum tenens,* the group made me an offer to join them. I gladly accepted this offer as I was familiar with Burnaby General Hospital where they all practiced and I knew Drs. Robertson and Gottschling very well. They had purchased a building on Royal Oak Avenue in Burnaby, just north of Kingsway and had renovated the second floor to create a large clinic with five doctor's offices, ten examining rooms, a small lab and sterilizing room, a coffee room, washrooms, and a very large reception office and waiting room for patients. The building also had a pharmacy, laboratory, physiotherapy clinic, a dentist, an orthodontist, two other family practice groups, and specialist offices for a general surgeon, a neurologist, two neurosurgeons, a urologist, an internist, and a plastic surgeon. This was like a gift from heaven for me.

We had to reorganize the use of the office space as now there were six doctors but only five offices. The solution was for the doctors to work in the office four days a week. The fifth day would be used to do minor surgery at the hospital, visit patients in nursing homes, make house calls, complete reports to insurance companies, lawyers, and compose referral letters to specialists. As I was the latest addition to the group, I used the office of the doctor who was not in that day and thus rotated through the various offices. It was a bit awkward, but this forced me to keep my pile of paperwork small and easily portable from office to office. Because I moved to all of the offices I became very familiar with all of the nursing staff and their issues. Gail Golz soon joined the group as office manager and I worked with her in staff management, including hiring and, on rare occasions, firing staff.

All the new patients looking for a family doctor were referred to me by my associates, so I built up a full practice in a matter of months. I thank God that such provision was made, enabling me to support my family and have a satisfying career as a doctor.

CANADA – OUR HOME AGAIN

A NEW ADDRESS

LIVING ON 49TH AVENUE BETWEEN Main and Fraser in Vancouver and having a medical practice in south Burnaby meant a lot of driving to and fro. We were also a bit cramped in the family house with four growing children, so we decided to move to Burnaby together with Oma. We searched a long time for a house with enough bedrooms plus a suite for Oma. There was nothing suitable in the price range that we could afford. Then someone directed us to an area on the south slope of Burnaby where the Van Dyke brothers were developing a site of large freestanding family homes. We contacted the Van Dykes and they still had some lots available in an area just east of Gilley on Brynlor Drive. They showed us various floor plans of homes that they were prepared to build. They were all similar in size and quality. We chose one that they were ready to build with a request to have four bedrooms instead of three. The plot available for this house was on Pynford Court, a cul-de-sac of six lots, three of which were still unused. Our house at 6341 Pynford Court was built in six months and we moved there in October of 1980. The new house had a main floor, an upstairs level, and a beautiful basement suite for Oma. The property had a slope such that Oma's suite was almost a ground level entry – just 3 steps down. The upper floor had a master bedroom with an en suite bathroom, three bedrooms occupied by Joyel, Lori, and Bruce, and a bathroom for the four kids. Paul had a bedroom on the main floor that opened to the family room with a fireplace. I had a desk in the family room that served as a home office. Marion enjoyed a large kitchen with an adjoining eating area. The rest of the main floor had a laundry area, formal dining room, and a living room. Oma also had a small but adequate galley kitchen, bedroom, dining-living room, and bathroom. There were two large storage rooms as well.

We were able to purchase this home without having a mortgage. Oma sold the family home in Vancouver for just above her asking price. We had listed the house with a realtor, but before the realtor could get the listing completed, a man came to the door and made a cash offer above the asking price with no subjects to the purchase. He only asked that we wait for three days so he could free up money from his investments. Marion and I had

AND THEN THE PHONE RANG...

been able to save a bit of money during our time in Africa and I was now earning a good income. The combination of these sources of money, plus payment in stages of construction made it possible to avoid a mortgage. Again we were amazed at how God had provided for us.

A new address meant a new school for Bruce and Lori at Clinton Elementary. A new address also meant new neighbours and playmates. We became good friends with Gino and Josie Polisi and their sons, Marc and David. Dan and Darlene Gunther and their kids, Shane and Shelby, were also great neighbors. The mayor of Burnaby, Bill Lewarne, and his wife, June, lived behind us. Our backyards were separated by a hedge with a gap in it to pass through. We had many friendly chats with them.

A new address did not mean a new church. We remained members of Bethany Baptist Church, even if we had a long drive to south Vancouver to get there. A lot happened in our first year back home in Canada. We sensed God's leading in all of it.

BUILDING OUR NEW HOME ON PYNFORD COURT IN BURNABY

CANADA – OUR HOME AGAIN

BUILDING AND LANDSCAPING COMPLETED

AT THE NAB TRIENNIAL CONFERENCE IN BISMARCK, NORTH DAKOTA

AND THEN THE PHONE RANG...

BURNABY FAMILY PRACTICE ASSOCIATES — GOOFING OFF A BIT

OUR MEDICAL BUILDING ON ROYAL OAK & KINGSWAY IN BURNABY

CHAPTER 17

Family Practice in Burnaby

My family practice grew very rapidly and I was seeing 25 to 35 patients on an average office day. My associates kindly referred new patients to me to help build the practice. Many of the patients were Christians because our group was known in the church community as the Christian doctors. I was careful to treat all people equally, without bias or special favors just as I did in Africa. I soon discovered that I had made the right decision to be a family doctor. I really enjoyed getting to know people and caring for families over extended periods of time. There were times when a patient came complaining of a headache or a cold, but I could sense there was a much deeper issue going on.

Our medical group was doing full service family practice. This meant that we were on call day and night for our patients. We took turns being on call for all the group's patients at night and on weekends. There were no walk-in clinics. We also cared for our patients who arrived in the emergency department before there were any emergency room doctors. It was a bit of an adjustment to realize that I could not do C-sections and other surgery any more as such privileges were only given to specialists. However, I did do a lot of minor surgery at the hospital such as excision of skin lesions, D&Cs for incomplete miscarriages, cervical biopsies, and suturing lacerations. I also enjoyed assisting both general and subspecialty surgeons with major cases on patients from our group.

I received admitting privileges at Burnaby Hospital shortly after joining our family practice group. At the time such privileges were not easy to obtain. The fact that I had worked at the hospital for three years in the 1960's was probably considered. I was able to admit sick patients and was responsible for their care during their stay in hospital. Complicated cases were referred to the appropriate specialist as required. By admitting patients with odd symptoms that needed investigation, I was able to get a diagnosis quickly and start appropriate treatment. An example of this was a patient with strange aches and pains and weakness. He was admitted on a Monday and by Wednesday he had undergone blood tests, X-rays, nuclear bone scans, and a bone marrow aspiration. A diagnosis of multiple myeloma was made and by Thursday a hematologist saw the patient to confirm the diagnosis and start treatment. Thus early diagnosis and treatment was possible, avoiding long wait times at home for each individual test and another long wait to see a specialist.

I also enjoyed doing obstetrics and after some time ended up having the second most deliveries per year of all family practitioners in Burnaby. I was available to my pregnant patients even when not officially on call on nights or weekends. I scheduled at least 45 minutes at the end of an office day to counsel a couple who were having their first baby. I walked them through a typical labor and delivery and then described some common complications and how they were handled. This time spent with them was very helpful later if problems in labor developed and we had to resort to special measures, including the ultimate C-section. They understood and could cooperate with necessary actions. I had learned how to use a vacuum extractor while in Africa to help deliver babies that were stuck despite the mother's efforts at pushing. The procedure involves placing a metal or plastic cup on the baby's head and attaching tubing to a suction pump. This sucked a bit of the baby's scalp into the cup and attached the cup firmly to the head. One could then pull on a chain attached to the cup to help extract the baby as the mother pushed during a contraction. Early in my time at Burnaby hospital I had such a case where a vacuum extractor was helpful. It so happened that one of the obstetricians had brought one back from an obstetrical conference but it had never been used. The head nurse knew of its existence and found it in storage. I used it with good success. The next day the two hospital obstetricians investigated this and began to use it too, as vacuum extraction is much less traumatic to patients than forceps. There

AND THEN THE PHONE RANG...

were limitations to this procedure that I pointed out to the obstetricians. This was never to be used on a head that was not fully engaged into the mother's pelvis. Also, to use the vacuum cup to rotate the baby's head from a posterior position to an anterior position was absolutely contraindicated as this would cut a big hole in the baby's scalp. Vacuum extraction became so successful that one of the obstetricians began to teach this procedure to residents in obstetrics at Grace Hospital and Women's hospital.

Having done a lot of surgery in Africa, I felt confident in surgically repairing vaginal and perineal tears myself rather than calling in the obstetricians to do it. I had a case of a fourth-degree tear in a woman that involved the tearing of the vagina, perineum, rectal sphincter, and up into the rectum. The case room nurse saw this and asked me which of the obstetricians she should call to come in. I declined this offer, and with double gloves, did a systematic repair of the rectum, sphincter, vagina, and perineum myself. The result was excellent and the lady returned a few years later and had a successful vaginal delivery with no tearing at all.

There once was a dispute between the doctors of British Columbia and the Ministry of Health regarding the fee schedule as well as other issues. The doctors decided to close their offices for a day in protest at some of the government's decisions. We were still available for emergencies and went to the hospital to make rounds on our patients who needed daily care. I arrived at the hospital early that day to make rounds and on arrival heard a loud voice on the intercom, "Any obstetrician in the building please go to the case room immediately." No specialists were in the building at such an early hour so, a few minutes later, there was another urgent message over the loudspeaker, "Any doctor go to the case room immediately." At that moment Dr. Ed Dubland, a fellow family practitioner appeared. I said to Ed, "Are we any doctors?" We went up to the case room and saw nurses rapidly pushing a pregnant lady on a gurney down the hall to the operating room. Apparently she was in early labor and the baby was showing signs of severe distress. An emergency C-section was needed to save the baby. We quickly got into operating room gowns and scrubbed up while the anesthetist prepared the patient. There were four or five family doctors scrubbed and gowned in the room. The question was, "Who is going to do this C-section?" I was selected because I had done hundreds of them in Africa. The other doctors were assigned to resuscitate the baby. I was about to make the incision when Dr. John Warner, a urologist, came into the operating room. I told him that he had a license to make scars, handed the scalpel to him, and told him that I would help him. As we proceeded I had to remind him to reflect the bladder down before opening the uterus. He said, "Oh yes, bladder, ...I know bladders." In the end, I probably did three-quarters of the operation.

The issue of abortions presented a challenge. I refused to do abortions because I believed in the sanctity of life. The question was, "If life is given to us by God, what gives us the right to take life away?" The rule of the day was that a woman could have an abortion if the family agrees to it and if a second opinion from an obstetrician supported the abortion. With two letters from the doctors, the hospital would permit the procedure. Some family doctors feared they would lose patients if they refused an abortion request. That potential was real, and I was trying to build a practice. I decided not to even refer a patient for an abortion as this would make me a party to something that I felt was contrary to God's will. Patients requesting an abortion were given an appointment at the end of the day for a long talk. I listened to the patient's reasons for wanting the abortion and then presented my view in a very gentle manner. The patients were free to go to Planned Parenthood to get the procedure done. I told them that I would continue to care for them after the abortion and that I would never metaphorically throw stones at them. In return, I asked them not to throw stones at me because I had to live with my conscience. Most of the women who went for an abortion did return to my care. I recall one lady who angrily stormed out of my office after the long talk. Some time later, after her abortion, she showed up for an appointment. I told her that I thought I would never see her again as she was very angry during her last visit. Her reply was, "I came back because I can trust you to be honest with me; I hate the people who did the abortion."

Part of full-service family practice involved doing house calls. These were done for elderly patients who had trouble getting to the office. Most house calls were done after office hours and at night for acute situations. I had a black bag with a stethoscope, otoscope, and some sample oral and injectable medicines such as analgesics, Gravol, antihistamines, and antibiotics. I could initiate

AND THEN THE PHONE RANG...

treatment that night and write prescriptions for ongoing treatment. At times the patients had to be admitted to hospital. This required a trip to the hospital to write a history and orders. Some house calls were done for palliative care patients who were basically bed-ridden. Such calls provided emotional support and advice to the family care- givers. I tried to be available for patients with urgent health issues. There were several blank lines in the morning and afternoon in my appointment book so that patients could be attended to the same day. This worked quite well most of the time. But one lady phoned my office in the middle of a busy day and demanded an immediate house call for her child who had an earache. We told her to bring the child to the office and that I would see the child immediately on their arrival. The lady said she couldn't come because she was too busy doing her laundry. I was definitely not impressed!

I visited my patients in about ten different nursing homes on a regular monthly basis to monitor their condition as they slowly declined. I became the medical doctor in charge at Carleton Hospital and Willingdon Private Hospital. At these facilities I held regular care conferences with the head nurse, activity coordinator, physiotherapist, and dietician where we reviewed the care of the residents. The resident's family was also invited to attend. I summarized the conference findings, giving suggestions for further treatment or investigations in a note in the patient's chart and sending a copy to the patient's personal doctor.

There seemed to be a great need for counseling. Psychological issues were very prevalent, especially depression. There were not enough psychiatrists available and referral appointments took a long time. So when deep depressions were diagnosed, I had to handle them myself. Such patients were seen at the end of the appointment schedule for long talks. I became quite familiar with the various antidepressant medications and dealt with most cases myself.

Some patients required extra time to deal with difficult and unhappy diagnoses such as cancer and diabetes. There were times of grief and bereavement with the death of loved ones. Broken marriages, addictions, sexually transmitted diseases, and anxiety disorders kept me busy. A Kleenex box was a necessary item in each examining room.

Other times of counseling were much happier. There was an opportunity to share my faith on numerous occasions. One man came to see me because he just did not feel right. A complete history and physical exam revealed nothing wrong. He was sent for screening lab tests and the results were all normal. I examined him again in case something was missed the first time. Again, all was normal. As he sat on the exam table in his underwear, I told him that his problem was not physical, it was spiritual. He confessed his spiritual emptiness. I was able to share the good news of the gospel with him. With tears running down his face he prayed to accept Jesus as his Saviour and Lord. On a prescription sheet I wrote John 3:16 and told him to read it in his heretofore unused bible and then to begin reading the four gospels. I sent him within the hour to see Dr. Carlin Weinhauer, senior pastor at Willingdon Church, for follow-up – phoning him right away to set up this meeting. At a later time this patient shared his testimony with the church and held up the paper I had given him saying, "I got a prescription that gave me new life." Incidents like this encouraged me to continue serving in God's kingdom, and to be sensitive to the Holy Spirit's guidance in pointing people to Jesus.

I very much enjoyed working with my associates in the office. We would often consult each other in the hallway about difficult patient issues. Other times we would share a joke or story to help relieve the pressures of our work. Gail Golz, our office manager, was fun to work with. She was very helpful in solving staff issues and kept the office running like a well-oiled machine. We would interview prospective new staff together and then decide on whom to hire. One time we decided to release a staff member who was incompetent and a potential danger to our patients. When informed about the termination, this person began to pound the table and yell, "You can't do this, I won't be fired!" After settling her down, we escorted her quietly out of the door. I appreciated all of the nurses and their help as I rotated daily to a different office. Judy Nears was particularly helpful and kind to me. About 10 years after I joined the group, Dr. Alec Robertson retired. Dr. Ian Cameron took over the practice, but after a short time he left the group and was replaced by Dr. Phil Hanam. Dr. Don Wagar gave his office to Dr. Hanam and insisted that I occupy Dr. Robertson's old office, saying that it was his turn to rotate through the five offices. Now I had an office that was mine. Soon after this Lisa Henry was hired to be my nurse. She and her husband had just recently joined

AND THEN THE PHONE RANG...

Bethany Baptist Church. Lisa was very energetic, efficient, and cheerful. I was totally spoiled as she made sure that I was well supplied with coffee at all times. After she became pregnant with her third baby she retired. I was sad to see her leave. Judy Nears then became my nurse and, with her cheerful efficiency, made my life in the office very pleasant.

All of the doctors took time off for vacations and to attend postgraduate refresher courses. I particularly enjoyed attending the postgraduate medical conferences that were held in the sunny and warm regions of California and Arizona. We engaged the services of young, newly graduated doctors to look after our practices as locums. Dr. Phil Hanam was one of these locums. Later Drs. Ed Dubland, Peter Golin, and Wi Guan Lim served as locums as well. They were all Christians and fit in very well. As I got older I began to consider retirement. It was my desire to ultimately turn my practice over to a Christian doctor who would provide continuity of care. My patients had become my friends over many years. I saw some of the baby girls I delivered grow up, get married, and then become pregnant. I had the joy of delivering their babies and so became a "grandpa doc." I became increasingly worried that I might not find a replacement as walk-in clinics had recently started up. New doctors gravitated to these clinics as they were easy to work in and required no financial commitment. I finally found Dr. Tim Foggin, a Christian doctor, who was interested in buying my practice. The value of practices had plummeted over recent years. So in November 2003 I sold my practice to Dr. Foggin at a bargain price, feeling content that my patients would receive good on-going care. I was only 62 years old when I saw my last office patient.

I was too young to totally quit practicing medicine so I semi-retired. I initially did locums for our group. There were many requests for my services from other doctors in Burnaby and New Westminster. One locum was for four months for a doctor who had hip replacement surgery. One positive thing about doing locums was that I did not have to do mind-numbing paperwork such as reports to insurance companies and lawyers. I just put the requests for reports on a pile for the "real doctor" to do upon his return.

We moved to a townhouse at Carrington in South Surrey in 2003. The Morgan Creek clinic was a two-minute walk away from our home and they were looking for locum help. So I did a lot of locum work there, including shifts in an adjoining walk-in clinic. One of the doctors developed a serious illness and was off work for many months. I did a locum for him until he recovered. I finally stopped all medical work in January of 2012 at the ripe old age of 70. It was good to quit before making serious mistakes!

MEDICAL OFFICE PAPERWORK

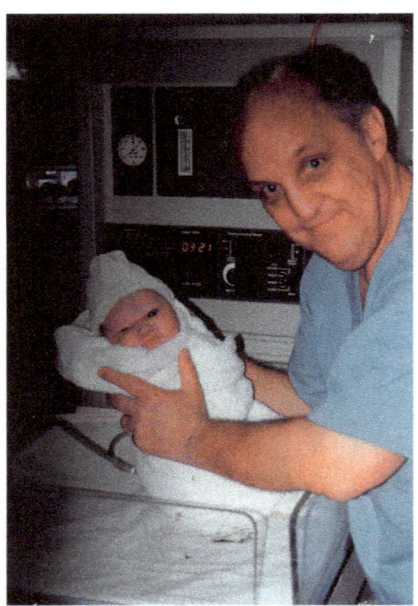

OBSTETRICS, A LARGE PART OF MY PRACTICE

AND THEN THE PHONE RANG...

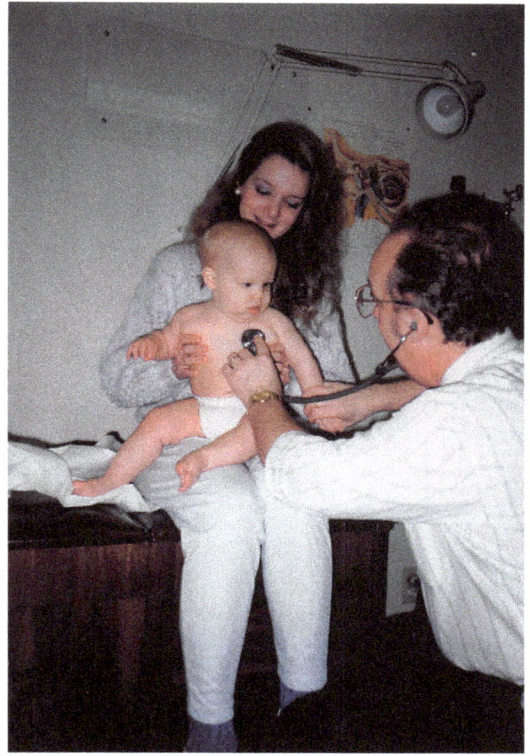

PEDIATRICS, A RESULT OF OBSTETRICS!

Jennifer, Bonnie, Tania, Patti, Judy
Gail & Melanie

OFFICE STAFF. FRONT LEFT - GAIL GOLZ (MANAGER), FAR RIGHT JUDY NEARS (NURSE)

FAMILY PRACTICE IN BURNABY

LISA HENRY (NURSE)

HALLWAY CONSULTATION WITH DR. KURT GOTTSCHLING

CHAPTER 18
The Family

We moved to our new house on Pynford Court, Burnaby in 1980. Our neighbours were also new to the newly developing area. We soon made friends. Our children had many playmates – Shane and Shelby Gunther, and Marc and David Polisi. Then old friends, Willi Strelau and Gordie and Irene Rathbun, moved into the neighborhood. Curt and Marva Radke, with their son Aaron, built a house behind us. Our kids and Aaron had easy access to both backyards via the gap in the hedge. The gang of children walked together to Clinton Elementary school with the older ones supervising the young when crossing streets. Later, my cousin Hans and his wife, Anita Hiller, moved into the Radke house with their boys, Bernie and Norm. There was a lot of exploring to do as our subdivision was located on the edge of a forested ravine. The boys built secret forts in the bush. We could hike down a steep trail on the edge of the ravine to the bottom where we crossed a wooden bridge over Byrne creek. At certain times we observed little fingerling salmon making their way down to the Fraser River. The top of the ravine had a long row of beautiful blackberry bushes which supplied us with fresh and frozen fruit and homemade blackberry jam. Two blocks away were a couple of tennis courts on the edge of the ravine. We used them often. A short walk from the tennis courts was the Edmonds SkyTrain station that provided rapid access to the Metrotown shopping center of Burnaby and to downtown Vancouver.

Marion developed close friendships with Josie Polisi and Darlene Gunther. They shared childcare, recipes, and coffee times. Marion started a Bible study with them plus Linda Sinclair and Mary Deans. It was good to see Josie and Darlene grow in their faith and ultimately join Bethany Baptist church. Marion had a small backyard vegetable garden and beautiful flowers in the front of the house. She also arranged music lessons for the children. Bruce and Lori had piano lessons with Irene Rathbun. They also had a few years of singing lessons. Joyel and Paul took violin lessons with Vic Wiens. At age four Paul wanted a violin, thinking it was just a toy. He was quite shocked when Marion signed him up for lessons. He also tried a trumpet but gave up when he got braces on his teeth. At age 14 he quit the violin because he thought it was not cool and instead started playing the guitar and drums.

As the children grew a bit older they each, in turn, made a public profession of faith in Jesus Christ as their Saviour and Lord. They were baptized at Bethany Baptist church at different times. They developed close friendships with their peers in the church. Joyel had a very close bond with Kristin Laser, daughter of our senior pastor Rick Laser. They had many sleepovers together. Paul and David were inseparable buddies. Bruce and Lori's friends included Troy Nikolai, Christine and Kathy Senges, Ron and Roger Liegmann, and many others. They enjoyed the youth activities and participated in a number of special musicals.

SCHOOL TRIP TO ISRAEL

BRUCE AND LORI ATTENDED BURNABY South High School which was within walking distance. They did very well academically, and while in grades 11 and 12 were enrolled in the International Baccalaureate (IB) Program which was an enriched educational course. This became a favourable resume item when applying for university admission. Bruce and Troy were in grade 11 when Fred Lepkin, their history teacher, arranged a tour of Israel for the IB students. This included Lori who was in grade 10. Fern Nikolai, Marion, and I went along on the trip as parent chaperons. There were about 25 students of different faith backgrounds on the trip. Fred Lepkin was Jewish and he brought his very orthodox Jewish mother along. We were impressed with the tight security when boarding an El Al plane in London en route to Israel. Our tour guide was an Israeli Zionist girl who grew up in the Oakridge area of Vancouver. She had to take a two-year university course to train as a registered guide. She knew the historical significance of all the sites we visited and their importance to Jews, Muslims, and Christians. Our bus driver was an Arab. The owner of the tour company was a Colonel of an elite Israeli paratrooper unit, so our guide was frequently in phone contact with him regarding safety issues on our trip. On one occasion we travelled in the middle of a tank brigade convoy, and another time travelled through a town that had been bombed by Katyusha rockets the previous day.

Among the many highlights on our trip were Masada; Jericho's archeological digs; the feast of Purim in Tel Aviv; a night at a kibbutz on Mount Carmel near Haifa; a trip up to the Golan Heights to Quneitra; swimming in the Red Sea, the Dead Sea and the Mediterranean Sea; a cruise on the Sea of Galilee; and finally seeing Nazareth and Bethlehem. We spent three days in Jerusalem during the passion week and visited the Shrine of the Holocaust (Yad Vashem), and the Museum of the Book containing the Dead Sea scrolls. We also toured the Knesset, touched the Wailing wall, got inside the Dome of the Rock built on the top of mount Moriah, and entered the Al Aqsa Mosque – the second most important Islamic site. Some thrilling moments were to see the Garden of Gethsemane with its 2000-year-old trees, and to climb the Mount of Olives to see the Kidron Valley below and the closed Eastern Gate of the temple mount. The view became even more interesting while sitting atop a camel. The highlight of the entire trip was to visit the supposed site of the garden tomb on Easter Sunday morning and see the empty tomb. It was raining at the time, but we went anyway to attend an English service at which the former Archbishop of Canterbury, Donald Coggan, spoke. In the middle of his sermon the rain stopped and suddenly a shaft of sunlight broke through the clouds. Donald Coggan paused his speech and then loudly proclaimed, "The Son is risen indeed!" That moment is etched in my memory forever.

THE FAMILY

AMUSING ESCAPADES

THE DAILY ROUTINES OF SCHOOL and work were punctuated by some amusing incidents. The following stories are only a few samples of events that became part of our family memories.

When Paul and David were about four-years old they discovered that tires had a stem with a cap on it. When the cap was screwed off they could press on the little pin inside the stem and hear an interesting hissing sound. One day there was a knock on our door. A workman on a house construction crew working next door asked Marion if we had noticed flat tires too. Apparently Paul and David made daily rounds on the worker's vehicle and flattened tires. There were some very stern words spoken to the boys by their Mamas! Another time the two rascals played demolition derby with their toy cars and completely ruined Paul's beautiful new Tonka truck that Oma had given him. Marion told the boys that they would have to earn enough money to buy a new truck. So she put them to work pulling weeds out of the garden for a half-hour. This was sheer drudgery for the little boys. They were paid a wage that was half the amount that Oma would earn in one hour. Marion then trotted them off to the store to buy a new truck. The boys were shocked that after all their hard work the money earned was barely enough to buy a tiny little matchbox car. They now realized how hard and long Oma had worked in order to buy the nice big Tonka truck. They never had another demolition derby!

Joyel had a terrible time in grade three. She was discovered to have a problem with dyslexia and really struggled to catch on to reading, writing, and spelling. One day she dropped her ruler on the floor just as the teacher walked down her aisle. The teacher tripped on the ruler, fell to the floor, and injured her leg. The teacher had to be taken to the hospital by her husband. Poor Joyel was terrified as she thought she had killed her teacher. To make matters worse, at a later time, Joyel felt unwell and suddenly vomited all over the same teacher's foot. It was not a good year for Joyel. However, she did learn that hard work brought her success and that ethic allowed her to enter into post-secondary education.

Lori wanted to learn how to drive a manual stick shift car, so Bruce offered to teach her. Somehow Lori just could not co-ordinate the clutch and stick-shift maneuver smoothly. The neighbours were all amused to watch the car lurching and jerking up and down the road with tires squealing in protest. On the way to the beach one day Lori was in the back seat of a car beside a young male friend. This friend suddenly put his arm around Lori's shoulders. Lori's reaction was to hold her hair brush, with stiff bristles, right under the young fellow's nose and threaten to push it up very hard if he did not remove the offending arm. As a father I was glad to learn that Lori could manage such a situation very well.

Joyel had her very own pet guinea pig named Piggy that she adored. One day the guinea pig died. Bruce was given the task of providing a suitable burial for the poor pet in the ravine next to our street. Bruce foolishly decided to take a short cut. Instead of burying the poor guinea pig as directed, he hurled it high into the air hoping that it would land out of sight deep in the ravine. The hamster soared high into the air but, instead of sailing into the ravine, it got caught up in the branches of a tree. There it hung in plain view and out of reach for retrieval. The following morning we all piled into our station wagon to go to church. There in the infamous tree was the guinea pig for all to see. I refused to stop the car and get the guinea pig down because we would be late for church. Bruce was certainly in the proverbial dog-house for a long time as far as Joyel was concerned.

The station wagon was a great family car but it had some disturbing quirks. On one occasion it suddenly lost power as Bruce was driving down a tight spiral parkade ramp. With no power brakes, Bruce managed to get the car down but in the process scraped the entire length of one side of the car along a cement barrier. This car also had the habit of spontaneously sounding the horn in a constant blare whenever the temperature plunged below freezing. One frosty night the phone rang, waking me up. A neighbour asked me to do something about my noisy car that was parked outside. I put on my kimono, went outside and, with a flashlight in my mouth, looked under the hood. I finally found a wire to pull to shut off the horn. I was glad to finally trade that car in for a new one.

One year our neighbourhood was infested by chafer beetles that settled in our lawns. The local raccoons were delighted. They proceeded to tear up the lawns to catch and eat the beetles. Mr. Ho, our next door neighbour from Taiwan, decided to trap the raccoons and save his beautiful lawn.

THE FAMILY

The next morning he was seen carrying his trap at arm's length towards the ravine. He was wearing a face mask and a full length smock. We nearly died laughing when we realized that he had trapped a skunk.

FAMILY TRIPS

WE ENJOYED TRAVELLING WITH OUR children and many fond memories were built. The following are short summaries of some special ones.

1980 Spring Break in Fernie

We drove to Fernie to visit Ben and Joy Warkentin. Wilf and Sharon Loch and their children, Janice and Darryl joined us on this trip. The mountains were beautifully covered in late spring snow. The Warkentin's home was on a hill, adjacent to a ski resort, and overlooking the town of Fernie. The kids loved swimming in their pool and being taken on 4x4 truck rides in the snow. We revived the hootenanny tradition of singing, accompanied by Ben's guitar and my ukulele. "Ticklish Reuben" was the children's favourite song. Their well water pump failed one day so we had to use their outhouse. The outhouse had no door on it because there was a spectacular view of the Fernie valley below. Needless to say, the ladies were not thrilled about this!

1982 Summer around British Columbia

With the station wagon loaded, we set off on a tour of B.C. We took the ferry to Nanaimo and drove up to Port Hardy to stay overnight. We then got on a big ferry that took us up to Prince Rupert. Part of this voyage was through open unsheltered waters of the Pacific Ocean. The waves were quite big and the rocking ship made Paul nauseated. As he vomited, Marion tried to hold him over the railing. I pulled them back for fear that Paul would accidentally be dropped into the ocean. A sailor with a water hose and mop came along and cleaned up the mess. The rocking helped us all get to sleep in our tiny staterooms. The drive from Prince Rupert to

AND THEN THE PHONE RANG...

Terrace and Hazelton wound along the bank of the Skeena River part of the way. The scenery was spectacular. After a night in Smithers, we travelled on through Prince George to Barkerville. Barkerville was a major site of the gold rush times. The old town had preserved buildings, including a chapel, general store, hotel, theatre, and a saloon. We enjoyed panning for gold dust. The boys were particularly interested in the dancing girls doing the can-can on a stage in the theatre and laughed heartily at the jokes and tall tales of the actors. A week at family camp in West Kelowna marked the end of our trip.

1983 Spring Break in Florida

We joined Bob and Nancy Hepting on a trip to Florida. Nancy's sister and brother-in-law owned a motel in Boca Raton that was made available for us to use. Orlando was our first destination and of course a visit to Disney World and Epcot Center was mandatory. We rented cars and drove to Cape Canaveral for a tour of the aero-space center. The rockets and launch gantries were immense. The next drive took us down the center of Florida to Lake Wales. We noticed many poor folks that lived in tiny shacks along the roadside. In Lake Wales we attended a performance of the life of Christ in an open-air theatre bowl. Live donkeys, sheep, camels, and cows were used. It was a very impressive production. We headed for the west coast to Fort Myers and Sanibel Island where beaches were covered with beautiful shells that the kids insisted on collecting. We managed to throw the shells out when they got too stinky. We then crossed over to the east coast via Alligator Alley. This road went through miles of swampland, home to alligators. The motel in Boca Raton was one block from a beautiful beach, so swimming was on the agenda. Unfortunately, Joyel got stung by a big jellyfish that caused a red welt on her leg. She howled loud and long. Marion finally told her, "Stop crying, you are not going to die!" Joyel blinked and said, "I'm not going to die?" Poor child thought this was a terminal condition and wondered why we weren't sad about her imminent demise. We found an aloe vera plant and squeezed out some soothing fluid to apply to her leg. Before returning home we drove to Fort Lauderdale for a short cruise on the inner waterway to see the huge private homes complete with yachts moored along the landscaped yards. We saw a man wrestling an alligator at a marine zoo which really thrilled the kids.

1984 Summer in Yellowstone

This was an action packed two-week trip. We drove to Spokane the first day. The next day was Sunday, so we had church in the car by listening to a sermon and music by Hale and Wilder. We drove through Coeur d'Alene to Missoula in time for lunch. Butte was the destination that day. On Monday we toured the Lewis and Clark Caverns, going 200 feet deep into the cave to see stalactites, stalagmites, and pop-corn formations. The scenery along the Madison River was beautiful as was Yellowstone Park where we stayed at a rustic cabin in Canyon Village. After supper we went for a drive to see wild animals – elk, bison, swans, Canada geese, bald eagles, herons, ducks, a moose swimming in a river, and a coyote that we almost ran over. The next day we drove to Roosevelt Lodge and got on a horse-drawn covered wagon for a ½ hour ride to Pleasant Valley where a cook had a huge breakfast ready for us. We did more hiking and horseback riding to see many more animals. We toured sulphur pools, mud pots, and painted pots on foot, and saw the Old Faithful Geyser erupting. A number of days were spent going on a hike, a boat tour on Yellowstone Lake, a three-hour raft trip down the Snake River, more horseback rides, and a tour through the Grand Teton mountains. There was one sour note on this trip. I got a speeding ticket as we left Yellowstone early on a Sunday morning. I was doing 59 mph in a 45 mph zone on a straight empty road. A park ranger stopped me and Joyel began to cry, thinking that he was going to put me in jail. The way home included a stop in Missoula, a visit with Ben and Joy in Fernie, a hill slide in Kimberly, swimming in both Fairmont and Radium Hot Spring pools, water slides in Vernon, and finally visits with Kelowna relatives.

1985 Summer in California

The NAB Triennial was to be held in Anaheim in 1985, so we planned an extended holiday in California. As Bruce was now 16 and the holder of a driver's licence, he got to drive considerable distances. He had to be very careful as we watched him like hawks! We spent three days visiting Shirley and Don in Oakland. Tours were made of Berkeley University, Fisherman's Wharf, and Alcatraz prison. Fun rides included the Bay Area Rapid Transit, cable cars, and the ferry to Alcatraz. The small cells and the solitary confinement area were scary. The next two days were spent in Carmel-by-the Sea. There we built a sand castle on the beach and watched the July 4th fireworks. Then on to Los Angeles via King City and Santa Barbara on highway 101. There was a lot of smoke from huge forest fires along the way. We stayed with A.G. and Vicki Sparks for three days, one of which was spent at Huntington Beach where we built another huge sand castle. Touring the Universal Studios movie lot was fun. San Diego was our next destination where we stayed for three days. We enjoyed Mexican food in the Old Town, as well as the lively mariachi music. Sea World and the San Diego Zoo were spectacular entertainment for the kids. On a cruise of the San Diego harbour we saw huge tuna fishing boats and the U.S. navy fleet, including an aircraft carrier. Heading north we had an all day tour of the Wild Animal Park near Escondido. It was interesting to ride a monorail through the park and see lions close-up and giraffes, elephants, zebras, and all types of antelopes sharing water holes. The monkeys and apes kept things lively.

The NAB Triennial was held in the Anaheim Convention Center. We stayed in a motel that was three blocks away from DisneyLand – very convenient. One night it was Paul's turn to pray before bed-time. His prayer included a request that God would protect Oma from being "low-jacked." He knew that lately several airplanes had been hijacked, so he explained that Oma was coming to the Triennial on a bus with a senior's group from Vancouver. Buses were on the ground and therefore could be "low-jacked." We laughed about that for a long time. There were some excellent speakers at the Triennial. Rev. E. V. Hill touched on the controversy between saving souls by only preaching the gospel versus winning people by first meeting their pressing needs first such as health, poverty, education etc. He explained that it was not one or the other but both, as in a baseball game, where getting someone to home plate first requires them to get to first base. We noticed this during our time in Africa as people were more ready to hear and accept the gospel after we dealt with their pain.

It was at this Triennial that I was elected to the NAB Board of Missions along with Dr. Jerry Fluth, Harold Lang, Wayne Bibelheimer, Herman Effa, Maria Rogalski, and Jim Biggerstaff. We had time to visit Disneyland, Knott's Berry Farm, attend the Evangelical Free Church where Charles Swindoll preached, and attend Calvary Chapel where Chuck Smith spoke. This long California trip really enriched our lives.

1986 Expo in Vancouver

We travelled on numerous occasions from Burnaby to downtown Vancouver on the new Skytrain to visit the many pavilions set up at the Expo site by False Creek. Bruce and his friend Troy Nikolai had student summer jobs there and were able to earn money for future school fees. People from all over the world came to Expo and this event really put Vancouver on the map as an international city of note. There was an air of excitement that was heightened by the visit of Prince Charles and Princess Diana. Many countries constructed pavilions to exhibit their unique special features. We noted that one Arabian pavilion had a large map of the Middle East that had the label Palestine in place of Israel. We asked an attendant about this and just got a blank stare in return.

1987 Spring Break in Arizona

It was nice to bask in the warm sunshine of Arizona in March and escape the cold and wet climate of Vancouver. We flew to Phoenix, rented a car and drove to Tempe where we made our headquarters in a nice motel with a pool and tennis courts. In Tucson we toured the Arizona Sonora Desert Museum and the Mission San Xavier del Bac. It was interesting to see all the types of cacti and desert animals. We also got to Sedona to see the arts colony and the many shops containing desert paintings, ceramics and fabrics. On the way back to Tempe we detoured east and up a steep climb to the famous Pinnacle Peak restaurant. It was famous as a place where patrons were not allowed to wear a necktie. If you arrived with one on, the staff would ring bells and blow horns and then ceremoniously cut the tie off with huge scissors and nail it to the rafters. Paul insisted on wearing one of my old ties so he could experience this event. The food was simple cowboy fare but very tasty.

1988 Triennial in Calgary

The meeting in Calgary was an opportunity for the extended Hiller clan to meet and enjoy each other's company. We spent the first night at Three Valley Gap and toured the beautiful gardens. The indoor pool was a hit with the kids. A Hiller reunion party was held at Harry Hiller's home in Calgary. The senior generation was represented by Oma, Bruno and Agnes, Herbert and Frohmut, Arthur and Ilse Hiller. The Triennial sessions were held in the Saddledome while 1100 youth held their gathering at the University of Calgary campus. Rev. Peter Jumvuh and Zebulon and Katy Wanmi from Nigeria attended as guests. We took them up an elevator to the 12th floor of our hotel to see the view. They were shocked to look down from the balcony to see people so far below. They had never been that high before.

After the Triennial we toured the Canada Olympic Park, site of the 1988 winter Olympics. We then spent a day in Banff before heading up to Edmonton. The kids really enjoyed the West Edmonton Mall water park with its wave pool and gigantic slides. The mall was too huge for Oma to walk in so she rented a scooter and ended up doing more shopping than the rest of us combined! Pete and May Schroeder hosted us for two nights. The next leg of our trip was to Jasper where we stayed in the Jasper House Bungalows with Rick and Lily Laser and Kristin. The beautiful scenery and wild animals reminded Marion and me of our honeymoon time in Jasper. We then travelled down the Columbia Icefield highway, stopping on the way to tour the glacier on a huge snow-mobile bus. At that time the foot of the glacier was only several hundred yards away from the highway. We spent a day in Radium Hot Springs with Ben and Joy Warkentin where we swam in the hot pools and went on horseback rides. The final destination was Green Bay for a week of family camp.

THE FAMILY

1989 Christmas in Hawaii

For a unique experience we decided to spend Christmas in Hawaii. Oma and her good friend Auntie Katie Sturhahn joined us. Coincidentally, Harry Hiller and sons Nathan and Drew had the same Christmas plan. So we enjoyed the expanded family time together in Honolulu. The Christmas decorations in the malls and stores were incredibly elaborate. On Christmas day the town looked like a ghost town with very few people to be seen. Swimming in the ocean with big waves was challenging. We soon learned to keep our eyes on the incoming waves to avoid getting bowled over when a large rogue one came. Feeding the fish at a bay near Diamond Head was fun. The huge number and variety of fish was impressive. With snorkel masks on we could follow them as they cavorted in the coral. On Christmas day morning we went to Waikiki beach for a church service. We sat on grass mats on the sand and watched Hawaiian ladies wearing muumuus and leis dancing hula style while singing Christmas carols. Their movements helped depict the story of the song. They were joined by cute little girls dancing along with them. A pastor then gave a nice Christmas message. On Boxing Day, which Americans don't know about, the streets and shops of Honolulu were filled with throngs of people. Many had flown to Hawaii that day to start their vacation time. For us it was time to say Aloha and Mahalo and head for our wintry home.

1991 June 4 – 25th Wedding Anniversary

Our children and Oma hosted a dinner for us at a local hotel and invited many of our family and friends. They even presented a bit of a programme with music and skits. They then helped us with an open house event at our home. Marion actually managed to fit into her wedding dress. Sharon Loch prepared a beautiful wedding cake for the occasion. Darlene Gunther poured tea for the many guests.

Marion and I went for a second honeymoon to Lake Louise and Banff. We wanted to repeat the honeymoon at Jasper Park Lodge, but the prices there were too high. We enjoyed getting away by ourselves to relax in the beauty of nature and to soak in a jacuzzi tub. The food in Banff Springs Hotel was fabulous.

1991 Triennial in Milwaukee

Triennials were a great time to have family gatherings and to meet with long time friends. This Triennial was no exception. A highlight at the conference was the missionary evening where we met with many fellow missionaries and swapped stories over coffee and sweets. The commissioning of new missionaries was especially moving for us. The youth had their own program at a separate location. We were able to get to a major league baseball game between the Milwaukee Brewers and the Kansas City Royals. The party atmosphere was interesting as people loaded up on hotdogs and beer and visited with each other. They only looked at the game when someone actually hit a baseball. After the Triennial the extended Hiller clan travelled to the Wisconsin Dells and enjoyed a Duck Boat river cruise before heading for home. Paul was thrilled to race go-karts and Oma even played a round of miniature golf!

Palm Springs

In the 1990's Marion and I travelled to Palm Springs in late March and early April. The kids were old enough to manage on their own for a week or two, with Oma's supervision. These times were relaxing. The hectic pace of family medical practice plus many church obligations tired us out. We enjoyed the company of many Bethany friends vacationing there as well. Poolside suntanning and dining out together were favourite activities, especially at restaurants like Tony Roma's and Marie Callendars. We played a lot of tennis, went shopping, and explored Palm Springs Canyon, Desert Hot Springs, Joshua Tree National Park, Rancho Mirage, Indian Wells, and Indio's weekly flea market. On one occasion we took an all-day bus trip to Lake Havasu in Nevada where we went on a paddlewheel boat trip followed by a buffet dinner in the casino. I borrowed some coins from Trudy Zindler and put a quarter in a slot machine on our way to dinner. The machine spluttered and coughed out a whole pile of quarters. I put another

THE FAMILY

one in the slot and out came another pile. I quit on the spot while I was ahead. My winnings totalled $25 which was enough to pay for the entire excursion for two ($8 per person for the bus and dinner). We visited local churches on Sundays and for the first time we experienced worship teams with guitars leading the congregational singing. At one church we were astounded that there was no prayer, no scripture reading, and sermons that were totally psychobabble.

1999 Summer in New York

Julie Pleines was getting married, and we were invited to attend. Marion and I took Lori and Joyel along and left the boys with Oma. Rich and Ruth Pleines graciously hosted. They rented a nearby home that we shared with Larry and Diana Hiller. The wedding reception was held in a most elegant setting. After the wedding Ruth and Rich took the Hiller clan on a fantastic tour of Manhattan. We started with a three-hour boat tour going all around Manhattan to get a general orientation. The tour guide was extremely humorous as he described what we were seeing. Among the sights were Ellis Island and the Statue of Liberty in the distance, the World Trade Center and its twin towers, Wall Street, the Empire State building, the United Nations buildings, Spanish Harlem, Columbia University, and Riverside Church to name a few. Using the subway system, Rich took us all over Manhattan. We saw the New York Stock Exchange, Little Italy, and went to the top of the Empire State Building to see the incredible view. Rich knew an official working in the United Nations complex and got him to take us on a personal tour inside, even into the Security Council Chamber. We then walked a bit into Central Park and also into the ornate atrium of the famous Astoria Hotel. We walked by the Carnegie Hall theatre and ate supper at the Carnegie Deli across the street. This deli was renowned for their rude waiters and huge servings of food. Our waiter came to us and snarled, "Wadda ya want?" The pastrami on rye was delicious and one slice of New York cheesecake was almost too big for four of us to share! T.V. cameras were filming a commercial and the girl speaking stood right behind me, so I photobombed one take by waving and mouthing the words, "Hi mom." We all had a good laugh, as did the T.V. crew. One night we went to the Gershwin theatre to see the Broadway show Peter Pan. We attended a New York Yankees baseball game in Shea Stadium. Aunt Frohmut came along and we were most amused by watching her chat at length with a young man who came with a girl on their first date. The girl was not too impressed with this older lady grabbing the attention of her beau! Oh yes, the game was entertaining too.

The Hiller clan travelled by car through Delaware to Hershey, Pennsylvania. The tour of the Hershey chocolate factory was interesting, but the best part was getting free samples of chocolate at the exit. We then drove into Amish country to see the well manicured farms of the Amish people. They were dressed in old fashioned clothes and travelled around in horse drawn buggies. It was funny to see a horse and buggy standing at a red light on a road with no cars in sight. A highlight was going to the Stoltzfus Farm Restaurant for supper. The food was served in large bowls that were passed around the table just like at home. The bowls were refilled as often as needed. The food was delicious. For dessert we had their famous Shoo-fly pie which was a molasses pie with many raisins (flies). We roared with laughter when we noticed that our road had to pass through the village of Intercourse to get to the town of Paradise!

2001 Alaska Cruise

Our kids had never been on an ocean cruise, so we planned a four-day Alaska mini-cruise and included Oma. She was 88-years old and unsteady on her feet. We borrowed a wheelchair from our church and wheeled her on board to her special stateroom with a wide door and easy-access bathroom. Our kids took turns pushing Oma all over the ship to ensure that she would not miss out on anything. We had our own dining table so we got to know the waiter very well. Everyone was impressed with the fabulous menu offerings in the Lido buffet and dining room. Oma always had a nap after lunch. We showed her how to order room service by pushing the special button on her cabin phone. After waking from a nap she would call room service and with delight receive a big carafe of coffee and several cookies. Bruce and Paul also called room service for hotdogs and hamburgers at midnight! We sailed the inside passage up to Ketchikan

Alaska where we shopped for souvenirs. The kids went on an excursion for a scuba diving adventure, wearing wet suits in the frigid ocean waters. We attended all of the evening entertainment shows and especially enjoyed the magician's performance. We were sad when the cruise came to an end as we had so much fun together. On disembarking Oma asked if she could take the phone with the special room service button home with her.

OLDER, BUT NOT OLD

BRUCE

Bruce graduated from Burnaby South High School in 1987, having completed the enriched International Baccalaureate program. He was accepted into the University of British Columbia (UBC) and graduated with a Bachelor of Science in Microbiology in 1991. He immediately started medical school at UBC and graduated in 1995 with his M.D. degree. At this time he moved out of our home to share an apartment with Ron Liegmann and Dezene Huber near Lougheed Mall. After one year, Bruce and Dezene moved to an apartment near Kingsway. After completing medical school he started a residency program in internal medicine. This involved four years of work primarily in Vancouver General Hospital. He then spent six months at the London School of Tropical Medicine and Hygiene and six months in Toronto doing peri-operative care of high-risk patients. In 2000, he received his Fellow of the Royal College of Physicians which qualified him to be a specialist consultant in internal medicine. He returned home to live with us for two years while doing *locum tenens* work for general internists in White Rock, Burnaby, and Penticton. He then settled into his own practice as a consultant at Burnaby General Hospital. During this time Bruce secretly took flying lessons. When we discovered this Marion asked in a panic, "Bruce, did you pray about this first?"

Oma, Marion, and I were planning to move to a townhouse in South Surrey where Oma could be on one level. Deciding to sell the family house in Burnaby, we gave Bruce the first right of refusal to purchase the home. He accepted this immediately, but I made him think it over for at least a week before making a final decision. So in 2002, he bought our family home. More importantly in late 2002 he became romantically interested in a very nice girl by the name of Kelly Marsh. On one date he flew Kelly to the Chilliwack airport that served excellent pies in their restaurant. Kelly was a brave girl! The romance blossomed into love. Bruce flew Kelly to Penticton where he proposed at the spot where they had shared the first kiss early in their courtship. They got married on September 25, 2004 at Bethany Baptist Church.

Bruce served as an elder at Bethany Baptist Church and Kelly was on the board of the Bethany Daycare Society. They later transferred to Faith Baptist Church where Kelly had many friends, and became involved in a new church plant in the River District of Vancouver. On March 17, 2009 Ben was born, followed by Abby on March 9, 2011 and finally Kaitlyn on December 26, 2013. We were most delighted to welcome these beautiful children into the family. Being grandparents is a real blessing.

Bruce became increasingly dissatisfied with the working conditions at the Burnaby General Hospital. After searching for a different place, Bruce and Kelly moved to Comox and bought a nice home in a quiet neighbourhood on the edge of a forest and a high school playing field. Within a year, Bruce was appointed chief of medicine at the newly built hospital. He then purchased one floor of a quaint building on the main street of Comox and renovated it to provide medical offices for five other internal medicine specialists who rented space from Bruce. The place is known as the Comox Valley Internal Medicine Clinic. Bruce and Kelly also became involved with a Baptist church in Courtney. We enjoy travelling to Comox to join them in their adventures and to play with our grandchildren.

LORI

Lori graduated from Burnaby South High School in 1988 also having completed the International Baccalaureate program. She was accepted as a student at UBC where she took one year of general science courses and then four years in the nursing program. Lori graduated in 1993 with a Bachelor of Science in Nursing degree. She worked as an on-call nurse at Burnaby General Hospital for a year. In 1994 she went to Capernwray Bible School

THE FAMILY

in Carnforth near the Lake District in England. After we dropped her off at the Vancouver airport I went home and cried, because my little girl was going all alone into the dangerous world with no daddy to protect her. She enjoyed her experience there, made lots of friends, and travelled much of Europe. On arriving home, she worked for the next two years as a nurse in Burnaby General Hospital. In 1997 Lori went on a six-week short term mission trip to Burkina Faso, landing first at the Ouagadougou airport. She travelled to places like Piela, Fada Ngourma, Diapaga, and Djibo (near the border of Mali). There were opportunities to help in a Bible school and a health center and to observe mission work among the Fulani nomadic people. She learned a lot about desert life and even sat out a sandstorm in Djibo. On returning home she used her nursing skills in the Burnaby Home Health program.

In 2000 Lori responded to God's call to short term missionary work in Cameroon. She worked in a village health program based out of Banso Baptist Hospital. This involved quite a bit of traveling to hold clinics in outlying areas. In 2001, she became a tutor at the Private Training school for Health Personnel at Banso Baptist Hospital. On returning home Lori resumed casual work in the Burnaby Home Health Program while also working on a Masters degree in Nursing and Midwifery. She completed this in 2005. Part of the degree program involved a six-month practicum in La Crosse Wisconsin. Marion and I drove with Lori to Wisconsin in a wintery cold February. A major blizzard followed us all the way through Idaho, Montana, Wyoming, and South Dakota. We managed to stay eight to 12 hours ahead of the storm.

Lori returned to Banso Baptist Hospital in 2005 to teach nursing and midwifery. She was able to take short trips home to see Joyel's baby, Elijah in 2006 and to attend Paul and Juliet's wedding in 2007. After a year of furlough in 2009 she returned to Banso for one more year during which she handed over her position of midwifery tutor to a capable Cameroonian midwife. Mentorship and transferring leadership to Cameroonians was a satisfying accomplishment for Lori and the NAB Mission.

In 2011, Lori came home to stay. She initially worked in a high risk out-patient antenatal clinic in Surrey. In late 2011 Lori was hired to the teaching staff in the nursing school at the British Columbia Institute of

Technology. Her area of teaching was Home Nursing Care. She continued to live with us until 2013 when she bought a two bedroom condo unit on the New Westminster Quay. Her place is on the 15th floor with a beautiful view of the Fraser River. Lori became active in Bethany Baptist Church, serving on the Missions Committee, Welcome Committee, Refugee Sponsorship Committee and also the Church Board. She also served a term on the board of the Evergreen Baptist Home in White Rock. Lori is a specially loved Auntie to seven nephews and nieces, whom she loves to spoil. She also insisted on doing the shopping for the elderly and vulnerable Auntie Shirley, Marion, and me during the COVID-19 pandemic lockdown in 2020.

JOYEL

Joyel graduated from Pacific Academy High School in 1993. She then attended Taylor University College in Edmonton from 1994 to 1997, obtaining a Bachelor of Christian Studies degree. She lived in the girl's dormitory and developed many close friendships including Tammy, Lisa, and Mel. Tammy Enockson graduated with Joyel and came to live with us for about six months before going home to North Dakota. During Joyel's time at Taylor she was part of a team that did two short-term mission trips to Poland. She returned to Poland alone in 1997 for another year of mission work. I was really concerned when we dropped her off at the airport as she seemed a bit confused about which way to go to the boarding gate. Her flight was to arrive in Warsaw at midnight and then she was to connect onto a flight to Gdansk. My fatherly instinct took over as I imagined her wandering around alone in the Warsaw airport trying to find the next boarding gate. After a few agonizing tears at home, I phoned the mission agency and discovered that someone was assigned to meet Joyel at the Warsaw airport. Joyel lived with a missionary family in Gdansk and quickly learned to speak and read Polish. My father, who grew up in Poland, would have been very proud of her.

After her return from Poland, she went to Simon Fraser University in Burnaby and graduated in 2001 with a Bachelor of Arts degree with a major in History and a minor in English as a Second Language. She then spent

THE FAMILY

a year at Regent College in Vancouver on the UBC campus. She earned a Diploma of Christian Studies in 2002. In late 2002, Joyel caught the eye of a young scholar, Dezene Huber. He had a Ph.D. degree in Biological Sciences from Simon Fraser University, and was involved in the youth and college age programs at Bethany. Joyel and Dezene went on several casual dates and decided to get more serious about their relationship over fine dining at the Bavaria Haus in New Westminster. The romance progressed rapidly. One day Marion and I were flying home from Palm Springs and Dezene firmly insisted that he would pick us up from the airport. On the drive home he asked our permission to marry Joyel. We readily agreed to this. The next morning as we were preparing a Sunday breakfast, Joyel appeared in a nice fancy dress and began to help with the preparations. We suddenly noticed a fancy engagement ring on her finger. Dezene had wasted no time! A few months later they got married on August 16, 2003 at Bethany Baptist Church. Joyel was not very interested in my suggestion of renting a wedding dress. I felt this would be much cheaper as she would only be wearing it for a few hours. Deep in my heart I knew my idea was not going to go very far. Walking her down the aisle was special and, part way down, I slowed her down so as to savour the moment.

DEZENE AND JOYEL MOVED TO Davis, California, after their honeymoon. In 2005 Dezene completed his work at the University of California Davis. Joyel taught at a Sylvan learning center for kids with learning issues. Dezene searched for a university teaching position and was accepted into the faculty at the University of Northern British Columbia in Prince George, British Columbia (UNBC). He gradually worked his way up the ranks from Assistant professor, to Associate, to Professor with full tenure. Joyel also taught ESL courses at UNBC. They initially rented a house for a short time and then bought a nice home in the College Heights area, just a short walk away from College Heights Baptist Church. In 2012, Joyel was hired from the church to become their part time Director of Children's ministries. This included organizing Sunday school, Junior church, and the annual vacation Bible school for children. Dezene became involved in church leadership positions and joined the worship music team.

AND THEN THE PHONE RANG...

On October 8, 2006 Elijah was born, and on January 31, 2009 Marcus appeared on the scene. These two boys, known as the classics, were the first two of our seven grandchildren. Our trips to visit them are fun and relaxing.

Joyel's friend, Tammy Enockson, came back to Burnaby in 2003 and lived with us for a number of years while she attended Regent College in Vancouver.

PAUL

Paul graduated from Pacific Academy High School in 1996. He particularly enjoyed the music program and learned to play the drums in the school band. He was chosen as the class valedictorian. We did not know this until the principal made a grand speech extolling the virtues of the valedictorian and then, to our surprise, called Paul up to make his speech. Along with his buddy David Polisi, Paul enrolled at NABC in Edmonton in 1996 and graduated in 1998 with an Associate of Arts degree. I was chosen to give the Baccalaureate Address at the Commencement Service. My topic was "A Reasonable Obligation" based on Romans 12:1-2. It was a call to the graduates to present their bodies as a living sacrifice to God, which is our reasonable service in view of all God's mercies to us. It felt a bit strange to wear academic robes and go down the aisle in the formal procession with all the college academics.

Paul then attended Simon Fraser University from 1998 to 2002 and graduated with a Bachelor of Arts degree in Communication. It was interesting to observe Paul's approach to assignments and exams. He would wait until one or two nights before the exam, then go to Tim Horton's and stay there all night cramming and drinking coffee. The next day he would ace the exam.

Paul's first job was with the Amyotrophic Lateral Sclerosis (ALS) Society of B.C. as the marketing and development director. He arranged fundraising and awareness events to support the work of the society, putting into practice his communications education. He moved out of our home, and with friends, rented a basement suite in Kitsilano. In 2005 he resigned from the ALS job and went on a pilgrimage. He trekked on the Camino

THE FAMILY

de Santiago route across northern Spain. From there he went to London hoping to find work to support himself while visiting England. There was no suitable job to be found, so when his money ran out he returned home, living with us again. He then got a job with a landscaping and lawn cutting crew to restore his bank account. Over the years Paul owned a number of old beat-up cars with interesting names like Dexter and Minerva.

Paul was blessed with an ear for music and played various instruments since age four. He started with a violin and added the following instruments: trumpet, guitar, drums, ukulele, mouth organ, mandolin, and banjo. A cello is waiting for lessons for him to play it correctly. He participated in a band with friends and did gigs at restaurants and special events. He also joined the music worship team at Bethany.

On Father's Day in 2006 Paul's life was changed forever. High school friends, Adam and Mary-Ellen Moore, set up a blind date for Paul with a delightful girl – Juliet Birth. She was an elementary school teacher with several university degrees and was a former ballet dancer. Paul was very impressed with her but felt he had no chance for any future relationship and so he just relaxed and enjoyed the date. A week later Adam and Mary-Ellen asked if he had called Juliet yet. Paul had not because he felt that she would not be interested. When he discovered that she was waiting for a call he sprang into action. Sparks flew and romance set in. Paul knew she was the right girl for him when they walked out on a point of land by the ocean in Whytecliff park. On the way back the rising tide forced them to wade back to shore and Juliet just laughed at getting her nice clothes all wet. Some time later, after a romantic dinner on Bowen Island, Paul took Juliet back to Whytecliff park to propose marriage.

In February 2007 Paul got a job with ACTIVE Network, initially as an account manager. Later he moved up to senior account manager and then senior technical sales engineer. Paul and Juliet got married on August 11, 2007 at St. John's Anglican Church in Vancouver. Paul moved into Juliet's tiny apartment in New Westminster. On June 24, 2009 Lucy was born. This was a great year for grandchildren as Marcus, Ben and Lucy were born in a span of five months. The apartment was too small so Paul and Juliet bought a three-level 14 foot wide house on Garfield Street in New Westminster. On October 28, 2012 Sebastian was born to complete the family. Both Lucy and Sebastian attend Pacific Academy where Juliet is a grade 4 teacher. Paul and Juliet are active members of Bethany Baptist Church and volunteer in music and children's ministry.

OMA

It was a real blessing to live together in the same house with Oma. She had retired from many years of work at Woolworth's and in the specialty foods section of Woodwards in the Oakridge Mall. By selling her house and joining us in the new house in Burnaby we became one family but two households, as Oma had her own suite. She did a lot of childcare for us and took kids to music lessons. On the way home from the lessons Oma usually treated them with milkshakes from McDonalds. Marion learned a lot of great recipes from her such as rouladen, streusel kuchen, kloese (dumplings), and pfeffernusse cookies, to name a few.

Oma started family traditions that continue till today. One was making an Advent wreath at Christmas time. Other traditions included Maundy Thursday spinach for supper, Christmas Eve chicken noodle soup with what we called "funny sandwiches" (rolled up grilled-cheese), and sauerkraut with turkey dinners. She had a wise rule that said there is only one boss woman in the kitchen, so she would never tell Marion what to do in Marion's kitchen and instead asked, "How can I help you?" Marion did the same with Oma in her downstairs kitchen. Oma loved music and was a wonderful alto singer. We enjoyed listening to her proficiently play her zither, but the instrument was too complicated for the family to learn to play. With many stories of the past, she provided a rich heritage for her children and grandchildren.

In later years her health gradually declined. In 1991 she had surgery for breast cancer. In 1994 she developed severe pains in her right leg with a drop foot type of disability. To improve this, a five-level laminectomy operation was done on her back. She suffered a heart attack during the surgery and was discovered to have aortic valve stenosis and regurgitation plus hypertension. Her vision deteriorated due to macular degeneration and thrombosis of her retinal artery. She had increasing difficulty reading even with the help of magnifying glasses. In 1997, she required

THE FAMILY

the insertion of a pacemaker. Her aortic stenosis got progressively tighter, resulting in congestive heart failure. In 2001 and 2002, she had a number of trips to the hospital emergency to deal with acute pulmonary edema causing extreme shortness of breath. We discovered that some of these episodes were related to very salty foods, such as her favourite pizza. By this time she was having her main meals with us. When she had difficulty in getting up the stairs we carried the meals down to her place and ate with her at her table. She was admitted to Burnaby Hospital in early September 2002 after baking cinnamon buns for Sunday breakfast. With this severe bout of pulmonary edema, her condition gradually declined. For several days we were unable to communicate with her. Lori was out of the country at this time. She hurried home to Oma's bedside. With loud voices we told Oma that Lori was here. Oma opened her eyes and reached out to Lori and smiled to see her. Several days later on September 21, 2002 Oma died and went to be with her Lord and Saviour. It was a very sad time for all of us as she was a very special and beloved Oma.

In October 2003 we moved to our newly built townhouse at Carrington in south Surrey. We had planned a nice master bedroom with an en suite bathroom on the main floor for Oma. Instead Marion and I now occupied it. The house had three levels. The upstairs had an open type office, two bedrooms and a bathroom. The walk-out basement had one bedroom, a bathroom, two storage rooms and a large family room. We enjoyed the fellowship of many old friends who lived in the Carrington complex and formed a Bible study group with them. Here our boomerang kids often lived with us on return from their various ventures.

THEN ONE DAY A TELEPHONE call ushered us into a whole new adventure.

AND THEN THE PHONE RANG...

HIGH SCHOOL TRIP TO ISRAEL

WAILING WALL AT THE TEMPLE MOUNT IN JERUSALEM

THE FAMILY

DR. BRUCE HILLER M.D.

BRUCE BEING CONGRATULATED AS A NEW INTERNAL MEDICINE SPECIALIST

AND THEN THE PHONE RANG...

BRUCE AND KELLY — HAPPILY MARRIED — SEPTEMBER 25, 2004

BEN, ABBY, AND KAITLYN JOIN THE FAMILY

THE FAMILY

LORI GRADUATES FROM UBC A WITH BACHELOR OF SCIENCE IN NURSING

LORI ON A MISSIONS TRIP TO BURKINA FASO IN AFRICA

AND THEN THE PHONE RANG...

LORI B.SC. NURSING & MASTERS IN MIDWIFERY — TEACHING IN CAMEROON

JOYEL — HIGH SCHOOL GRADUATION

THE FAMILY

DEZENE HUBER & JOYEL JOYFULLY CELEBRATE — AUGUST 16, 2003

ELIJAH AND MARCUS OUR FIRST 2 GRANDCHILDREN

AND THEN THE PHONE RANG...

PAUL CHECKS HIS B.A. IN COMMUNICATIONS FROM SIMON FRASER UNIVERSITY

PAUL AND JULIET'S SPECIAL DAY — AUGUST 11, 2007

THE FAMILY

LUCY AND SEBASTIAN JOIN THE FAMILY

THE ENTIRE FAMILY PLUS AUNTIE SHIRLEY (MARION'S SISTER)
AT GREEN BAY BIBLE CAMP – SUMMER OF 2019

AND THEN THE PHONE RANG...

OMA — THE MATRIARCH OF OUR FAMILY

OMA — CELEBRATING HER ADVANCING YEARS

CHAPTER 19
The Phone Rings Again

As mentioned before, the phone rings very often at our house. However there are some phone calls that, in response, cause one's life to take a sharp turn in direction. One of those calls occurred in 1970 when Dr. Schilke asked us to consider medical missions in Nigeria and Cameroon. We accepted this call with considerable trepidation as we did not feel that we were the spiritual giants that missionaries were supposed to be. After a period of hesitation and much prayer we accepted this call from God and agreed to go to Africa. This launched us into the incredible journey already described.

Then in the summer of 2004, we got a similar phone call. This time it was Carol Potratz calling on behalf of the NAB Missions department, asking us to consider going to Nigeria for six to seven months. They needed a doctor to replace Dr. Wim and Marleen Munting who were going on a six-month furlough. The Muntings worked at a small hospital near Gembu that was started by the Mambilla Baptist Convention Medical Department. Dr. Munting was a pediatric surgeon from the Netherlands who had worked in Cameroon prior to going to Mambilla. *Fear* was my reaction to this proposal. I had not done major surgery for 25 years, and now I would be expected to do what a pediatric surgeon did. Also, safety was a concern. I was aware that there had been a recent civil war on the Mambilla Plateau between the Mambilla farmers and the Fulani herdsmen. There was also strife between Christians and Muslims in the Jos area where some Christians had been killed. Finally, the scourge of HIV infections and a rise in the number of malaria infections resistant to usual treatment made me doubt my ability to deal with these conditions.

Once again, after much prayer Marion and I felt that this phone call was another call from God. We needed to obey this call despite our fears. We were reminded of the great commission where Jesus promised, "Lo, I am with you *always*, even to the end of the age." We knew from prior experiences that God is in the business of making divine appointments.

Before going we corresponded several times by email with the Muntings. They described the facilities in the hospital and the house in which we would live. They also suggested some medical equipment that we should try to bring with us. We sold our two cars and sent the money to the NAB Missions department as a charitable donation to cover the costs of our trip and the purchase of food and supplies while in Nigeria. Bethany's women's ministry generously purchased surgical instruments, including two doptones to listen to fetal heartbeats, gel foam, and sutures. They also funded the extra costs of this accompanying baggage on our flight. Our Bible study group passed around the hat and collected enough money to purchase malaria prophylaxis medicine for us. Our total cargo consisted of two large suitcases, four carry-on bags, and three large rubber-maid bins, each weighing 70 pounds.

I kept a daily diary of our time in Nigeria and Cameroon and made copies of newsy emails that we sent home. This material made it possible to write the following account of our venture back to Mambilla.

GETTING THERE

AFTER A WONDERFUL FAREWELL DINNER with our family at the Seasons in the Park restaurant on Little Mountain we did our final packing. At 4 AM on June 5, 2005 our alarm clock awakened us. Our friends Bob and Nancy Hepting drove us to the airport for our Air Canada flight to Toronto. In Toronto we had to claim all our cargo, put it on carts, and go outside to pile everything onto a bus. People crowded ahead of us onto the bus. We finally got on the third bus taking us to the international terminal and our flight on Air France to Charles de Gaulle airport in Paris. Again, bus trips to another terminal for our final flight to Douala. The airport in Douala was hot and humid and full of aggressive porters. All our baggage arrived intact and we easily passed through customs and immigration. Vincent, the Cameroon Baptist Conference driver, took us to the European Baptist guesthouse for a bath, a meal, and a sleep. We were very tired after 24 hours of non-stop travel.

The next day, after a hearty breakfast, we loaded our cargo into the mission vehicle and Vincent drove us to Bamenda. On the way we noticed that Douala had grown in size and was filled with people on motorcycles. Going inland we saw large plantations of palms, bananas, and rubber trees. We passed through Bafoussam which was also big and busy. Signs of relative prosperity were evident – women in fancy clothes, fancy cars, and many cement buildings. Dennis and Nancy Palmer hosted us for several days while we shopped for staples and produce. We made a day trip to Mbingo driving on a nicely paved road. The hospital had grown since last we saw it. There were many new buildings, including a large new operating room complex.

Preston Hartwig, the Mambilla Baptist Mission (MBM) Field secretary, arrived to take us the rest of the way to Mambilla. He shared his many frustrations with the leadership of the Mambilla Baptist Convention of Nigeria (MBCN). He felt they were corrupt and out of touch with the local churches. They rewrote the constitution and imposed central control of all church funds so they could pay the pastors. Some churches refused to send money to the MBC office and other churches simply left the MBCN and joined the Southern Baptists. He also felt unsupported by the NAB Missions department stating that he had inadequate funds to carry out evangelism. We did not know how to evaluate all this information and found it strange to be informed of all this before we even arrived in Mambilla.

On our way we stopped at Banso Baptist Hospital and had a great supper meal with Betty Mantay. I was asked to see Dr. Pokey Cleek, a surgeon, who was quite sick with probable staphylococcal septicemia. He felt a bit improved with I.V. cloxacillin. I discussed his situation with Dr. Julie Stone, an internist, and we decided to send Dr. Cleek home to America for further treatment, cultures, and an echocardiogram.

THE PHONE RINGS AGAIN

Zebulon Wanmi joined us in Banso for the journey to Mambilla. Zebulon was an invaluable worker at the Warwar Hospital during our time there in the 1970s. Our journey took us past the famous tea estate near Ndu. The next fork in the road took us down to the Mbaw plain and on to Sabongari where we signed out of Cameroon. The road from Sabongari up to the Mambilla Plateau was indescribably terrible. It was very steep and so deeply rutted that we had to stop numerous times to fill the holes with rocks and shovel in sand. The road was also slippery as the rainy season had arrived. We got stuck several times and had to push the vehicle. We finally hit such a large deep hole that we couldn't proceed. On the horizon I saw dark rain clouds gathering and feared that we might end up sleeping there. Several men showed up to help and we finally got the Toyota moving. The driver did not stop for us to get in, fearing that we would be stuck again. So we trudged up the steep slippery road to the top, sweating profusely from the exertion in the hot muggy weather. I was totally exhausted, panting, soaked in sweat, and covered with dirt. I even felt some chest pains and wondered if my heart was really happy with all of this. Marion fared better as we did not let her push the vehicle, but told her to take pictures. The Nigerian officials were quite rude and gave us visitor's visas for only 30 days.

On our way through Mbamga we met Zebulon's wife Katty who gave us a warm welcome. It was good to see a familiar smiling face. We then crossed the Donga River by a small raft powered by men with bamboo poles. Driving through axle-deep muddy ruts on both sides of the river brought back memories of the 1970's. A bridge over the Donga River had been promised by politicians for at least 35 years. Driving into Gembu in the rain we noticed how gloomy the place looked with its mud block buildings and rusty metal roofs. Gembu town had grown since we left 26 years ago. It looked impoverished – a shanty town of 40,000 residents with no running water, no dependable electrical power, no sewage disposal, and a high rate of HIV infections. Marion and I both felt a sense of darkness and oppression, a place of spiritual warfare. After much needed showers and a short nap, we had supper with Preston and Irene Hartwig, and Art and Dorothy Helwig. The following day the Helwigs gave us a tour of their home and offices and introduced us to their work of AIDS education, prevention, counselling and ministry to orphans as Baptist General Conference missionaries. That afternoon Dr. Wim Munting and Dave Burgess returned from a trip to Jos and after supper we drove to the hospital site, five miles out of Gembu town. After seven days of travel we had finally arrived. We were completely bushed and quickly set up a mosquito net and fell into bed.

SETTLING IN

THE HOSPITAL COMPOUND WAS SET on a plateau high above the Donga River about 5 miles east of Gembu in a rural area. The doctor's house was built by Bernie Lemke and was a well-designed, split level, three-bedroom home. The three bedrooms and bathroom were on the upper level and the kitchen, dining room and living room on the main level. There was a solar panel on the roof of the house that charged up a series of car sized batteries that powered a small fridge containing chemotherapy medicines and vaccines as well as bags of donated blood. The batteries were also connected to an inverter that converted the 24 volt batteries to 120 volts. This gave power to appliances and light to the house at night. The roof had an interesting leak that dripped on the dining room table during very heavy rain storms. We had to position our plates carefully to avoid diluting the food! There was a small garden with vegetables and two chicken coops that kept Marion busy. We had a night watchman, Lot, who also did garden work as directed by Marion. Charity, a teenager, helped in the kitchen and with house cleaning and laundry.

The hospital building was set across the main dirt road. The outpatient area contained two consulting rooms, a dispensary, a laboratory, an administration office, and a large store room for medicines and supplies. The in-patient section was contained in two wings separated by an inner courtyard. One wing contained three wards with ten beds each for men, children and women. The other wing had an operating room with scrub-up area, a treatment room, a sterilizing area, a delivery room, a ten-bed maternity ward, and a small empty room for an X-ray machine in the future. A separate building housed two generators- a big diesel one to

THE PHONE RINGS AGAIN

power the entire hospital and a small one to power just the operating room at night. There was some staff housing available but many of the staff lived in Gembu. Every day the hospital vehicle was loaded with Gembu staff coming to work in the morning and going home in the late afternoon.

The next day was Sunday so we drove to First Baptist Church in Gembu. We were introduced to the congregation by Wim and we brought greetings from the NAB churches and Bethany in particular. The English service was very lively with a worship team that used multiple types of drums, electric guitars, a synthesizer and a sound system. Worship time included several choirs, each singing at least two songs. After the service we met many old timers from our Warwar days in the 1970s. We toured the Bible school at Mbu and had lunch with Dave and Mary-June Burgess who served there. The Bible school had 52 students enrolled. A number of new buildings had been added since 1979, including a beautiful multistory library.

Part of properly getting settled involved meeting with the MBCN president, Philip Sol, who accompanied us as we visited the immigration officer, the state security service, and the Chief of Mambilla. The immigration officer was willing to help us stay in Nigeria until Christmas as planned. The Chief of Mambilla was happy to be recognized, especially when I requested his protection while we were there to help his people. The state security service officer also assured us of his watchful protection. It was always good public relations to give proper respect to the local rulers. They are honoured and we gain their support.

I was introduced to the hospital staff by Wim and followed him on ward rounds. I found that Wim did a lot of good medicine with limited resources. This included blood transfusions, chemotherapy for Burkitt's lymphoma, and multiple drug therapy for tuberculosis. I was glad to have Wim stay for a couple of weeks of orientation regarding the hospital administration, staffing, budgets, maintenance of drug supply lines, and supervision of outlying community health clinics. The typical week day schedule was as follows:

- 6:15 - the alarm rings, preceded by obnoxious roosters crowing

- 6:45 – 7:15 breakfast and devotions

- 7:30 – staff devotions and prayer lead by the chaplain

AND THEN THE PHONE RANG...

- 8:00 – meeting with Director of Nursing and Administrator to plan the day

- 8:15 – 9:45- ward rounds in the maternity, men's, kids, women's, and private wards. This was often a time for teaching the staff and the referral of specific cases to the chaplain for spiritual counselling.

- 9:45 – 10:00 – run 100 yards home for a quick coffee

- 10:00 – mid-afternoon - doing out-patient consultations, admitting very sick patients, and any emergency surgery. Elective surgery was done on one day of the week while senior staff saw out-patients.

- 4:00 – main meal followed by administrative work, counselling, and repairing stuff.

- 8:00 – light supper, read a bit, and fall into bed all tuckered out.

After quick ward rounds on Wednesdays, Marion and I travelled to Gembu where I saw between 40 and 80 patients at the Primary Health Clinic (PHC) operated by the MBCN medical ministry. The most critically ill patients were referred to the hospital for admission. We also checked the large medical store room in Gembu that contained bulk supplies of medicines, equipment and White Cross material. Marion did child vaccinations with Mary Wanmi and a bit of shopping for food. Once a month Marion met with the heads of the 12 Primary Health Clinics (PHC) who came to town to deposit their drug fees with her and receive medicines that they required. The PHC's are scattered over the entire Mambilla Plateau. When Marion and Mary Wanmi's work was done they walked into town for shopping – typical women!

We had well-trained staff in the medical work. The Medical Director was Daniel Samuel who was a deeply committed Christian, and a good manager, with very high ethical standards. He was capable of consulting sick patients and assisting at surgery when required. He had some difficulty in commanding total respect from some of the Mambilla staff because he was from the Tiv tribe. Tribalism was a real problem in Mambilla. He became a very close friend of mine and we had many long talks and prayed together. His wife, Charity, was a very competent midwife. Gideon

THE PHONE RINGS AGAIN

Menyah was the administrator in charge of the medical supply stores, hospital equipment, hospital vehicle, and supervised of all the heads of the PHC's. He was able to do basic consultations and assist at surgery. Gideon was a playmate of Bruce and Lori when we were at Warwar Hospital in the 1970's. Elias Zephaniah was the Director of Nursing and in charge of all the hospital staff. He was capable of doing basic surgery like hernia repairs, skin grafting, and even C-sections in the absence of a doctor. Jezreel Wanmi was in charge of the operating room equipment and sterilization. He was also able to do spinal anesthetics. His wife, Mary, was a capable midwife and nurse. She spent time with Marion in the kitchen teaching each other recipes. Felicia Wanmi was in charge of the medical stores at the hospital with some assistance from Marion.

TAKING OVER

DR. MUNTING STAYED AT THE hospital for about two weeks in order to hand over the medical and administrative work. He was perturbed at the absence of Dr. Ogwu, a Nigerian doctor, who had worked together with him. He apparently went to see his sick father in the southwest part of Nigeria. There had been no further communication from Dr. Ogwu for months despite the fact that he left all his belongings here. Wim felt badly that I would have to handle everything on my own. I had forgotten how primitive the hospital facilities were compared to those at home, but I felt that with God's help we would manage. I knew that God had sent us here.

There were new medical situations that did not exist when we were here in the 1970s. I even had a tinge of culture shock as I witnessed the ravages of HIV-AIDS and the opportunistic infections that caused young people to die within hours of admission to hospital. People with AIDS were rejected by their families and left to die in the gutters in Gembu. One mother, with HIV-positive testing, delivered a premature baby that had a failure to thrive syndrome with chronic diarrhea. This baby was also found to be HIV-positive. We had no drugs to treat HIV-positive patients, except for Nevirapine. We gave it to pregnant women in labour and to the newborns to prevent transmission of HIV. Unfortunately HIV can, in some cases, be transmitted to babies via breast milk. The situation was so grim that churches refused to conduct marriages until the couples were tested for HIV. I had the horrible task of informing some couples that one was positive and the other negative. A church deacon usually accompanied the couple to ensure that they were properly tested at the hospital. Tuberculosis was one of the opportunistic infections in AIDS patients. This required multiple drug therapy with PAS, streptomycin, rifampicin, and isoniazid (with vitamin B6 to prevent neuropathy).

It was the rainy season and there were a lot of very sick kids with malaria as people tended to wait before coming to the hospital. Some of the kids arrived convulsing and in a coma. Most were very anemic with hemoglobin levels of two to three grams instead of the normal level of 12 to 14. Malaria was not new, but what was new was the fact that the malarial parasite had mutated over time. Now most cases were resistant to the time-honoured treatment with chloroquine. We had to use quinine which was much more toxic especially when administered intravenously. We had a new drug, Artesunate, that was produced in Hanoi, Vietnam. It was very effective in treating malaria that was resistant to the usual drugs. I kept a small supply of this locked up in our house to be used for missionaries who had no immunity to malaria. Most local people develop some partial immunity from repeated exposure over time to malaria.

Burkett's lymphoma was also a new condition in Mambilla. This was a cancer found mainly in children and thought to be associated with the Epstein-Barr virus found only in parts of Africa. Most of these kids presented with huge tumours of facial bones (mainly jaws) and abdominal tumours. Without treatment this condition was uniformly fatal. We were the only hospital in the entire Taraba State that was able to treat this disease. We had no pathology services for diagnosis by biopsies, so we had to make a clinical diagnosis by careful physical examination. Treatment consisted of intravenous chemotherapy with three drugs – cyclophosphamide, methotrexate, and vincristine which we kept in our little refrigerator by our house. To avoid renal damage, we gave intravenous fluids for a day and then gave triple-drug chemotherapy for three days. The dose required was based on a calculation of the meter squared of the body surface area of the patient. This cycle of therapy was repeated every three weeks for a total

THE PHONE RINGS AGAIN

of six treatments. It was remarkable to see rapid shrinking of the tumours even after the first cycle of treatment.

One new thing we were grateful for was the ability to send and receive email messages. Wim had a laptop computer and a satellite phone set up. We had to go outside the house and aim the screen to get a strong enough signal from the Atlantic satellite that would transmit the emails.

I followed Wim on rounds and started doing some simple operations. It did not take long to get the feel of dissecting and suturing tissue back in my hands and head. My first C-section was on a woman eight-months pregnant and bleeding. Her hemoglobin was only eight grams (normal 12 grams), and we only had a half a unit of compatible blood to give her. The surgery went well and her hemoglobin the next morning was seven grams. Over the next few days I dealt with a lady in diabetic ketoacidosis, a baby girl in coma with cerebral malaria who died despite treatment, a number of kids with malaria – one with a hemoglobin of three grams, and did a C-section on a woman with an arm presentation. An elderly woman arrived having been injured in an accident with a motorcycle. She had a concussion, a supracondylar fracture of her right femur, and a compound fracture of her left tibia and fibula with the bone ends protruding through her skin. She was referred to us by the government hospital in Gembu with no notes and no treatment. So I got busy reducing the tibia-fibula fracture and resuscitating her with IV fluids and blood transfusion. These cases all gave me a reality check on the situation I was inheriting.

One morning we had an interesting incident. The staff vehicle bringing hospital workers from Gembu suddenly lost its braking power. Instead of gearing down and going in circles to slow the vehicle, the driver decided to stop by ramming into the wall of the out-patient department. This made a big hole in the wall of the room where all the hospital money was kept. So now we had to figure out how to repair the vehicle and find a bush mason to fix the wall. I also watched Wim deal with some other administrative problems:

- the generator man not doing proper maintenance
- a carpenter making an absolute mess in hanging an office door

AND THEN THE PHONE RANG…

- an interpreter/screener working in the out-patient department who was totally useless – he was incapable of reading a scale to weigh children

Marion had her own adaptations. As she found out what was growing in the garden, a tick decided to bury itself in her leg. We lit a match to heat up the little guy's tail end to encourage him to leave the premises – we got him all out. After her first shopping trip to Gembu after the PHC clinic, she saw it was a far cry from Metrotown, the large mall back home in Burnaby! The meat market was quite smelly. Sugar was scarce and cost $80 for 100 pounds. She spotted a lemon tree full of beautiful ripe lemons beside our living room window. She harvested them and found a recipe for making lemon curd. She enjoyed our kitchen and spent time with Mary Wanmi and Charity Samuel, teaching them how to make guava sauce. To do laundry she had to start up a small generator to run the washing machine. Clothes were dried by hanging them outside on a line, with a watchful eye on gathering rain clouds. Ironing was done by heating an iron on a wood-fired stove top.

VISIT TO WARWAR

AFTER QUICK WARD ROUNDS ONE Sunday morning, Marion and I went to Warwar with Wim, Gideon and Mary. We crossed the Donga River on a pole-driven raft and drove through a long stretch of mud on the other side. Halfway to Warwar we started to cross a stream on a wooden bridge when the bridge collapsed and both front wheels fell into deep holes. We spent about an hour piling rocks and bits of wood so we could jack up the front end of our vehicle and back off the bridge with the aid of a group of men who had come to observe our predicament. We walked up and down hills until we got to Warwar. Marion got a ride on a passing motorcycle part of the way. The hills and valleys were extensively cultivated for farms of corn and even large areas of pineapples. We learned that the people got pineapple starts from our original garden in the 1970s and were now growing them for sale in the markets.

We attended the church service at Warwar. They had numerous choirs singing several songs each, then followed by a very long sermon. We met many of the former Warwar hospital workers who were now retired, and saw the grave site of Pastor Daniel Njilmer. Pastor Peter Jumvuh and his wife treated us to a nice lunch of fufu and palm oil chicken in their house. They had a nice parlour with easy chairs and a carpet.

On our way back to our vehicle we detoured a bit to visit Warwar Hospital which was still being run by the government. The compound was very run down. The out-patient, surgical, and maternity buildings that were built by the mission were still in fairly good shape. The buildings constructed by the government later were deteriorating badly. The general in-patient ward was empty and had broken windows and a leaking roof. There were very few patients present. This was sad to see! Dr. Dauda, the government doctor, kindly let us see our former house. The place was neglected, dirty, and dark. We just peaked in the entrance and did not want to see more. The sight brought tears to our eyes.

ON OUR OWN

WIM LEFT AT 3:30 AM to go home and join his wife on furlough. Dr. Ogwu was still absent. With no communication from him, we realized that we were now going to run the medical work with just one doctor – me! The day Wim left, I saw a deaf-mute woman who was pregnant. She had a C-section for her first pregnancy, for a presumed big baby that turned out to be premature twins who died at birth. Now her hemoglobin was only 6.4 grams. She was too poor to pay for medications, transfusions, and a repeat C-section. What sorrow! We did not charge her any fees. For such cases we had a poor-and-sick fund that covered the costs. By mid-morning a doctor and three officials from Abuja, the capital city of Nigeria, arrived to investigate how we dealt with HIV. We showed them how we did testing and told them that we had no antiretroviral drugs for treatment except for nevirapine for pregnant women in labour. All we could do for HIV positive patients was counselling and antibiotic therapy for opportunistic infections. I pleaded with them to supply us with a CD-4 counter (to measure immune cells) and drugs.

The next day a very sick sixteen year old girl was referred to me from the government hospital in Gembu. She apparently had an abortion done in Gembu and several days later developed a fever and abdominal pain. She was treated with antibiotics and IV fluids but her condition deteriorated. On arrival at our hospital she was found to be very sick, weak, thin, and pale. I examined her and found a tender abdomen. A pelvic exam revealed fullness in the right cul- de- sac. A primitive ultrasound test showed something in the pelvis to the right of the uterus. This girl must have had a perforation of the uterus during her procedure and now had a pelvic abscess. This needed to be drained before she would recover. There is an old surgical maxim that says where there is pus there must be steel. Antibiotics are useless in treating abscesses without prior surgical drainage.

Two days later I experienced a particularly *wild day*. I quote from my diary as follows:

A wild day! Rounds took till almost 11 AM with 2 surgeries being done by Elias, which I supervised by running in periodically to check on his progress.

- *skin graft of a boy with glove avulsion injury of his hand*
- *debridement of a man's infected leg that looked like necrotizing fasciitis*

Out-patient consultations took till 2 PM. Several patients were admitted.

- *a 25-year old boy who was thin, unable to stand, coughing, and had a blood pressure of 70/50. He was HIV positive.*
- *a woman arrived in labor with premature twins weighing 1.8 and 2 kg. She popped them out before I could get there.*
- *a woman in poor labour – needed a pitocin drip to deliver her baby.*
- *a woman in labour at 41 weeks with twins. She had a huge cyst on her labia that required aspiration. One of the babies*

developed profound decelerations of it's heart rate. A vacuum extraction attempt failed. We gave her 1500 cc of normal saline and then did a C-section. Unfortunately the spinal anesthetic that Jezreel put in was not very successful. The patient nearly leaped off the table when I pinched her skin to check the level of anesthesia. So I injected local anesthetic and began to cut. She squirmed and raised her knees. This was tough as her abdomen was huge. Once I got her abdomen open I put her to sleep with IV Ketamine. The uterus was levo-rotated to 90 degrees which made it hard to orient and even find the bladder. It looked like a ring twisted around the neck of the first twin, whose head was molded and jammed into the pelvis. It was very difficult to get the head out and delivered. The baby was quite limp. The second twin came out easily – what a gratifying sound to hear them cry. The twins were both over 7 pounds. There was some difficulty in controlling the bleeding, but we succeeded in getting it stopped. I was soaked in sweat and blood right through to my socks and underwear. When I initially could not get the first baby's head out, even with a nurse trying to push it up from below, I thought that the babies and the mom were going to die. I sent up a bullet prayer – "God help me." Another attempt to get the baby's head out was successful.

Yes, I was really on my own. But not really – *thanks to God for answered prayer*. I began to see this episode as a divine appointment. God had me come here, and God brought this lady here too for His special purpose.

AND THEN THE PHONE RANG...

TERRIBLE ROAD AT THE CAMEROON-NIGERIA BORDER

SENIOR STAFF AT THE HOSPITAL NEAR GEMBU

THE PHONE RINGS AGAIN

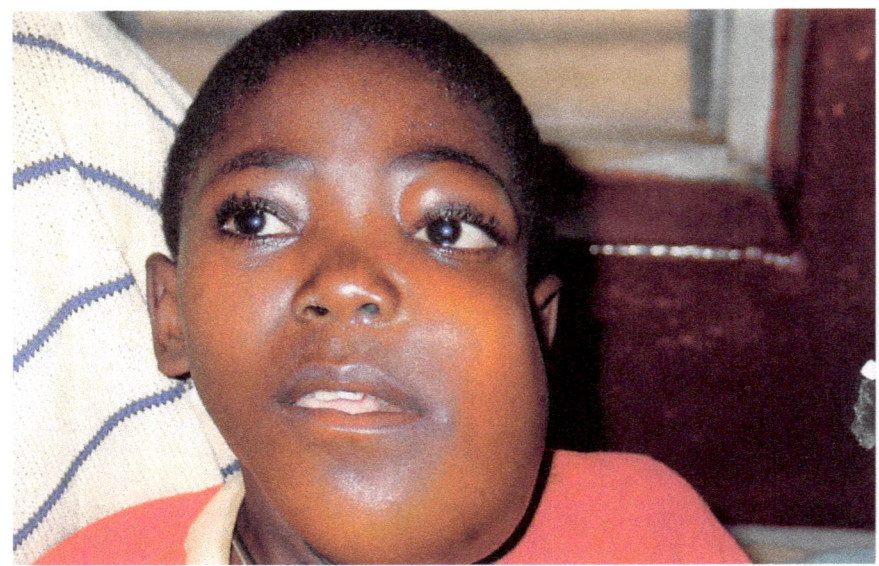

BURKITT'S LYMPHOMA OF THE JAW

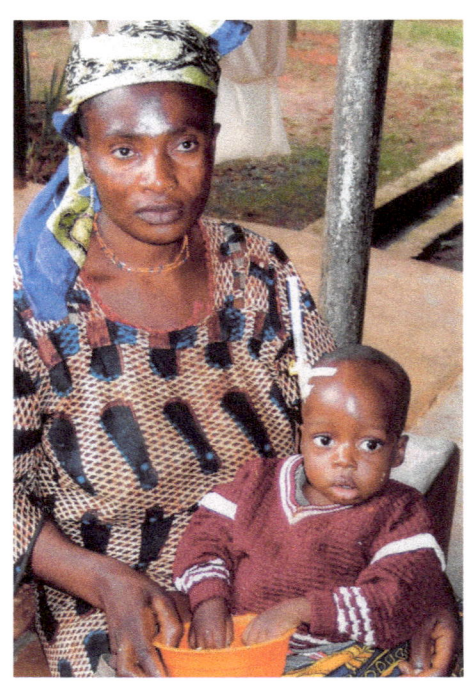

CHEMOTHERAPY FOR BURKITT'S LYMPHOMA

AND THEN THE PHONE RANG...

RESTORED HEALTH MAKES EVERYBODY HAPPY!

HOSPITAL PATIENTS ENJOYING SOME SUN

THE PHONE RINGS AGAIN

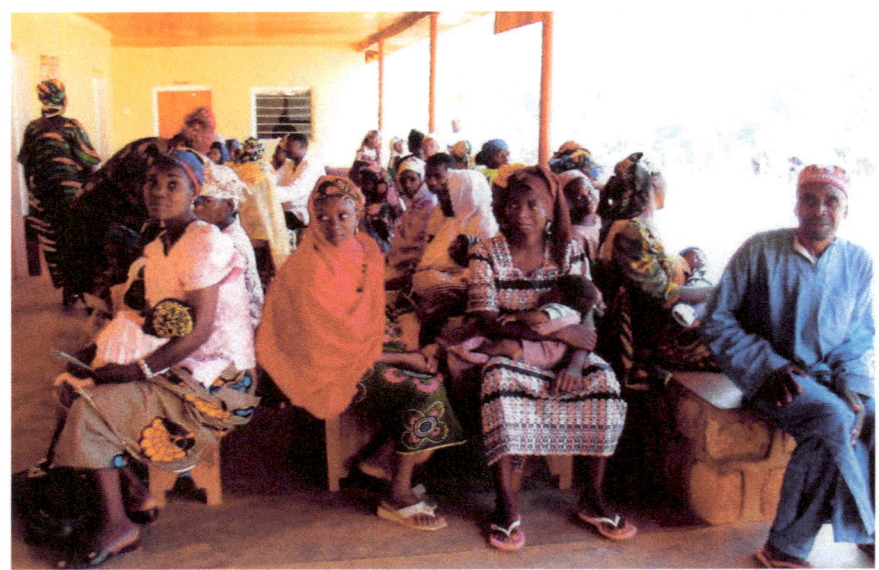

OUTPATIENTS WAITING FOR CONSULTATION

DR. MUNTING BACKING VEHICLE OUT OF A BROKEN BRIDGE

AND THEN THE PHONE RANG...

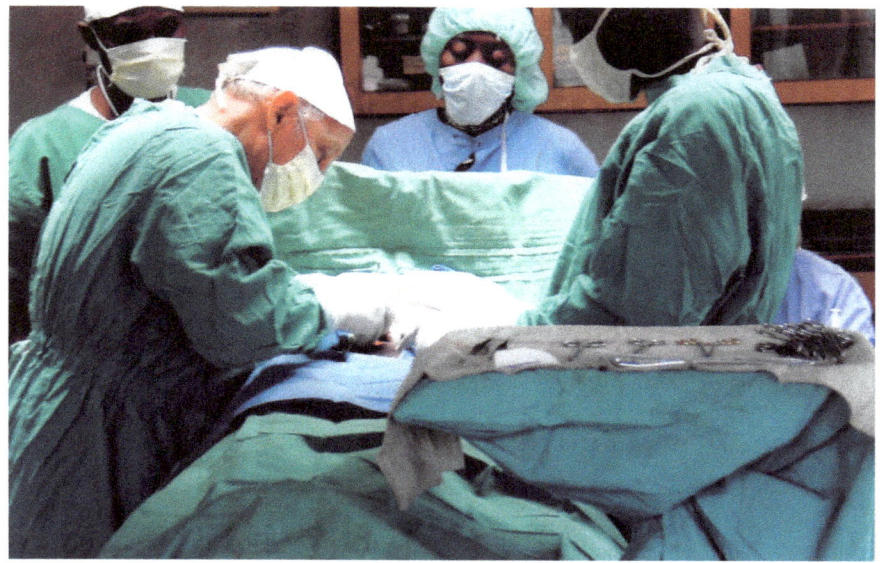

SURGICAL SKILLS RETURNED QUICKLY

HEALTHY MOM AND TWINS AFTER VERY DIFFICULT C-SECTION

CHAPTER 20

God's Help Every Step of the Way

JULY 2005

THE RAINY SEASON WAS FULLY established making the dirt roads to PHCs in outlying villages nearly impassable. Trips to the villages were cancelled until the start of dry season in November. The road from the hospital to Gembu was still passable and we were glad for the ruts that kept our vehicle from sliding off the road into the bush or rolling down a hill. With clinics cancelled, I could focus on the medical and surgical work and administration of the hospital.

We became regular attendees at Vision Church located near our PHC in Gembu. This church was only about five months old and had grown rapidly to a membership of 350, with average attendance of 450 people. The service time was lively and long – from 9 AM until noon. The services start with choir singing – they had five choirs and they all sang two numbers. The kid's choir was first and really lively with rhythmic dancing. The two vernacular choirs used local instruments such as shakers, drums, and calabashes. The formal English choir used sheet music and sang four-part harmony. Finally, the contemporary choir sang accompanied by an electric keyboard, bass guitar, and very intricate drumming. Announcements followed and were very lengthy – almost like reading business meeting minutes, including the names of next Sunday's ushers! Then a very lively offering was held as everyone danced up the aisle to the front to put money in a bucket held by an elder. Scripture reading, prayer, and a lengthy sermon in English followed, with translation into Fulfulde

(Fulani). By September the church had grown to almost 500 members. We learned a very meaningful song that they often sang at communion time:

> "There will be another fellowship in heaven
> I will be there. Will you be there?"

These words were repeated over and over and over. They made us think of the marriage supper of the Lamb and His bride (Rev. 19:7-9).

Some interesting clinical situations occurred in July among the many patients seen. The following were some examples.

During an especially busy day I admitted 14 very sick out-patients to hospital, causing a customs official to complain bitterly that he had to wait to be seen. He totally did not comprehend the concept of triage that was happening as we picked critically ill children out of the waiting line to be seen as priorities.

We did an above-knee amputation on a man who had gangrene of his lower leg and was HIV-positive. I was double gloved and wore safety goggles which had to be removed as they fogged up. I had some difficulty in isolating the femoral artery and vein. Then as I was sawing, half way through the femur (thigh bone), the saw fell apart. We declared time out in order to repair the saw. Luckily the patient was not aware of this problem. His hemoglobin was only nine grams and the following day after three units of blood his hemoglobin was only seven grams. We loaded him with flagyl, gentamycin, and ampiclox – all antibiotics. He recovered without infection of the wound and eventually was sent to Mbingo Baptist Hospital in Cameroon for an above-the-knee prosthesis.

Another man arrived with a fractured ankle, having stepped in a hole. We sent him to the government hospital in Gembu for X-rays. He returned with the films that were poorly developed, but did show a trimalleolar fracture of his ankle. We gave him ketamine and attempted a closed reduction of the fracture and applied a cast which was split to allow for swelling. His blood pressure soared to 220/120. A dose of I.V. hydralazine settled the pressure back to normal. He returned for follow-up with X-ray films in hand showing 80% improvement of position of the fracture. I did another manipulation of the fracture. We again gave him ketamine anesthesia and his blood pressure rose to 220/120 again. I ordered IV hydralazine.

AND THEN THE PHONE RANG...

The operating room attendant brought an ampoule of adrenaline instead of hydralazine. Luckily, we caught the mistake before the adrenaline was given. That would have killed the patient! Some very stern words were spoken to the attendant after all was done.

Two children arrived on subsequent days with a history of being bitten by a rabid dog. Fortunately we found some anti-rabies vaccine in the fridge. I was reminded that rabies was still endemic. To this day I have an aversion to unfamiliar dogs.

A girl in her 20s was brought to the hospital by her family. She was comatose and had pitting edema of her legs extending up to her mid back. She had obvious fluid in her abdomen, rales in her chest, and malodorous breath. She had been in hospital in Jalingo, the state capital. Her aunt produced a referral letter from the Jalingo hospital addressed to the consultant nephrologist at the University Teaching Hospital in Maiduguri. The family brought her here instead for treatment. Her kidney function tests were markedly abnormal. Her hemoglobin was only six grams and she was HIV-positive. We catheterized her and found that after six hours her urine output was only 70 cc despite an IV dose of lasix, a diuretic. I spent a lot of time with the family explaining her pathology of end-stage kidney failure and that she was near death. Only kidney dialysis might extend her life a bit. She would never survive a trip to Maiduguri or Jos. Her HIV status would also likely preclude her from a dialysis program – if one even existed. The only options were for the family to take her home to die or stay for palliative care. They stayed and she died the next morning. What a sad, sad waste of a young life!

One day a man arrived at suppertime with a history of falling out of a tree. He had been cutting dry branches to sell as firewood in the market. He was sitting in a wheelchair complaining of severe chest pain and gasping for air. He had a fractured right clavicle and multiple fractures of his ribs on both sides of his chest. I could hear the grating sound of broken ribs with my stethoscope. He was pale as a ghost. I also noted absence of air entry into his right upper chest. I suspected a tension pneumothorax (trapped air in the chest cavity). We had to do something quickly as he was close to dying. We found an underwater seal bottle in our store that we quickly set up. The patient was hustled into the operating room. There was no time for scrubbing up or skin prep. I quickly put local anesthetic into his right upper chest and inserted a large trochar. To every one's relief, including the patient, we heard a mighty rush of trapped air escaping from his chest. Immediately his breathing became less laboured. I inserted a chest tube that was connected to the underwater drainage bottle. The patient was put to bed with a transfusion of blood running as he was very anemic as well. The man survived the night, but several days later his breathing became more difficult. He had developed a flail chest due to several fractures of his left ribs such that his chest wall sucked inwards when he inhaled and popped outward when he exhaled. We needed to fix this. We had enough time now to give him a ketamine anesthetic. I found a large towel clip that I used to grab a rib (through the skin). We then tied a White Cross roll bandage to the clip, ran it over a stick tied to the bed, parallel to the mattress, and tied the other end to a bag full of stones to provide traction. With this in place he was able to breathe better. Needle aspiration of his left chest revealed no fluid or blood. With local anesthetic injected into the rib fracture sites the man was comfortable. Two weeks later his chest tube was removed and three weeks later the towel clip was removed. After a period of mobilization, he was discharged home – happy as a clam!

TRIALS AND TRIBULATIONS

VARIOUS ISSUES CROPPED UP JUST to make life more interesting. The butane tanks used to heat bath water ran dry. The replacement tanks had stripped threads making attachment impossible. We only had cold water until a man showed up with a hacksaw blade to fix the problem.

The laptop computer died. That meant no more easy communication with the outside world. I was no technological genius, but I took the battery out, unplugged everything, waited a while and then reassembled it all. To my amazement it worked!

WE ALSO HEARD STRANGE NOISES in the night coming from somewhere in our roof. Investigation revealed an attic full of bats, bat dung, and bird's nests. This did not appear to be a healthy situation at all. Robert, a local contractor came with a crew and removed the bats and head-pans full of dung. They then repaired the soffits and closed any holes that were present.

The mission vehicle died – a dead battery. Fortunately, Preston Hartwig showed up a few days later with a small 45-amp battery that would work until we got a big one from Jos.

To my horror I discovered that some of the hospital staff had become lax in their work. They were admitting new patients to beds that had not been cleaned after the previous patient was discharged. I put the entire hospital on lock-down. The ward staff were ashamed when asked if they would admit their own family members to such contaminated beds. No staff were allowed to leave that day until they took all the mattresses outside and washed and disinfected them. There was also a general clean-up of the latrines and minor operating room. Elias was instructed to write up a protocol for Dettol scrubs of all mattresses after patients were discharged.

Preston and Irene Hartwig showed up (on my birthday) to announce that they were resigning – effective December 2005. I spent a long time counselling with them, and it became obvious that they would need to be repatriated as soon as August. I sent a letter to the NAB Missions director with my advice. This was a sad day for all of us, leaving me as the only doctor in a two-doctor situation, and Dave and Mary-June Burgess at the Bible school as the only other NAB missionaries in Mambilla.

Some hope on the horizon appeared when Dr. J. D. arrived and stated that he would consider working with us at the hospital. He was a Mambilla Christian who wanted to serve his people. To do this he would arrange to be seconded to our hospital by the State Governor, who was also a Christian. He stayed for a week to help with the work and then left to make arrangements for his secondment. In that week I had enough time to do a complete drug inventory in preparation for ordering further supplies.

AUGUST 2005

THIS MONTH BEGAN WITH A big bang. We were in the depths of heavy rains and thunderstorms. One afternoon we heard several very loud cracks of thunder and flashes of lightning right above us. This was so intense that my whole body tingled. Our compound had taken two direct hits of lightning. The solar inverter at our house was fried as the lightning hit our lightning rod and travelled down and arced to the inverter ground wire. There was no light in the hospital and there was plaster on the floor near a light switch. The electrical line from the hospital Lister generator to our house was also hit and hanging very low. Fortunately, the solar panel on our roof still worked enough to charge the bank of batteries. This was used to power the small fridge full of vaccines and chemo drugs. We were able to get power from the big Lister generator to the delivery room and the operating room. Amos, an electrician, came and worked on burned out circuit breakers at the hospital. He reconnected our house to the hospital with an underground cable. I insisted that this be at least three-feet deep and inside a PVC pipe. I also had him install a steel post in deep holes dug near the hospital and our house. The posts were attached to weld-mesh in the bottom of the holes. Salt was poured into the holes before they were refilled with dirt. These posts would serve as lightning arrestors in the future.

Later more big bangs were heard at night. Lot, our night watchman came to our door wide-eyed. With a shaking voice he told us that armed robbers were on the road just above the hospital. We heard gunshots. We felt a bit nervous and locked all our doors. The next morning the staff were all buzzing with various versions of what had happened. The armed robbers were harassing people on the road between Gembu and our hospital. At gunpoint they would force people to lie face down while they robbed them. One night at 8 PM we had the Nigerian army descend on us. They brought a soldier to us who had been shot by the armed robbers. He was initially taken to the government hospital in Gembu, but no doctor could be found so he was brought to us. It felt strange to walk to the hospital with my little flashlight and umbrella, surrounded by huge army guys with automatic weapons fully loaded. The soldier had been off duty and riding his motorcycle in civilian clothes. He was on his way to an army camp near Gembu when he was accosted. He gunned his motor to escape. The robbers jumped aside but shot him in the right lower back with a pellet gun or shotgun. He was bleeding quite a bit and made a mess of our treatment room. All the wounds were superficial and I stopped most of the bleeding with good old fashioned pressure – a forgotten form of treatment. The secret of success is to not let go and peek for at least 15 minutes. He made a lot of noise, howling on and on. He finally stopped when I told him to be quiet and that he would still be the father of many children. He thought he was dying. After treatment with antibiotics, IV fluids, tetanus toxoid, and several days of recovery he was discharged. All his armed buddies left with him.

Three of the suspected robbers were caught by the army and roughed up before being transferred to the police station in Gembu. They were to be taken to Jalingo for a trial. Before that happened the local people of Gembu surrounded the police station and demanded that the robbers be turned over to them. The people feared that the robbers would either escape or bribe the police to release them on the way to Jalingo. The police initially refused to turn the men over to the mob, but eventually did let them out when the mob began to threaten the police. The mob then took two of the suspects to one side, beat and kicked them, hung tires around their necks, poured gas on them and burned them to death while the other suspect watched. Then they called the surviving suspect over and said, "Now it's your turn." I was shocked at this vigilante form of justice. The next day after the Sunday church service I met with several pastors and asked what they thought of these events. All the pastors agreed that this was a good thing to do, even though there had not been a proper trial to establish guilt. They felt that a lesson had to be taught to their youth that armed robbery was not going to be tolerated in Mambilla!

A man arrived with a large tumor in his left thigh. A biopsy in Jos showed that it was cancer that had already metastasized to his lungs. He was admitted to our hospital with severe coughing, blood tinged sputum, and rales throughout his chest. He was put on IV ampicillin in the hope that he might have some temporary benefit. I had a long talk with him and he was ready to accept Jesus as his Lord and Saviour. After he prayed to Jesus we saw that he was much happier. He died two weeks later.

On one tragic day I again witnessed the ravages of malaria on children. One child arrived with a hemoglobin of three grams and obviously needed a transfusion of blood. Another child dropped his hemoglobin from eight grams to four grams in the space of six hours. A 12-year-old boy came in with cerebral malaria and urinary retention. A beautiful little girl with malaria was improving on artesunate when she suddenly vomited, aspirated, and died of subsequent cardiac arrest. Her grieving mother had waited nine long years to get pregnant. What horrible suffering! The suffering was not limited to children. On another day a young woman arrived at the hospital in a semi-comatose condition. She came as a passenger on a motorcycle, strapped to the driver so she would not fall off. Her hemoglobin was four grams and she had a stiff neck. Our staff flew into action and within 10 minutes she was in bed with an IV set up, vital signs taken, and blood samples taken to the lab. Her spinal fluid was turbid, blood smear positive for malaria, and she tested positive for HIV. She died within two or three hours despite IV rehydration, quinine, ampicillin, and chloramphenicol. Malaria was certainly on the rampage now that rainy season had arrived. One day it rained so hard that water flooded the wards. The staff furiously tried to sweep it out.

We were dismayed to see the suffering of patients who had AIDS. One day we had four such cases in the wards:

- A young man with paraplegia, huge pressure sores on his back, and HIV-positive.

- A young pregnant girl with malaria, a hemoglobin of four grams, and HIV-positive. Her unborn baby was at high risk of intrauterine death and/or getting HIV in future as a nursing infant.

- Two women with AIDS had intractable vomiting and wasting. One of them was urinating blood.

What a helpless feeling as we had to watch this suffering and know that we had little to offer these people. Antibiotics seemed powerless to deal with opportunistic infections. We had no antiretroviral medications available or affordable to deal with AIDS. There was a faint glimmer of hope when a representative from The Evangelical Church Association of Nigeria (TECAN) came for an interview regarding a five-year supply of antiretroviral drugs. The medical arm of TECAN had funding for these drugs from President George W. Bush, so we filled out an application but never heard anything more about the offer.

AND THEN THE PHONE RANG...

I was happy one day to have a successful serious surgical case. A man presented with a large right testicular tumour. I did a right orchidectomy (removal of the testicle) and the surgery went surprisingly well, despite the fact that I was not a trained urologist!

We started a Sunday evening Bible study for our staff that lived on the hospital compound. We based it on a study of John's gospel. Our new hospital chaplain and his wife were regular attenders. He was very active in visitation of patients, doing morning devotionals with the staff and then with the outpatients waiting to be seen. He reported 19 decisions for Christ in August. One evening he and his wife made a special request to Marion and me. They wanted us to adopt Omega, his last son, and take him to Canada when we returned home. We were to keep him, raise, and educate him. We had to respond very tactfully because to say a direct no to them would be seen as a rejection of them as persons as well as their request. We gently pointed out that the Canadian Immigration officers would never believe us if we claimed that Omega was our son. If he was not our son, we would then be accused of child trafficking or kidnapping. They seemed to understand that officialdom was the obstacle to their request.

Another request came from our NAB Missions director who asked us to consider a posting as Interim Field Secretary in Mambilla after Wim and Marleen Munting returned. It was suggested that we have a furlough in Canada for one month, and then return for one year. The NAB Missions department would find the money to pay for our flights and various churches would be asked to raise enough funds for our living expenses. I really did not feel equipped to handle all the administrative details of the job and the necessary trips to Jos and Abuja. Also, the Burgess's were scheduled for furlough, so I would probably have to take on the Field Treasurer's work as well. Finally, I needed to have a good medical checkup as my aortic stenosis was becoming symptomatic. This might require surgery for an aortic valve replacement. After some prayer, Marion and I felt led by God to decline the proposal.

A few worrisome issues developed that required action:

- Marion needed a haircut. My offer of assistance was accepted after her prolonged deliberation. I thought I did a pretty good job. She looked a bit like Julie Andrews, but her singing needed a lot more work!

- Our visas for Cameroon were about to expire. Frantic efforts were made to get them renewed in Yaoundé. We faced the prospect of leaving Mambilla quickly to get flights home from Douala. The visa extensions arrived just days before the deadline.

- We had a number of key cases:

- Friday night – no key for the fuel store to get diesel for the generator.

- Sunday night – no key for the lab to get urgent tests done.

- Monday – no key for the treatment room. We needed to do dressing changes on the shot-up soldier.

- Monday – no key for the morgue. Relatives came to collect the body of a 17-year-old boy to take home for burial.

It was very frustrating to waste so much time looking for keys that the staff were negligent in handing over at shift change time. I spoke some very firm words to them. I also discovered that some of the staff had issues with overconsumption of alcohol as I could smell it on their breath. This required tactful counselling.

Marion became a midwife and nurse when she supervised the hatching and care of a bunch of chicks. She also discovered lice on our chickens, so she caught them one by one and rubbed palm oil on their little heads and eyelids.

I awoke one morning to find an anopheles mosquito on the wall beside my bed. It was shaped like an SST Concorde jet. This type was responsible for transmission of malaria. I declared that I was the lord of this house and vengeance was mine, so I smashed him with my hand. To my dismay I found blood on my hand. This critter had got to me first. I was glad we had our Doxycycline antimalarial prophylaxis.

SEPTEMBER 2005

THE RAINY SEASON WAS BEGINNING to ease up a bit, but in early September a huge cloud burst caused water to pour into our carport and threaten our small fridge. Marion got thoroughly soaked as she tried to redirect the flow of water away with a garden hoe. Being good Baptists, we were not afraid of a bit of water! We did begin to visit outlying PHCs to see patients booked by the local health officer. The first of the weekly visits was a 175-kilometer round trip from Gembu to Maisomari on a paved road. We saw 100 patients there and another 108 the following day in nearby Ngurogi. A few weeks later we went to Yerimaru for their clinic. The scenery on the way was beautiful. After seeing 61 patients we stopped at the Kakara Tea Estate on the way home. We bought some packages of tea to take home as gifts. Marion took a picture of the main gate and was immediately arrested by a security man who hassled her and wanted to confiscate her camera. I did not see her being hauled away and after a while I went looking for her. I found her in the security house by the main gate. I sensed that the security guy was trying to shake us down for a bribe to get our camera back. I gave him a very stern look and in a loud voice told him to cut out the baloney and give the camera back to us immediately. He gave it back and I escorted Marion out of there.

I saw many people in the out-patient department and in the hospital. The following are a number of interesting and difficult medical and surgical cases.

I saw a very sick lady with asthma and pneumonia who improved with cefuroxime, zithromax and a symbicort inhaler. I had a long talk with her husband who was a tribal elder and represented the Mambilla tribe as an advisor to the State Governor and to Obasenjo, President of Nigeria. I asked him if he would persuade the local government officials to fix the terrible dirt road between Gembu and our hospital. He was impressed to see a five-year old boy admitted with a huge mass of his right cheek, swelling of his palate, and loose teeth – all due to Burkitt's lymphoma. He also saw another boy with the same disease who came for the second cycle of chemotherapy, who by this time looked almost normal.

A young man came complaining of a painful tender mass in his right lower abdomen and a history of an appendectomy done two years ago. He had been in Gembu hospital for several days, but nothing had been done for him. His hemoglobin was only six grams and his blood smear was positive for malaria, so he was not a candidate for immediate surgery. He was given treatment for malaria and a blood transfusion was started. The next day we did a laparotomy, opening his abdomen with a right paramedian rectus splitting incision. A thick band of adhesion from his small bowel to the peritoneum was divided and large towels were used to pack off his intestines. I opened a large pocket of pus in the right paracolic gutter with blunt dissection. There I found a thick gangrenous retro-caecal appendix adherent to the back of the caecum. A large hard fecolith (particle of stool) was impacted in the neck of the appendix. Now a real appendectomy was done, the abdominal cavity washed out with copious saline, a drain inserted, and the abdomen closed. The skin layer was left open for later closure. He was given IV flagyl and chloromycetin and put to bed with his head raised. I showed the rotten appendix to the family waiting outside. They were absolutely furious at the people who treated the boy two years ago and then lied about doing an appendectomy. I later discovered that there were doctors in parts of Nigeria who would make a skin incision and sew it up on patients with abdominal discomfort. The patients would be told that the supposed doctor had saved their lives by doing a supposed appendectomy, and then would charge a huge surgical fee! This young man recovered and went home happy.

At the end of a Sunday night Bible study I was called to see a woman who had a postpartum retained placenta. I saw a trail of blood the entire length of the verandah to the delivery room. The lady was semi-comatose and in profound shock with no pulse or blood pressure. A large amount of blood was draining from her vagina. Our staff found a vein for an IV and had 5% dextrose/saline pouring in. The room was full of people who brought the lady to the hospital. They were all sent to the lab for cross-matching and we got three units of donated blood from them. We had no time to get a generator going for light, so I examined her by the light of a kerosene lamp. I found a retained placenta and got most of it out. I then raised her legs to get her own blood to stay centrally and perfuse her vital organs. I put pressure on the aorta, massaged the uterus to get it to contract, and hollered orders for IV ergot, pitocin and antibiotics. A second IV was started in her other arm for blood transfusions. We finally got a pulse and a firm uterus. She was put to bed with a foley catheter inserted to measure her urine output. This lady miraculously recovered and the next day she was cuddling her newborn baby that had come with her. This was a real hair-raising experience, and I did not have a lot of hair left to raise!

We did quite a few C-sections and some of them were very unusual. I was called at 1 AM to see a lady in labour whose baby was lying transversely and the presenting part was an arm. Vaginal delivery was impossible in such cases. Jezreel's spinal anesthetic did not take very well so I opened the lady's abdomen using local anesthetic, and once the uterus was opened, we gave her an IV ketamine general anesthetic. The baby's other arm protruded out of the uterine incision and this caused great difficulty in the delivery of the baby. I finally got a grip on the trunk and teased the baby out, bum-first, like a breech delivery. I was drenched in sweat from the effort and was so pumped with adrenaline that I couldn't sleep much after getting to bed at 4 AM.

ONE DAY I REALLY GOT depressed at seeing so many seriously ill people. All of the following cases arrived on one day:

- A Fulani girl with a painful distended abdomen of unknown cause. I even wondered about typhoid fever.

- A boy with polymyositis. He had eight abscesses, all of which I drained.

- A man in a semi-coma, a stiff neck, and HIV-positive. He did not respond to multiple IV medications. His family took him home to die.

- A Fulani boy with cerebral malaria. He was comatose and had widespread rales in his chest. We treated him with everything we could think of, but he died.

- A boy with huge Burkitt's lymphomas on both sides of his neck that almost occluded his trachea. We got chemotherapy going within two hours of admission as there was no time for IV hydration first. He was on the verge of choking to death.

This was a grim day! The Fulani girl with the distended abdomen was afebrile the next day and had a normal white blood count. We gave her an enema to evacuate rock hard stool and her abdomen got softer. Several days later she suddenly deteriorated. I opened her abdomen under ketamine anesthetic and discovered thin brown fecal matter in her abdomen. We found a perforation in her terminal small bowel and a distended loop of bowel with a strange band of fibrous tissue across it. We resected a part of her bowel and cleaned out the abdominal cavity with saline and instilled tetracycline in it before closing her up. She was given IV fluids, blood, and antibiotics. By the next morning she had very little urine output and her extremities were cold. She died. I really felt awful about this case and beat myself up mentally and emotionally. This girl might have lived if I had operated sooner. It was a lesson to me to put aside my personal fears and misgivings about my limitations as a surgeon. This was really tough for me.

Administrative issues also required attention. The MBCN Medical Board met periodically, and I had to attend these meetings. They took several meetings to finally decide to terminate a nurse who had been suspended for several months. He was guilty of reckless drunk driving of the staff vehicle and then going on a rampage of verbal and physical abuse of staff members. The termination was difficult for the board members to do because the nurse was the son of a prominent member of the convention who was sitting in on the meetings. The medical board also decided to build a new hospital at the site of the PHC in Gembu and use the present hospital site for a secondary school and a rural development center. A new hospital in Gembu would better serve the needs of the large population center by providing easier access to medical care. Obviously, there would have to be a fund-raising campaign for this project.

We were on a very tight budget and diesel fuel was very expensive. In order to reduce hospital operating costs, we only ran the big hospital generator for 4 hours, two nights per week. On those two nights Gideon and Jezreel set up a projector and a screen on the hospital verandah and showed the Jesus film, adding another evangelistic opportunity to these evenings. Patients and their caregivers gathered to watch. It was interesting to see their reactions and applause when Jesus healed someone. They moaned at the sight of the crucifixion and cheered at the resurrection scene. The chaplain followed the film with a devotional thought and an invitation to accept Jesus Christ as their Saviour too.

AND THEN THE PHONE RANG...

Dr. J. D. came back in late September with Daniel Samuel to discuss the possibility of joining the staff of our hospital. His salary demands were outrageously high and in negotiation he did not lower his request very much, even after we raised our salary offer. We reminded him of his vow to come and serve his Mambilla people, which made him a bit nervous. He left to discuss our final offer with his wife. We never saw him again. So much for his vows.

Marion also had administrative issues centered on animal life. One evening a bat got stuck between the window screen and the louvre window slats. She was not very impressed with the situation and I could see the whites of her eyes all around as she warned me about rabies and bats. Just then our good friend Daniel Samuel walked in and assessed the situation. He grabbed the bat with a haemostat clamp, took it outside, and introduced the bat to the sole of his shoe. The bat died an untimely death. Marion also got the urge one day to do some house cleaning. She cleaned two wicker chairs full of spider webs on our patio. As she sprayed them with insecticide, four huge black widow spiders waddled out, rolled over and died. We had been sitting on those chairs to relax after supper, totally unaware of our danger. Another time the Chief of Mambilla came to the hospital, in his Mercedes, as a patient. He was grateful for our care and to thank us he sent a gift of two roosters. Now where would we put them, as they would get into huge fights with our own roosters? Marion had to decide which one to kill and put in a pot for supper. Suddenly she gave me a strange look and said, "Hey, your hair has a rooster-tail too." That got me worried so I quickly left to check on a few patients. I returned when the right rooster was in the pot. A short time later I got a haircut to get rid of my own rooster tail and was able to relax again.

WE WERE VERY TIRED AFTER months of work and being on call day and night. We took a weekend off and accepted the offer from the Burgesses to visit them at the Bible school in Mbu. On the way we stopped in Gembu to tour the government hospital. Dr. Alexander Okan was the doctor in charge – the same Alexander who was on staff at Warwar hospital in the 1970s as a ward attendant. Sabina Mamla, Rachel Jeminda, and Faye Chufor, all previous members of our Warwar staff, were now in senior positions in the Gembu hospital. The hospital was in very poor condition with broken up floors, rotting ceiling boards, old beds, and no running water. There were few patients in this 100-bed hospital. It was a sorry sight. We did a bit of shopping in Gembu before going to Mbu. We were able to sleep in and had a lazy breakfast. The Bible school had a beautiful chapel and a two-story library. It was a treat to see some CNN news on TV and to play some Rook card games. We attended church the next day in Mbu and after lunch headed back home to the hospital feeling more relaxed and rested.

OCTOBER 2005

THERE WERE AN UNUSUAL NUMBER of obstetrical cases during this month, and some of them were quite dramatic. In one memorable week we had the following cases:

- A delivery of premature twins weighing 1.5 and 1.7 kilograms

- A deaf-mute pregnant lady in labour with a history of three normal vaginal deliveries and then a C-section for twins. We did a trial of VBAC (vaginal birth after C-section). This was scary as she could not communicate with us regarding her level of pain. She also made very slow progress, such that I had no sleep that night. She finally delivered the next day.

- The same night as the above case, a lady in her first pregnancy, had an extremely long slow labour. This added to my loss of sleep. She delivered at 2:30 AM.

- A lady in labour with a history of a previous C-section. All four of her children had died of various diseases. We did a difficult repeat C-section as the spinal anesthetic was ineffective and we had to resort to local freezing. Once the baby was delivered, we gave her ketamine anesthesia. As I was sewing her up, I was informed that another lady in labour had a baby with a very slow heart rate. I had my assistant finish sewing up the C-section wound while I ran over to see if we had to do another C-section on this new case. Fortunately, she was fully dilated. I got her to push the head down far enough for me to do a vacuum extraction.

- A lady in labour that the midwife thought had the umbilical cord presenting. On examination I found a face presentation in a transverse lie. I knew it was not a breech as the little kid bit my finger during my examination. I rotated the head into a mentum-anterior position and with pressure on the mother's levator muscles I got her to push the kid out. The baby's face looked like he had run into a brick wall!

- For an encore that week, a woman came in with a retained placenta, having delivered nine hours previously. She had a hemoglobin of six grams and a blood pressure of 80/30. IV's were started and ketamine was given so that I could do a difficult manual removal of the placenta that was densely adherent to the uterine wall. The baby, her firstborn, died shortly after despite our efforts of chest compressions and ventilation. It was heartbreaking to see and hear the mom's agonizing cry. I was in tears too.

All of the above cases occurred in one week, in addition to a number of normal deliveries. The most dramatic event happened about a week later, around 9:30 PM. A party of 20 men carried in the chaplain's sister on a litter. She had been in serious labour for two days for her fifth pregnancy. She was in shock with a blood pressure of 60/40 and a hemoglobin of six grams. She was pale and cold and no fetal heart could be heard. The baby was in a transverse position and its limbs were very easy to feel. I suspected that she had a ruptured uterus. IV's were started in both arms and the 20 men were sent to the lab for blood-typing. Jezreel was put in charge of getting blood transfusions started while I drove like Jehu to Gembu to get Elias to assist with surgery. Two units of blood and 1500 c.c.'s of IV fluid had been given by the time we got back. Her blood pressure was now 80/60. We gave her a ketamine anesthetic. As we opened her abdomen, we noticed how white her tissues looked. Blood gushed out of the wound and the first thing we saw was the placenta, which we removed. We then pulled out a huge dead baby girl that was in the mom's abdomen outside of the uterus. The uterus had ruptured on the right side, into the broad ligament, through the cervix and into the upper vagina. With some difficulty we managed to close the large ragged tear and stop further bleeding. Without prior permission we did a tubal ligation to prevent any further pregnancies which had a very high probability of a fatal outcome. By the next morning she was in stable condition with copious urine output.

NOT ALL OBSTETRICS WAS AS grim and difficult as the above-mentioned ones. One day a man driving a motorcycle was bringing a passenger to the hospital. This passenger was a lady in labour. He got the lady to the top of a hill very near to the hospital when the lady stopped him because her contractions were very intense and she felt the urge to push. The resourceful man found an old wheelbarrow in a nearby compound, put the lady in it, and wheeled her to the hospital. The old wheelbarrow was rusty and had a squeaky wheel. The people at the hospital heard them approach by the rhythmic squeak, squeak, squeak, and the lady's moans. She delivered the baby on the doorstep of the hospital. The baby was not happy with the bumpy ride and decided to moon everyone by coming out breech – bum first! Mom and baby were fine. The next morning the women in the maternity room roared with laughter, the mom included, as I walked in muttering "squeak, squeak, squeak." The baby was named Squeakie.

A young boy was admitted with an eight-month history of coughing and had been paraplegic for the past two months. His chest was full of rales and he had a deformed spine. I suspected that he had tuberculosis and we tried to confirm this by checking his sputum for TB bacteria. We did not have an X-ray machine which would have been helpful in diagnosis. We started him on multiple drug therapy for TB. I really felt sorry for this poor neglected kid. We found an old beat-up wheelchair for him to get around. After two-and-a-half weeks he was able to move his legs, so we got him onto his feet using a walker for support. It was gratifying to see this little guy get stronger almost on a daily basis.

Another young man was admitted with a four-day history of epigastric pain. To treat this pain, he drank gasoline! We obviously had to change his treatment plan!

I was in a real quandary one day when we admitted two children with Burkitt's lymphoma and there was enough cyclosporine for only one person. Who should get the medicine – first come, first served, or who needed it most? I emailed Lori at Banso Baptist Hospital in Cameroon to see if she could find some to send us. She was able to send 20 bottles of cyclosporine free of charge.

We were not immune from illness ourselves. Marion stayed home from church one Sunday as she had a headache and an upset stomach. The next day I felt dizzy, fatigued, fever, sweats, headache, and woolly-headed. I was so tired making morning ward rounds that I sat on the edge of every bed I came to. Marion and I both tested positive for malaria despite the fact that we were on doxycycline as prophylaxis. We both took artesunate and felt better after a long nap. I was glad that we kept a small part of the artesunate supply aside for missionary use.

I began to realize that being the only doctor and on call 24/7 was starting to wear me out. I had lost about 25 pounds since arriving in Mambilla. I had to take better care of myself, and Marion, in order to finish our assignment. So, we took another weekend off to recuperate at Mbu with Dave and Mary-June. Again, it was good to sleep-in, watch current news on TV, play Rook, and just lay back and relax. There was a glimmer of hope when Dr. Dele Owoyele came for an interview regarding the possibility of joining our staff. I gave him a tour of the hospital and then had him assist me in an appendectomy. We discussed salary and showed him the PHC site in Gembu where a new hospital was to be built. He left without making a commitment about working here, saying he would consult with his wife. Another physician showed up and expressed some interest in working with us, but his salary demands were way too high for us to consider. He wanted a special bonus for working in a rural situation. This did not sit very well with me at all.

Thanksgiving time at Vision Church was a joyous event. We had a message on Psalm 100 listing the reasons for giving thanks to God. One quarter of the people went outside to pick up their offerings and danced enthusiastically back in, to the beat of drums. They formed a line down the aisle carrying corn, beans, rice, firewood, and yams as gifts to God. One boy even carried a case of soda pop on his head. The rest of us joined the conga line and brought money to a basket in the front of the church. After the church service we all went outside where all the gifts were auctioned off. The money from this went into the church coffers to fund ministries.

Marion had brought a loaf of bread, bundles of cookies and jars of guava sauce. These items were highly sought after and brought in a lot of money.

We hosted a special reunion of former Warwar hospital staff who now lived nearby. We had fufu, bean cakes, chicken, and vegetables. Marion also served homemade ice cream, much to their delight. It was great to talk about the old times, and about the present situation they were in, as they had all achieved senior positions in rural health care and hospital work. We were proud to have been part of their early lives and development.

Daniel Samuel, Marion, and I paid a visit to Mr. Gideon Kataps, the Attorney General of Taraba State, in order to resolve a minor legal matter. He lived in a huge beautiful mansion on a walled estate property. There were turkeys, eaglets, and a peacock strutting on the lawn. He owned several vehicles including a beautiful Mercedes sedan. He and his pregnant wife were gracious hosts and we enjoyed the visit. Several weeks later his wife came to our hospital. She was eight months pregnant and had leaking membranes. She had a history of premature rupture of membranes in her last pregnancy and a C-section for a baby in a breech position. I gave her some ampicillin and sent her to Jalingo where she could be with her husband and be monitored at the government hospital there. She returned to our hospital about three weeks later to show us her new baby. She had a C-section after three days observation in the Jalingo Hospital.

WE HAD GREAT JOY ONE day when the chaplain informed us that two Fulani Muslim Maalams (Islamic teachers) accepted Christ as their saviour. This was a huge step of faith for them as they would be shunned by their family and tribal community. I was aware of some small house churches consisting of former Fulani Muslims who had become Christians. Hopefully these two Maalams would find fellowship and support in these groups.

NOVEMBER 2005

FINALLY, SOME GOOD NEWS! DR. Dele Owoyele sent a message that he had agreed to come and work with us. He did not show up for a week and that gave Gideon time to put his considerable organizational talent to work. He

AND THEN THE PHONE RANG...

got a crew to clean the second physician's house, paint it, fill it with furniture, linens, and stock the kitchen with appliances. Gideon wisely got the generator running when Dr. Dele arrived so that the house was brightly lit up. He also arranged for the chaplain's wife to cook meals for him. I made ward rounds with Dr. Dele the following day and then assigned him to see out-patients while I did surgery. He seemed to be a capable doctor and, some time after his arrival, I witnessed him doing a reasonable job on a C-section. His presence took a lot of strain off me and gave me the opportunity to do some other projects.

One of the other projects was to do a complete drug and supplies inventory with Felicia so that I could restock the hospital stores and pharmacy. We placed several orders with Basil, an agent in Gembu, who went to Onitsha to buy and transport supplies to us. Other orders were sent to Jos. The hospital owed a large sum of money to the NAB mission and were also in debt to Basil. In discussion with Daniel, we restructured the hospital finances and managed to pay the debt to Basil and make a large reduction in our debt to the Mission. I also had time to do a detailed inspection of the hospital facilities with Elias and Gideon. The latrines and garbage pits were very dirty. We made a list of work for the security guards and grounds keepers that kept them very busy. The clutch in the staff vehicle gave out, so a new one was added to Basil's shopping list.

As it was dry season now, I was able to visit a number of outlying PHC's to do mobile clinics. With Dr. Dele 's presence at the hospital, I was able to add a couple of new clinics. One of them was a day at the Bible school to do check-ups on all of the children of the students as well as any sick adults. Daniel and Gideon came along to help. Of the 75 kids we saw, eight of them had pneumonia and others had malaria, intestinal worms, and some were malnourished. All the kids were given fansidar and albendazole to treat malaria and worms. The school was given 1000 doses of vitamins to dispense to the children. Even Dave Burgess required treatment for bronchitis. The parents were all poor struggling students, so money was found to pay for the medicines given to the kids.

A special visit was arranged for me to see all the prisoners in the Gembu jail. It was a dingy place with high walls, iron double doors, and armed guards who held flexible canes in their hands. There was an eerie silence as I entered.

All the prisoners were crouched in rows on the grounds of the inner courtyard. The inmates moved very quickly when guards, bearing their flexible canes, barked orders at them. I saw bunk beds through barred windows of a building along one side of the courtyard. It looked like there were bunks for about 40 people in each room. This was definitely not a pleasant place. I examined about 109 inmates in addition to the guards, who insisted on being seen first. Two of the prisoners were women. I asked one man how long he had been in jail. He said about three years, and had no idea of when he would be released. I felt sorry for these guys. The way they cowered when guards came near suggested that they experienced regular beatings.

Among the many sick patients that we saw at the hospital were several that I will never forget, and have described in the following four paragraphs. They again illustrated the suffering of the people of Mambilla.

A tall, pregnant Fulani girl arrived one night with a history of bleeding for a week. She spent five days at the Gembu hospital in observation. Her hemoglobin was only eight grams. She had another major bleed at night and after two units of blood her hemoglobin was still only eight grams. She needed a C-section and more blood. I appealed for donors among a large group of women who had come to the hospital with her. They all refused to even be cross-matched. In frustration, I yelled at them and told them if they didn't donate blood, they could take her back home to die in their house. A Mambilla man overheard this and offered his blood. The women were ashamed and they also were cross-matched. I proceeded to do a C-section and found that the patient had a complete placenta previa, where the placenta completely covered the opening of the cervix. She would not have survived an attempt at a normal delivery. I felt a bit sheepish about hollering at the Fulani women and apologized to them the next day. The staff and others nearby were amazed to hear the doctor, a big important man in their eyes, apologize. I wondered later if this was yet another way to be a testimony as to what a Christian should do.

A beautiful little four-year old girl arrived with a distended abdomen due to bowel obstruction. At laparotomy I found an intussusception of her entire colon from caecum to descending colon. This is where the bowel collapses in on itself like a telescope. As a result, she had hugely dilated, fluid-filled loops of small bowel. I reduced the intussusception and used a rectal tube to milk the fluid out of the small bowel, thereby decompressing it. She was given IV fluids, blood, and antibiotics. We then prayed for her healing. I was crushed and in tears when she died several days later. I wished that we had the ability to measure electrolytes.

A woman came with multiple burns of her abdomen, arms and thighs. Her husband was a particularly meddlesome, know-it-all type. He interfered with our treatment by putting rabbit hair and egg whites on the burns. He was warned not to do things that would potentially cause infection. We got her all cleaned up but the next day discovered that the husband had put honey and feathers on the wounds. He even refused our plans to debride necrotic tissue prior to skin grafting. At this point I threatened to discharge the woman into his care at home if he continued interfering.

A woman arrived in early labour with a fetal heart rate that was very erratic, a sign of fetal distress. To complicate matters, she had a hemoglobin of under eight grams and a history of a previous C-section for a dead baby. This baby was already in distress and the only hope for survival was an immediate C-section. Marion came to the hospital and donated a unit of blood, making her quite light-headed and weak in her legs. The baby was very lethargic and pale and required prolonged resuscitation. Sadly, the baby died 12 hours later. The mother was heartbroken. Two C-sections and two dead babies! If only we had a proper incubator for such babies.

On a particularly busy day we admitted the following patients while trying to do ward rounds:

- A woman in diabetic ketoacidosis.

- A man with severe pneumonia.

- A pregnant lady with pneumonia, a hemoglobin of six grams and HIV positive.

- A psychotic man with his hands tied behind his back and stamping one foot like a soldier.

- A wild man, raving loudly and fighting. It took six men to hold him down while Jezreel gave him a shot of Largactil, 100 mg. which slowly settled him down.

GOD'S HELP EVERY STEP OF THE WAY

We attended the Warwar Field Bible Conference with our chaplain and a number of hospital staff. We sat under a canopy made of old flour sacks sewn together. It was such a hot sweltering day that Marion got quite nauseated and had tingling in her arms and legs. She headed for the cooler kitchen where she helped the women who were cooking for the 600 people at the conference. I was a bit nauseated too, but had to stay as I was unexpectedly called upon to address the conference. We enjoyed a meal of fufu and chicken livers in palm oil at Pastor Peter Jumvuh's home. On arrival home I was immediately called to see a semi-comatose lady who had just had a convulsion. She had pneumonia and possible malaria. I then did a C-section on a short lady under five feet tall who had been in labour for a long time and the baby's head was still unengaged. She was also HIV positive. I was really tired that day after non-stop sweating. I fell into bed, asleep before my head hit the pillow.

The next day we crossed the Donga River again to attend the wedding of Charity, our house maid, and Naphthtali, a recent law school graduate. The road was very rough, but we managed, somehow, to arrive with a four-tiered wedding cake intact. Marion and Mary Wanmi had spent a long time building that cake! The church service was two hours long. It took the wedding party a half hour to dance down the aisle. The dancing was very vigorous and caused a lot of sweating. Charity, dressed in white, came a quarter of the way down the aisle and crouched down when her groom approached her from the front. He gently lifted her up and they danced to the front together. The message was from Song of Solomon. The vows were hilarious as the pastor asked Charity if she would vow to stay with her husband even if his tie was crooked, his beard straggly, and his teeth had fallen out. We then drove the couple to the groom's compound where an outdoor service was held, complete with another message. Cutting of the cake and light refreshments followed.

We were looking ahead to December with mixed feelings when our time in Mambilla would be done. News came that extensions to our visas for Cameroon had been approved. The Nigerian immigration officer also allowed us to stay till Christmas. I sent an email home to inform our family that we would be able to complete our assignment. I noted that we still had one-and-a-half small jars of peanut butter left. When that was finished, we would be finished!

AND THEN THE PHONE RANG...

DECEMBER 2005

WITH DR. DELE WORKING AT the hospital I took the opportunity to hold a medical clinic for the people of the so-called needy Church. These were people with leprosy, both active and cured, that lived in a small community on the edge of Gembu. They were very poor and for the most part shunned by the rest of society. I examined 41 of them using the bedroom of Genesis Keke as a consulting room. He was the man who fell out of a tree and fractured his ribs and had now recovered. Several of the people were found to have pneumonia and many of them had various deformities of hands and feet as a result of leprosy. One man had a badly infected leg and was sent to our hospital for further treatment. They were extremely poor people so I did not charge them for any of the medicines we supplied them.

ONE EVENING A LAND ROVER tipped over and crushed the pelvis of a man who was sitting on top of the vehicle. He had a huge perineal laceration, fractured pelvic bones, severed urethra, and bladder damage. We inserted a suprapubic catheter, stabilized him with IV fluids and antibiotics, and transferred him to the Jalingo Hospital where a urologist could see and treat him. Another passenger had a supracondylar fracture of his left hip, and other people had lacerations and bruises, making for a very busy night.

Zebulon Wanmi's sister came to the hospital with out-of-control diabetes and a very swollen leg due to deep vein thrombosis (blood clots). We had very little stock of anticoagulant medicine. Her prognosis was very poor and the following day she had multiple pulmonary emboli, clots from her leg travelling to her lungs. After a brief struggle to breathe she died.

One busy surgery day we did the following surgical operations:

- A laparotomy on an elderly man who had a pus-filled abdomen. There were many adhesions between loops of bowel, but no source of perforation was evident. We cleaned out his abdomen with copious saline irrigations and placed two drains and saline with tetracycline before closing him up. I suspected a possible diagnosis of typhoid fever and ordered IV chloramphenicol and flagyl. He rallied for a few days, and then slowly deteriorated and died.

- A hernia repair done using lidocaine, a local anesthetic. Two other elective hernia repairs booked for that day were cancelled due to lack of heavy marcaine that we used for spinal anesthesia.

- A laparotomy on a cute little six-month old girl with a history of vomiting and passing blood rectally. Her abdomen was hard and distended. We decompressed her stomach with a nasogastric tube and anesthetized her with ketamine. On opening her abdomen, we found a distended small bowel and a volvulus (twisted) terminal ileum. There were perforations of the distal small bowel as well. I did a resection of the affected part of her small bowel and decompressed the rest of the bowel using a foley catheter. After washing out the abdominal cavity I instilled saline with tetracycline and closed her wound. We did not have a suction machine, so I instructed one of the nurses on the night shift to aspirate the nasogastric tube every 30 minutes through the night to prevent gastric distension. Three days later the baby passed some stool and was able to swallow infant formula. Her abdomen was soft and bowel sounds were detected. She gradually improved over the next few days, but 11 days after surgery she suddenly died. We did not know the cause of death. I again went home and cried.

The day after the busy surgery day I admitted a pregnant lady with a huge spleen, another pregnant lady with a liver mass and schistosomiasis, an eleven-month-old baby with tetanus, and a man with a painful abdominal mass, AIDS and severe anemia. These last two days completely exhausted me to the point of nausea, dizziness, and headaches. I had already noticed episodes of light-headedness after getting up from a crouch or prolonged sitting. I thought that my aortic stenosis must be getting tighter, and that I should get an echocardiogram done as soon as we got home.

December 1 was World AIDS Day. We watched as the Deputy Governor of Taraba State cut the ribbon to dedicate the Gembu Center for HIV-AIDS Advocacy that the Helwigs had established. A big rally was held in the Mansur Stadium. Much of the time was taken by boring, long speeches by various governmental officials. There was some good choir music and a hilarious skit by the Youth Corps about the serious effects of AIDS. Marion was busy doing immunizations that day but did manage to get to the rally by hitching a ride on the back of a motorcycle.

After seeing patients at the Gembu PHC we walked about a kilometer up a gentle slope to the upper end of the property. Robert, a local contractor, had a crew of men digging into a hillside to tap into a spring that produced a good flow of water even in dry season. He was building a catchment for this water that was to be piped down to the PHC building and to the area of the proposed new hospital buildings. It was interesting to see how creative and efficient Robert was in designing this project.

I was asked to preach at the Warwar church on December 18 during the advent season. To get there I had to drive three-quarters of the way through the Donga River to get to the raft as the river level was very low by this time of dry season. My message was based on Isaiah 9 and Matthew 24:29-44. The main point of the message was that we celebrate Christ's coming to earth at Christmas, but He is going to come again – are you ready to meet Him?

I had many long talks with our staff. Both Gideon and Elias were encouraged to support Daniel who was the Medical Director. They needed to work as a united team and avoid the scourge of tribalism. I had many discussions with Daniel about staffing, financial management, and relationships with the state government and the convention medical board. He was in tears at times with the various frustrations that he faced. We had precious prayer times together. Daniel and his wife Charity were a mature and dedicated Christian couple and became our close friends.

WE ALSO HAD SOME DISCUSSIONS with Felicia who had fallen in love with Larry. Larry was a handy-man and builder working with Art and Dorothy Helwig, missionaries of the Baptist General Conference (BGC). Larry and Felicia were planning to get married. This caused complications because the BGC had a policy that did not allow such relationships between missionaries and local people. We also feared that the huge cultural differences between them could pose a considerable strain on their marriage in the future. We shared several meals with them and tried to help them understand and work through some of the issues involved.

GOD'S HELP EVERY STEP OF THE WAY

Our time in Mambilla was coming to a close. The peanut butter jars were empty. We had a farewell time with the MBCN Medical Board and were given gifts of appreciation. We also enjoyed dinners in the homes of some of our staff. At the staff Christmas party, we enjoyed rice, goat meat, sweet rolls, and Fanta (soda pop). After a number of speeches from the staff I thanked them all for their work in bringing treatment and comfort to many sick people in the name of Christ. I also exhorted them to avoid tribalism and to truly love each other. I privately had farewells with Elias and then with Daniel, giving each of them a few gifts.

GOING HOME VIA CAMEROON

THE DAY OF DEPARTURE, DECEMBER 23, had come. Dave and Mary-June Burgess arrived to load up the vehicle for our trip together to Cameroon. The entire staff gathered at our house at 7:30 to say good-bye. There were a lot of handshakes, hugs and tears. I gave the house keys to Gideon. Daniel said a word of prayer, and off we went wiping tears from our eyes. We crossed the Donga River by raft for the last time and drove on a reasonably good road through several villages to the border of Nigeria and Cameroon. We were signed out of Nigeria by the same rude border officer who in June had signed us in. We had to drive past an army post and were stopped by some officious officers who threatened to make us unpack all our cargo for inspection. Suddenly they seemed to lose interest and let us pass through. The French officials on the Cameroon side were also very unfriendly, but they did not detain us. A few minutes later we were in Mayo Darle and met the chief immigration officer who officially signed us into Cameroon. We finally got to Allat, our destination for the day.

In Allat there was a missionary compound where Cal and Susie Hohn and their two daughters were stationed, as well as a health center. We stayed in the rest house and enjoyed a great supper meal with the Hohns in their beautifully designed home. Lori and Kathy Kroll came to Allat from Banso to spend Christmas with us. We had a great time relaxing, touring the health clinic, eating, going to church, eating some more, opening gifts, eating, having a carol sing, and doing a Christmas pageant. Cal was King

Herod and Lori was chosen to be Mary, so she put a pillow under her clothes to look pregnant. Ysabelle Hohn was the reluctant angel. I don't recall who the designated donkey was. We also celebrated Kathy Kroll's 60th birthday.

The next leg of the trip was to Banso, where we stayed with Lori. She gave us a tour of Banso Baptist Hospital and showed us the site of the planned three-story school of nursing and midwifery. The tour included a hike down to the Banso market to shop at the famous Patrick's Supermarket that had an amazing variety of foods and supplies. At the hospital we also met a number of resident doctors from various parts of Africa who were doing post-graduate training to become surgeons. Banso had a number of qualified Cameroonian specialists on staff as well as Dr. Pokey Cleek and his wife who were from the U.S.A.

We went to Bamenda for the annual Cameroon Missionary Fellowship conference from January 2 to 6, 2006. There was great fellowship, good food, and inspiring presentations and devotionals. Marion led a 90-minute devotional and discussion for all the women on the topic, "What is a world Christian?" Fred Folkerts, a former missionary and Missions Director, gave me a small jar of peanut butter that Carol Potratz sent to us. She apparently saw some of my emails stating that when our jars were empty, we would go home. We were already on the way home so I gave the jar to Dave Burgess and we all had a good laugh. While in Bamenda we went to the military fort on a nearby hill and found the gravesite of Johannes Sieber. He was my mom's uncle and a pioneer Baptist missionary in Cameroon.

After the conference we returned to Banso to spend a few more days with Lori, her fellow missionaries, and hospital staff. The time came to fly home, so after a tearful farewell with Lori, we drove to Bamenda. The next day we headed to the Baptist Mission rest house in Douala for a shower and change of clothes. We ate a supper of hamburgers, fries, and ice cream in a fancy restaurant. This was a very expensive treat! The airport was most uncomfortable. The boarding gate area was small and stifling hot, with standing room only. We had to join in the pushing and jostling to get on the plane. I was so soaked with sweat that I had to change my shirt. The flight to Charles De Gaulle airport took seven hours. The next flight took us to Toronto where we had to take our baggage outside to catch a bus to the domestic terminal. The temperature was –4°C. What a shock going from stifling hot to freezing cold. It was wonderful to see family and friends who met us at the airport in Vancouver.

Well it was over – our assignment was done by God's enablement. Our faith in His call and His provision was severely stretched many times by difficult medical cases, fear of the unknown, and the sense of being overwhelmed. It was only our weak faith that produced fear, anxiety, and sleepless nights. The exercise of obedience to God's call deepened our faith and put a new perspective on what life is all about. We do serve a most wonderful God. All praise and honor belong to Him alone. Yes, we helped the Muntings get a furlough and helped many sick people, but I think we got more out of this experience than we realized. So, what would come next? HIV tests, echocardiogram, a new ministry?

HIV PATIENT REQUIRED AMPUTATION OF BADLY INFECTED LEG

HIV A MAJOR HEALTH ISSUE IN MAMBILLA

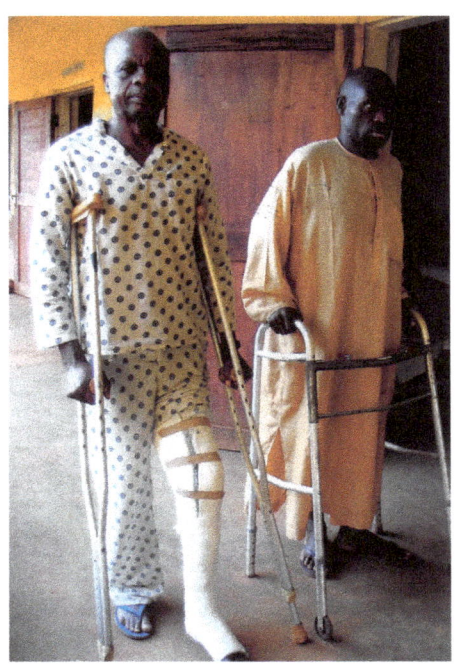

PATIENT WITH ANKLE FRACTURE AND PATIENT WITH PELVIC FRACTURES

GOD'S HELP EVERY STEP OF THE WAY

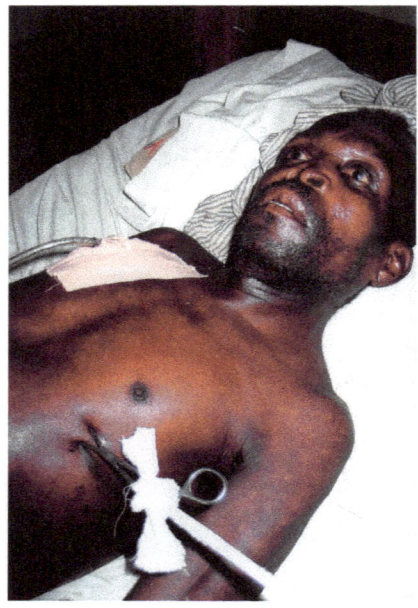

PATIENT WITH RIGHT PNEUMOTHORAX AND MULTIPLE LEFT RIB FRACTURES

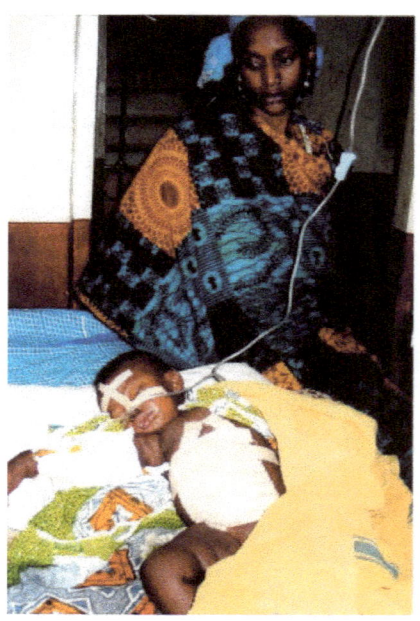

CHILD WITH BOWEL OBSTRUCTION AFTER EMERGENCY SURGERY

AND THEN THE PHONE RANG...

HELP AT LAST! - WELCOMING DR. DELE OWOYELE

MAMBILLA BAPTIST THEOLOGICAL SCHOOL & SEMINARY (MBTS)

DAVE & MARY JUNE BURGESS IN THE MBTS LIBRARY

CHILDREN OF MBTS STUDENTS LINED UP FOR EXAMINATION & IMMUNIZATIONS

AND THEN THE PHONE RANG...

LORI, MISSIONARY NURSE AT BANSO BAPTIST HOSPITAL

LORI WITH MIDWIFERY TEACHING AIDS

CHAPTER 21

Retirement is Not Resting

LOCUMS

PAUL HAD RETURNED FROM HIS walk across northern Spain and trip to London. He had our house nicely cleaned and waiting for us. It did not take us long to settle back into routine life in Canada. I had retired from full-time family practice, but now I continued to do *locum tenens* for family doctors who needed someone to care for their patients while on vacation or study leave. Most of the locums were for two to three weeks at a time. I helped the doctors in my former group practice as well as several other doctors in Burnaby. One locum was for a doctor who had a lot of drug addicts in his practice. He often prescribed huge amounts of opioids to patients. I refused to refill such prescriptions and gave these patients just enough pills to last until their doctor returned. As we now lived in South Surrey, I found it difficult to do the long drive to and from Burnaby in the rush hour traffic morning and evening. I started doing locums for the three doctors in the Morgan Creek Clinic on a regular basis. The Morgan Creek Medical Clinic and Walk-in Clinic were a two-minute walk from our house. The family practice doctors at this clinic were on a rotation to work in the adjoining walk-in clinic for one day a week. This was an excellent set-up to provide medical care for all the patients even when their regular doctor had a day off. One of the doctors had a serious illness so I took over his practice for an extended locum while he slowly recovered. I continued doing locums until age seventy.

RETIREMENT IS NOT RESTING

NEW HOSPITAL

THE PROJECT OF BUILDING A new hospital at the PHC site in Gembu was approved by the NAB Missions Board and required major funding. I felt burdened about this and began to publicize the project and raise funds. At the request of Pastor Tim MacIntosh, our senior pastor at Bethany Baptist Church, I gave a long report to our church about our recent experiences in Mambilla. I presented the need for a new hospital in Gembu so that sick people would have access to much needed care. The existing hospital was five miles out of town and difficult for sick and poor people to reach. They had to walk or pay exorbitant fees to a motorcycle driver to take them there. I imagined a night where a woman in labor was having some complications. How was she going to get to the hospital in the dark on a rough muddy road perhaps in a rainstorm? The Primary Health Clinic in Gembu had a number of facilities already in place, including an out-patient clinic, two-room eye clinic, physician's house nearing completion, lab, treatment room, pharmacy, and clean gravity-fed spring water. To upgrade the PHC to hospital status would require the following buildings and equipment.

Maternity	$51,000	Laundry	$52,000
Admin. offices	$65,000	Surgical suite	$120,000
Bulk Store	$68,000	Patient wards	$156,000
Guest house	$85,000	Generator house	$17,000
Chapel	$78,000	Kitchens	$78,000
X-ray Room	$39,000	Spring catchments	$195,000
Beds and mattresses	$32,500	X-ray machine	$65,000
Solar power system	$97,500	Solar refrigerators	$32,000

The total funds needed for the project were about $1,200,000. I spoke in various churches in British Columbia to help raise money for the hospital construction. In the presentation I challenged people to give up one cruise that year, or reduce the number of expensive gifts put under the Christmas tree, and instead, give towards helping the poor and sick in Mambilla. Dr. Phil Yntema headed the NAB fundraising drive, and together we raised over one million dollars. Bethany Baptist Church members contributed over $120,000. Churches and individuals in Prince George, Chilliwack, Kelowna, and Vancouver also made donations.

GRANDCHILDREN

ON OCTOBER 7, 2006 BRUCE, Kelly, Marion, and I drove to Prince George in order to help Joyel and Dezene welcome their first baby. We left early in the morning and by the time we reached Chilliwack, Joyel had progressed well into her labour. We tried to phone Dezene for an update when we stopped in Cache Creek three or four hours later. There was no answer. We began to imagine all kinds of scenarios. As we got into cell phone range outside William's Lake, Dezene called to tell us that Elijah had just been born. That called for a celebration of coffee and doughnuts at Tim Horton's in William's Lake. Paul also arrived in Prince George later that day to meet his first nephew. The arrival of Elijah was the beginning of a new era of being grandparents. By 2009 three more grandbabies were born within the space of five months – Marcus, Ben, and Lucy in that order. In the next several years Abby, Sebastian, and Kaitlyn arrived to complete the list of blessings. It was a real joy to see each one of them progress through infancy and early childhood.

AORTIC VALVE SURGERY

DURING 2007 WE WATCHED AS Paul and Juliet's romance progressed. Early in their relationship Paul warned Juliet that he was still living with his parents, had a temporary job cutting grass, drove a beater of a car, and snored. His honesty must have captivated her interest in him, because they continued to see each other.

I had developed more lightheaded episodes and an echocardiogram showed severe and progressing aortic valve stenosis. In June the cardiologist recommended surgery for aortic valve replacement. His prognosis was that, without surgery, I would have a major stroke or heart attack within

RETIREMENT IS NOT RESTING

a year. I had heard of patients dying on the operating table during this type of surgery. One who that had happened to was Dr. Hildebrandt, a prominent vascular surgeon in Vancouver. In order to remove the diseased valve and insert a prosthetic one, the beating heart muscle is chemically stopped, and the blood is bypassed to a mechanical pump and oxygenator. Dr. Hildebrandt's surgery went well but his heart would not restart at the end of the procedure. Despite two hours of resuscitation attempts, he died on the operating table. I requested a delay of my surgery until after Paul and Juliet's wedding in August. I did not want to run the risk of missing this event in case I also died on the table.

I saw Dr. Hilton Ling, the cardiac surgeon, in September after an angiogram showed a good caliber of the coronary arteries. I opted for a porcine valve instead of a mechanical one that would require a life-time of anticoagulant medication and frequent blood tests. On October 4, 2007, I was admitted to St. Paul's Hospital for surgery that day. The night before I watched a video of cardiac surgeons in Texas doing the same operation. I really wanted to know exactly how that was done. My kids thought I had gone nuts when they heard about this!

As I lay on the stretcher waiting for the surgery, I felt perfectly calm and at peace. I told Marion that it was very simple. I was going to go to sleep and then wake up, to see either her or Jesus. She was not amused when I asked if I had a choice. They wheeled me into the operating room that was filled with all kinds of fancy equipment. A nurse was holding a urinary catheter and I asked the anesthetist to put me to sleep before it would be inserted. I did wake up with a tube down my throat, abdominal drains, IV's, arterial lines, a central venous line, monitor leads and yes, the urinary catheter too. My family members were allowed to see me briefly, two at a time. They were quickly rushed out when my heart monitor showed an erratic heartbeat. It felt much better when the tube in my throat was removed so I could talk. The following day all the tubes and drains were removed except for the IV, and I was transferred to a four-bed room in the cardiac step-down unit. There were two patients in that room with open infected wounds that required frequent dressing changes every day. The floor was sticky and, for the five days I spent there, I never once saw the floor being mopped. Someone's urine specimen in a container in the washroom was left there for several days before it was removed. I was not to be discharged home until I had a 24-hour period of a normal cardiac rhythm. Being anxious to go home, I stopped drinking regular coffee, thinking why should I dump a bunch of caffeine on an irritated heart. I was glad to get out of there and head home!

Bruce arranged to elevate the head of my bed as lying flat was impossible. I was so weak that I could just barely walk from the bedroom to the kitchen table for breakfast. After dressing, I was so tired that I had to have a nap. On my first walk outside I was able to go slowly around the Carrington compound. I was grateful for the bench on Ruth Liegmann's front porch to rest on, as I had ventured a bit too far. Over the next few months my strength and stamina gradually returned and I resumed doing locums.

MINISTRY INVOLVEMENTS

PASTOR FRANK BERTO, MARION, AND I ran an Alpha Program at Bethany which was an evangelistic tool to introduce people to the gospel. We did Alpha programs as a team for 14 years. Pastor Frank was the emcee. I led table discussions, set up the rooms, and ran the videos. Marion organized a beautiful three-course supper every Tuesday night for the participants. She supervised a crew of over ten kitchen helpers, including her sisters, Jocelyn and Shirley. It was wonderful to see people come to faith in Jesus and then to see their baptisms. After 100 we lost count of how many folks made this step of faith. In the last few years of the Alpha program a grief support group joined us for dinner, and then the two groups went to separate rooms to conduct their sessions. Alpha was discontinued when the number of participants dwindled down to two or three people. After 14 years it seemed that people had invited all the unsaved friends and family that would come.

A short time later I started a class called Discovering Jesus for seekers and new Christians. The course was based on the book, "On the Road to Emmaus." The book described Jesus meeting the two men on the road to Emmaus after his resurrection. The author imagined Jesus telling the men what the Old Testament scriptures said about the Messiah and God's plan for his creatures. The author described the creation, the fall into sin and separation from God, various futile attempts by humans to reach God, and God's provision for restoration. The tabernacle and temple sacrificial system of atonement for sin by shedding the blood of lambs was described. By the time the class heard the words of John the Baptist, "Behold the Lamb of God, who takes away the sin of the world," they totally understood that Jesus is that Lamb whose death on our behalf takes away our sin. The course was done with video clips and discussion as we worked through the Old Testament. I taught this for several years and really enjoyed the class.

I also took turns with others in teaching the adult Sunday school class. My sessions were devoted to a study of a book of the Bible. These included Romans, Galatians, Ephesians, Hebrews, First Peter, James, First John, and letters to the seven churches in Revelation.

Another class I enjoyed was a preparation for church membership. This was a Sunday morning class for five weeks that dealt with the concept of church, the ordinances, responsibilities of members, and the organization and ministries of Bethany. Included was a review of the NAB statement of faith that Bethany endorses, and the mission work of the NAB. Class members were encouraged to discover their spiritual gifts and to use them in Bethany's ministries.

BOARDS, BUT NOT BORED

MY FIRST EXPERIENCE WITH CHURCH board activity was in the 1960's when I was a Bethany church board member-at-large. This 30-plus member board was huge, containing all the deacons, elders, trustees, and members at large. The agendas were so long that meetings often went from 7 PM to midnight. It was really impossible to do justice to all the issues of finance, building maintenance, member discipline, ministries, programs, membership care, accountability of pastors, policies, and event planning. After some time, we agreed to divide church leadership into separate boards. The deacons dealt with member care, visitation, and discipline. The elders were responsible for policy, oversight of pastors, theological positions, and difficult membership discipline referred from the deacon board. The trustees looked after building maintenance and budgets. An executive board made up of the moderator, vice-moderator, chairmen of the trustees, elders, deacons, and treasurer met to present issues to the church membership as needed. I served two terms as church moderator and spent many years as an elder, some of the time as chair of the elder board.

A major decision for Bethany was to move from south Vancouver, 50th Avenue & Quebec Street, to the Hamilton area of Richmond. The church building at the Vancouver site was too small to accommodate the growing congregation. Expansion of the building was cost-prohibitive as we would have had to buy up a whole block of neighbouring houses. Many of our young families were moving eastward to get more affordable housing. Also, there were four NAB churches within a one-and-a-half mile radius in the area. We found a large parcel of land in Hamilton-Richmond for sale. We felt God's leading to move to this new site where there were no other churches. The location was easily accessible from Richmond, Vancouver, New Westminster, Surrey, and North Delta. Funds were raised to purchase the new site, which was preloaded with sand in preparation for building the new church. Further fundraising, sale of the old church, and loans from the NAB Church Investors Fund and a bank financed the project. The architect designed the building based on the facility needs of the various church ministries planned for the future. We had many volunteer work-parties on Saturdays to help keep construction costs down. In 1998, we moved into the new building. Initially Sunday services were held in the gym while the sanctuary was being constructed. This was a great time of the church uniting for a common cause. The vision was that Bethany would be God's lighthouse in the community. Some people from the neighbourhood joined Bethany. Others brought their children to the daycare and a Moms and Tots program. Street parties were held in the parking lot to which neighbours were invited and introduced to our ministries. This brought a number of people to Alpha sessions and youth events. It was a great experience to be involved at the elder board level as many decisions were made. I was an elder from the 1980's to 2017 with a year off after every two terms.

RETIREMENT IS NOT RESTING

FOR A FEW YEARS NOT all church experiences were joyful. Some divisions arose in the church regarding how we should do church. This included music style preferences, the role and authority of leadership, and divergent theological views. This led to grumbling, judgmental attitudes, pride, and divisiveness. A result of this was the resignation of the senior pastor and later the adult ministries pastor. We engaged the help of the Deeper Waters Congregational Health and Conflict Assessment people to do an in-depth analysis of Bethany and present a report to the church. The church accepted all 14 recommendations from Deeper Waters. This included the calling of a transitional pastor for a two-year term, developing a process of healing, and providing opportunities for spiritual and relational renewal. Some people left the church, but new members were gradually added, bringing a more peaceful atmosphere. I found this period of troubles to be a most difficult time and I had many times of tearful prayer to God for His guidance.

I served on the NAB Board of Missions for six years in the 1980's. These were held twice a year at the NAB office in Oakbrook Terrace, a suburb of Chicago. I learned a lot about how boards work from this experience. On one occasion there was discussion on the appointment of a couple as short-term missionaries who had a history of divorce prior to becoming Christians. The chairman wisely tabled this discussion and had the board make a policy regarding the qualifications for missionary candidates. Once a policy was established, the consideration of appointment of this couple could proceed without a long and detailed discussion. We also worked on a statement of mission priorities for all of the fields that emphasized the planting of indigenous churches that were self-supporting. Mission work in medical and educational areas would continue as the expression of the gospel to the sick, poor, and underprivileged.

Another 10 years, in the 1990s to early-2000s, were spent on the board of the NAB College and Seminary in Edmonton. Many changes occurred during this time. The College was basically an undergraduate Bible school with many students taking just one year of courses before pursuing further studies at a university. An attempt was made to provide university level education by establishing various faculties in the humanities and sciences. This proved to be very difficult financially as a full complement of professors and programs had to be approved by the Alberta Ministry of Higher

AND THEN THE PHONE RANG...

Education before classes could start. Thus, the enrollment was initially first year-students only, but the budget requirements were for a full four-year program. A faculty would only be fully funded by tuition when there were students in all four years of the bachelor program. Several faculties were started, but due to financial constraints and low enrollment, the university program was discontinued.

The board also worked on a name change to Taylor Seminary. The use of the Taylor name came from the life and work of Hudson Taylor, a missionary to China, who identified with the Chinese people by dressing and living like them while bringing the gospel of Christ to them. His life exemplified the Taylor Seminary's motto of, *"Producing Christ-minded people who make a difference in the world."* The loss of the Bible school program was not popular with many people. To replace this, the Wahl Center was established, named after the founder of the Christian Training Center (CTI), the original name of the school. This center provided educational opportunities for a wide range of people.

In 1997, I joined the board of the North America Indian Mission (NAIM). The name was later changed to North America Indigenous Ministries. The purpose of the mission was to reach out with the gospel to the Indigenous peoples, mainly in western Canada and USA. The work was started by Bill Lottis and others, using a boat and sometimes an airplane, to reach Indigenous settlements on the west coast of North America. The work spread inland to Alberta and Saskatchewan in Canada and in the U.S.A. to Washington, Idaho, Montana, and New Mexico. There were two boards, U.S. and Canadian, that met four times a year in a joint council of boards to deal with governance issues, policies, and budget decisions. Right after that meeting the two boards met separately to endorse the joint council decisions, thus satisfying the legal requirements for the NAIM boards in both countries. Initially I drove to Mount Vernon for the board meetings and later to Bellingham. Kuno Dreger and Bob Hepting were also on the Canadian board so we would often carpool for the trip.

A separate entity called Thetis Foundation was set up to invest funds that gradually accumulated from the sale of NAIM owned properties. A training school on Thetis Island was no longer viable and the sale of this property initiated the formation of the Thetis Foundation. Further funds were added by the sale of an office building in Ladner and The Gladstone Conference Center near Pincher Creek in Alberta. The foundation assets of about $3 million dollars (US) continue to earn enough money each year to pay the rent of the NAIM office in Abbotsford and to fund various special ministry projects.

I served as president of the Canadian Board for a number of years. During one of those years I had to apply to the Canadian government for a certificate of continuance as a charitable organization. This required an entire revision of our bylaws in order to comply with government regulations. This was a tedious job, but necessary. The work of the board seems very secular at times in dealing with policies, budgets, government regulations, investments, and supervision of the executive director.

I came to understand that our work with all these administrative issues made it possible for the mission to exist and enabled the missionaries to do their work of evangelism and discipling. Without the board there would not be a mission. I also learned that to have an effective board there needs to be a balance of gifts among the board members. Boards need some members who have a cause and are visionaries who drive an agenda with a purpose and a goal. Other members need to have a corporate mindset and ask appropriate questions such as how will this cause be realized? Who will do it? How will it be done? And where is the needed money coming from? The third group brings a concern for the community. How will the proposed cause affect the rest of the church or mission community? A good balance of the three Cs on a board enables it to be effective. The realization of the value of board work in the kingdom work of God brought joy and satisfaction to me. Retirement was definitely not relaxing. The concept of retirement is not found in the Bible.

AND THEN THE PHONE RANG...

MARION & SISTERS JOCELYN AND SHIRLEY – ALPHA COOKS

MORE COOKS IN THE ALPHA PROGRAM

RETIREMENT IS NOT RESTING

CAROL POTRATZ WITH US AT AN NAB TRIENNIAL CONFERENCE

CHAPTER 22

Trips and Travels

While working full-time, I took an average of three weeks of vacation per year, some of which was spent in postgraduate refresher courses. We took a number of trips to Palm Springs for times of total relaxation and rest. We enjoyed the warm weather and the fellowship of friends at the poolside. Our favourite restaurants were Tony Roma's and Marie Callender's, which had delicious pies on the menu. After retirement from fulltime medical practice there was more opportunity to go on various wide-ranging trips.

CARIBBEAN CRUISE – 1995

IN NOVEMBER WE CELEBRATED OUR thirtieth wedding anniversary in advance by going on a cruise in the Caribbean. I was still doing full-time family practice at the time, but the special occasion warranted a bit of extra time off. We flew to Fort Lauderdale the day before the start of the cruise and stayed in a hotel near the beach. After breakfast we enjoyed a short walk on the beach before boarding a bus that took us to the Holland America ship. It was very exciting to be on a cruise for the first time. After lunch at the fantastic buffet in the Lido Restaurant we explored the entire ship. There was a large contingent of folks from Bethany on the same ship with whom we could mingle. Barb Hass brought some choir music along and got permission to have us sing some choir numbers in the Sunday morning chapel service. We discovered a group of musical performers who played violins, bass, piano, and a harp. They were willing to take requests from the audience, so we requested some Christmas carols. We joined in singing in four-part harmony to the astonishment of fellow shipmates. It became obvious that the musicians were Christians too.

We sailed through a storm and the rocking of the ship was so marked that we had to hold our arms out to both sides of the stateroom hallways to stay upright. The rocking put me to sleep in a hurry. The captain altered the itinerary so as to avoid the worst of the storm. As a result, we missed visiting St. Thomas. Saint Lucia was a very beautiful island and we went on a bus tour to see the vegetation and little bays. Bridgetown in Barbados was the place for the gals to enjoy shopping. Tortola in the British Virgin Islands had a fantastic smooth sandy beach with clear, warm water for swimming. A big fish came very near to us in knee-deep water and we tried to catch it. It was the big one that got away!

The dinner meals in the formal dining room were amazing. The menu was so large that it took several minutes just to scan the contents. On the last night of the cruise the dessert chef prepared a midnight buffet of incredibly fancy desserts. It was so elaborate that people were given time to take pictures before loading up their plates. Ben and Joy Warkentin were on this cruise as well. Ben and I discovered delicious bread pudding in the Lido buffet. Our wives knew exactly where to find us. Needless to say, we all gained too much weight. We had such a good time that the 10 days of cruising seemed too short.

MEXICO CRUISE – late-1990s

SOME YEARS LATER WE WENT on a cruise to Mexico. The cruise started in San Diego, so we had the opportunity to shop in Horton's Plaza and walk along the harbour before getting on the ship. We stopped in Cabo San Lucas, Mazatlán, Puerto Vallarta, Manzanillo, and Acapulco. We enjoyed watching the cliff divers in Acapulco who dove into fairly shallow waters from incredible heights. In Puerto Vallarta we got on a small boat to sail across Banderas Bay to a sandy beach area where waiters from a nearby restaurant ushered us to beach chairs. They served food and drinks while we soaked in the sun and swam in the warm water. In Cabo San Lucas the cruise ship had to anchor some distance off shore due lack of docking provision for such a large ship. We got on shore by lifeboats used to tender us to the center of town. I resisted the temptation to buy stuff in the market, but agreed to some Mexican food.

PANAMA CRUISE – early-2000s

KUNO AND IRMA DREGER, AND Norbert and Gerda Wessler, joined us for this cruise that originated in Fort Lauderdale and ended in Vancouver. Our first stop was in Cancun where we took a bus excursion through Cancun and down the coast to Playa del Carmen. The many resorts looked inviting and we considered going on a vacation there in the future. Going through the Panama Canal was most interesting. The ship was gently guided into locks which were then filled with more water that raised the ship to the level of the next lock. After a series of locks the ship was raised to the level of Lake Gatun which we crossed. The set of locks at the western end of the lake lowered the ship down to the level of the Pacific Ocean. The lake level is kept up by many rivers and streams that flow into it so that the locks can be in use constantly. In Punta Arenas, Costa Rica, we went on a bus tour inland to San Jose to see the countryside. On the way back we stopped at a small hotel where we were entertained by some musicians. Drinks were available, both alcoholic and non-alcoholic. I did not pay attention to which was alcoholic and ended up taking a rum cocktail that made my head spin. I was mercilessly teased by Marion, Ben, and Joy. Costa Rica was really a beautiful place. We had further visits in towns along the west coast of Mexico and the U.S.A. and reached Vancouver after 21 days of sailing. The food on board the ship was terrific. The calories piled on and so did the weight.

TRIPS AND TRAVELS

ALASKA CRUISES

WE WENT ON THREE CRUISES to Alaska. A short four-day cruise was done with our children and Oma as described in Chapter 18. Marion and I went on a seven-day cruise on our own. Later we invited Dave and Mary-June Burgess to fly to Vancouver for a visit. We bribed them with an offer to pay for a seven-day Alaska cruise for them as a thank-you for their hospitality to us in Mambilla. Of course, we had to cruise with them to serve as tour guides! The ports-of-call were Ketchikan, Juneau, and Skagway. The scenery was stunning along the inner passageway. We were so close to shore that we could see bears on the shore looking for food. We saw dolphins playing in the wake of the ship. We also saw whales, including a mamma whale with her little baby whale. Eagles, hawks and gulls accompanied us on the journey. The only bit of rough water was between the northern tip of Vancouver Island and Haida Gwaii. In Ketchikan we walked through the town to a large creek where we saw a salmon run. There were so many salmon going upstream that the water was churning. I have never seen so many fish in one place. We walked up the side of the creek to see the old town with little shops and even a brothel. On the dock where our ship was tied up was a large emporium full of souvenirs that Marion had to explore in depth. Juneau, the state capitol, was less interesting as it was a typical modern town. Our favorite port was Skagway, the little town that became a boomtown during the gold rush days that started in 1898. Thousands of people came to Skagway to travel inland to find gold. We went on a bus excursion up the White Pass, a steep climb up the coastal mountains to the Yukon River and beyond. We saw deep valleys where thousands of worn out horses died during the gold rush. The trees were stunted and bent due to annual snow packs of over 20 feet. The trip took us into a corner of British Columbia and on to Carcross in the Yukon. Carcross (Caribou Crossing) was the site where prospectors would bring supplies that would last them for many months as they rafted down rivers in the spring to the gold field area. We had a delicious meal of chicken in an open-air restaurant. Nearby was a museum filled with stuffed animals and birds in action poses. There were wolves, cougars, deer, elk, rabbits, moose, and even a woolly mammoth. We spent a long time looking at this beautiful exhibit. Behind the museum was a huge kennel for sled dogs. One could pay for a ride on a sled with wheels (summer tires!) that was pulled by some of the dogs. Part way back to Skagway we left the bus and got on a narrow-gauge train for the ride down the steep incline. The railway track included trestles, tunnels, and sharp bends, making for an exciting trip. We could certainly make this trip again.

MEDITERRANEAN CRUISE – 2009

THIS TRIP WAS ALMOST A total disaster. The plan was for Marion and me to fly to Rome two days prior to the start of the cruise. Lori was to join us for the cruise one day before embarkation. She was on her way home from Cameroon for a year of furlough. Marion and I got to the airport in Vancouver and at the check-in we were told that the flight to Rome was delayed. By the time we cleared immigration and got to the boarding gate the delay was over two hours. Five hours later the flight was cancelled entirely. We were put up in a hotel in Richmond and were told to return around noon the next day and British Airways would see what they could do for us. We were given a late supper at the hotel, at almost midnight. A couple sitting near us told us that they phoned Air Canada and got an early morning flight booked. I phoned Air Canada as soon as I got to our room and was told that the booking office was closed and would open at 7 AM Eastern Time. I set the alarm for 4 AM our time and in a half-hour got a flight booked to Rome via Toronto. We arrived at the San Valentino hotel in Rome in the mid-afternoon, one day late but still in time for the cruise the next day. We expected to see Lori at the hotel as her planned time of arrival was in the morning. Lori was not there. We had no idea what happened to her. We agonized over what we should do. Do we go on the cruise the next day without Lori? Was she in trouble? I could not rest or relax in our tiny hotel room and decided to go for a short walk outside. I checked with the hotel desk again to see if Lori was in a different room. Finally, I stepped out of the front door and spotted someone unloading a van. It was Lori. She got a huge daddy-bear hug from me. Her flight from Douala to Tripoli was delayed as the Libyan plane was late getting to Douala. The reason for the delay was that President Muammar Al-Gaddafi was celebrating his fortieth anniversary as president and was flying important guests to Tripoli for a party. The airport was lavishly decorated, and a huge picture of Gaddafi was hung on a wall. With all this commotion, Lori's flight from Tripoli to Rome was also delayed. All our fears melted away as we rode in a van to the ship.

The cruise on the Holland America ship, Noordam, was in the Eastern Mediterranean with visits to Dubrovnik, Corfu, Olympia, Santorini, Kuşadası, Athens, Messina, and back to Rome.

The old town of Dubrovnik was a walled fortress with a small harbour. We walked through courtyards, narrow alleys, and into a monastery. There were interesting shops and restaurants with inside and patio tables. After lunch we toured an old monastery and walked along the wall of the fortress. The old town was a world heritage site and, fortunately, most of the town was preserved during the recent war with Serbia.

Corfu was the next stop. A bus tour took us to a Greek Orthodox Monastery in Paleokastritsa on the west side of the island. After viewing the ornate icons and paintings there we returned to Corfu. We walked through the cobblestone alleys of the town and found a quaint outdoor café for lunch.

The following day we docked in Katakolo and went on an excursion to ancient Olympia, the site of the original Olympic games. It was all in ruins, but signs indicated what the remaining structures were. We saw where the Olympic torch is now lit every two years, using mirrors to focus the rays of the sun on the torch. The actual games were in a flat field with surrounding sloped embankments covered with grass where 40,000 spectators could sit to watch. We even did a little jog on the racetrack. The ancients used to run races naked, but we kept our clothes on!

Santorini used to be a round island that turned into a C-shape after a huge volcanic eruption. The town was high up on a ridge accessed by a donkey ride on a very steep path or in a gondola. We had a lazy lunch on the edge of the cliff with a fantastic view of three cruise ships below. After a guided walk through narrow streets to see the whitewashed homes all piled on top of each other, and some time to swim at the beach, I returned to the ship via the gondola. Marion and Lori did some shopping and then walked down the path. They had planned to take a donkey ride down but due to rain the donkeys were taking a break. To their dismay the path was covered in donkey dung.

Kuşadası is a port on the west coast of Turkey very near to the ancient ruins of Ephesus. The bus tour to Ephesus was one of the highlights of the trip. We saw ruins of once glorious buildings where over 250,000 people used to live. Among the sights were the Odeon (parliament), Trajan's building, public toilets, Hadrian's temple, the Celsus library, and the huge open-air theater that seated 25,000 people. I stood on the sweet spot of the stage and Lori, high up in the seats, could hear every soft-spoken word I said. This was the place where Apostle Paul faced the riot, started by Demetrius, the upset silversmith. We also saw the little stone house where Mary, the mother of Jesus, lived and was protected by the Apostle John. In the same region we saw the museum of Ephesus containing marble heads of several emperors, a huge statue of Artemis, and many other artifacts. The nearby Church of St. John contained his burial site. The tour ended in a Kuşadası hotel with a fancy 4-course meal and a performance of lively dancing guys and gals dressed in traditional costumes. Lori bought a small woolen rug as a souvenir.

From the port of Piraeus, Greece, we took a one-and-a-half hour bus tour to Cape Sounion to see the ruins of the temple of Poseidon. Along the winding road were beautiful homes, beaches, and little villages in the numerous bays. After a buffet lunch of Greek food in Athens, we drove into old Athens to see the Olympic stadium built in 1800 when the modern games were re-established. We also saw Hadrian's Arch, St. Paul's Church, the Temple of Zeus, parliament buildings, and many prestigious hotels and embassies. We climbed the Acropolis, a huge black rock, to see the ruined Parthenon that was being restored. Beside it was the Temple of Athena with the porch of six maidens. The view of the city of Athens from this height was stunning. To the northwest was a small hill that we were told was Mars Hill where Apostle Paul made his famous speech. We sneaked away from the tour group and climbed to the top of Mars Hill. Below was the agora (Greek market) and an ancient synagogue. What a thrill to be in the place where Paul witnessed so many centuries ago.

Messina in Sicily did not impress us at all. We climbed a long hill, taking care to avoid the many dog droppings, to tour the big church at the top. It was closed. Marion and Lori had another aimless shopping trip in mind. So, I returned to the ship to bask in the sun and swim in the ship's pool. While sailing we saw Mt. Etna, and later, passed close by the volcanic island of Stromboli where puffs of smoke and ash spewed out of one of the three craters. People actually lived on the side of this volcano!

In Rome, a Mercedes Benz transfer car arrived at the dock. The driver, dressed in a fancy suit, emerged holding a big sign labelled Hiller. He took us back to the San Valentino Hotel. We had three days to tour Rome before our flight home. Our hotel was within walking distance of old Rome and also the Vatican. That first day we hiked to the old city, crossing the Tiber River on a bridge to see the huge white stone monument of Victor Emmanuel on horseback. He was the first king of a united Italy in the early 1800s. Just beyond were the ruins of the ancient Roman forum. There we saw the remains of Constantine's Basilica, the Mamertine Prison where Apostle Paul was jailed, the site of Julius Caesar's assassination, the Roman Senate, the house of the vestal virgins, and the ruins of a medieval church. We climbed the Palatine Hill to see the palaces and gardens of the Caesars and then descended the hill to the Colosseum and the Arches of Titus and Constantine. The Colosseum had many levels including rooms and passages beneath the main floor where prisoners and lions were kept. Our final visit that day was to the Pantheon, built by Hadrian in 120 AD. It had massive columns and a huge dome with a round hole (oculus) in the top to admit light. Originally it was a temple for the many Roman gods, but later it was turned into a church. After a meal of bruschetta, antipasto, and pizza we dragged our weary bones back to the hotel, stopping only for gelato.

The next day we walked to the Vatican to tour the museum. Fortunately, we pre-booked our tickets and avoided the line-up of thousands of people waiting to buy their tickets. A knowledgeable and humorous guide took us on the three-hour tour. The many rooms contained tapestries, sculptures, and paintings on walls and ceilings by masters like Bernini, Raphael, and Michelangelo. The rooms were ornately decorated with tiny floor tiles, mosaics, marble columns, and carved wooden door frames. Some early tapestries had woven figures of people, including one of Christ, with eyes that looked at you regardless of where you were standing. This type of weaving became a lost art. The high point was the Sistine Chapel with Michelangelo's ceiling painting depicting the Biblical accounts of creation, the fall of man, the flood, the life of Christ, and the huge final judgment day. No photos were allowed because the Fuji film company paid for the cleaning and restoration of the painting and in return had exclusive photo rights. Surly, rude guards hustled people through, not allowing any talking or photos. The tour ended in the huge St. Peter's Basilica with its soaring arches, domes, tile and marble floors, and many sculptures and statues. After lunch in a hole-in-the-wall pizzeria, we headed back to the old town. Our walk took us to the Spanish Steps that we had to climb – all 132 steps. We got lost in the narrow streets and alleys but eventually found the Trevi fountain with its wondrous sculptures of marble figures and rocks and the water cascading down to a pool. Folklore says that tossing a coin into the pool backwards over your head ensures that you will return someday. So, we all tossed some coins.

The last day was spent walking along the Tiber River to Trastevere where we climbed a winding hill to the ornately decorated Santa Maria church that was dedicated to the Virgin Mary. We crossed the Tiber to the island of Tibernia to see the ruins of the Jewish ghetto where thousands of Jews had been once forced to live on just a few acres. After a siesta at our hotel we had a nice supper at Perilli in Prati, a highly recommended restaurant to celebrate the end of a wonderful trip. The next morning, we transferred to the airport in another Mercedes Benz for our flight home via Heathrow airport in London.

WASHINGTON D.C. – May 2010

LORI WAS TO ATTEND A midwifery conference in Washington D.C. and invited us to accompany her. We flew into the Baltimore-Washington International airport and took a bus to our bed and breakfast. It was located across the street from the hotel where the conference was to take place. The location was ideal as we could walk a block to the subway line that went directly to the center of town. We were also able to walk to the National Zoo that was well laid out with many animals in quarters similar to their natural habitat. Another walk took us to the beautiful Washington National Cathedral where many state events take place. The subway station by our B&B was very deep underground- a bit spooky in semi-darkness. We visited many interesting places including the Mall, the National Monument, the Lincoln Memorial, and the Vietnam war memorial wall with the many names of fallen soldiers. We walked around the White House and saw Michelle Obama's vegetable garden that she planted together with her children. We were allowed into the ground floor of the Capitol Building by the back door and were able to see some exhibits. Only U.S. citizens were allowed to tour more parts of the building. Close to the Capitol Building was the Canadian Embassy in a place of prominence. The Mall was lined with many buildings of the Smithsonian Museums and the National Art Gallery. Entry was free in all of the buildings, but there was not enough time to visit all of them. We took a hop-on-hop-off bus across the Potomac River to the Arlington National Cemetery that contained the graves of fallen soldiers and prominent people. The landscaping was beautiful. We found the headstone of John F. Kennedy on our way back to the bus and had to stop to take a picture. On another bus tour we saw the Embassy Row, a tree lined street that had numerous embassies on both sides. This tour took us through Georgetown, an area inhabited by the ultra- rich people. We wished that we had more time in Washington as there were many more highlights to be seen.

THE MARITIMES – August 2010

DEZENE AND JOYEL INVITED US to join them in a visit to a cottage near the fishing village of Miminegash on the west end of Prince Edward Island. The cottage was owned by Dezene's parents, Eugene and Irene Huber. We made this a family event, travelling there with Lori and Shirley. Paul, Juliet, and baby Lucy also joined us for the occasion.

Marion, Lori, Shirley, and I joined Dezene, Joyel, and the boys to fly to Charlottetown and checked in to the Islander Guest Rooms & Suites that included breakfast. We spent a day walking around the town to see the sights, including a tour of the building where the fathers of confederation met to form the country of Canada. A priority was finding the famous Cows Creamery for ice-cream. The next day we drove north through rolling green hills with country homes. All had beautifully manicured very green lawns. Our destination was Cavendish, the site of Lucy Maud Montgomery's house – the author of "*Anne of Green Gables*" and other books. In preparation for this trip, I read all of the Anne books and was well prepared to tour the famous house and the haunted forest trail. We ate a meal at Rachel's Ristorante and slept in the Kindred Spirits Country Inn. On our way to Miminegash, on the extreme western edge of P.E.I., we made a short detour to see the PEI National Park with its red sand beaches. The Huber cottage was quite large and on several acres of land right on the beach. We stayed there for a week, going for walks, swimming in the ocean, and building a huge sand castle. The sand castle moat was so deep that little Lucy and Marcus could not climb out on their own. We went to explore Miminegash and saw fishermen preparing lobster traps and loading their boats, as the lobster season was about to open. At 6 AM the fisheries officer shot a pistol in the air to signal the start of lobster fishing. We returned later to buy fresh live lobsters right off the returning boats. They were put in the bathtub to wait while we collected sea water and heated up the lobster pot. What a delicious meal! Poor Joyel discovered that her intestinal system does not like lobsters. One evening we went to St. Mark's Hall to attend a cèilidh, where local performers gathered for singing and dancing. All was led by fiddlers playing in an exuberant Maritime style. After the intermission, Paul and Juliet were called to the stage to play and sing a song. It was a great week of family time.

 We rented a car and drove over the long 13-kilometer Confederation Bridge from P.E.I. to New Brunswick. We drove through Moncton to visit the famous Hopewell Rocks of the Bay of Fundy. A long series of steps took us down to the beach where we wandered along between huge eroded pillars of rock. The enormous Bay of Fundy tides had carved these rock formations over the centuries. Travelling further, we stayed at the Eagles Landing B&B in Truro, Nova Scotia. The next day we drove on the Cabot Trail to see the wonderful scenery and smashing waves along this coastal drive. We stayed at the Colby House B&B in Sydney. The next item on the itinerary was a tour of the Fortress of Louisbourg on the Atlantic coast. The Fortress was established by the French and served as a base for cod fishing and later as a military post. It was captured by New Englanders but three years later the French regained it, only to ultimately lose it to the British. It was reconstructed and now is staffed by people dressed in costumes of the 1700-1800's. A cannon is shot daily at noon. Cafes serve simple food items of the era. A military salute to the flag is performed in a square outside the barracks. An actor portraying a criminal is led to a pillory by a squad of soldiers and public charges are announced. The whole experience made one enter into the spirit of the olden days. This was a long day, so we only got as far as Port Hawkesbury for the night. Lunenburg was the next destination and while walking along the harbour we saw Prime Minister Stephen Harper on the sidewalk. Further along we saw the famous Bluenose sailing ship that was being repaired. We drove to Halifax and on the way made a short detour to see Peggy's Cove and its famous lighthouse. A Swiss Air plane had recently crash landed near this place and many lives were lost. In Halifax we met with Bill and Gerry Styles and their two adult children. Marion and Gerry were friends since grade school. They showed us around Halifax, including Pier 21 where my dad landed with two brothers Herbert and Bruno, and their sister, Hannah, on May 9, 1930 as they immigrated to Canada. We saw their names listed among the passengers and made a copy to take home. The Styles booked a tour on an amphibious vehicle that drove all over town and then went down a ramp into the water to tour the harbour. This was a most interesting trip, experiencing a part of Canada over 3000 miles away from home.

BALTIC CRUISE – 2011

MARION AND I WERE JOINED on this Baltic cruise by Lori, Shirley, Len and Charlene. We flew to Heathrow Airport and took a bus to Dover where we boarded a Holland America ship, the Eurodam. The white cliffs of Dover and the huge castle on a hill built by King Henry VIII were an impressive sight. Once again, we were impressed by the fine dining provided on a Holland America ship. There must have been an infection previously as the crew were wiping down railings and door knobs and dispensing hand sanitizer. The food in the Lido buffet was served by gloved staff.

We took a bus tour to the center of Copenhagen to see the Citadel, the Amalienborg Castle, home of Queen Margarete, the Charlottenberg Palace, and the Christiansborg Castle. The ultimate destination was Tivoli Gardens. This was a large amusement park with restaurants, shops, open-air theaters, and a playland with rides. There also was a lake, gardens, and winding pathways. Apparently, Walt Disney got some of his ideas for Disneyland from this place. After a treat of ice-cream, we returned to the ship with a short stop at the seaside to see the famous bronze statue of the Little Mermaid perched on a rock. There were heavy showers of rain that day but we managed to stay dry.

Warnemünde is a little resort town in Germany with beautiful beaches. We took a three-hour train ride to Berlin and had a six-seater booth for all of us. The countryside was beautiful with farms and little villages dotted along the way. The gentle rolling hills gradually gave way to flat lands as we neared Berlin. The bus tour in Berlin included a stop at remnants of the Berlin Wall that was covered in murals. In other areas a double track of paving stones marked the course of the former wall. The present Berlin is quite new as the city had to be almost totally rebuilt since the devastation of WW II. The Brandenburg Gate was an impressive arch. Protesters were making speeches in the Plaza as we arrived. We enjoyed a German-style lunch in a restaurant on the Kurfürstendamm. The lunch included chicken, potatoes, sauerkraut, soup, salad, and an apple-strudel dessert with a cherry sauce topping. Very delicious! We had an hour to do some shopping in the upscale shops along the Kurfürstendamm. The bus tour resumed with stops at the Charlottenburg Palace, Check-Point Charlie, and the Holocaust Memorial. The tour went through both East and West Berlin. The buildings of the East were very drab and dreary looking. We were very tired after the three-hour train ride back to the ship.

After a restful day at sea we arrived in Tallinn, Estonia, and toured the old city area. Our bus took us up to the top of Toompea Hill. From the top of the hill we had a panoramic view of the old city and the deep-sea harbour in beautiful sunshine. A guide took us on a walking tour down the hill, stopping at St. Mary's church where many famous people were buried.

TRIPS AND TRAVELS

The next stop was the town square that contained sidewalk cafes and restaurants. The town hall had no downpipes, so rainwater from the roof drained into eavestroughs and spouted out the mouths of gargoyles onto unsuspecting people below. Further down the hill was a smaller square where I sat down in an outdoor café and enjoyed a strong coffee while the others went shopping. We got into an old church for a short concert of medieval singing, accompanied by some very ancient instruments. We found a dark little restaurant in a narrow street for a lunch of stew, dumplings, and bread in a ceramic crock. Len and I walked back to the ship for coffee while the gals dealt with their voracious appetite for shopping.

A visa was not required to enter Russia as we were passengers of a cruise, but we had to show our passports to get through the immigration check. We carefully put our passports in money belts under our shirts as we were warned that St. Petersburg was known as the superbowl of pickpockets. Our bus tour took us along the wide Neva River that runs through town. There were a lot of bridges and canals, rivalling Venice in number. After a drive through the old town we headed south of town across a low flatland that was the demarcation line of the German army during the WWII siege of St. Petersburg (Leningrad). We toured Catherine the Great's summer palace on a large tract of park-like land with gardens, hedges, pools, and riding paths. The palace was restored after being ruined by communists in 1917 and again by the German army in WWII. The palace was a place of extravagant grandeur. The rooms were huge with high ceilings, large chandeliers, and ornate carvings covered with gold leaf. Many of the 1000 rooms were filled with paintings, murals, tapestries, statues, and carvings. One room had amber covering all the walls and ceiling. This was so special that no photographs were allowed in the room. We went back to town for a ride on the subway that was 100 feet underground. The stations were decorated with fancy tilework. The trains were tightly packed with passengers and it was a miracle that we all got off at the right station. After lunch at Stockman's, an upscale department store, we continued our bus tour to see the statue of Peter the First, St Isaac's Church, and The Church of the Spilt Blood, which was especially ornate with many onion shaped domes and spires. A torrential rain forced us back to the ship for supper, a show, and a night's sleep.

AND THEN THE PHONE RANG...

The next day we got up early to get to the Hermitage for a special early entry. Apparently 17,000 people visit daily. This was Catherine the Great's museum to store all the art she bought with her tons of money. The 350 rooms contained masterpieces of art – Dutch, Flemish, French, German, and Italian. A highlight for me was to see Raphael's "*Mary Magdalene*" and Rembrandt's "*Return of the Prodigal Son*." The building itself was a work of art with its tapestries, lapis lazuli, malachite columns, marble statuary and tile mosaics on the floors. After a Russian lunch of borscht, chicken, and potatoes, we drove to Peterhof Palace, a 500-acre park-like estate on the banks of the Gulf of Finland. The palace was built by Peter the Great. There was a large garden with tree lined walkways that led to the palace. We skirted around the palace to the great marble verandah that overlooked the sea. Two large marble staircases led to the lower gardens. Between the stairs was an enormous cascade of water and many gold-covered statues and spouting fountains. The water was gravity fed from a small river above the property. All the water was channeled into a canal, about one kilometer long, that flowed to the sea.

A man in our tour group had his passport stolen right out of his zipped-up shoulder bag by a pickpocket. We helped him search around in case he had dropped it. As a result, he could not get through the immigration checkpoint and onto the ship. All this diversion made us late in getting back to the ship. The immigration guys just waved us through and we had to run to get on the ship as they were already untying the docking ropes. The man who was robbed saw his wife get on board but he was left behind as we sailed away. A shore agent of Holland America helped him find a hotel room (normally hotels there require a passport to admit a foreigner). The next day he was taken to the U.S. Consulate to get a temporary passport in order to get a visa for Russia. All this enabled him to fly to Stockholm two days later and rejoin the cruise.

We were deeply impressed with the enormous wealth of the Tsars of old as we saw the palaces and the Hermitage. The contrast with the humble dwellings of the peasants was huge. No wonder that there was a revolution in 1917!

We decided to tour Helsinki on our own and took a shuttle bus for $10 round trip from the ship to the city center. The day was spent walking

TRIPS AND TRAVELS

along the waterfront marina, and up a hill to the botanical gardens. We then wandered down the Kaisaniemenkatu road to explore the railroad station. Some shopping was done along the Mannerheimintie road and then we stopped for lunch in a cafeteria. A huge rain storm descended on us and I hiked back to the shuttle bus to get to the ship for a good cup of coffee and a cookie. The gals still had shopping in their blood and stayed for a while to look at stuff they didn't really need. Helsinki was a very clean city and worth further exploration.

On the voyage from Helsinki to Stockholm we encountered gale-force headwinds, so we did a bit of rocking. We anchored at Nynäshamn and tendered ashore on lifeboats and took a one hour bus trip into Stockholm. The freeway took us from the edge of town to the center via a long tunnel, thus avoiding traffic lights and intersections on the surface. What a novel idea! It was a national holiday and many people had left town for their country cottages. There were parties and maypole dances. Many gals adorned their hair with flowers and wore national costume dresses. We visited the Vasa Museum to see an old wooden warship that was the largest of its kind in the world. It was so top heavy with guns that the ship sank within 20 minutes of being launched. This was a huge national embarrassment. It lay on the bottom of the sea for 300 years before it was discovered and was raised and restored. We walked around the old town and ate lunch in a little hole-in-the-wall cafeteria. We explored some narrow streets to see souvenir shops and cafes and then returned to the ship by bus. We enjoyed a nice relaxing day.

We spent two days at sea going from Stockholm to Dover. The scenery looked peaceful and pastoral as we passed through the narrows between Copenhagen and Malmo. One evening we had an entertainer from Romania who called himself Count Dimnia. He was an excellent pianist and also played a woodwind and an accordion. For one act he put on a coat that had numerous squeaky balls attached that sounded different notes when squeezed. He actually played complicated tunes by squeezing those balls. He called this his Draculaphone.

We took a bus tour from Dover to Canterbury. On the way we saw a huge castle on the hill above Dover built by various kings, including Henry II, Henry VIII, and William of Orange. Canterbury was a quaint small town, very neat and clean. It had narrow cobblestone streets lined with shops, cafes, and pubs. Canterbury Cathedral was immense with high towering spires, while inside were many alcoves and tombs. Thomas A. Becket was assassinated here and a special crypt area was constructed to memorialize him. A rusty broken sword hung on the wall by his tomb. The history of the cathedral goes back to St. Augustine who came in A.D. 596. We explored the church and the streets of the old town and then took the two-hour bus trip to the huge Heathrow Airport for the flight home. Of course, our final meal in England was fish and chips.

GERMANY – 2015

LORI, MARION AND I DECIDED to travel to Germany to see our relatives and to finally return to the land of some of our ancestors. The three-week trip was in four stages. The first was to visit Marion's niece, Susan and her husband Gunther Seyfried in Bad Teinach, second was to Ursula and Markus Von-Linden in Furth, third was to Konrad and Adelheid Krause in Potsdam, and fourth to meet Carol Potratz in Amsterdam for a river cruise up the Rhine River.

We flew to Frankfurt via Calgary and were met at the airport by Susan, Marion's niece. This was our first experience on the German autobahn. Susan drove her father-law's Mercedes Benz at 120 to 130 km/hour and cars passed us like we were just crawling along! We made a side trip to Heidelberg on the Neckar River and walked through the old town center and entered the ancient cathedral. A tram took us up a steep hill to the old crumbling and massive Heidelberg Castle with its thick walls, and a deep moat spanned by a bridge to the gate and portcullis. The view from the castle was breathtaking. We could see the entire town of Heidelberg and the valley of the Neckar River that flows into the Rhine. Inside the castle we saw many wine vats, one of which was the size of a small house. Finally, we wandered back to town going down a long series of steps and ending up in a Bäckerei for lunch. Susan then drove us to her home in Bad Teinach-Zavelstein by a scenic route through parts of the Black Forest with its quaint little villages along the way. After supper in the backyard we strolled through the tiny village to see the hot springs and the hotel built around the spring. It was a long day and we fell into bed exhausted.

The next day Susan and Gunther drove us south through the rolling hills of the Black Forest with its cute little villages nestled in the valleys. Each one had a town center, a church with a steeple, and restaurants with patios. We got to the Schwarzwald Freilichtmuseum at Vogtsbauernhof. This museum was on a large parcel of land containing many old wooden farm houses built on multiple levels with thatched roofs made of rye stalks. The ground level was a place for animals, the second level was the family home with cast iron wood stoves, and the top level was a storage place for farm produce. The houses were heated with ceramic-tiled wood burners with air vents. Smaller buildings served either as outhouses or storage places. This place reminded me of stories my dad told me about life on the farm in Poland in the 1910s and 1920s. We had a snack of Schwarzwälder Kirschtorte (Black Forest cake) and coffee while sitting in the real Black Forest area – a special moment! On the way home we visited Gengenbach with its ancient monastery and church and tons of restaurants. Supper was in a restaurant on the hill above Bad Teinach-Zavelstein. Again, we enjoyed authentic German food – Wienerschnitzel and Spätzle with mushroom sauce.

The following day we toured an ancient monastery near Calw that was built in 1000 A.D. In the afternoon we explored the ruins of an old castle tower above Bad Teinach-Zavelstein. We enjoyed selections of various torten and coffee at the home of Gunther's parents. I managed quite well in German conversation. I was surprised at my recall of many German words that I had not heard since childhood. They smiled at some of the old-fashioned expressions that I had learned from my mother's 1930 style of German.

Gunther took us to a local train station and showed us how to buy tickets for our trip to Nuremberg via Stuttgart. The trains were fast, smooth, quiet, clean, and precisely on time. The excellent signage and oral announcements of the next station helped us figure out where we were. The hills and forests of the Black Forest area gradually gave way to flat lands and large grain and dairy farms as we neared Stuttgart. The main train station was on multiple levels and it took us a while to find the IC/EC platform with its 16 different lines. I had my first experience with W/C pay-washrooms. I pretended to not know what to do to see what kind of help was available. There was absolutely no assistance. I was quite disappointed to pay a Euro just for a preemptive pee. The train to Nuremberg was very fast with only five quick stops on the way. We were relieved to see Ursula standing on the platform with three roses in hand. It was great to see her again after 30 years. Ursula was my second cousin on the Paschold side of the family. Her dad and my mom were first cousins. We drove to her apartment for lunch and a short nap. When Marcus Von-Linden came home from work we toured the old town of Furth and enjoyed supper in a Spanish-Andalusian tapas bar.

Ursula drove us north to Bamberg, a very important medieval center of power. It had the grave of the only Pope buried outside of Rome. There was a huge church in the center of town for the ordinary people. The Dome Church on a high hill was reserved for the elite only. On that hill was a large monastery with a beautiful rose garden and a panoramic view of Bamberg. We walked the winding narrow cobblestone streets of the town with its many shops – goldsmiths, tailors, clothing stores, tons of restaurants, outdoor cafes, and beer halls. The city hall was on a tiny island in the middle of the Mainz River, with a small stone bridge for access. We then drove to Bayreuth to visit Ursula's Uncle Franz Dietzel and his wife Margot. Franz was a first cousin to my mom and a specialist and professor of radio-oncology. They lived in a large home in an up-scale neighborhood. He was only two years older than me and understood English quite well. Interestingly, he also had a stenotic aortic valve which was replaced with a mechanical one. We had a wonderful visit in which we compared family trees, diagrams and all, and shared many stories. His wife, Margot, had multiple sclerosis but was quite mobile. She prepared at least three different fancy torten, and insisted that we sample each one as we enjoyed coffee. On our way back to Furth, Ursula drove on winding back roads through hamlets and farms, passing occasionally between the house and the barn. The farms were well manicured with wheat and corn crops. We had supper at the Brauerei Gasthof Rothenbach in Aufesser. This was a small local brewery, restaurant, and tiny hotel. I had a small delicious pint of beer (the first one since age 15), and we enjoyed cordon bleu pork schnitzel, dumplings, and pureed cabbage. This was ultimate gemütlichkeit.

The next day, after doing laundry, we went to Nuremberg's old medieval town and on the way passed by the imposing courthouses where the World War II war crimes trials were held. The old town was surrounded by a stone wall with a number of arched entry ways. The streets were all cobblestoned and a small river with stone bridges bisected the town. There were many restaurants of all descriptions and sizes, some with outdoor tables. Many old stone buildings from 1000 – 1300 A.D. were still in use. We toured the Lorenz Kirche that was previously a Catholic cathedral but now an evangelical church. Above the entry door was a stone façade with carved figures of Adam and Eve holding fig leaves and above them more carvings of the birth and life of Jesus, His passion, crucifixion, burial, resurrection, rapture, and judgment. Above all this was Christ with the sun and moon at His feet. A hospital, containing a senior's home, was built over the river. Lori jokingly planned to check us in there and promised to visit us often. Lunch was at the Bratwuersthauesle where I ordered the famous drei im wechsel (three small Nuremberg sausages in a bun). We climbed a steep cobblestone road up to the Kaiserburg Castle, one of the major homes of German emperors. There were 45 buildings with displays of ancient armour and weapons. We got home to Furth in time to help Ursula prepare a barbecue and potato salad supper in their backyard for us and Konrad and Adelheid Krause. The Krauses came all the way from Potsdam to pick us up for the next stage of our trip. Adelheid was a second cousin to me on the Sieber side of my mom's family. Ursula and Adelheid did not know each other, so I had the interesting pleasure of introducing them to each other and showing them how they were related by my family tree drawing.

After a hearty German breakfast Konrad and Adelheid drove us to Schneeberg in their Skoda. The countryside was a mix of forest and farms with hamlets and villages dotted along the way. Schneeberg was a large village on a hilly site near the Czech border, and was the place where my mom spent her childhood. Adleheid also grew up in Schneeberg years after my mom and her family left for Canada. We checked in at the Methodist church rest-house with its four bedrooms and fully stocked kitchen. We walked to the old Sieber house and Pagoda garden house. The Sieber house was remodeled and accommodated handicapped people. We were allowed to tour the three levels of the old Pagoda garden house which was quite run down. The lower garden was neglected and full of morning glory and weeds among the many rhododendrons. I was sure that mom would be very sad to see the present state of the property. We then went to Ehberhard and Brigitte Neuman's home (Brigitte is Adelheid's cousin) for an afternoon Kaffe-Klatsch with torte and ice-cream cake. A short drive took us to the Lutheran church on the top of the Schneeberg hill. It was badly damaged in WW II and was still in a state of restoration. Wedding decorations were being put up, but they let us tour the beautiful interior. We walked down the hill and bought some wood carvings in a souvenir shop. Schneeberg was famous for its intricate wood carvings. We returned to the Neuman's for a wonderful supper of bratwurst, pork, and potato salad. I sure love German cuisine! We were able to share our story of how Marion and I met, and about our time in Cameroon and Nigeria. There was a connection with Cameroon as my mom's uncle, Johannes Sieber, a pioneer missionary in Cameroon, also had roots in Schneeberg. Lori also shared about her work in the Banso Baptist Hospital in Cameroon.

We drove with the Krauses to Potsdam via Dresden. The countryside got progressively flatter as we travelled north. There were large farms, and outside some of the towns were huge fields of solar panels. Many homes also had them on the roof tops. Krause's home was a third-story apartment near the center of Potsdam. We went for a long walk and climbed 100 steps in the ruins of a Norman tower so we could take in the 360-degree panoramic view of Potsdam. Right below was the San Souci complex of castles and palaces in a large park setting. As we walked home, we saw a home with the name Hiller on the door. I was not allowed to knock on the door to say hello.

On Sunday we attended the Potsdam Baptist church where Konrad was the Pastor prior to retirement. There were about 200 people in attendance. We were warmly greeted and I was called forward to say something. I managed to express our joy at being able to visit the land of my mother, and brought greetings from Bethany Baptist Church in Richmond. I did all this in German! We sat in the back and had English translation of the service via headphones. At coffee time down stairs after the service we met a professor, and his wife, who taught missiology at the Baptist Seminary in Berlin. They had spent time as missionaries in Cameroon with the European Baptist Mission. We were able to share some of our experiences with them. Later that day we drove around Potsdam to see the KGB headquarters building that the Russians used during their occupation after WW II. We saw many beautiful homes and embassies and toured the ornate palace of Cecilienhof where Churchill, Stalin, and Truman held their famous Potsdam Conference at the end of WW II. Here they carved up control of much of the world. Supper was at Christel and Martin Faber's home south of Berlin. Christel was Adelheid's younger sister and thus another second cousin of mine. They had a huge garden and greenhouse. The menu was fantastic – filled mushroom caps, BBQ pork cutlets, Berlin sausage, fancy tomato slices with cheese, bread, non-alcoholic beer, special kaffe, and fruit with cream. I sure love German cooking!

The next day we toured the St. Nikolai church in Potsdam and took a boat tour on the Tiefer See to see the many palaces and huge ornate homes of kings and nobles on the shore and the hills above. Lunch was in a fancy Italian restaurant at the base of an old windmill tower. We also visited Manfred and Margit Krause nearby and saw their summer home with its beautiful garden that had little labels on white stones for each plant. The evening was spent touring the Sanssouci Park to see the various palaces, statues, and fountains.

Our final day was spent touring Berlin with Konrad. We travelled there by train and then a double-decker bus, arriving at the Alexanderplatz with its many cafes and bakeries. We went into the Maria church which was a very dark and gloomy place. There were many depictions of death on the walls, paintings of souls and skeletons in hell, and plaques on the walls depicting dead heroes. The big Berliner Dom (cathedral), an evangelical church, was much nicer. There was a large set of pipes on one side. Fortunately, we were able to hear the majestic organ music and listened to a short devotional message in German that I easily understood. We also found a small Catholic church one block off the main Unter den Linden Avenue. The church had a dome reaching to the ground which people called the upside-down teacup. The pews were arranged in a circle on the main floor. In the center of that floor was a staircase going down to the basement where the pulpit and the rest of the sanctuary was located. Our walk took us along Unter den Linden to see various embassies, the Brandenburg Gate, the Reichstag, the Tiergarten, and the Governmental Administration building which was nicknamed Angela Merkle's washmachine because of all its curved glass windows. The Berlin Hauptbahnhof , the main train station, was a big beautiful building with five levels of train tracks. There were many shops and cafes, bakeries, and restaurants, so we had to indulge in a snack. Konrad and I enjoyed pickled herring and raw onions. Marion and Lori ended up with sweet pastries. Adleheid spoiled us with another great German meal – pulled beef, red cabbage, sauerkraut, kloese (dumplings), and cherry cake. We were totally spoiled.

WE FLEW FROM THE SCHOENEFELD Airport south of Berlin to the Schiphol Airport near Amsterdam. It was a no-frills flight, not even water was provided. We took the train to the Amsterdam station that was within walking distance of our booked Hotel Brouwer. It was a quaint old building constructed in 1652 on the edge of a canal. The floors were not level, probably due to settling of the building over many years. Carol Potratz was to meet us there at 4 PM in order to join us for the Rhine River cruise. Carol was not to be seen. We walked the streets hoping to spot her. The desk clerk phoned the room where she and Lori were to stay, but there was no answer. Finally, at 4:30 the clerk checked the room using a master key to get in. Lo and behold, there was Carol, fast asleep while we were sitting in the lobby waiting for her to arrive. We walked over canal bridges and down narrow cobblestone streets lined with shops and cafes. There were row houses about four stories high with facades that were tilted forward so that furniture could be hoisted to the upper floors by pulleys and then pulled inside through windows. This was because the inside spiral stairs were too narrow for furniture to be moved in or out. Our hotel elevator was so small that only two people, or one person with a suitcase, could enter. We ate at a restaurant where the chef was from Texas and spoke to us with a very loud American twang. Our walk through the Jordan area brought us to Anne Frank's house. The lineup to get inside was too long, so we just took pictures. We had to be careful on our walks to avoid being run

TRIPS AND TRAVELS

over by the hundreds of cyclists. Amsterdam has a population of 750,000 and a total of 1,000,000 bicycles! After shopping in a large cheese store, we headed home for some sleep. The next day we explored the neighborhood around our hotel and ended up in the red-light district that surrounded The Olde Church that was built in the 1300s. The church was locked and empty and surrounded by sex shops. A bronze breast with a hand on it was mounted in the pavement by the front door of the church. Beside this was a green statue of a prostitute. The streets were littered with rubbish from the revelry of the night before. Men with pressure washers pushed the debris onto the road where street sweepers scooped it up. There was such a sense of oppressive evil with an empty church and objects of perversion surrounding it. I stopped to pray to God that He would break Satan's hold on this place. Further along we found a secret garden at the end of a narrow path that had a tiny hidden church in it. This was an island of peaceful serenity.

In the late morning we dragged our bags to the Gérard Schmitter river boat run by the French CroisiEurope line. We were most impressed by the cuisine presented by the ship's French chefs. I was over the moon when the first course of lunch was a large heap of potato salad topped with strips of pickled herring. I got extras as Lori and Carol gave me their herring. We had another day in Amsterdam, so we toured the Rijks Museum to see the collection of original art by Rembrandt, Vermeer, and Van Gogh. We also went through the second oldest Jewish synagogue in Europe and toured the Jewish Historical Museum. About 80% (over 100,000) of the Jewish population in Amsterdam, in the 1940's, were sent to concentration camps and killed by the Nazis. We went on a night time canal cruise to see only some of the 1200 bridges and 100 Km of canals. There were numerous permanent houseboats lining the canals and some very beautiful mansions with huge chandeliers in the windows.

The ship left Amsterdam at midnight, and we woke up docked in Nijmegen. We walked up a hill and through the town to see the big church that was built in 1602. It was ornate and beautiful with a tall steeple. I had a sore knee so I wandered back to the ship to rest while the gals explored some old Roman ruins from the time of Charlemagne. It was Lori's birthday, so at supper time the lights were suddenly dimmed and our waiter brought a fancy cake with a flaming torch to Lori. Everyone on board sang happy birthday, and an elderly French man came to kiss Lori's cheek. There was musical entertainment that night and I joined the conga line to dance around the room.

The next day we sailed through the modern industrial center of Dusseldorf and past the flat farms and villages to the south. By noon we docked in Köln, a city of 1 million people. We walked along the riverside promenade past tents and kiosks selling beer, trinkets, and ice cream on our way to see the famous cathedral of Köln. It was huge with two main spires and many smaller ones giving the impression of a candle with wax dripping down. Between the spires were many sculpted figures. The stained-glass windows were very elaborate. Legend has it that the bones of the three magi were buried here in golden caskets. Our walk took us through the Alte Markt and the Fish Market that had wall-to-wall restaurants. The cruise continued on to Königsberg for the night.

We awoke the next morning to find our ship entering the Romantic Rhine. The river now flowed through an area of small mountains covered with forests and vineyards. There were many small towns, each with a church and often a castle on a hill above the riverside town. There were two castles near St. Goar called mouse and cat for Mausburg and Katzburg. The river made a sharp S-curve at the Lorelei Rock which was in the center of the river. A statue of the maiden Lorelei combing her hair was on the center of the rock. In the past this was an area of frequent shipwrecks as, according to folklore, sailors crashed into the rock because their attention was diverted by the singing of the beautiful Lorelei. As we passed the rock the ship played the song, " *Ich weiss nicht was soll es bedeuten das ich so traurich bin*" (I don't know the meaning of my deep sadness). Then we passed the picturesque river towns of Kaub, Oberwesel, and Bacharach with their steeples, castles, and vineyards. We docked at Rüdesheim am Rhein, a stretched-out village on the east bank, where we walked up the Doesselgang street. The narrow alleyway was lined with restaurants and souvenir shops with inflated prices.

We sailed past several nuclear reactors on our way to Mannheim, our next stop. We walked through a park to get to the center of town to explore the most beautiful Jesuiten Kirche. It was partially destroyed in WWII, but was now restored. We entered to hear a magnificent organ recital. The interior was a pale green and large windows brought in a lot of light. The place had a sense of beauty and worshipful serenity. Later the gals went shopping on the Kurplatz Strasse which was a sign for me to head back to the ship for coffee, solitude, and sanity.

OUR FINAL DESTINATION WAS STRASBOURG in France. With our bags in hand, we walked from the ship to a train station and rode into the central station that was close to the Best Western Monopole Hotel. We strolled all over the old town situated on an island. The main attraction was the imposing Cathedral of Strasbourg with its ornate façade of stone sculptures, which was celebrating its 1000 year anniversary. The huge stained-glass windows survived the World War II bombing by being stored in bunkers until the war was over. There was a large astronomical clock with fancy gears that moved carved figures around at 12 noon. At 11:30 a very rude priest unceremoniously evicted everyone from the church. On the outside I saw a line of people waiting to buy tickets to see the clock strut its stuff at noon. I was not impressed and thought that a house of prayer had been turned into a den of thieves. Rain forced us to seek shelter and lunch. Unfortunately, the ladies had another irresistible urge to shop in a three-story shop. I stood outside to watch a mime entertaining the crowds. After a short nap at the hotel we ventured out to explore the Petit France area with its canals, apartments, shops and restaurants. We all had spätzle with toppings as we sat outdoors under an umbrella and watched the setting sun. On our way to our hotel we came upon a brass band that put on a wonderful free open-air concert which was most enjoyable.

The next day we met Dr. Wim and Marleen Munting in the Heiligestein patisserie for a short visit. They came to pick up Carol who was going to visit them prior to her journey to Albania. It was great to see the Muntings again and to catch up on each other's history and news of Mambilla. At noon we walked to the curbside bus depot to board the Lufthansa non-stop bus to the airport in Frankfurt. We were impressed with the miles of wheat and corn fields. The three-hour trip was mainly on country roads so as to avoid the busy autobahns. We checked into a very posh hotel that informed us that all the rooms for three adults were taken. So, to our delight, we were put into a huge suite with another connecting room for Lori. We splurged on a fancy meal at the hotel to celebrate the end of a wonderful trip. Our flight home from Frankfurt was via Heathrow airport in London. The security lines there were very long and slow. We finally pushed our way to the front and pleaded for help to make our connection to Vancouver. We had to run on the moving belts to get to the boarding gate as we were the last ones to board the plane. We ended up in row 58 on the huge 777-300 Boeing jet. This was a trip that will forever be etched in our memories.

ENGLAND – 2017

LORI, MICHELLE LANGE, MARION, AND I decided to pay a visit to jolly old England. Our itinerary was devoted to the south-west, including the Cotswolds. We chose three weeks in July in order to have good weather. Michelle left Vancouver earlier than we did so that she could visit Iceland before getting to England. We settled in for a nice peaceful flight to London-Heathrow. However, when we were flying over Ontario our peace was broken by a flight attendant calling for any doctor or nurse to please come and help with an emergency. I responded and found a very heavy-set middle-aged man lying supine on the floor by the emergency exit door. He was semi-conscious and very pale. He responded, slowly, and with slurred speech, when stimulated. His pulse, pupils, and hand grips were normal. He did not have a seizure or a fall. I finally got a history of left and central chest pain that radiated to his left upper arm. All this suggested the diagnosis of a heart attack. An internist with a specialty in perioperative care and anesthesia and a nurse also arrived at the scene. The flight attendant produced an emergency medical kit that had various drugs in it. A fellow passenger gave us an aspirin for the man to chew and we sprayed nitroglycerine under his tongue. I got the oxygen cylinder and mask set up to maintain an airway and raise his blood oxygen level. The internist started an intravenous drip to provide another route of drug administration if required. The man felt better for a while, but his pain returned, so we gave more nitroglycerine and covered him with blankets. Contact was made with an Air Canada doctor by radio who advised weaning the man off oxygen. This resulted in a marked drop in his oxygen saturation from 98 to 85. We persuaded the captain to divert the flight to Goose Bay where paramedics removed the man and took him to a hospital. The plane sat on the tarmac for one hour waiting to be refueled. Thus a nine-hour flight became a twelve-hour flight. We got a 4 PM bus from Heathrow airport to Oxford and another bus to Woodstock and finally arrived at Hope Cottage at 7 PM where Michelle was waiting for us. After supper at the Star Inn Pub (pot pie and mushy peas) we fell into bed.

Blenheim Palace, the home of the Churchill family, was within walking distance of our cottage. The palace was set on a two-thousand-acre plot that had a lake full of fish and swans, green hills with sheep, and small forests with a mix of mighty oaks and fir trees. The palace and grounds were a gift to John Churchill from Queen Anne in appreciation for his defeat of French forces led by King Louis at Blenheim in Bavaria, hence the name for Blenheim Palace. This victory saved England from French domination. We toured the palace and saw the room where Winston Churchill was born. There was a WWII museum and many great state rooms with painted portraits and hanging tapestries. The highlight of the day was having tea and scones with clotted cream and jam in the Water Terrace Café overlooking the water fountains.

The next day we took a bus to Oxford, a vibrant place full of young university students. Oxford has about 35 colleges that make up the University of Oxford. We toured Blackwell's bookstore, one of the largest in the world with several floors full of bookshelves. We entered the Divinity School, a rectangular hall with desks along the walls. The hall was used to film some of the Harry Potter movies. We tried to get into the Church of St. Mary the Virgin. When we got there a stream of students emerged, some of them wearing robes with flowers pinned on their shoulders. They were followed by professors in academic regalia. A college graduation was in progress. Thus thwarted, we went for lunch in a covered market, similar to Granville market in Vancouver. An attempt to tour Christ Church College also failed due to many tour groups of prospective students lined up to enter. We then walked to Magdalen College, a beautiful college of Oxford University, where C.S. Lewis lectured before moving to Cambridge. The small chapel with stained glass windows contained small figures of early church fathers and a large one of Christ sitting in judgment, with saints going up on His right and the ungodly going down on His left. The inner court had a nice lawn with many blooming hydrangeas, and the River Cherwell on one side. Student dorms and classrooms were on another side, while a herd of deer lived behind a fence on the fourth side. Magdalen College had such a quiet and peaceful atmosphere that it really invited meditation. We rented a car and Michelle bravely drove back to Woodstock managing to stay to the left side of the road, even around traffic circles.

With Michelle driving and Lori navigating, we drove the winding, narrow roads through the hills and plains of the Cotswold region. The Cotswold is famous for its production of wool and textiles. The fields along the way had large pastures for the many sheep. The homes were made of yellow honey-colored limestone with straw-thatched or tile roofs. Every village had a church with a tall steeple. The drive took us through Chipping-Campden, Stow-on-Wold, Lower Slaughter, Upper Slaughter, and Burton-on-Water. Coffee and scones with Devonshire cream and jam was our treat.

The next day we drove to Stratford-upon-Avon, home of the Royal Shakespeare Theater. On a guided two-hour walking tour we saw where Shakespeare was born, the church containing his birth and death records, and the place of his burial. We ate a picnic lunch on a park bench behind the Royal Theater and watched the many swans and geese swimming in the Avon River.

We took a bus from Oxford to Bath and walked to our third-floor apartment. We avoided the 90-year-old lift with a metal sliding door. It often got stuck and guests were required to sign a waiver in order to use it. There was a one-page list of instructions to deal with getting stuck in it. We had a view of the Avon River and a cricket field from our window. After a sandwich lunch we went on a two-hour guided tour to see the Thermal Spa, Victoria Square and the Crescent, which was a huge arc of five-story apartments. Supper was at the famous Sally Lunn's bun bakery. The next day we walked across the old Putney Bridge that was lined on both sides with shops and eateries. On the far side was the fashionable Great Pulteney Street with its ritzy six-story apartment buildings. At the end of the street was the Holburne Museum full of paintings and ceramics. We then toured the Bath Abbey, a famous old cathedral built by the Normans in medieval times on the grounds of old Roman baths. We arrived in time to hear a wonderful pipe organ recital and to listen to a devotional talk by the chaplain. In the evening we explored the Roman Baths where hot mineral spring water bubbled up through the Avon River silt. The Romans had cleared the silt and built a system of baths with gradually decreasing temperature until the water eventually drains into the Avon River. When the Romans left, the baths deteriorated and were gradually covered in 20 feet of mud and silt, becoming totally forgotten. The baths were rediscovered when a man noticed a lot of water in the basement of his house and began to investigate. City engineers finally discovered the baths as they dug down to find the source of the warm water.

The next day was restful. Laundry was done, and lunch was in a small bakery on the Pulteney Bridge. Then we relaxed for three hours in the Thermal Spa. The spa had three pools, hot and cold showers, several saunas, a steam room, and even an ice room that had a trough full of ice chips to rub on one's skin! I tried out all of the facilities and left feeling very mellow, relaxed, and ready for supper and bed.

The train ride from Bath to St. Ives in Cornwall went through rolling hills with corn, grain, and grassy fields. Every farm had sheep and cows. We travelled through Bristol and Exeter to St. Erth where we got on a small local train for a fifteen-minute ride to St. Ives. We dragged our bags up steep hills and steps to the Olive Branch B&B. The hosts, Justin and Julia, greeted us warmly and carried our bags up to our-third floor room. Within minutes of arrival Julia appeared at our door with a tray of cookies and coffee. She also had a map to show us the major attractions in the town. We were warned about the numerous opportunistic seagulls that swoop down to snatch food right out of the hands of people. We wandered around town to see the many shops, galleries, bars, tea rooms, and pizza parlors. There were many tourists on the narrow cobblestone streets. The English breakfast at the Olive Branch was fantastic and included sausage, ham, sautéed mushrooms, hash browns, poached eggs, tomatoes, cereal, and fruit. Michelle had smoked salmon on scrambled eggs and Lori ordered eggs benedict. We explored the entire town and saw the harbour with its

AND THEN THE PHONE RANG...

fishing boats, the coast guard observation post, and old canon mounts. An afternoon was spent on Porthminster beach with its fine sand – excellent for sand castle building, but we were too lazy to build one. The water was extremely cold and it took a lot of determination to actually get in all the way for a swim.

One day we took a double-decker bus for a tour around the peninsula to Land's End, the Minack Theater, and Penzance. The road wound through the rural countryside with small farms. The road was so narrow that approaching cars had to back up to a farm driveway to allow the bus to pass, often with two to four inches of clearance. The hills were covered with ferns, blackberries, flowering bushes and various grasses. Many homes had hedges of huge colorful hydrangeas – I have never seen such big ones. Land's End was on a high bluff above the ocean. In the distance we could see a small island with a lighthouse on it. Beyond was the open ocean with North America on the other side. The Minack theater, named for the lady who built it, was an open-air amphitheater carved out of the side of a rocky cliff overlooking the ocean. Up to 700 people could be seated on the stone benches to view stage productions. We had lunch in a café overlooking the theater and I had my first taste of the famous Cornish Pasty, which was quite filling. Nearby was the Telegraph Museum at the site where underwater telegraph cables connected to France and North America. After supper in St. Ives we walked along Wharf Street and noticed about 35 men in blue blazers gathering in a courtyard. As we approached, they began to sing in four-part harmony with a conductor leading them. This Cornish male choir proceeded to entertain the crowd with a 40-minute concert that concluded with a hymn.

Another day we went by bus to Penzance and took a small ferry to St. Michael's Mount which was a rocky island on which a castle and chapel were built. At low tide it was accessible by a narrow causeway. We toured the village at the water's edge and then climbed a steep cobblestone path to the top, stopping frequently to catch our breath. The castle on the top was still inhabited by its owners and had beautiful terraced gardens and a breath-taking view. Suddenly it became very windy and a huge ominous cloud appeared bringing a big storm with lightning, rain and hail causing flash flooding nearby. The rain barely missed us so we managed to stay dry.

TRIPS AND TRAVELS

We celebrated our last day in St. Ives with a fancy dinner at the Pendova Hotel restaurant.

Marion's ancestors on her mother's side originated from St. Ives, so we asked Justin and Julia if there was a church that would contain family records. No such church existed in this St. Ives, but we discovered that there were three towns called St. Ives in England. Marion's ancestors apparently came from the St. Ives near Cambridge.

Hosts Justin and Julia made us an early breakfast and gave us ham and cheese croissants and drink cartons for our lunch on the train to London. The trip took over six hours and we checked into our apartment at 70 Inverness Terrace. We were disappointed in the place as it had old worn out furniture, torn curtains, a tiny poor shower, and only two rolls of toilet paper for four people for six days. Just after our arrival, a pest control officer arrived to inspect the baited traps for rats and mice. The back door had a rotten sill and a huge chain with a padlock held the iron bar door closed. The apartment door had two locks, two deadbolts, and a chain. We were definitely not impressed especially as we were paying $250 per day. We decided to make the best of the situation as this place was still better than some of the African places in which we had slept. Also, the location was great as the tube station was only two blocks away and there were a lot of good restaurants nearby. We walked into Kensington Park and saw a playground dedicated to Princess Diana and then strolled on to Kensington Palace, the home of Prince William and Kate. On one side of the palace was a special rose garden dedicated to Princess Diana. Adjacent to the palace was a long tree lined street with many huge embassies of countries from all corners of the globe. Later we joined John and Chris Riley (nee Leman) for a delicious Lebanese meal.

We took a train for a day trip to Cambridge and met Ruth Empson, Lori's good friend from her time at Capernwray. Ruth guided us all over town to see Christ College where Charles Darwin taught, and took us on a punting ride on the Cam River on a shallow draft boat propelled by a young man with a long pole. From this vantage we saw King's College and Queen's College among others. We then walked to King's College to see the beautiful stained glass windows of the chapel and the fan shaped arched ceiling. Ruth discovered that the St. Ives of Marion's ancestors was a short

AND THEN THE PHONE RANG...

distance away, but we did not have time to go there as our train to London was leaving shortly.

The next day we took the tube to Tower Hill to see the Tower Castle with its high stone walls and deep moat. We saw the royal jewels, including several magnificent crowns and elaborate regalia. There was an open square where several of the wives of Henry VIII were executed. The castle also had a tower prison where Queen Elizabeth and Sir Walter Raleigh were incarcerated. There was a basement torture chamber with a rack, a compression device, and manacles to hang people by the wrists on a wall. The nearby Tower Bridge that spanned the Thames River had a center section that could be drawn up to allow boats to pass through. We were able to climb the tower bridge and get to a walkway that crossed the river to an opposite tower. Part of the walk was on thick glass that caused some concern to nervous people for it was a very long way down to the traffic below. After a pizza lunch we boarded a tour boat going up the Thames to the Parliament buildings and Big Ben. On the boat ride we saw the Globe Theater, the Anchor Pub, Cleopatra's Needle, the London Eye (a huge Ferris wheel), and the two silver griffins guarding the entrance to the old city of London. A tube ride took us to St. Paul's Cathedral where we participated in a 5 PM high Anglican evensong with a liturgy of scripture readings and the recitation of the Lord' Prayer and the Apostle's creed. There was no music or devotional thought. We could not explore the elaborate building as we were ushered out quickly due to it being closing time.

We returned to Westminster the following day and toured the underground Churchill war rooms and museum. This was a tiny secret bunker under a building and covered with a thick slab of steel and concrete. Top secret war maps and communication centers were set up for conversation between the allies during WWII. The museum contained pictures and artifacts that chronicled the history of the war. We then made our way to Trafalgar Square, passing under the Admiralty Arch. We wanted to tour the famous St. Martin's in the Field Church, but a wedding was in progress. A sudden rainstorm had us seek shelter and lunch in the Café in the Crypt, a wonderful cafeteria deep under the church. The food was excellent. As we sat eating lunch, we noticed many grave markers in the stone floor and suddenly understood why the place was so named. We walked in the rain to Westminster Abbey to see the wonderful architecture of the high, arched ceiling. Inside were countless tombs of famous generals, lords, royalty, and poets. Some notable ones we saw were tombs of C.S. Lewis, Handel, Livingstone, Wilberforce, Newton, Faraday, and Chaucer. It was a full day!

A visit to Windsor Castle was on the agenda the next day. We joined a long line of people waiting to get into the castle. We had to go through a security check like in an airport. Many heavily armed police were present as well as security guards wearing bearskin hats. The castle had very high walls and a deep moat. We were able to tour the Terrace building with its many elaborate state rooms used for formal dinners and balls. The walls were covered with paintings, tapestries, portraits, and arms. Across a grassy field was the building containing the Queen's private lodgings, but she was not at home. English cuisine was the order of the day with a lunch of Cornish pasty and an apple tart in a Windsor bakery, while supper was a steak and ale meat pie with mashed potatoes at the Redan Pub in London.

The next day was full of special events. We toured the British Museum for three hours and were impressed with the Egyptian mummies, the Rosetta Stone, Assyrian and Babylonian wall friezes, African juju costumes and masks, and even carvings from Cameroon and Mambilla, Nigeria. Near the museum we saw the London School of Hygiene and Tropical Medicine where Bruce did some of his postdoctoral fellowship studies. We then walked through St. James Park along the lake with its many types of waterfowl. We came upon the large statue of Queen Victoria in front of Buckingham Palace. The surrounding area was a real tourist trap with shops selling a coffee mug for 20 pounds! After a nap in our apartment, we took the tube to Piccadilly Circus and walked up Shaftsbury Avenue along theater row and had pub food for supper at O'Neil's tavern. The day's climax was the very enjoyable musical, "Les Miserables," in the Queen's theater. It was a fabulous performance done on a rotating stage that enhanced the sense of movement and location. The Jean Valjean actor had a fantastic tenor voice with excellent diction. Without microphones I was able to understand every word. Lori and Marion used a lot of Kleenex tissues to mop up all their tears, and I was really moved by Jean Valjean's songs, especially, *"Take me home,"* as he lay dying. This show was one of the top highlights of our time in London.

AND THEN THE PHONE RANG...

The day before flying home we walked around Kensington Park and along Embassy Row. We celebrated Lori's birthday with four sweetcakes and coffee in our apartment. For a candle we lit a match and stuck it in a cake until it burned out in five seconds.

One could spend a month in London, Oxford, Windsor, and Cambridge and see something different every day, but it was time to go home.

BRITISH ISLES CRUISE 2019

WHEN KELLY HEARD THAT LORI, Marion, and I were planning a cruise of the British Isles in August, she persuaded Bruce to join us. What a nice surprise! On our flight to Gatwick airport near London, a woman became quite ill. The flight attendant called for a doctor to help with a medical issue. Bruce and I looked at each other to see who would get up first. I told him that he was a specialist and I was only a general practitioner, and so he should go ahead and see the lady and I would back him up. He got her to stop vomiting with an injectable antiemetic and some oxygen. He got a $250 voucher towards a future flight on WestJet for his efforts. We were met in the airport by a Princess Cruises hostess who connected us with a charter bus for the two-and-a-half hour trip to Southampton, via Portsmouth. Boarding the Crown Princess ship was quick despite the 3000 passengers booked on this cruise. After a nice dinner in the classy Michelangelo dining room, we got to bed early and slept soundly as the ship sailed to St. Peters Port.

St. Peter Port was a quaint little town on the island of Guernsey, a place that was fought for by the English and the French for centuries. It was even occupied by German forces in World War II. We were tendered ashore in groups of 150 passengers in lifeboats. A short walk took us to Castle Cornet that was perched on a huge rock in the ocean and connected to the town by a causeway. The staff in the castle were dressed in medieval costumes, one of them as King John. Marion bowed before him and he asked her if she had paid her taxes! There were tables full of medieval suits of armour, helmets, and weapons. We saw gun emplacements all over the castle, and at noon a soldier marched up and shot a canon to mark the time. The view was beautiful and we could even see the faint shoreline of France far off in the distance. We enjoyed steaks and fancy desserts in the Crown Grill that evening. The choppy sea gently rocked us to sleep that night as the ship sailed to Ireland.

Lori went on a tour to Tipperary and the Rock of Cashel while Marion, Bruce, and I took an excursion to Killarney on a comfortable bus with a talkative guide who gave a non-stop commentary of Irish history and politics. The countryside was lush and green due to the rainy climate, giving rise to the name, the Emerald Isle. The pasture land supported many herds of sheep and cattle and the area became known for woolen textiles, beef, and dairy products. The bus climbed rolling hills and went through Moll's Gap between two mountains. The road descended to Muckross House, a fancy old manor house on a large groomed estate that included three lakes. We finally came to Killarney, a beautiful small town where we enjoyed a three-course lunch. We took a different route back to the ship through small villages with ranch-style homes and very tidy well-kept yards.

After an early breakfast, we went on an excursion to Glendalough south of Dublin. It was the site of a very early church founded by St. Kevin, a monk circa 550 A.D. in the days of St. Patrick, who evangelized the Irish Celtic animists. The countryside had many little stone churches and tall round stone towers built for protection against raiders. These churches became the cradle of Christianity during the Dark Ages in Europe. After exploring the ruins of one of these churches, we returned to Dublin, a modern city of a million people, and roamed the streets. In the late afternoon we found St. Patrick's Cathedral and attended the evensong service which was very formal, stilted, and hard to hear. There was a bridge over a small river in town that looked like a harp. A large curved beam arched over the bridge and the cables from it, that supported the span, looked like harp strings. We discovered that the Irish national emblem was a harp, not a shamrock.

The next day we walked to Trinity College that was opened by Queen Elizabeth I. We arrived early enough to avoid the crowds in order to tour the ancient library which contained a display of the Book of Kells. This book was a Latin version of the four gospels written on vellum calf leather in 800 A.D. The pages were beautifully engraved and painted with

AND THEN THE PHONE RANG...

elaborate drawings. It was lost at one time and nearly destroyed by fire. It was finally given to Trinity College for safe keeping. We were able to see two open pages in a glass covered case. This book was another example of how the Irish helped preserve the gospel records during times when a lot of books were destroyed. The library itself had a high vaulted ceiling on a long building. There were stacks of shelves on either side of the room. Circular stairs gave access to more shelves on the second level. Apparently, the library had a copy of every book ever written in the U.K. After exploring the university grounds and buying a mug and a calendar with pictures of the Book of Kells in the gift shop, I returned to the ship for a rest. Marion, Bruce, and Lori stayed in town for more shopping. Bruce was anxious to find just the right gifts for Kelly, Ben, Abby, and Kaitlyn. They also did a tour of Dublin Castle.

In Belfast we toured the city hall museum to see a description of the development of the city. Originally the town was a center of textile production and later developed a large manufacturing industry, including aircraft and ship building. A hop-on-hop-off bus tour took us past the Titanic Museum (which was built in Belfast), the Stormont parliament, and through fancy and poor neighbourhoods. The tour went through both Catholic and Protestant areas which were separated by walls and high fences. Gates topped with barbed wire were closed at night. Many of the high walls had murals and graffiti painted on them that contained political slogans. Our tour guide described the complicated political turmoil in Belfast. The Catholic faction wanted to leave the United Kingdom and join with the republic of Ireland in the south. The Protestant folks were loyal to the crown of England. The guide described The Troubles, as a time of conflict, war, riots, shootings, bombings, and just plain bad blood between the two sides. People identified themselves as either Catholic or Protestant which also defined their political position. The guide joked that a man once identified himself as Jewish and then was asked, "Are you a Catholic Jew or a Protestant Jew?" In 1998, President Bill Clinton and Secretary George Mitchell helped to broker a peace agreement, signed on a Good Friday. This finally brought peace, but the memories and hurts still linger to this day.

TRIPS AND TRAVELS

An overnight sailing brought us to Greenough Port in Scotland. We walked a mile to the train station for the 40-minute ride to the center of Glasgow. A taxi took us to the beautiful Glasgow Cathedral that had an interesting display of stained glass windows that described the story of Matthew, chapter 25. A steep climb up to the top of the Necropolis gave us a panoramic view of Glasgow. On top of the hill was a 12-foot statue of John Knox holding a bible. We wandered down the streets to George Square where we met Brenda Hass, who became our tour guide. She took us by subway to Knightsbridge station near her home and we had lunch in a quaint upstairs restaurant. I tasted Haggis for the first time and rather liked it. Andrew Hass joined us for coffee and hearty conversation. He was a Professor at the University of Stirling, Reader in Religion, and Deputy Director of Postgraduate Studies for the School of Arts and Humanities. I remember a time when I taught him in my Sunday School class! After lunch we walked up a hill to the 600-year-old University of Glasgow, and went through the Cloister for another view of Glasgow. Another long walk took us to the Kelvingrove Museum. I sat sipping camomile tea and resting my sore back and hip while the rest toured the exhibits. Another long walk to the subway got us back to the center of town for a fancy high tea at the Willows Tea Room. Then came the train ride back to the ship and another long walk to get to the dock. Bruce recorded 26,000 steps on his fit-bit that day. The next day was at sea as we sailed by the Isle of Skye and the Hebrides on our way to Inverness.

We docked in Invergordon and took a bus to Inverness, a beautiful town with many old buildings of black and red stones. We toured the castle on a hill to get an overview of the town beside the Ness River that drains the famous Loch Ness. Behind the hill was the small Baptist Church of Inverness with about 100 very friendly people. We entered in time to enjoy the first half of the Sunday service. The worship songs were contemporary and familiar. After a fish-and-chips lunch we explored an old cemetery, walked along the Ness River, and peeked into the big cathedral before getting on the bus for the ride to the ship.

We tendered ashore and took a taxi to the train station for the twenty-minute ride to the center of old Edinburgh. We walked to Holyrood Palace, the home of Scottish Kings, and now Queen Elizabeth II's home.

AND THEN THE PHONE RANG...

The staterooms and bedrooms were all wood-panelled and covered with tapestries and portraits. Marion and Lori were particularly interested in one room that had a display of Megan Markle's actual wedding dress. There was very fancy lace stitching in the long veil. In the same display cabinet were dresses of the flower girls. We also saw the ruins of an old cathedral that abutted the palace wall. In proper style we had tea with scones covered with jam and clotted cream in the palace courtyard. We made our way up the Royal Mile with its many shops, cafes, bars, and restaurants. The stores were full of souvenirs and beautiful woollen scarves, sweaters, kilts and cashmere blankets. The street was full of tourists and entertainers doing music and juggling acts. At the top of the Royal Mile were bleachers set up for the annual Edinburgh Tattoo that had ended the previous day. Beyond was the huge Edinburgh Castle with its thick walls, turrets, and moat set on a huge, black rock hill. We saw the Scottish crown jewels in a dimly lit room. Every day at one o'clock a soldier fired the castle's cannon. It is said that the Scots find it cheaper to fire one shot at one o'clock than to fire twelve of them at noon! It was interesting to sit and watch people as we sipped an afternoon coffee on the Royal Mile. We entered the ancient St. Giles Cathedral and saw the life-size black statue of John Knox, the famous Presbyterian reformer. On the ship we got to bed early as we had to set our clocks one hour ahead. The next day was at sea as we sailed into a new time zone and docked in Le Havre, France.

There were many excursion choices from Le Havre, including a trip to the Normandy beaches where Canadian soldiers landed in 1944. However, the consensus was to go to Claude Monet's home in Vernon-Giverny. Our bus took us past the busy industrial port of Le Havre into the flat French countryside with its many farms. We gradually got into low rolling hills as we approached the home of Claude Monet, the famous French painter. He was an avid gardener and planted beautiful flower beds arranged in long rows, each row having the same color of blooms. There was a Japanese water garden with floating lilies and a small wooden bridge. In one corner of the pool was an old rowboat with oars, obviously a subject in one of his paintings. We toured Monet's house with his paintings covering many of the walls. Our tour bus then drove us to a quaint guest house restaurant in a bucolic setting by the bank of a stream that turned a picturesque water wheel. Lunch was served in a large gazebo with open sides, and included a salad with trout terrine, chicken, mashed potatoes, and an apple torte with ice cream for dessert. This was all washed down with a small glass of white wine. The French sure know how to cook!

We drove north to Rouen and toured the Notre Dame of Rouen, a huge cathedral with very ornate designs, sculpted figures, and statues. A walk down a busy pedestrian-only street took us to a garden monument honoring Joan of Arc who was burned to death at that very spot. A modern church with a curved, low, white roof was built adjacent to the garden.

A late supper on the ship was followed by entertainment from a fantastic jazz combo of saxophone, trumpet, trombone, guitar, bass, piano, and drums. Several vocalists sang to the lively accompaniment of the combo.

We sailed from Le Havre to Southampton during the night. The transfer bus trip from the dock to Gatwick Airport took two-and-a-half hours in some very heavy traffic. We checked our bags and went through security. On our way to the boarding gate Marion checked her purse and noticed that her passport was missing. We searched all our pockets and found nothing. We returned to the security checkpoint to see if her passport had fallen out of a bin that went through the scanner. The security personnel were not interested in helping us as the place was teaming with people. We were terrified at the prospect of Marion not being allowed to board our plane. Finally, a lady who seemed to be a senior official checked around for us and found the missing passport. Apparently someone had seen it lying on the floor and turned it in. What a relief! The flight home was smooth. A nice meal was served and a later snack included a scone with clotted cream and jam – a most fitting way to end our British Isles trip.

AND THEN THE PHONE RANG...

"ANNE OF GREEN GABLES" HOUSE

LOBSTER FEAST AT THE HUBER HOUSE IN MIMINEGASH P.E.I.

TRIPS AND TRAVELS

TRADITIONAL HILLER SANDCASTLE IN MIMINEGASH

AIN'T LOVE GRAND!!!

AND THEN THE PHONE RANG...

CRUISE TO ALASKA

CRUISING THE PANAMA CANAL

TRIPS AND TRAVELS

ENJOYING A MEAL IN CORFU ON THE ADRIATIC SEA

THE PASCHOLD PAGODA HAUS IN SCHNEEBERG, GERMANY

AND THEN THE PHONE RANG...

LONG DISTANCE CALL FROM CAMBRIDGE, ENGLAND

PROPER HIGH TEA IN LONDON, ENGLAND

CHAPTER 23

Retired, but Not Resting

ORGAN RECITAL

AS WE GET OLDER THE wear and tear of life catches up with our bodies. Various symptoms appear that tell us things are not as they used to be. I have already documented my surgical adventure in having a sclerotic aortic valve replaced with a porcine valve. Marion and I did a lot of walking for exercise but in time my knees began to object to the punishment. As a result, I had to have arthroscopic surgery on both knees (not at the same time) to deal with torn medial menisci. I was happy to be able to go walking again. I also noticed that I was missing out on bits of conversation around a crowded dinner table. This became worse over time, such that I did not always hear Marion's instructions to me. Audiometry testing revealed significant hearing loss, such that I needed hearing aids. I jokingly blamed the loss of hearing on job related noise damage from doing obstetrics for many years. Listening to women in the final stages of labor and delivery can be quite noisy. I did not appeal to the Worker's Compensation Board for help with the purchase of hearing aids. Next in the complaint line was my back. I developed low back pain that gradually got worse. One morning I literally fell in the bathroom due to sudden sharp back pain that radiated down my left leg. Marion half carried me back to bed. The symptoms got worse and even caused a mild degree of left foot-drop. An MRI showed several bulging discs, spinal stenosis, and arthritis of facet joints. I elected to try physiotherapy including traction. This gradually reduced the pain and increased my mobility. I had to rely on a cane to walk short distances for a number of weeks. Back pain continues to be a problem but I am still able to walk four or five miles a day for exercise. My eyes were next to join in the organ recital. My vision got increasingly more blurred. The solution was cataract surgery for both eyes, one at a time. It was great to see clear colors again, especially whites and blues. The improvement was temporary as the capsular material holding the new lenses became opaque. The solution was for the ophthalmologist to burn holes in the posterior capsules of both eyes with a YAG laser. This allowed light to get through to the retina at the back of the eye. I also had numerous surgeries to remove basal cell carcinomas and squamous cell carcinomas from various parts of my face. It was not very amusing to have needles poked into my nose and upper lip. It brought a new meaning to the word hurt. In 2018, I developed some chest pain with exertion. A cardiac angiogram showed some narrowing of several coronary arteries. As my symptoms had subsided, the decision was to wait and watch. I suppose there will be more organ recitals as I will soon celebrate my eightieth birthday. I really look forward to my new heavenly body promised by God.

RELOCATION

WE LIVED IN OUR CARRINGTON townhouse in south Surrey for ten happy years. We had four bedrooms so we could accommodate Paul, Lori, and Tammy Enockson. Tammy lived with us for several years while she attended Regent College. All three of them ultimately moved out, leaving us with 3200 square feet of house for Marion and me. We did not need that much space, especially when it came to cleaning! Marion had begun to babysit our grandchildren, Lucy and Sebastian, who lived in New Westminster while Paul went to his job and Juliet to her part-time teaching at Pacific Academy. This involved driving in rush hour traffic both morning and evening once a week. This was difficult driving in the dark and rainy months of the year. Lori also had a job as instructor in the nursing department at the B.C. Institute of Technology in Burnaby and wanted to move closer to work. We helped Lori find a beautiful fifteenth-floor condominium unit near Quayside Drive in New Westminster. In the process of helping Lori, we stumbled onto a nineteenth-floor unit for sale in the same area. That unit had 2000 square feet of space, a long balcony, and a beautiful view of the Fraser River and Mount Baker. Norm Hiller, a young realtor and relative, helped us with the purchase. The interior of the unit was quite dated with flowery wallpaper and pink bathroom tiles. We embarked on a major renovation of the kitchen and bathrooms and a new paint job for all rooms. During the renovation period we lived with Bruce and Kelly in Burnaby, occupying the basement suite in which my mother used to live. After moving into our unit we continued renovating by replacing the hardwood flooring. The cement floor under the old hardwood was so uneven and wavy that over 50 bags of levelling cement were used to get things even! A year later we removed the broken tiles of the balcony, levelled it, and put down a rubberized surface.

We were very happy with the new location as Marion had just a short drive for babysitting, and we were much closer to church. The Quayside Drive area had a long, beautifully landscaped boardwalk, and hanging flower baskets on ornamental light posts. The New Westminster SkyTrain station was a 10- to 15-minute walk, as was Safeway, Save-On Foods, three pharmacies, a bank, and at least 25 restaurants. We enjoyed getting to know our neighbours in the same building and entertained them with coffee breaks and occasional meals. One neighbour often reciprocated with special homemade borscht. Several neighbours cared for our plants while we were on various vacations. We also had opportunities to counsel some of them as they struggled with serious health issues. Marion was able to invite some of the gals to Bethany's annual Spring Tea where they enjoyed special food, a fashion show and heard a gospel presentation.

FIFTIETH WEDDING ANNIVERSARY – June 4, 2016

IT WAS HARD TO BELIEVE that we had been married this long, another sign that we were getting older. We decided to celebrate, so the church lounge was booked and we invited old friends and family to come for a catered meal and a short program. The only wedding attendant unable to come was Wilf Loch who had died some years earlier. Bruce and Paul were the emcees for a program that included speeches and a gift presented by two of our grandchildren. A lot of pictures were taken of our family and the wedding attendants, and it was great to mingle with our many friends and catch up on their stories.

Following the party, we went on a week-long retreat with the entire family to a lodge near Port Alberni that Kelly had booked. The lodge was built with logs and situated on a large property on the edge of the Stamp River. There were enough bedrooms to accommodate all 17 of us with rooms to spare. Marion and I were not allowed in the kitchen as our kids had planned all the meals and had a duty roster for cooking and cleanup. The dining table was huge and we could all sit together at once. Several St. Bernard dogs visited us daily and allowed the kids to pet them. Deer roamed the property as well. The grandchildren inadvertently stirred up a wasps' nest and several of them were stung, resulting in howls of anguish. Dezene boiled some water, and in the evening, he dumped the piping hot water into the nest, killing the nasty guys. One day was spent on the beach in Parksville and on other days we explored the areas around Port Alberni. We even saw a bear coming out of the woods some distance across a river from us. It sniffed a bit and wandered away into the bush. That week was a wonderful time of building memories.

CEDAR SPRINGS

FOR A NUMBER OF YEARS, we attended an annual retreat in May for retired pastors and missionaries held at Cedar Springs near Sumas, Washington. The retreat center was available to Christian groups and churches in Canada and the USA. It was situated in a rural area with several large ponds, beautiful landscaping, and acres of rhododendrons in full bloom. There was a hiking path along an abandoned railway track with several old rail trestles spanning some deep gorges. The food served by the staff was exceptionally good. It was always a joy to visit with the many missionaries we had worked with in Cameroon and Nigeria. The speakers and testimonies were challenging, the music inspiring, and the fellowship sweet. There came a tinge of sadness as over time some of the older pastors and missionaries became too frail to attend and some of them had passed on to be with Jesus.

GROUP MINISTRY INVOLVEMENTS

PRIOR TO MOVING TO NEW Westminster, we enjoyed the regular Bible studies and fellowship with our neighbours in the Carrington townhouse complex. We rotated through the homes of Don and Betty Ainslie, Norbert and Gerda Wessler, and our home. It was great to deepen friendship with fellow Christians. After moving to New Westminster, we continued to meet at the Ainslie's for about a year. We found the travel distance in bad weather taxing. A decision was made to start a new fellowship group in our new home that included newcomers to Bethany Baptist Church. We soon had a group of about 16 to 18 people that met in our home every other month for a meal, fellowship, encouragement, and prayer time. We then varied our meeting places to homes large enough to host the group. At times we met in the church lounge, together with other fellowship groups, for special meetings with visiting missionaries.

These group meetings led to the idea of hosting a special Christmas day dinner for people who were lonely at that time of year. The invitation to this included people in the immediate neighbourhood of the church. We were surprised at how many non-church people showed up for this dinner. Entertainment included singing of well-known Christmas songs and simple gifts. A short devotional was also given. The attendance grew over the next few years to well over 100 people. We planned our family Christmas dinner on Christmas eve so that we could help on Christmas day. It was a special joy to share the good news of Christ with lonely and unchurched people.

UNION GOSPEL MISSION

THE FOLLOWING WORDS IN MATTHEW 25:34-40 really challenged me:

> Then the King will say to those on His right hand, "Come you blessed of My Father, inherit the kingdom prepared for you

RETIRED, BUT NOT RESTING

from the foundation of the world: for I was hungry and you gave Me food; I was thirsty and you gave Me drink; I was a stranger and you took Me in; I was naked and you clothed Me; I was sick and you visited Me; I was in prison and you came to Me."

The disciples responded, saying "when did we see You like that?"

And the King will answer and say to them, "Assuredly, I say to you, inasmuch as you did it to one of the least of these My brethren, you did it to Me."

Those words made me wonder where these hungry, sick, and thirsty people were today. I soon realized that there was a Union Gospel Mission (UGM) in New Westminster within a 20- minute walk from our home. They distributed clothing to the poor and homeless people on our streets, and served breakfast and lunch on weekdays. I simply had to get involved. Initially I set up donation boxes in our church so that people could donate jackets, sweaters, socks, shoes, toques, gloves, and toiletries. I would inspect the donations to make sure they were appropriate, and then deliver them to the UGM. On entering the facility, I saw the many people who were being fed, and I realized that volunteers were needed to help with this. I asked if we could be involved and before I knew it, Marion and I were signed up. Marion was initially concerned that we might get lice and bring them home on our clothes, but we quickly dismissed that concern. The routine involved walking to UGM at 7:30 in the morning in order to toast a huge pile of bread donated by local bakeries. After a short prayer of blessing by the staff, the doors were opened to receive between 100 and 200 hungry people. We poured coffee for them and loaded the breakfast plates with generous portions of scrambled eggs, sausages, hash brown potatoes, and toast, plus ketchup as desired. They came for many refills of coffee. We then served donated tarts, pies, and cakes from a cart that we rolled between tables. A large row of shelves on one wall contained donated bread and rolls that we put in plastic bags for people to take. There were boxes of fruits and vegetables as well that the people could take home along with their bread. The staff gave a devotional while Marion and I went into the kitchen to wash dishes and dice up vegetables used to make a hearty soup. Leftover toast and eggs were made into sandwiches that we served at lunch, along with the soup. Then came time to clean up, as we washed the tables and chairs in the dining room. After walking home, we had a bit of lunch and a little nap because, with our advancing age, we were very tired, but happy to serve. The staff at UGM also did counselling, employment searches, and conducted Alcoholics Anonymous meetings. We got to know some of the UGM attenders on a first name basis and enjoyed serving and visiting with them until late in 2019 when my health issues interfered.

REFUGEE SPONSORSHIP

IN LATE 2015, WE BECAME aware of the desperate situation of refugees in the Syrian conflict. This was highlighted by a news video showing a policeman picking up the body of a dead child washed up on a beach. The child was separated from his family that was fleeing to the Greek island of Lesbos in a boat filled with refugees. The plight of refugees haunted me and I wondered what we could do to help them. The problem of over 60 million refugees worldwide was overwhelming. Several other members of Bethany were also concerned and we met with the adult Sunday school class to discuss the matter. A small committee was formed to investigate the possibility of our involvement in sponsoring refugees. We attended a seminar at the Rock Church, formerly Alta Vista Church, to hear what other folks were doing. We then invited Rev. Jamey McDonald to speak to our Sunday school class about issues involved in refugee sponsorship. Our ad hoc committee decided to proceed with sponsorship under the umbrella of the Mennonite Central Committee (MCC) as they have been involved with refugee work for decades. The MCC had a sponsorship agreement with the Immigration and Visa Office of the Canadian Government. We were glad that the MCC would be responsible for all the paperwork with the Government.

We drafted a proposal for refugee sponsorship, complete with a budget, and presented this to the Elder Board of Bethany. They unanimously approved this as a ministry of Bethany to be done under the umbrella of the MCC. The arrangement with the Government was a blended one in which the Government would provide some funds for six months of the one-year sponsorship. This ministry was presented to the church and within a week we had pledges of over $25,000 and in a month collected over $50,000 for the sponsorship fund. Bill and Rosella Vanee offered the use of the upper floor of their house for the refugee family. There were three bedrooms, a large kitchen, dining area and living room. The house was situated on over an acre of land with vegetable gardens and a lawn on which the children could play. Bethany member Rev. David Fearon was moving into a care facility and donated dishes and cooking utensils that he no longer needed.

After we signed a memorandum of understanding with MCC we began to organize. I looked at a long list of issues that sponsors need to deal with and divided them up into the following eight categories:

1. Settlement Services and Employment- job search, SIN
2. Finance and Money Management – banking and budgeting
3. Shopping and stocking - clothing, food etc.
4. Education – school, English classes
5. Transportation – bus, SkyTrain
6. Health – Medical Services Plan, immunization, dental, physician
7. Social and cultural issues
8. Housing and furnishing

A team leader for each category was chosen and they recruited volunteers for their team. The Migration and Resettlement Coordinators from MCC came to Bethany and conducted an evening training session for all of the 40 volunteers. We were now ready for sponsorship. With the help of MCC we chose to sponsor a Syrian refugee family. The Canadian Government was willing to pay for the flights of Syrian refugees at that time.

On February 14, 2016, we went to the Vancouver Airport to welcome the family - a father, mother, and their four children. They originally lived in Idlib, Syria, and fled to Lebanon when the war in Syria intensified. They applied for refugee status and were put on a list of approved refugees for Canada. After some paper work was done at the airport, they were given Permanent Residence status. They were very tired after a long journey from Beirut to Vancouver via Amman and Toronto. We took them directly to the Vanee home and got them settled for a long sleep.

The Refugee Support Teams did a remarkable job with shopping, enrolling the older three children in school, getting SIN numbers, MSP registration, applying for the Government Resettlement Assistance Program and child tax credits. A bank account was set up and immunizations were brought up to date. Many of the family required dental work that was provided for free by local dentists. One child's dental surgery was extensive and required general anesthesia. ESL classes were arranged that included babysitting. This was especially challenging as the parents were illiterate, even in Arabic. They knew very little English, but we were amazed how quickly the eldest daughter learned to speak it. She soon became an interpreter for the family. We were also helped with interpretation by Dr. Edward Amin, a Christian retired doctor from Egypt who attended Bethany. We were fortunate to find an Arabic speaking family doctor who accepted the family as patients.

The family were Muslims and soon began attending a local mosque where they formed a circle of acquaintances. Assistance in shopping for food required finding shops that sold Halal meat products. They were taught how to find bargains at Value Village and Walmart and how to access the Richmond food bank. They were happy to come to Bethany Baptist Church to see the people who were sponsoring them. The mother had a birthday shortly after arrival, so we arranged a lunch for them after the church service, together with the volunteers in the support teams. She was very moved when we brought a birthday cake with candles and sang happy birthday. They were very social and we often shared meals with them.

By November 2016, we helped the father find a job in a Richmond green house. This job was full time and permanent. He was able to get to this job on his bicycle. With this income plus the child tax credits, the family was now financially independent. They paid rent for their housing at current rates and paid for their clothing, food, and transportation. This independence was a relief to us, as our legal sponsorship responsibility was for one year. However, we continued to support the family beyond February 2017 in non-financial ways such as preparation of tax forms and some transportation issues.

By late 2017 the family moved to a basement suite in Surrey near to some Arabic speaking friends and the Middle Eastern Friendship Center. After a few months they suddenly moved to Red Deer Alberta to be near some relatives who had arrived there from Syria. To date we have had occasional contacts with the family. We were happy to have helped them get out of a dangerous situation in Syria and bring them to Canada. They progressed from a state of paralysis and culture shock to full independence, with a job, renting their own home, and functioning in our society.

We were now ready to consider sponsoring another refugee family. We had about $50,000 in the refugee fund and Bill and Rosella Vanee were willing to house another family.

We approached the Migration and Resettlement Coordinator for the MCC for her help with a new sponsorship of refugees. Five of us travelled to the Abbotsford office to arrange this next venture. We discovered that there were more refugees from the Democratic Republic of Congo (DRC) than any other single country due to years of tribal and civil wars. We were shown lists of refugee families approved for sponsorship to Canada from the DRC. Most of the family groups were three to six in number and some of the groups contained people fluent in English. However, there was one family of 9 that caught our attention. We wondered who would ever sponsor such a large family, especially to Metro Vancouver where the cost of housing was extremely high. We tried to focus on the smaller families, but God did not give us peace about them. We definitely felt His leading to take on the family of nine, despite our misgivings. Our faith in God's leading would be stretched by this choice. God would have to provide the means. This reminded me of the Israelites crossing the Jordan river to enter the land that God had promised to them. The Jordan river did not part until the priests actually stepped out into the water in faith. The decision was made unanimously by the refugee support team leaders to sponsor the family. We had to trust in God's provision.

The family had been living in a refugee camp in Mozambique for about 6 years prior to coming to Canada. They originally lived in the DRC near

AND THEN THE PHONE RANG...

the border with Rwanda. This area was particularly dangerous due to tribal raids and on-going civil war. The Hutu and Tutsi strife also created a lot of trouble. An armed raid in the area where the family was living resulted in them fleeing the violence. They traveled for over a month through Burundi, Tanzania, Malawi, and finally got to the refugee camp in Mozambique. The United Nations Commissioner for Refugees declared the family to be bona fide refugees as they could not safely return to the DRC. With this declaration the family applied to go to Canada. They were screened by the Canadian immigration people and given permission to come to Canada if someone would sponsor them. They waited for a long time in the refugee camp until Bethany Baptist Church became their sponsors.

On May 10, 2018 the family arrived at the Vancouver airport. They had flown from Mozambique to Vancouver via Addis Ababa, Ethiopia, and Toronto. We met them at the airport and noticed that they had only 2 small suitcases and 3 small back-packs for the nine people in the family. The children had no shoes, just flimsy flip-flops. On the way from the airport to the Vanee home, the driver of the van pointed out Bethany Baptist church as they drove by. We managed to communicate with simple English and, with the help of Josie Polisi, some French that the father understood. He made a request that he and his family be allowed to attend Bethany Baptist Church on Sunday. We discovered that they were Christians and were aligned with an Apostolic church. Marion had prepared an African style meal of fufu and a meat sauce for them on their arrival. The children did not start to eat until the father asked me to pray. We all felt a closeness as fellow believers in Jesus Christ.

Our refugee support teams swung into action and within a week the children were enrolled in school and a major shopping trip supplied clothes and shoes for the entire family. The day after their arrival they were registered with the Medical Services Plan of BC and paper work was done to get SIN numbers for everyone. ESL classes were also arranged. There were some major health concerns. Within a week of arrival, two children were admitted to the BC Children's Hospital with high fevers, chills, and weakness. When the first one arrived at the hospital she was met by staff wearing protective clothing as they heard that a girl with a fever was coming from the Congo. They feared a possible Ebola fever diagnosis.

They all relaxed when it was discovered that she came from Mozambique. Both children had a potentially fatal type of falcipara malaria and both had become severely anemic. Fortunately, I was able to discuss treatment with the doctors, based on recent experience with this disease in Nigeria. They both recovered after a week in hospital. All the children were found to be mildly anemic and required iron supplements. Immunizations were brought up to date and dental work arranged for the entire family. We also discovered that we inadvertently were sponsoring nine-and-a-half refugees, as the mother was pregnant. Antenatal care and delivery of a baby boy was done at a local hospital. All of this kept Gail Golz, the health team leader, very busy. I helped with driving people to numerous appointments.

The family faithfully attended Bethany Baptist Church. The children especially enjoyed Sunday school, family night activities on Fridays, and vacation bible school. The two oldest girls also attended a youth gathering at Green Bay Bible Camp.

In February 2019 the father obtained a job with a company that makes a chemical additive to cement rendering the cement waterproof. After a three-month probationary period the job became permanent and full-time. His salary plus Child Tax credit income was sufficient to make the family financially independent. With the help of the shopping and transportation teams, the family became independent in using buses to access the food bank, shops for clothes and food, and their bank. The children had bikes that they rode to elementary school.

There was never a dull moment in our refugee sponsorship activity. We definitely saw the hand of God guiding the process and felt God's call to us to get involved. We were very fearful about sponsoring the large family, but we learned to trust God and His provision. Any further refugee sponsorship plans were put on hold due to travel restrictions imposed by governments in response to the COVID-19 pandemic.

COVID-19

IN JANUARY 2020 THE WORLD became aware of a novel viral infection that came to be named COVID-19. This infection probably started in Wuhan,

China, and quickly spread to the rest of the world. This infection was spread mainly by inhalation of virus-containing droplets and less commonly by touching contaminated surfaces and then touching one's face. The infection initially involved the respiratory system causing respiratory distress with consolidation of the lungs and diminished blood oxygen levels leading to death. In time it was found that other organ systems could also be affected, including the liver, kidneys, brain, intestines, blood coagulation, and an immune storm response. The people most vulnerable to severe forms of infection and death were the elderly, the immune-compromised, and people with chronic illnesses. Italy was one of the first European countries to have a severe wave of infections, such that ambulances were lined up outside hospitals waiting for a vacant bed. People were dying at such a fast rate that mortuaries could not keep up with the demand for their services. Bodies were stored in refrigerated trucks to wait for proper burial. New York City was one of the early epicenters of the pandemic in the U.S.A. There was a desperate scramble to provide ventilators for the compromised patients in intensive care. Elective surgical cases were cancelled in order to free up doctors, nurses, and hospital beds to deal with the huge number of COVID-19 patients. There was a lack of protective equipment such as N-95 masks and gowns for the front-line health workers. It soon became apparent that this virus was spreading across the entire world and that we were woefully unprepared to deal with it. Tragically there were many deaths in nursing homes due to the vulnerable elderly residents housed in close quarters. Intensive efforts to produce a vaccine were started by many countries.

For our protection we put ourselves in isolation. Our children were concerned about our heightened vulnerability and insisted that we stay confined to our condominium unit. Lori went shopping at Save-On-Foods for us and Paul went to Costco with our shopping lists. They did the same for Auntie Shirley. We were moved by their expression of love and concern. We continued our daily walks and made sure to keep a good distance away from other people. Once the initial wave of new infections subsided, we did our own shopping, being careful to wear masks, disinfect purchases, wash hands frequently, and keep a social distance from others. By the summer of 2020 we ate meals together on Sundays with Lori, Shirley, Paul, Juliet, Lucy, and Sebastian. This was our bubble of contacts.

Church services were cancelled in March 2020. Instead, our pastors provided virtual services with music, prayers, announcements, and a message that we could watch on our computers. It was really strange to observe communion virtually, using a glass of juice and a cracker in front of the computer screen. In June 2020, the Public Health authorities allowed meetings of up to 50 people with adequate distancing, wearing of masks, and keeping a list of contacts for future testing if necessary. Our Seniors group began to meet at church every other Tuesday for a short program and lunch. We sat with a maximum of 4 people to a table and brought our own sandwiches and coffee. Masks were worn whenever there was any singing. Bethany church also had a maximum of 50 people attend Sunday services at 9 and 11 AM.

At the end of July we drove to Prince George, together with Lori and Shirley. Bruce, Kelly, Paul, Juliet, and all the grandchildren joined us for several days of visiting. To accommodate everyone, we used the home of Dezene and Joyel, a tent trailer, and the home of generous neighbours and friends of Dezene and Joyel who were away on vacation. We enjoyed going to a lake, and to the ancient forest at Chun T'oh Whudujut Provincial Park with huge old growth trees. We celebrated Lori's fiftieth birthday by feasting on a steak dinner and cake, and then making smores at the firepit that the Hubers had built in their backyard. It was great to see all the grandchildren enjoy each other's company.

In early September 2020, the leaders of Bethany Baptist Church decided to conduct Sunday worship services at 9 AM and again at 11 AM for a maximum of 50 attendees per service. Marion and I preferred to stay home on Sundays and watch the service on our computer. This made more space for extroverted people, who were desperate for some socialization, to attend.

Unfortunately, September 2020 brought a huge rise in the number of new cases of Covid-19 infections. As a result, Marion and I were again isolating ourselves into a smaller bubble of contacts until this second wave was brought under control. Thankfully, a safe and effective vaccine became available in early 2021. This will help everyone to return to a more normal way of life.

AND THEN THE PHONE RANG...

GRANDCHILDREN

ELIJAH, MARCUS, BEN, LUCY, ABBY, SEBASTIAN, AND KAITLYN – you are very special. It has been a real delight to see you grow into the great people that you are. Grandma/Oma and I, Grandpa/Opa, pray for you every day. We rejoice when we hear of your desire to ask Jesus into your heart and to follow Him.

CONCLUSION

I HAVE COME TO THE end of writing my story to date. Obviously, the future and ending of my story will have to be written by someone else. Everyone has a life story to tell. In my case the story was directed by God when I surrendered my body, mind, and will to Him. There were some lessons I learned along the way as a result of this commitment.

- Such a life may not always be easy, but Jesus stays with you through it all.

- Such a life may bring disappointments, but God is in charge of the results.

- Such a life can bring you to the end of your rope, but God gives us what we need.

- Such a life can show God at work as we see changed lives in people to whom we minister.

- Such a life sets us on the path that God has planned for us.

My advice to my children and grandchildren is found in Proverbs 3:5-6:

Trust in the Lord with all your heart and lean not on your own understanding; in all your ways acknowledge him, and he shall direct your paths.

My words of blessing to you are from Hebrews 13:20-21 and Numbers 6:24-26:

RETIRED, BUT NOT RESTING

Now may the God of peace who brought up our Lord Jesus Christ from the dead, that great Shepherd of the sheep, through the blood of the everlasting covenant, make you complete in every good work to do his will, working in you what is well pleasing in his sight, through Jesus Christ, to whom be glory forever and ever.

The Lord bless you and keep you; the Lord make His face shine upon you, and be gracious to you; the Lord lift up His countenance upon you and give you peace.

STILL ROMANTIC AFTER 50 YEARS OF MARRIAGE

OUR WEDDING PARTY (MINUS WILF LOCH) AT OUR 50TH ANNIVERSARY

AND THEN THE PHONE RANG...

LOOKING FORWARD TO MANY MORE YEARS TOGETHER

OUR FAMILY AT THE 50TH WEDDING ANNIVERSARY

RETIRED, BUT NOT RESTING

VOLUNTEER AT VACATION BIBLE SCHOOL

REFUGEE FAMILY FROM SYRIA ARRIVE AT VANCOUVER AIRPORT

AND THEN THE PHONE RANG...

BETHANY REFUGEE SPONSORSHIP TEAM GREET THE FAMILY

GREETING THE FAMILY — REFUGEES FROM THE DEMOCRATIC REPUBLIC OF CONGO

REFUGEE FAMILY EMBRACED BY BETHANY CHURCH

OUR FAMILY — SUMMER OF 2020. GRANDCHILDREN GROWING UP RAPIDLY

CPSIA information can be obtained
at www.ICGtesting.com
Printed in the USA
BVHW020302180222
629282BV00003B/6